Praise for the Work of David Evanier

"Amazing perception."

—Elie Wiesel on *Red Love*

"As much as Tony Bennett's music is appreciated, so will be this insightful book about the man behind the music."

—Gay Talese on *All the Things You Are: The Life of Tony Bennett*

"Irreverent, unflinching, and almost disgracefully entertaining."

—*Kirkus Reviews* on *Red Love*

"Evanier has written a book so charged with intimacy, so heartbreakingly ebullient with life, that you feel that any moment the pages are about to snap their fingers and break into song."

—*The Boston Globe* on *Roman Candle: The Life of Bobby Darin*

"David Evanier commands skills to merit our attention and wonder."

—George Plimpton on *The One-Star Jew*

"Evanier exhibits mastery. . . . His stories boil with a satisfying sense of rage, stoked by sharp observations."

—*Publishers Weekly* on *The One-Star Jew*

## Also by David Evanier

*The Nonconformers*
*The Swinging Headhunter*
*The One-Star Jew*
*Red Love*
*Who's Sorry Now* (with Joe Pantoliano)
*Making the Wiseguys Weep: The Jimmy Roselli Story*
*Roman Candle: The Life of Bobby Darin*
*All the Things You Are: The Life of Tony Bennett*
*The Great Kisser*

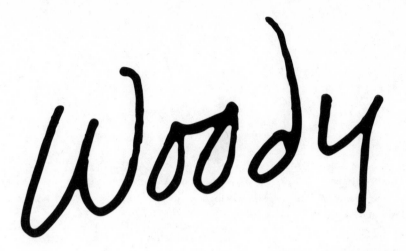

# Woody

## David Evanier

St. Martin's Press 〰 New York

www.stmartins.com

The photography credits that appear on page 367 are a continuation of this copyright page.

Designed by Steven Seighman

Library of Congress Cataloging-in-Publication Data

Evanier, David.
    Woody : the biography / David Evanier.—First edition.
        pages cm
    ISBN 978-1-250-04726-7 (hardcover)
    ISBN 978-1-4668-4762-0 (e-book)
    1. Allen, Woody, 1935–   2. Motion picture producers and directors—United States—Biography.   3. Motion picture actors and actresses—United States—Biography.   4. Comedians—United States—Biography.   I. Title.
    PN2287.A53E93 2015
    791.43'092—dc23
    [B]

                                                            2015030395

Our books may be purchased in bulk for promotional, educational, or business use. Please contact your local bookseller or the Macmillan Corporate and Premium Sales Department at (800) 221-7945, extension 5442, or by e-mail at MacmillanSpecialMarkets@macmillan.com.

First Edition: November 2015

10  9  8  7  6  5  4  3  2  1

*To Dini Evanier, Andrew Blauner, Gary Terracino, and Mark Evanier*

# Contents

Acknowledgments ix

Introduction: How I Got to Woody 1

1. Enchantment Was the Reason 33

2. "Writing Saved His Life" 51

3. The Real Broadway Danny Rose 86

4. "Woody, *C'est Moi*" 113

5. Bathing in Honey 144

6. "As Tough and Romantic as the City He Loved" 178

7. The Woman Who Saves Leonard Zelig 225

8. Dick and Woody 251

9. "Startling Intimations of Greatness" 267

10. Sex, Lies, and Videotapes 284

11. Woody Pulls the Rabbit Out of the Hat—Again 323

12. Balls of Steel 339

Epilogue: Touching the Entire World 349

Filmography 353

Bibliography 363

List of Illustrations 367

Index 369

# Acknowledgments

With deep appreciation to Javier Aguirresarobe, Harlene Rosen Allen, Peter Bart, Elizabeth Beier, Jennifer Belle, Dr. Maria Bergmann, Dr. Michael Bergmann, Walter Bernstein, Andrew Blauner, Donna Brodie, Brad Burgess, Frank Buxton, Dick Cavett, Jerome Chanes, Lynn Cohen, Stephen Dixon, Dr. Gerald Epstein, Dini Evanier, Mark Evanier, Elaine Evans, Linda Fairstein, Michael Fiorito, Eva Fogelman, Jason Fraley, Dorothy Friedman, Vincent Giordano, Shelly Goldstein, Elliott Gould, Charles Graeber, Robert Greenwald, Eamon Hickey, J. Hoberman, Ilana Howe, Annette Insdorf, Neal Jesuele, Carol Joffe, Jerome Kogan, Andrew Krents, Judith Liss, Phillip Lopate, George Lore, David Lowe, Judith Malina, Ric Menello, Marilyn Michaels, Elliott Mills, Barry Mitchell, Theodore Mitrani, Craig Modderno, Micah Morrison, Bill Mullins, Mel Neuhaus, Diane O'Leary, Eric Pleskow, Norman Podhoretz, Craig Pomranz, Richard Powers, Tim Pratt, Dorothy Rabinowitz, Hugh Raffles, Kathleen Rogers, Francesca Rollins, Hillary Rollins, Jack Rollins, Susan Rollins, Cynthia Sayer, Jimmy Scalia, Richard Schickel, Stephen Schrader, John Simon, Sharon Simpson, Steve Stoliar, Heather Stone, Howard Storm, Juliet Taylor, Gary Terracino, Vicky Tiel, Lennie Triola, Paul Ventura, Jack Victor, Jeff Weatherford, Sid Weedman, Robert Weide, Alan Zweibel.

Special thanks to the brilliant executive director of the Writers Room, Donna Brodie.

Woody

## Introduction
# How I Got to Woody

I RANG HIS DOORBELL.

I'd been told by a friend of his that he never looked at his mail. Whether that was true or not, I wanted to be sure he knew I was writing a biography of him and that I had some questions for him. So I wrote him a letter and took it to his house.

A pleasant-looking fellow peered down and checked me out from an upper story. "I have a letter for Mr. Allen," I said. "Hold on," he said, and a moment later opened the door. He smiled, took the letter from my hand, and said, "Perfect."

I was in. Well, not really. I got to Allen and I didn't get to him.

In my letter I had introduced myself and told Allen that I had already interviewed Jack Rollins, his longtime manager; as well as the film critics John Simon, Annette Insdorf, and Richard Schickel; the former banjoist in his band, Cynthia Sayer; and Sid Weedman, who had seen Woody in his early days when he wrote and performed at the Tamiment resort in the Poconos. I also said that I considered *Crimes and Misdemeanors* and *Zelig* to be his masterpieces.

I received an e-mail from Woody the following day. (He allegedly does not use e-mail, so I assume he dictated his letter to his assistant, Gini.)

Since then I have had a limited back-and-forth correspondence with Allen. He has picked the questions he chooses to answer, but he has been unfailingly courteous.

After writing five biographies I have learned at least one essential thing: The iconic image for which we know such a figure has little to do with what he or she actually is. No one has struggled with the problem of being really known more than Woody Allen, whose public persona is instantly and eternally assumed to be his real personality. I will never forget undertaking the biography of Tony Bennett, the sweetest and most lovable of personalities, and being told by Lennie Triola, a New York concert producer and music manager, "There's an ogre behind that door." True or not, I gave that observation a lot of thought. Woody Allen has compounded the problem by being the most confessional of writers-directors-actors, borrowing from his life in so many of his films while insisting that although a few details might be true, he has exaggerated and embellished most of it. He is also the only comedian in Hollywood history to insert the same unchanging comedic persona into every genre of filmmaking—comedy, romantic comedy, satire, drama—and yet have it effectively blend in. It is always the same character/persona. No one else has ever succeeded at this. It is remarkable, and it makes him liminal.

Groucho was always Groucho, doing Groucho stand-up within a film. Jack Benny was always Jack Benny, doing Benny stand-up. Every Bob Hope film is built around Hope's comedic shtick. According to the screenwriter-director Gary Terracino, "Today's comedians (Will Ferrell, Adam Sandler) go in the other direction. They give us their tried-and-true comedic shtick within comedies, but ditch that persona altogether in dramas to demonstrate that they are 'real actors.'"

Woody is Woody in all of his films, he is the same unchanging comic persona, yet each film works in its own way. Unlike Groucho, Bob Hope, and Jack Benny, in addition to being an actor Allen was also a writer and director. He knew exactly how his persona could blend in. *Zelig* can be seen as a sly commentary on his own career and acting.

Allen has carved out exactly what he wants to do and has total control of his films. "I have control of everything, and I mean everything," he told John Lahr. "I can make any film I want to make. Any subject—comic, serious. I can cast who I want to cast. I can reshoot anything I want to as long as I stay in the budget. I control the ads, the trailers, the music." Lahr asked him what would happen if he wasn't able to completely control his films. "I'd be gone," he said. There is no doubt that he meant it.

As an artist, Allen was never tempted to sell out or to try to outdo himself; nor did he care to ingratiate himself with the powers that be. He cares only to express himself without apology. He has managed to be current without being trendy and to be a genuine artist who almost always embraces classic storytelling over cerebration and abstraction.

He is the most amazing phenomenon in the history of American show business. John Ford, William Wyler, Charles Chaplin, all had a major output. No one has covered the gamut as Allen has, from downright laugh-aloud funny to poignantly, startlingly moving.

"Sometimes it seems as if Allen has explored every shade of longing in Western man," Kent Jones wrote in *Film Comment*, "for deliverance from the disappointments of the present, for transport to another more fulfilling realm, for solace from the drudgeries of shared existence, for recovery of the past, for consummation of love, for a little bit of luck."

"Only Chaplin comes close," Gary Terracino said, "and Chaplin, too, endures. He also had an astounding almost thirty-year run of global popularity. But even Chaplin ditched the Tramp in later years, only to see his popularity wane. Woody never ditches Woody."

Allen, like Chaplin, was "self-educated, reclusive, melancholy and meticulous," wrote John Lahr. "Both are comic geniuses who give life without actually loving it."

Allen defined the difference between Chaplin's screen persona and his own in his interview with Lahr. "I came along after Freud," he said, "when the playing field had shifted to the psyche. It was interior. What was interesting to people suddenly was the psyche. They wanted to know what was going on in the mind."

"It's almost Shakespearean in terms of volume," Alan Zweibel, a comedy writer for *Saturday Night Live, It's Garry Shandling's Show,* and *Curb Your Enthusiasm,* says about Allen's body of work. "Look at the number of movies, the books, the plays, the albums. The breadth of the whole career: writing, directing, performing, and everything else."

Everything about Allen is unique, not only in cinema but in pop and celebrity culture. There is no one like him. He portrays the kind of man that was never seen in film before. "Woody Allen helped to make people feel more relaxed about how they looked," Pauline Kael wrote, "and how they really felt about using their fists, and about their sexual terrors and everything else that made them anxious. He became a new national hero. College kids looked up to him and wanted to be like him."

The richness of his films, their layered texture, bears watching again and again. There is always more to glean. And there is the matter of integrity in his business dealings and in his relationships to actors. He doesn't care if an actress is over forty. He doesn't care if an actor hasn't worked in years, as was the case with Andrew Dice Clay in *Blue Jasmine*. An actor does not have to be hot to be in an Allen film. Allen doesn't care who the actors' agent is. All he cares about is quality. This does not make him soft and fuzzy. He never will be that. He is saying, in effect, I'm an artist; deal with me on that level.

Allen's work presages so many things that came after it: *Borat* and *Bruno* could not exist without *Zelig* and *Stardust Memories*, nor could the work of Albert Brooks, Larry David, or Garry Shandling. Allen became the new, the template for a generation. "The old comics were funny," Alan Zweibel told me, "but then came Woody. And wow! A page had been turned. A new reality, totally, that somebody can live in and talk about from within. He created his own world, and given his persona, you bought into it, the illogical fantasy."

According to Zweibel, "You just let him take you for a ride, that it was possible for it to start to rain in his apartment. You look at this guy, and of course it could happen to him. And it was hysterical. And he is the thinking man's comedian. So when he alludes to the Holocaust, to anything philosophical, to life's big questions, you know that a point is made, that something is being debated. So there's an honest intelligence that the subject itself is being treated—in and around the jokes. Even when I was writing for *Saturday Night Live*, even when I created the *Garry Shandling Show*, Garry and I idolized Woody. So it was, What would Woody do in a case like this?"

No one *has* ranged in his work so consistently from the sublime to the wretched. He is willing to gamble with failure, to extend and deepen the formal and substantive elements of his films.

"You look at the body of work," Zweibel says, "and you can see how he had to make this movie or that movie in order to get to make the great movie. His growth as a writer, as a director, as a filmmaker, as a human being. The fact is that part of the creative process is that sometimes you have to fail. Sometimes there are foul hits, in baseball terms, or he wouldn't hit the next home run. You have to do certain things in order to get to that big thing, that great thing. Some years ago I heard Rob Reiner say, 'Look, we all do what we do. We all write, we make movies, this and that. And then there's Woody.' And he's right. Woody's in a class by himself.

"I look at Carl Reiner, Woody, Buck Henry, Larry Gelbart," Zweibel relates. "They didn't just write for one medium. They wrote for everything. They were writers. They wrote something and then decided what form will this idea be best expressed in: books, plays, TV shows, magazine pieces. And so Woody is among those guys: You're a writer, write! Let the piece tell you what it wants to be, as opposed to trying to shoehorn it into being something else. This is the best way this certain story can be told. It should only be a three-page story in *The New Yorker*. Or this should definitely be a play, for whatever reason. And Woody told us all of that. In 'The Kugelmass Episode,' his timeless story, here's a guy who's unhappily married for the third time. He's got this shitty life, he's a professor, he reads *Madame Bovary*, and he falls into the book because it's a better place for him to be! Woody has the uncanny knack of knowing when you should use your imagination, as in 'Kugelmass,' or when it's best for him to visualize it, make it appear on the screen, like the Jewish mother floating over him in *Oedipus Wrecks*. Doesn't that speak volumes?"

Allen is of the moment, but his subject matter is timeless: the recurrent insolubility and sorrow—and momentary glories—of the human experience: "The same things come up time after time," Allen has said. "They're the things that are on my mind, and one is always feeling for new ways to express them. What sort of things recur? For me, certainly the seductiveness of fantasy and the cruelty of reality. . . . What interests me are always the unsolvable problems: the finiteness of life and the sense of meaninglessness and despair and the inability to communicate. The difficulty [of] falling in love and maintaining it. These things are much more interesting to me than . . . I don't know, the Voting Rights Act."

He was part of what author and film critic J. Hoberman dubbed the Jewish "new wave" between 1967 and 1973, starting with Barbra Streisand in *Funny Girl* and continuing to *The Way We Were*, during which "Jewish humor reigned confidently supreme. . . . This presupposition of a new Jewish-American cultural visibility informs the dozen or so movies—all characterized by their insolent black humor and social satire—that featured (mainly) young, (sometimes) neurotic, and (by and large) not altogether admirable Jewish male protagonists cut off from their roots but disdainful of a white-bread America. Self-hatred merged with self-absorption, narcissism seemed indistinguishable from personal liberation, and alienation was a function of identity." Hoberman was referring to *The Producers, The Graduate, Take the Money and Run, Goodbye, Columbus, The Angel Levine, Portnoy's Complaint, Where's Poppa?, I Love You, Alice B. Toklas, The Heartbreak Kid,* and *Bye Bye Braverman.* Hoberman contended that *The Heartbreak Kid* marked the twilight of this golden age, "Ethnic Jewish characters lost their prominence, although ethnic characterizations did not." Blaxploitation films and Italian-American films followed. He wrote, "With the end of the Jewish new wave, the urban neurotic anti-hero disappeared as well. Or, rather, this figure was subsumed into the person of Woody Allen—at least until he resurfaced, a less abrasive wise guy, in the TV sitcoms of the 1990s."

Allen was—and remains—forthrightly Jewish, and he did so at a time when Jews were only then coming to the forefront of matinee-idol status. Jews had been shticky, almost parodistic comedians (Groucho Marx) or made to seem like WASPs (Lauren Bacall, John Garfield). Allen was an unapologetically Jewish movie star, and in so doing represented a new emerging multicultural America.

As early as 1969, Allen was unashamedly apolitical, although his followers ascribed to him whatever they believed in at the moment. In an interview that preceded *Zelig* by many years, he expressed his contempt for rock and roll, Woodstock, and the mass herd mentality of utopian political movements that lead to fascism, and held out for the solitary independent vision of the artist. "When I was in *Play It Again, Sam,*" he told writer Robert B. Greenfield, "I didn't work on Moratorium Day [an anti–Vietnam War event], for my own reasons. Kids came to me and said, 'That's great, man.' It seems so easy now, to salt things with relevant themes. The kids are exploitable. They've made a lot of millionaires in the last ten years, what with drugs and records and clothes. Music is just too easy. I like it, but their excuse for not reading, for not thinking . . . and then they hang it on McLuhan's global electric thing. I went to see *Woodstock*. The kid in front of me kept saying, 'Beautiful, beautiful,' as though he were trying to convince himself. John Sebastian sings a song about kids, and everyone shouts. There's no discrimination or real art involved in it at all. The truth is, there have never been very many remarkable people around at any one time. Most are always leaning on the guy next to them, asking him what to do."

"Woody managed to be groundbreaking as a comedian and a film-maker yet was never out to overturn the old order," Gary Terracino said. "He did his own thing and was thoroughly new and modern—yet was no hippie or revolutionary or even Hollywood lefty. He was new and fresh without being dangerous; he was a great artist, yet totally accessible; he was cutting-edge, yet safe."

Pauline Kael was the most entertaining of film critics; her enthusiasm for film, which seemed to be her life, communicated itself to the readers of *The New Yorker*. Who else could title a book with semi-innuendo *I Lost It at the Movies* and provoke no surprise whatsoever in the public? (After all, her writing often sounded almost orgasmic.) "You have to be open to the idea of getting drunk on movies," she wrote in 1990. "Our emotions rise to meet the force coming from the screen, and they go on rising throughout our movie-going lives." She was that rare critic who was capable of great acuity but also of writing captivating sentences even when she was completely wrong; she was so swept up in her feelings she could sweep the reader away with her. (Allen told director Peter Bogdanovich that "Kael has everything that a great critic needs except judgment.") She was so good she sounded at times more like a novelist than a critic; when she was wrong one could forgive her, since she was creating her own universe. She called *Take the Money and Run* "a limply good-natured little nothing of a comedy, soft as sneakers." Dead wrong, but what a great sentence! More judiciously, she wrote in 1980 that

> *Woody Allen, who used to play a walking inferiority complex, made the whole country more aware of the feelings of those who knew they could never match the images of Wasp perfection that saturated their lives. He played the brainy, insecure little guy, the urban misfit who quaked at the thought of a fight*

*because physically he could never measure up to the big strong silent men of the myth—the genuine beefcake. Big strong men knew that they can't live up to the myths, either. Allen, by bringing his neurotic terror of just about everything out front, seemed to speak for them, too. In the forties and fifties, when Bob Hope played coward heroes the cowardice didn't have any political or sexual reso-nance, but in the late sixties and the seventies, when Woody Allen displayed his panic he seemed to incarnate the whole anti-macho mood of the time. In the sloppy, hairy counterculture era, Americans no longer tried to conform to a look that only a minority of them could ever hope to approximate. Woody Allen helped to make people feel more relaxed about how they looked and how they really felt about using their fists, and about their sexual terrors and everything else that made them anxious. He became a new national hero. College kids looked up to him and wanted to be like him.*

According to Kael's biographer Brian Kellow, Kael thought that de-spite his jabs at the NRA and the Nixon administration in *Sleeper*, and his popularity with young people, Allen was "anything but subversive. Quite the opposite: He was too much of a misfit to be a genuine hero of the youth movement, and he was a nostalgist with a deep love for traditional pop culture." Allen saw Kael socially when he was filming in California, and corresponded with her. He sent her the script for *Everything You Always Wanted to Know About Sex*, asking for suggestions and criticism. "He wasn't afraid to disagree with her," Kellow wrote, and cultivated her strenuously. "He also knew that he always had a sympathetic ear whenever he com-plained to her about the indignities suffered by talented directors in Hollywood, writing to her in the summer of 1973 about the creative bank-ruptcy that he found so stifling."

Kael, who was Jewish, liked Allen and Streisand at first when, as Jewish actors, they were broad and funny. (She also liked Dustin Hoff-man.) She turned on Allen when he asserted himself, assimilated, and went after the shikse. That was her attitude about Hoffman in *The Gradu-ate* as well. As late as 1980 she flayed Allen for portraying Jewish charac-ters as clowns and frantic stereotypes, citing his flashback to his Jewish family while eating at the table with Annie Hall's family. Kael, as usual, was perceptive about this. Yet Allen would actually move on and create the same scene nine years later—of people from the present walking into the past—in *Crimes and Misdemeanors*, drawing a Jewish family that was serious and real. Allen, whose devout atheism had caused him to be in rebellion against Judaism in his early work, was able here to write of an Orthodox Jewish family with respect and almost rueful regret for not being able to share their hopeful beliefs in a living and compassionate God.

Kael quoted Michelangelo, who observed, "He who walks behind others will never advance." She went on to write that there are two kinds of great directors: Jean Renoir "with his masterly simplicity and unobtrusive visual style [who] has helped people to find their own way. You don't have to walk behind Renoir because he opens an infinite number of ways to go." Renoir blazes a path and creates a template for others to follow. The other kind of director is Jean-Luc Godard, "whom you can only follow and be destroyed. Other filmmakers see the rashness and speed and flamboyance of his complexity, they're conscious of it all the time, and they love it, and, of course, they're right to love it. But they can't walk behind him. They've got to find other ways because he's burned up the ground." Allen is closer to Renoir in this regard. He has changed pop culture and influenced Hollywood in myriad ways.


Allen's comedic persona works in everything he does. Whether it is Virgil in *Take the Money and Run*, Isaac in *Manhattan*, Mickey in *Hannah and Her Sisters*, Cliff in *Crimes and Misdemeanors*, Boris in *Love and Death*, Fielding Mellish in *Bananas*, Danny in *Broadway Danny Rose*, Sandy Bates in *Stardust Memories*, Joe in *Everyone Says I Love You*, Sheldon in *Oedipus Wrecks*, or Alvy in *Annie Hall*, we watch the total alarmist played by Woody Allen, a character who hated school and still hates bugs, the country, sun, crickets, cocaine, pretentious intellectuals, New Age panaceas, death, Los Angeles, marijuana, mechanical devices, rock and roll, hippies, right-wing zealots, Nazis, and catching a cold. In case there is any doubt that we are seeing at least a part of the real Woody in his films, consider this haunting and troubling response to a question by Stig Björkman, a Swedish filmmaker and film journalist, about Boris's attitude toward nature as opposed to urban life in *Love and Death* as it related to Woody's own feelings: "When you look at natural beauty you look at a beautiful pastoral scene. If you look closely what you will see is pretty horrible. It you really could look closely, you would see violence and chaos and murder and cannibalism." And you may see urban beauty, but up close you will see "what happens between man and his fellow man. It's a pretty miserable, ugly, horrifying thing."

This character will often be obsessed by the Holocaust, but he will also, perhaps, regard the concentration camp as a metaphor for ordinary human life. After all, we all wind up in the ashes anyway, don't we? But we know that he thinks of life as meaningless and love as transitory, that "love fades." We know he would never take a shower in front of other men "of his gender." We expect to see in all his films relationships in which "the heart doesn't know from logic," a character is passionate about someone who rejects him or her. The person who rejects is in turn passionate about someone else who is also rejecting her or him. Someone passionately desired by someone always passionately desires someone else. Everybody's looking over their shoulder.

We know that Allen loves Ingmar Bergman, Marcel Ophuls, Frank Sinatra, Jean Renoir, Anton Chekhov, Satchmo, basketball, Fyodor Dostoyevsky, Sidney Bechet, *Rashomon, Shoeshine, The 400 Blows,* and *The Bicycle Thief,* and is drawn, if ambivalently, to magic, psychics, fortune-tellers, and séances, rainy, gloomy days, and always wholeheartedly to New Orleans music and the American Songbook of the Gershwins, Irving Berlin, Cole Porter, and company, to high-strung, neurotic, crazy women, to pairs of sisters, to "polymorphously perverse" women as well as young, beautiful women of all varieties. And we will be reminded that he is disdainful of his comic gifts—"I am cursed with the clown's approach . . . I put a higher value on the tragic muse than on the comic muse"—that he regards drama as the truly serious art form—"I wish I was born a great tragedian, but I wasn't"—and that he regards himself as an unfulfilled artist because he has not written a work that has the grandeur and epiphany of an Ingmar Bergman, a Federico Fellini, a Vittorio De Sica, a Roberto Rossellini, or, for that matter, Tennessee Williams, Eugene O'Neill, or the Arthur Miller of *Death of a Salesman.* Sarah Boxer, who covered Allen's appearance onstage at the 92nd Street Y in New York, reported in the *New York Times* in 2002 that Allen said, "I'm not kvetching. I'm glad I got any gifts at all. But I would like to do something great. . . ." He continued, "I'm not overly humble. I had grandiose plans for myself when I started out. And I have not lived up to them. I've done some things that are perfectly nice. But I had a much grander conception of where I should end up in the artistic firmament. What has made it doubly poignant for me is that I was never denied the opportunity. The only thing standing between me and greatness is me."

But Tennessee Williams and Arthur Miller petered out after the initial flames of their talent burst on the stage; so did O'Neill, although he reemerged triumphantly at the end with *Long Day's Journey into Night*, *The Iceman Cometh*, and *A Moon for the Misbegotten*. Allen, on the other hand, has stayed the course.

Allen respects (but does not love) Preston Sturges's American comedy *Sullivan's Travels*. In that film the movie director comes to the conclusion that comedy is a noble art form because in a world of intense suffering and pain, it lightens people's load and gives them brief moments of happiness and relief. Allen likes the film but reaches the exact opposite conclusion: Comedy is to him a sellout, a compromise with reality that renders it secondary—candy, rather than ballast for the soul. (He told Kent Jones that the end of *Sullivan's Travels* was "a commercial cop-out, because life does *not* have an ending or a resolution. It's an unearned optimism.") Speaking to Michiko Kakutani of the *New York Times* in 1987, he said, "I always enjoyed comedians when I was young. But when I started to read more seriously, I enjoyed some serious writers. I became less interested in comedy then, although I found I could write it. These days I'm not terribly interested in comedy. If I were to list my fifteen favorite films, there would probably be no comedies in there. True, there are some comic films that I think are wonderful."

He has the highest aspirations for his work but despairs that he will achieve them. He has said that he wants to reach the level of O'Neill's *Long Day's Journey into Night* but fears he will wind up with *Edge of Night*, a soap opera. "There is that constant aspiration toward the magical moment," Allen begins, "but in the end . . ." Discouraged, he is unable to finish the sentence. He told Eric Lax in *Conversations with Woody Allen:* "I have a very realistic view of myself. Some people think it's too much or even fake humility when I say I haven't made a great movie. . . . I'm telling the truth. I don't see myself as an artist. I see myself as a working filmmaker. . . . I'm not cynical and I'm far from an artist. I'm a lucky working stiff." Allen spoke even more pessimistically about his artistic limitations in a *Paris Review* interview in 1995. He concluded by stating:

*I say this with no false modesty—that I have done no really significant work, whatsoever, in any medium. I feel that unequivocally. We've been sitting and talking about Faulkner, say, and Updike and Bergman—I mean, I obviously can't talk about myself in the same way at all. I feel that what I've done so far is . . . the bed of lettuce the hamburger must rest on. I feel that if I could do, in the rest of my life, two or three really fine works—perhaps make a terrific film or write a fine play or something—then everything prior to that point would be interesting as developmental works. I feel that's the status of my works— they're a setting waiting for a jewel.*

Some critics agree with his self-assessment and some go even further, computing Allen's late age and the unlikelihood that he can strike gold now: "Basically, for me he's just become an underachiever," J. Hoberman told me. "He makes these movies too quickly and I just think that whatever depth was there has kind of evaporated."

But many others disagree. When I asked film critic and historian Annette Insdorf, director of undergraduate film studies at Columbia University and author of a seminal book about Holocaust films, *Indelible Shadows,* where she would place Allen among American directors, she replied, "He has made a real place for himself in the pantheon. Like Clint Eastwood, his persona has become part of our culture. Both of these actor-musicians were not content to act in other people's films; they became prolific, efficient directors. When I was interviewed for the *American Masters* [PBS documentary about Woody Allen], I compared him to Chaplin and Orson Welles: All three are genuine auteurs whose on-screen personae make them recognizable to audiences.

"I think that—like Preston Sturges and Billy Wilder before him—he is a writer-director with a distinctive voice and a satirical thrust. I appreciate his tone, which is bittersweet and self-conscious. At their best his films reflect on the process of cinematic storytelling. It's no surprise that he and François Truffaut were a mutual admiration society."

When I told Allen that John Simon, who had been extremely harsh toward some of Allen's early films, has reassessed his work, he said:

*I have always liked John Simon. The truth is he is one critic who while being very critical of me over the years, I have still respected and liked personally the number of times I've met him. He is so acerbic that he can be difficult to warm up to but I've always enjoyed reading him and have never held against him, that friends have told me he frequently criticized my work. Incidentally, I do not believe for a second that he reappraised the work and is full of praise. Still, he is an interesting, highly intelligent, insightful, and entertaining critic to read and in person rather likable despite his withering contempt for imperfection.*

I responded by sending him excerpts from the comments Simon had given me in which he had indeed done some reappraisal of Allen's work. Allen answered: "Thank you for sharing John Simon's comments with me. I'm told he has always been tough on my work and perhaps that stringency is a good thing and keeps writers, directors, and actors honest." (Allen, of course, fits admirably into all of the three categories he listed.)

"He hasn't made a great film yet," Simon told me. "But if you make enough good films, that will take the place of one or two great ones. It is amazing how he turns them out. There's no set pattern to them. He is aware of the world. He does pay attention to what's going on."

What seems indelible are our memories of Isaac's face at the end of *Manhattan,* the mingling of hope and fear at Tracy's departure; Broadway Danny Rose's expression when he is told by Lou Canova that he is moving on to greener pastures; Alvy Singer's suggestion to Annie Hall on their first date that they kiss for the first time and get it over with so that they can digest their food better; Isaac and Mary in silhouette seated on the bench overlooking the Fifty-ninth Street Bridge at twilight; Cliff's expression at the sight of Hallie married to Lester in *Crimes and Misdemeanors;* Annie Hall singing "Seems Like Old Times"; the haunting words of hope expressed by Professor Levi at the end of *Crimes and Misdemeanors;* Steffi beside the Seine levitating in *Everyone Says I Love You.* And countless others. These are scenes we will carry with us for the rest of our lives. And in all of these films Allen has been the writer, director, *and* actor.

He is locked into his aloneness. "Woody is very private," film editor Ralph Rosenblum wrote in his memoir, *When the Shooting Stops.* "Very reserved, excruciatingly—at times maddeningly—controlled. The public reports stress his unhappiness, but despite all the words that have been written about his two decades of psychoanalysis, only a few intimates know the particulars of his pain." There are reserve, coldness, and sorrow, but there are generosity, kindness, compassion, and soul as well. *Broadway Danny Rose*, one of his greatest, most personal, and deeply felt films, is a portrait of an Allen that might have been: a loser on the fringe of show business, just the opposite of what Allen has become. But there are aspects to Danny Rose that reflect Allen's philosophy and morality: his loyalty to those who helped him, his feeling for the man who saved his life, Jack Rollins, who gave unstintingly to others—and who helped Allen above all. There is no coldness here. There is tremendous warmth, too, for the struggling denizens of outer show business, the old vaudevillians, the magicians, the jugglers, the tap dancers, those who played the old Keith Vaudeville circuit and the Catskills. When Danny inadvertently causes the mobsters to beat up his ventriloquist, Danny visits him in the hospital and insists on paying his medical bills. He does it simply and without pretense. This is his moral code. Allen does not sentimentalize these sweet losers—he lightly satirizes them—but he loves them.

Few screenwriters are quoted as often as Allen. Yet another example of Allen's finger on the pulse and the social ethos of his liberal audience occurred in October 2014, when David Greenglass, the brother of Ethel Rosenberg, whose testimony against his sister landed her in the electric chair, died at the age of ninety-two. The *New York Times* concluded its front-page obituary of Greenglass with a famous quote from Allen taken from his sarcastic reference to Lester (Alan Alda), his pompous brother-in-law in *Crimes and Misdemeanors:* "I love him like a brother—David Greenglass." Allen has managed to be one of the most widely quoted cultural figures. Even his rare allusions to current events, apolitical as he really is (his friend Marshall Brickman has said that as a kid when he was protesting the execution of the Rosenbergs, Allen was hoping to become an FBI agent someday), never grow stale and are always pointedly, irresistibly, inimitably funny.

Allen celebrated New York at a time when New York was crumbling, when the city doubted itself. He thought the city was a great place to be at a time when Howard Cosell proclaimed, "Ladies and gentlemen—the Bronx is burning!" At the height of white flight Allen said, in essence, "I'm not going anywhere. Why would anyone want to leave?"

What else do we know about Allen? That he passionately, unconditionally, and romantically loves, celebrates, and embraces Manhattan, especially rich Manhattan and its inhabitants, "this bourgeois bubble," J. Hoberman calls it, the Manhattan he saw in Hollywood movies of the

1930s and 1940s, the Upper East Side stretching from Fifty-ninth Street to Ninety-sixth Street, and Central Park, especially the spot where he and Mariel Hemingway in *Manhattan* ride a horse-drawn cab. It is the exact spot he first saw as a boy, watching the scene in which James Stewart sang "Easy to Love" in *Born to Dance* (1936).

He is realistic about his penchant for romanticizing the Manhattan he loves. "I tend to romanticize people and culture heroes, and the island of Manhattan," he said in 1986. "I never grew out of that. New York is not exactly the way it appears in *Manhattan*. I know that at two or three o'clock in the morning if you're sitting down by the Fifty-ninth Street Bridge, you do take a risk. I thought of doing the scene where Mariel Hemingway and I take a carriage ride through Central Park, and having screams in the background, and people yelling 'Stick 'em up.' But in the end, I went for a very romantic piece of Gershwin music. So I do tend to create certain moments of escapist perfection. When I was doing *Manhattan*, I was going all over looking for great places, and it was hard to find places that weren't broken down. . . . I was very selective, and I did the same thing with *Hannah*, choosing the best locations. I presented a view of the city as I'd like it to be, and as it can be today, if you take the trouble to walk on the right streets."

In 2008 Allen went on to elaborate on his love affair with Manhattan. Nothing had changed in his attitude. One can feel the intensity, the excitement of his love for the city as he hopscotches in his mind from Times Square to Bank Street in Greenwich Village to Fifth Avenue to Central Park West, a love he felt initially as a small boy coming to the city with his father. He told James Kaplan in *New York* magazine:

> *I always regretted that I was born too late for New York City in the twenties and thirties, because once the war started, it started to degenerate. Places started to close, the city slowly started getting sucked up into problems of huge welfare payments and narcotics problems, the crime problem mushroomed, television induced people indoors, and the city didn't have the vitality it had when there were so many Broadway shows going and so many nightclubs that you could go to.*
>
> *When I was a child, I lived in Brooklyn, and we were a half-hour away by train. In the early forties, my father would bring me from Brooklyn into Manhattan for a Sunday. . . . You'd walk up into Times Square and look in every direction, and there would be lit marquees from movie houses . . . east and west on 42nd street, and up Broadway. I never saw anything like it in my life. It*

*was just one movie house after another, all lit up, a number of them with stage shows, and the streets were jammed with soldiers and sailors, because it was during the war. And it was just what a choreographer would choose to exaggerate if he was choreographing a ballet about New York. There would be the guys with the apparently stringless dancing dolls that they were selling, and sailors picking up girls at, you know, papaya stands. It was just amazing to look at it. . . .*

*Paris is the only city, I think, that can compete with New York. Paris is a more beautiful city, but it's not more exciting. I still fantasize that a million interesting stories are occurring in those apartments on Fifth Avenue and in those redbrick houses on Bank Street and on Central Park West. You know, it's still so vibrant that I've never felt any diminution of intensity for the city. It's always Manhattan, this little, compact island, where everything is going on.*

Allen/Isaac adores Manhattan unconditionally. But he speaks about the intellectual decay of the city, the problems of an "expedient" culture, and the tendency to "take the easy ways out." Since he spent a lot of years of his youth reading only comic books, and comes to philosophy, art, and literature late, there is a deference on Allen's part to those he considers the heavy thinkers—the artists, the philosophers, the Marshall McLuhans—who periodically decry the deterioration of American culture. And he still maintains he doesn't get pleasure from reading serious literature. And he is still guilty about it. He makes obeisance to the "intellectuals" and, like Alvy Singer, he recoils at the idea of challenging those great minds as the shallow academic on line at the New Yorker theater in *Annie Hall* does, ridiculing Fellini and McLuhan. (Alvy has to summon the real McLuhan to put down the pedant—obviously neither he nor Allen could bear to read McLuhan for himself.) Similarly Isaac/Allen is appalled at the way the academics Mary (Diane Keaton) and his friend Yale (Michael Murphy) put down the "Academy of the Overrated," that gallery of great minds: Isak Dinesen, Carl Jung, F. Scott Fitzgerald, Lenny Bruce, Norman Mailer, and Walt Whitman. Isaac is aghast: "I think those people are all terrific, everyone that you mentioned."

Has Isaac/Allen actually read all these people and genuinely come to the conclusion that they are sacrosanct, or is he name-dropping or following the literary crowd? An autodidact (as he admits) with many gaps in his education, Allen knows that he should revere them, but despite his deep intelligence, he has apparently dipped into literature only dutifully, and not often been enthralled by it except for Dostoyevsky and Tolstoy. He told Stig Björkman: "I never liked to read but I still read a lot. But I have never read a lot for pleasure. I read because it's important to read. Every now and then something gives me pleasure, but mostly it's a chore for me to read." It is hard to know what is true. Allen has a photograph of Dostoyevsky by his bedside (as well as ones of Sidney Bechet and Cole Porter) and clearly reveres him. It all started when he was trying to pick up girls in Greenwich Village, and he'd never heard of Camus and Sartre, and he still defers to the "intellectuals." There isn't the slightest indication that Isaac's cretinous friend Yale (who betrays him in the end) has the intellectual depth, never mind the self-discipline and work ethic, to write a decent study of Eugene O'Neill. Yet it isn't clear at all that Isaac/Woody knows this. He perceives Mary's hollowness as an intellectual, yet he falls for her and is deeply hurt by her rejection.

In both *Annie Hall* and *Manhattan* Allen is holding out for a moral and intellectual rigor, an integrity, decency, humanity that he senses is fading from the world around him, but he doesn't quite know what those high standards are or should be. He senses inauthenticity and phoniness, but his own best friends, Rob (Tony Roberts) and Yale (Michael Murphy), are empty suits. His vision is inchoate. Isaac and Alvy recoil from the vulgarity of TV writing (as Allen did), from all the panaceas that somehow find their apotheosis in Los Angeles (and threaten to permeate Manhattan), and he tries to think they are above it all. But Allen is a quipper, an entertainer, not a sage, and he has no solutions. He is a set of judgmental attitudes; he does not fully know himself. When Alvy Singer's relationship with Annie Hall is broken off by Annie, Alvy, who has driven her away, says, "I don't know what I did wrong." The visionary lacks the self-discipline to penetrate the mysteries of the human condition. He can stab at them, and sometimes when he does, he achieves an artistic epiphany, as in *Crimes and Misdemeanors*.

Allen, who is sly and aware, continues to insist that his life is a simple one built entirely around his work, and he bridles at attempts to psychologize about him. In some ways he is right. Ralph Rosenblum, who worked with him as his film editor for some years, writes perceptively that Allen "has

Prussian discipline. He's the only director I know who finishes a film and then, without any time off, without drinking or drugs or philandering, without celebration, gloating, or self-punishing regrets, goes quietly to work the following day on his next script. He practices his clarinet seven days a week. He finds time to write short stories for *The New Yorker*. He reads voluminously." Mia Farrow, in her memoir, writes of one occasion when Allen was involved in one way or another with juggling four scripts at once.

And we know that Allen, like many artists, borrows liberally and repeatedly from his own life. For a sty in his eye Allen had really gone to a Chinese physician, who advised him to use a cat's whisker in his tear duct, and he had actually done so. Allen lends this event to a guest at a dinner party in *Crimes and Misdemeanors*. (The woman says that she had a friend who consulted a Chinese physician for "an eye problem. And he inserted a cat's whisker into her tear duct and cured it.")

We know that he is a staunch liberal Democrat, and more recently we have learned that while he has no patience whatsoever with organized religion, he passionately loves the state of Israel. He told the Israeli newspaper *Yedioth Ahronoth* in 2012: "I support Israel and I've supported it since the day it was founded. Israel's neighbors have treated it badly, cruelly, instead of embracing it and making it part of the Middle East family of nations. Over the years Israel has responded to these attacks in various ways, some of which I approved of and some less so. I understand that Israelis have been through hard times. I don't expect Israel to react perfectly every time and that doesn't change the fact that it's a wonderful, marvelous country. I'm just worried about the rise of fundamentalism in Israel, which I think damages its interests. I also have questions about your leadership, which doesn't always act in Israel's best interests. But even my criticism of Israel comes from a place of love, just like when I criticize the United States." In 2013, referring to the double standard applied in the barrage of criticism of Israel, he told Israeli television that political criticism of Israel can conceal the deeper hatred of anti-Semitism. "I do feel there are many people that disguise their negative feelings toward Jews, disguise it as anti-Israel criticism, political criticism, when in fact what they really mean is that they don't like Jews."

Earlier, in February 1988, he published a letter in the *New York Times* objecting to Israeli treatment of rioting Palestinians. He expressed his fury about the Holocaust in an article in *Tikkun* magazine in 2002.

But Allen has expressed his feelings about Judaism and the Holocaust most often in his films, where his references to the Holocaust have been frequent. But since his films often have comedic texts, many people may have not taken his comments about the Holocaust or Judaism all that seriously. As astute a critic as Annette Insdorf told me that "Woody Allen's Jewish identity in films like *Annie Hall* is presented in comic terms: we are invited to laugh with and at his 'nebbishy' Jewish persona rather than taking Judaism seriously."

Allen's public comments about Israel, excepting in 2002 and in the recent period, have been few and far between. His caution may be due to his concern about being used as a propaganda tool by others or in some other way tarnishing his artistic vision by being pressured to engage in agitprop projects or to become a "public spokesperson for the Jews." In 2013 the editor of a small Jewish newspaper in Los Angeles began a short-lived campaign to raise funds for Allen to film in Israel—a highly dubious project, since Allen decidedly makes his own artistic decisions without taking advice from anyone except a few close friends like Marshall Brickman, Dick Cavett, and Douglas McGrath, cowriter of *Bullets over Broadway*—has based his entire career on that artistic independence, and has his own secure funding sources.

But the Holocaust remains for him the central horrific event of the twentieth century within a snake pit of nightmarish events. David Dobel, a central character in *Anything Else,* an excellent, unjustly underrated film, says: "The crimes of the Nazis were so enormous it could be argued that it would be justified if the entire human race were to vanish as a penalty." This statement is repeated twice in the film, once orally and once written on a chalkboard. Allen expressed the same sentiments in a letter to me about the Holocaust: "Since the Holocaust was such an immense event in my lifetime it couldn't help but wind up as a sporadic or even frequent issue in my work. . . . There are certain crimes that are simply unforgivable. I believe we are a species that would very easily die out with nobody to thank for it except for ourselves."

The film has many other references to the Holocaust, and Allen told Douglas McGrath in *Interview* magazine that the character of David

Dobel has aspects of himself in it. Dobel, a schoolteacher, is a mentor to Jerry Falk, a young writer in his thirties. Dobel constantly refers to the Holocaust and to anti-Semitism. Coming out of a comedy club with Falk, he tells Falk that a couple of men looked at them and one said, "Jews start all wars." He tells Falk, "We live in perilous times. You got to stay alert to these things. You don't want to wind up as black and white newsreel footage scored by a cello in a minor key." He urges Falk to purchase a gun and a survival kit. He has a gun in every room of his apartment. "The day will come when you need a weapon," he says. Jerry asks why. "Why?" Dobel replies. "So they don't put you in a box-car."

Jerry Falk: "Dobel, you're a madman."

David Dobel: "That's what they said in Germany. There were actually groups called 'Jews for Hitler.' They were deluded. They thought he would actually be good for the country. . . . You are a member of one of the most persecuted minorities in history."

Falk tells his girlfriend that Dobel "is still convinced that the slaughter of six million Jews is not enough to satisfy the anti-Semitic impulses of the majority of the world." Dobel tells him, "What you don't know will kill you. Like if they tell you you're going to the showers. But they turn out not to be showers."

"The issue is always fascism," Dobel insists.

Another thing I am certain of is that Allen is not a schlemiel, a nebbish, a sad sack, or a Kafkaesque character, nervously treading the world as a freaky outsider. "I remember when I first saw Woody on the street," Norman Podhoretz, the former editor of *Commentary*, who lives in Allen's neighborhood, told me. "I was struck by how utterly different his posture was from his image: strong, stiff, upright. The schlemiel he plays is a persona. He does it well. It clearly isn't him." This view of Allen was echoed by John Lahr: "There's a difference between the magician and his bag of tricks. Allen does not stammer. He is not uncertain of what he thinks. . . . He is courteous but not biddable. He is a serious, somewhat morose person who rarely raises his voice, who listens carefully and who, far from being a sad sack, runs his career and his business with admirable, single-minded efficiency." The director Sydney Pollack observed, "He's *very* intransigent—in the best sense of the word. For all the mild-manneredness, the Mr. Peepers thing, I have always felt he was a very strong man."

He was unquestionably shy at the beginning. "I remember when I started," Juliet Taylor, Allen's casting director for more than thirty years now, told me. "I was working as an assistant to [casting director] Marion Dougherty. And Woody literally wouldn't talk to me. He brought his line producer with him. And Woody sat in the corner, and the producer spoke because Woody couldn't do it. He sat in this little rocking chair, and he had this funny little Victorian house. And Freddy Gallo, who was assistant director, did the interviews. It was so funny.

"So back then—he's much less shy now—Woody really wouldn't talk to people very much," Taylor continued. "He kept thinking he didn't want to waste people's time. He'd say, 'I don't want to ask somebody in and maybe get their hopes up and then disappoint them.' I would say, 'Well, if you're legitimately thinking of them, an actor likes nothing more than the opportunity to prove to you that they're the person for this part.' Sometimes I think he can overdo it in that way. But my experience is that many directors who have also been performers are like that. They really don't like to put actors through the paces because they've been there. This was true of Sydney Pollack and I hear this about Clint Eastwood. They are really uncomfortable in the casting process. They just feel embarrassed by it.

"And Woody still definitely does his own thing. 'Aloof' is too strong a word. But he doesn't engage and he doesn't rehearse and he doesn't spend time with people; he doesn't shmooze. Actors are used to it by now; he's got that reputation, and they're all kind of ready for it. But if they aren't, it can be upsetting to people. And he's a hands-off director; that's what I think makes actors anxious. He doesn't do a readthrough. He doesn't rehearse. And he doesn't spend any big chat time with them. So they're nervous that they're going to arrive on the set and he's not going to be pleased with their performance. So he's hands off in the sense that he'll say to people, 'If the dialogue doesn't make you comfortable, change the words. Make it your own. Just do it.' But more and more he's getting a little bolder. He's starting to be rather specific with people if he doesn't feel they're getting it."

I asked Taylor if it had taken Allen this long.

"Yes! Yes, I think so. He went through a period years ago where people would be fired. There was quite a bit of firing that went on earlier on. *September* was a movie in which he said he wasn't happy with the writing. He reshot the whole thing. And he couldn't get all the cast back. Some he didn't ask back. I felt and so did everyone else involved that he wasn't really doing the due diligence before hiring people. He was hiring people without meeting them or without really exploring the situation. I found that, if I brought an actor in, the most important thing was to tell Woody what that person's capabilities were—I'd say, 'Okay, this person has this strong quality and this strong quality, but you know, you really need to read them, because I've never heard them do something like this.' Or I'd say, 'This person can definitely do it.' Or 'You have to hear it, you have to hear it.' So he does read people, which he didn't use to do. It's been going on now for a number of years. So it's changed and he's become more responsible. He hasn't replaced anybody for a long time. Also financially it wasn't a doable thing.

"After so many years together, the casting process is sort of more of an ongoing conversation. Because we're old friends, really. And we've been doing this for so long. Usually he starts to think about what he might write around the Christmas holidays. We sort of start talking about the idea he has before he's really finished writing. He feels me out about whether I like the idea, whether it feels right in terms of what he did just before. Or whatever else he's thinking of.

"Sometimes he'll have two ideas. Sometimes he'll send me two scripts. Or he'll talk about two ideas. And then if we're talking about one, the conversation might lead on to, 'Well, if we did this, who would be right for it?' Obviously you always want to have the perfect person for everything. He's not someone who waits for an actor. He's on a schedule, so he will keep pushing forward. If we haven't gotten an actor who he thought was going to be really remarkable, he may have thought of doing something else he had in mind. Usually we keep going until he fills it. This is rare, but occasionally you'll get the feeling that if we can't get the best for this, the person that's really going to make it their own and special—he'll say, 'Well, this is what I've written and I think it's a good idea. But I'm going to take a few weeks and I'm going to fool around with this other idea.' And then he'll come back to it. Or not.

"But you can really say anything to him. I don't think I've ever worked with anyone who was as easygoing about stuff like that, listening and taking advice without ego. I think my experience is that the better, the more talented the director is, the more open they are to hearing what people have to say. He's very open. He's great to work with in the sense that you can really suggest some pretty far-out ideas and he responds. It's great to work with a director who makes you feel safe in bringing up outlandish ideas, not somebody who shuts you down right away. I also think he's got a wonderful, even work process. You can deliver the worst piece of news, that somebody just dropped out, and he'll just say, 'Okay, so what are we gonna do?' He's not all upset. I don't think I've ever seen him lose his temper. Very even tempered, very steady."

Ralph Rosenblum also mentioned Allen's flexible ego. "Unlike so many directors I have known," he noted, "Woody simply has not allowed the ego issues to get in the way. He's kept focused on his main concern, which is the work, and has refused to fall into playing The Director. Repelled by anything resembling authoritarian posturing, he's gone overboard at times to avoid it, appearing on the set in the frowsiest outfits and speaking in the softest, most uncommanding voice."

Yet we also know that, by his own admission, he has "burned over a low flame of depression my whole life." He has never had "clinical" or suicidal depression, but what he has defined as a "low-level depression." The pilot light is always on. He has devised strategies over the years to work around it, he told Eric Lax: working, relationship, and distraction strategies. He calls his aloof, withdrawn attitude an aspect of his depression.

But there is a certain self-acceptance in his more recent reflections. He told Robert Weide in *Woody Allen: A Documentary* in 2011: "I've lived out all these childhood dreams. I wanted to be a movie actor. I became one. I wanted to be a movie director and comedian. I became one. I wanted to play jazz in New Orleans and I played in street parades and joints in New Orleans and played opera houses and concerts all over the world. There was nothing in my life that I aspired toward that hasn't come through for me." He added laughingly with gentle, self-mocking irony: "But despite all these lucky breaks, why do I feel I got screwed somehow?"

We know too that Allen's work ethic has been ingrained in him and that it has, as he freely admits, saved his life. "I knew this when I was in my late teens," he told Stig Björkman in 2000. "That there were always going to be distractions as well. And I felt that anything that distracted from the work and minimized your effort on it was a self-deception that was going to be detrimental. So to avoid getting caught up with a lot of writing rituals and time-wasting, you've got to get there and just work. Art in general, and show business, is full to the brim of people who talk, talk, talk, talk. And when you hear them talk, theoretically they're brilliant and they're right and this and that, but in the end it's just a question of 'Who can sit down and do it?' That's what counts. All the rest doesn't mean a thing."

From that work ethic emerged a work pattern that he has adhered to throughout his life. The hardest work of writing for him is the "pre-work," finding the ideas, the conception of the entire story. He is home free after that. "When I get up the day that I'm going to start the actual writing," he told Björkman, "I can celebrate. Because that's the day when everything is over." All the agonizing work has been done. Writing the rest is "pure pleasure." He writes quickly; he has to hurry to keep up with his thoughts. But he's done the hard work already. He can write the script anywhere, on scraps of paper, on laundry slips, on menus, on hotel stationery, the backs of envelopes, sitting on a park bench. He can travel through Europe from town to town and virtually construct a film script on hotel napkins before he boards the plane to New York. (He did that with *Crimes and Misdemeanors.*) "Writing is a complete pleasure for me," he told Björkman. "I love it. It's a sensual, pleasurable activity that's fun."

"The other person who keeps working all the time is Bob Dylan," J. Hoberman told me. "And he's by all accounts very strange. Driven in a certain way and isolated. People who have talked to me about Woody say he only comes alive when playing his music."

He is in love with the creative process; it may be almost as good as sex for him. "It is culmination, it is flying, it is being wholly alive," he related to Björkman. "I start to think. I walk up and down [his living room] and I walk up and down the outside terrace. I take a walk around the block. I go upstairs and take a shower. I come back down and think. And I think and think. . . . I work every day. And even when you're not thinking about it, when you get it going, your unconscious is cooking, once you've turned it on." He takes breaks to play the clarinet, but even when he is not consciously thinking of writing the unconscious is percolating.

He is still most inspired by the Russians. He feels that he must, he told Björkman, "aim at very, very high material. And that to me would be the spiritual, existential realm." Aiming high has been both a virtue and a trap for him, yet it was a triumph for him in *Crimes and Misdemeanors.*

He has stayed skeptical of political movements because he views change as death. "I'm against change," he related to Björkman. "Because change equals aging, change equals the progression of time, the destruction of the old order. Now, you can say that somebody in a certain station in life wants nothing more than change, because they want the destruction of the old order. But ultimately, to me, change is not your friend. It's like nature. Change is your temporary friend sometimes. People who live in poverty and misery, of course, long for change. And when they get change, change is their friend for that period of time. But change beyond that is not going to be their friend. Change is a fair-weather friend, a short-term friend."

Among independent filmmakers, he stands alone. Others have had, and some continue to have, memorable moments—Richard Linklater, Nicole Holofcener, Alexander Payne, the Coens, Wes Anderson—but Allen has persevered and triumphed over a period of forty-six years with endless diversity and inventiveness. His continuity and high rate of productivity are unprecedented.

He is closest in some ways to the late Claude Chabrol, one of the best of the influential French New Wave directors. Like Allen, Chabrol made an enormous number of films (more than sixty) and would have a few stretches of unsuccessful, weak films but then bounce back with a slew of good-to-near-great films in a row, with an occasional masterpiece. Then he would return to the weak but usually interesting ones, and back again to the good ones. Chabrol loved working all the time, just like Allen. He admitted that for him shooting a movie was like a drug, and that he'd rather make a bad film than not make any film at all. (Allen's *Match Point*, one of his better later films, is very much like one of Chabrol's thrillers. The section of *Crimes and Misdemeanors* involving the murder of the mistress is influenced by Chabrol.) Among American directors, Allen is perhaps most like Robert Altman, who also worked constantly until he died and went through many peaks and valleys. This was also true to some extent of John Ford, although he was working within the studio system, and of John Huston.

Kafka is like the grandfather of Allen's generation of comic artists, from Philip Roth to Jules Feiffer to Lenny Bruce, Joan Rivers, Shelley Berman, Mort Sahl, and Elaine May. Allen can be linked to all these other people of his generation; he is central to his times. But one of the most facile psychological comparisons that has been made over the years has been that of Allen with Kafka. Yes, Woody hid himself in the basement of his Brooklyn house because he had little to say to his parents, and there are superficial similarities in Kafka's and Woody's self-derision. But there the parallels end. He was not afraid of his parents. "Woody's father was more a buddy than a father," Jerry Epstein, Woody's childhood friend, now a psychiatrist and an author, told me. He recalled that one of Marty Konigsberg's frequent affectionately teasing jokes was to say to Woody, "I hope you'll be the champ of the world." Woody asked why, and Marty replied, "Because then I'd be the next champ." Woody loved and seemed to be loved by his Runyonesque, somewhat goofy father, who resembled the French comic actor Fernandel, was happy-go-lucky, a good-time Charlie and hustler who played the numbers and carried a gun. He'd run a pool hall and been an egg candler, a bookmaker and gofer for the mob boss Albert Anastasia, a jewelry engraver, and a cabdriver (as in *Radio Days*). Woody got many different answers from his parents when he asked them what Marty did for a living. One response was that he was "a big butter-and-egg man," the explanation Joe's parents give him in *Radio Days*. Marty played all the angles at Sammy's Bowery Follies, a funky Gay Nineties joint in the pit of the Bowery, beneath the rumbling Third Avenue El. He tended bar, was a bouncer, and was later promoted to night manager. "I know that Marty was on a firing squad at some point in his life," Jerry Epstein told me. "I don't know the circumstances. He also helped to make the badges for the New York City Police Department, together with his uncle."

Marty was easy with money and gave Woody a generous seven-dollar weekly allowance when he was a teenager, often slipping him more money when he felt like it. Sammy's attracted many celebrities, rich people and tourists who came from all over to mix with the servicemen on leave to watch the raucous, saucy scene at the club with its showgirls and zaftig red-hot mamas in big floppy hats who stood atop the bar belting out the old saloon songs, waving large white handkerchiefs. Weegee, the famed news photographer with an eye for the exotic and the macabre, hung out at the club and took many photographs of the goings-on there.

It was easy to park on the Bowery, with its abandoned buildings and scores of SRO hotels for the homeless. Hoboes and alcoholic bums lined the streets, sleeping in hallways and cadging drinks from the tourists. They waited for the elegant cars to arrive and park on the street, and after their owners hurried into Sammy's, they often broke into the car windows and stole anything in sight. They brought the merchandise to Woody's father in the early morning hours after the club shuttered for the night, and traded the merchandise for drinks. He often brought home all kinds of gadgets, valuables, and nice clothing for Woody, his sister, Letty, and his mother. "His father could get you anything you wanted without a serial number," Elliott Mills, a boyhood friend from Woody's teenage years, told me. "When we started playing music, these instruments appeared with their serial numbers filed off." Woody said of his father, "He never let a thought enter his head. When he was young he spent every cent he ever made. Never thought about whether he could pay the bills. He was an affectionate guy, but he never cared about anything."

"One time we were driving with Marty," Jack Victor, another boyhood friend, remembered, "and he was upset because people would park a car and they opened the door on the roadside. He said, 'If I hit him there wouldn't be a thing he could do about it.' I said to him, 'Well yes, he'd be dead.'"

"Woody's father was very doting on him," Jerry Epstein said. "Very accepting of him. No question. The mother wasn't but the father definitely was. Woody treated him like a friend rather than like a dad. We used to come home from school at three p.m., and Woody's father, who came home very late from Sammy's, was there in a chair watching the old grade-B black-and-white Westerns. He was mesmerized by them. Woody's mother worked days as a secretary in the flower district. She would bring home very beautiful flowers."

In his later years, after Woody became a client, Marty Konigsberg became a messenger for Jack Rollins's office. "My father had to give him something to do. Marty was driving everyone crazy," Susan Rollins, Jack's daughter, told me. "And he liked to walk. So that's what he did. He was a blustery simpleton. A great intellectual he wasn't. Working as a messenger didn't seem beneath him. He seemed well suited for the job. He'd come all dressed dapperly in a suit, with a diamond tie pin. He looked like a horseplaying gambler. Woody thought his father being a messenger was sort of great because it gave him something to do. There was an affection there combined with some shame."

The mother would always remain ambivalent, but there may have been a hardening toward Allen on his father's part as well in the later years. In the documentary *Wild Man's Blues*, Woody and Soon-Yi visit his parents in the twilight of their years. It would appear from the documentary that the father and mother have a lot to do with that underlying lifetime depressiveness that Allen acknowledges. The parents' behavior is joyless as they behold their son, a star beloved by half the world, who has been good to them and to his sister Letty. Their attitude toward Allen seems almost pathological in its complaint and bitterness. There is no acknowledgment, no recognition of what Allen has accomplished. One has to imagine that for all the family closeness and love they gave him in the Jewish family way, there was always this element. The chronically unhappy man and wife in the film—who, Allen has said, did not speak to each other for months or perhaps even years at a time—may have gotten worse with age. But the depression and bitterness seem to have always been hovering there.

In Franz Kafka's monumental story, "The Judgment," as in so much of his work, Kafka deals with the castrating attitude of his father and his own inability ever to surmount his father's tyrannical domination. His father rebukes him for wanting to marry and condemns his "devilish" ways. At the conclusion of the story, Georg, Kafka's protagonist, consumed by guilt and the compulsion to try to please his father, obeys his command to jump off the bridge and drown himself. It is the culmination of a story in which the father's ravenous hatred and condemnation of his son reach lunatic proportions.

Woody was not a creature out of Kafka. He had a strained relationship with his strict and punishing (but loving) mother—perhaps the "castrating Zionist" in *Oedipus Wrecks*—and his carefree, careless father who played the numbers every day. But he was not consumed or enthralled by great literature, reading Dostoyevsky in his basement room, afraid to go outside. He was a creature of the pool halls and the streets, a habitué of vaudeville shows and the Magic Shop on Times Square and every movie theater in Brooklyn and the Paramount Theatre in New York, and a fairly good athlete. He told the *New York Times* that as a boy he had been "interested in being a gambler, a card hustler, a dice hustler." He added that he "was aiming to a life of borderline crime." One of the few references to him in his high school newspaper was this warning from the editor: "A motto among Red's [Woody's] friends: 'Never play cards with Konigs-berg!'" When he read, he read only comic books. He was not even a pas-sive victim of his mother. He wheedled his way, struck back, teased and tormented her, and followed his own path. When he was twenty, he was seated at the kitchen table talking of his coming marriage to Harlene Rosen. He showed his engagement ring to his mother. His mother held on to it while lecturing him on the foolishness of the impending marriage. Woody grabbed the ring out of her hand and ended the conversation by storming out of the house.

Allen was never a victim. He set about very early defining and working at his goals. He was indefatigable, resourceful, and tenacious. Whatever he did he did completely, working long hours from the beginning. "Woody has very little in common with the characters he portrays in his films," Ralph Rosenblum noted. "The insecurity and fears are truly his own, but the behavior is not. He is not a bumbler. He is not ingratiating. He rarely makes an effort to be affable to strangers. He is not particularly 'Jewish' in his mannerisms, speech, or personal habits. Despite his scuffed shoes, ill-fitting chinos, army fatigues, and dilapidated felt hat, he is, when working, much more the style and image of the detached corporation executive."

"Woody was a go-getter," Elliott Mills, now a research scientist at Duke University Medical School, told me. "He was a hustler. He worked hard. I admire him for the determination he showed at a young age. We went on these dates, and Woody used to wear his trench coat and dangle a ciga-rette from his lips. To look like Bogart. Tucked it in the trench coat and smoked the cigarette. You had to know how to take them out of a pack-age. How to stick it in your sleeve. All kinds of cool things. He could make a nice production out of a cigarette."

"Woody was a pretty good athlete," Jack Victor, now a research psy-chologist, recalled. "He was a pretty good baseball player, and he was a very fast runner. He had an overdeveloped calf muscle, and one of his problems was that the muscle would pop. Before I knew Woody well, there was a track meet in junior high school, and Woody ran against the guy everybody knew as the fastest guy on the track. But Woody beat him. I remember saying I'll eat my paper bag if this guy Larry loses. And I had to eat the paper bag."

"We played a lot of board games together," Jerry Epstein recalled.

" 'Cabbie' was one of the great games we played. Part of the game stipulated you had to steal passengers from other cabs, and be caught by the police. So Woody always wanted to take the position of the cab that stole the passengers. There were the police and there were the cabbies. Woody always took the position of wanting to get away with something. There's a trickster element that's always there in him. With Woody it's 'Me real, you shadow.' "

The story of Woody Allen is the story of the triumph of the very small, unattractive guy, the most unlikely, the most neurotic, the nebbish. In his youth he loved to do magic tricks (they reappear in a number of his films).

"As a kid I loved magic and might have become a magician if I hadn't been sidetracked," Allen told John Lovick in *Genii* magazine in 2015. "When I got my first magic sets, and there were cups and balls and Chinese boxes and sponges, I was intrigued with the equipment. And then when you go to the magic store and you see all these wonderful things, candle tubes and production boxes and changing bags with red velvet and the tassel. It all looks so luscious to you, so inviting that you become turned on by it, and I was turned on by it. And I read all the magic books. And then you would read about [the] magicians . . . the feats sounded very heroic and amazing, naturally the Houdini things, the vanishing of elephants, and the sawing women in half, and mummy cases . . . and all of that stuff . . . I don't mean to be stretching here [but it] just had a religious quality to it. . . . It's ritualistic—you lay the woman down and you cover her up and then you take the saw and put it through her, and she's restored. Or you put the person in a mummy case and they appear at the back of the theater. So it was the exotica of the equipment that was so fascinating to me."

"There's a very close bond between magic and stand-up comedy," the comedy and TV screenwriter and biographer Mark Evanier told me. "They are two of the only professions that are self-starting. You don't need assistance, you don't need props. You can do your magic act anywhere. There are people who do magic acts and comedy acts. It kind of blurs which they are. One bleeds into the other very easily. There are some comedians who are more magicians and some magicians who are more comedians. Many people like Johnny Carson and Dick Cavett segued from magic to comedy.

"Magic has a punch line," Evanier continued. "For the most part you're working toward a punch line. You're setting it up. There's that skill you need to cultivate: how fast or how slow to get there. Because one of the worst things you can do in comedy is rush a joke. One of the worst things you imagine in magic is rush a trick. Ideally in magic as in comedy, you want to surprise the audience in an expected way. Unless you're doing a classic trick they already know, like sawing a lady in half, your goal is to not have them know what's going to happen but to accept it as logical when it does. 'Oh yeah! I should have seen that coming!'"

Soon Allen moved from magic tricks to the magic of the movies, and he has never strayed from his love of that form of magic. He reverses the usual male-female stereotype; he appears to be the weak, needy one. The Woody Allen schlemiel was a first for American comedy despite its derivations from Chaplin, Buster Keaton, and Laurel and Hardy: a man who is vulnerable, inadequate, insecure, and often helpless, as when he tries to drop a lobster into a lobster pot, or kill a water bug in Annie Hall's bathroom. It is easy to hurt him. He is often pathetically dependent on his lover, begging her to not leave him even when he has manipulated her into doing so. His attempts at machismo seem ridiculous. This insecurity is what made Allen's male personae such a startling change from traditional Hollywood stereotypes.

This irresistible scamp, this desperate chaser of women, this eternal adolescent trying to prove his manhood, has now become one of the elder statesmen of comedy. The whole generation of Bob Hope, Milton Berle, and Jack Benny is all gone. The next generation of living comedians is Don Rickles, Bob Newhart, Mel Brooks, Jackie Mason, Carl Reiner, Jerry Lewis, and Woody Allen. A mere handful, they are all in their eighties or nineties (Reiner). Of the entire group, only Allen—whose eightieth birthday is imminent—is still starring in movies.

He derived his screen and stage personae partly from Chaplin's tramp and Stan Laurel's naïf, men whose inadequacies were considered unmanly and who were desperately shy. They displayed needy, "feminine" characteristics. Stan Laurel often wept when he was unhappy or when he was criticized. These characters encouraged both men and women to empathize with them; they felt themselves invisible to a society focused on strong, masculine winners. In reality Chaplin and Laurel created characters whose inadequacies are many men's. Chaplin spotlighted aspects of men's personalities that had traditionally been regarded as unmanly: a desperate eagerness to please and to be loved. Shyness with women, physical incompetence in the workplace. Laurel also emphasized the feminine side of his character: He was so deferential to Oliver Hardy that he seemed almost to be playing his wife. Yet today audiences do not feel more than a remote affection for Chaplin's tramp or for Laurel and Hardy. The world *loves* Allen.

There was that fundamental difference, however, between Allen's screen persona and the archetypal wusses who did not seek physical intimacy with a woman, just as there was a wide difference between Allen and Kafka: Allen was a sexual aggressor. For Allen physical intimacy is a constant goal. Defying his fate, psychological chains, and deformations (which he has chronicled endlessly and hilariously)—an apparent inability to associate with people often lest he come into contact with germs that could kill him, a fear of elevators and enclosed places—despite these, he was a *tough* heterosexual man with a rampaging lust that in his early years rendered him shy and self-conscious with women. But he was not shy or uncertain in his art. Unlike so many writers, Allen did not grapple with the demons of drug abuse, megalomania, and crippling self-doubt. His self-assurance always won the day. This is the story of an artist succeeding against difficult odds, a story of resurgence, resilience, and steely determination: as a person, screenwriter, director, prose writer, actor, and playwright.

# 1. Enchantment Was the Reason

THIS IS NOT a blow-by-blow or a standard critical biography. Other writers have connected all the dots of Woody Allen's personal life and his work. Allen has been explored, dissected, and analyzed, and has eluded the grasp of biographers who have explored him that way. I want to add what has been missed about his work while sketching in some essential brushstrokes of his life and career. There is a great deal that is new. I hope that these discoveries and insights will make Allen known and understood in a deeper way.

Allen was one of a select group of men enormously rich by their thirties, used to getting what he wanted, doing whatever he wanted, and getting away with it. But *what* did he want? Apart from artistic freedom and independence, it has never been clear. He was never beholden to normal moral boundaries. There were no boundaries, no remorse. Yet he has proceeded morally. He was withdrawn and brooding, and he has stayed that way. "I think he's essentially the same person he was when he started out," Richard Schickel told me. "I don't think his essential sensibility has changed much over the years. He really will do what he wants to do.

And he doesn't really care what other people think. He simply lives his life by his own lights. It's a completely moral life. I've known him since the sixties. He's never disappointed me. I have the highest regard for him.

"When he finishes one movie, I don't think he really takes any time off," Schickel continued. "He's probably thinking about the next one when he's making the one he is making. He just goes ahead. I don't think, health issues aside, I can't imagine him stopping. I think he'll go forever. Those who are really unstoppable as artists, I think, like Woody, are a little bit taken for granted. People don't really appreciate the consistent high quality of what he does. So many people falter quite early and fall into their various funks. But he does not. It's an amazing body of work."

But Allen remains painfully shy. "The most difficult aspect of filmmaking for Woody is *people*," Ralph Rosenblum wrote. "Meeting them, dealing with them, managing them. . . . Socializing, schmoozing, kibitzing are anathema to him. He'd prefer not to be introduced to the sound editor's new assistant, and he will do almost anything to avoid a handshake. Those he gives—watery handshakes, no grip in them at all—seem to be moments of torture during which he won't know what to do with his eyes." The concentration is always on his work.

And Allen seems to disappoint himself even in that. He has always walked away from what he has succeeded at. It's never good enough, in his own estimation. He didn't let himself be swayed by the passion for acceptance and money. He has turned his back on success in a way that no other major filmmaker has. They would be both unwilling and unable to do it. In terms of early white-hot mainstream successes—*What's New Pussycat? Casino Royale, What's Up, Tiger Lily?, Love and Death, Annie Hall, Manhattan*—his career can be compared to Alfred Hitchcock's. But Hitchcock loved the hits. It mattered to him to have an audience. In the Truffaut-Hitchcock interviews in *Hitchcock* (1967), he shrugged off *Vertigo* because it was not a big hit. He had success as a producer and director in filmmaking and TV for decades, and he was somewhat addicted to that. Allen's addiction is to the work alone. Allen has constantly segued from commercial hits (*Manhattan*) to Bergmanesque esoterica (*Interiors*) to beautiful and heartfelt personal films (*Broadway Danny Rose*) without batting an eyelash, just as he has constantly experimented with new types and styles of films so that he would not sacrifice his freedom to invent and create something new. He has been aesthetically and thematically groundbreaking in ways that we have tended to forget or take for granted. There's no linear arc to *Annie Hall*: Allen uses animation in it; he plays with time; he uses a split screen. He breaks the fourth wall. Annie moves outside her body to observe her lovemaking with Alvy.

Walking away has been a recurring motif in Allen's career—and life. "Woody had developed over the years an absolutely killing stand-up act," Mark Evanier recalled. "He gave it up. There are other guys with that kind of material who would have lived the rest of their lives off that act. Woody was opening at one point in Las Vegas for someone else. He didn't care about the billing. Very few people in his position would not say, 'I'm not going to take second position on the marquee; it's bad for my career.' But for Woody, stand-up didn't matter; he wasn't going to do stand-up for the rest of his life. At that point it was clear he was moving toward movies and stage. There was a moment in his career when he was on everything. He was on game shows. He was guest host for Johnny Carson. He was on *I've Got a Secret, What's My Line?* And there seemed to be nothing he wouldn't do. He was turning up in *Playboy* all the time. And that all stopped. One day he was not available anymore."

Allen was a hit in Las Vegas, extremely popular with audiences, and he walked away from it. No other film artist has walked away from the mainstream in this way. Allen has always walked away. He walked away from being a hugely successful TV writer. Harlene, his first wife, urged him to persevere and keep building on his success in television, but he turned his back on that to do stand-up, where there was initially no money at all. That was part of the tension between them. He was very popular on the talk-show circuit. He walked away from that. Then from stand-up he segued to become a very successful Hollywood writer. When he wanted to become a writer-director, there wasn't real support for that; his budget was only a million and a half dollars for *Take the Money and Run*. That wasn't his salary; that was the total budget. They wouldn't pay him a fee, and people were asking him, Why are you doing this? Go cash your checks and be a Hollywood rewrite guy.

"There's some self-loathing in Woody," according to Gary Terracino. "Groucho Marx's 'I would never want to join a club that would have me as a member.' It's there in what he's walked away from. It's there in the way he doubts his own work. It's there in terms of how he blew up his personal life. But he has always known how to fan the flames of his own celebrity but not be a fame-chasing whore.

"While there's that aspect of Woody, it's not quite self-destructive because he's always done things the same way," Terracino continued. "There's something contemptuous, a need to upend things without upending things—shake things up, let people know he can walk away. You don't think I can walk away from Hollywood? I can walk away. You don't think I can walk away from Vegas? Yes I can. You don't think I can abandon the working-class and middle-class shtick of *Take the Money and Run* and *Sleeper?* Watch me. He walked away from Mia even with the kids. I can be nominated for the Academy Awards every other year. I won't go. He can do it. And most people *can't*. Most artists hold on to everything. Everyone else chased the hits. There's no other mainstream writer or producer who has not been intoxicated by the mainstream. Orson Welles, of all people, was in love with his celebrity. With other artists, self-loathing manifests itself as a more desperate need for success and adulation. Scorsese cares about success. Hitchcock lived and died by temporary success. People like Coppola or Hal Ashby spun out of control in more drugs and alcohol or more blatantly self-destructive behavior chasing the hits."

"And Woody doesn't pander to easy money," Mark Evanier said. "Think what Woody could make tomorrow if he suddenly decided to endorse a product or do a TV special. Or make a really commercial movie. Even if it's not money, sometimes there's a desire for activity and notoriety. Not Woody. He must be constantly approached by people who want to break into his lifestyle, have him appear in their movie, direct their movie, be on their specials. I don't know if he's ever done a talk show since the early days on Carson and Cavett. There was a period when the staff that worked for David Letterman were determined to get Woody on the show. David had made it clear that he wanted no guest more than Woody Allen. People had the attitude, I'll be the hero; Dave will love me if I get Woody. And I'd guess they probably made some pretty rude, harassing approaches. I would guess when they called Woody's office it's like, Thanks very much; Woody is very appreciative of the honor but he just doesn't do that. There are only a handful of people who are ungettable. There aren't too many people who ever place limitations on their own careers. Who just say, I'm going to do this. I don't care if I do anything else."

I will mention in passing but not dwell on Allen's lesser films (good as many of them are), and I will focus on some of his best: *Annie Hall, Manhattan, Zelig, Broadway Danny Rose, The Purple Rose of Cairo, Hannah and Her Sisters, Husbands and Wives, Radio Days, Crimes and Misdemeanors, Bullets over Broadway, Alice, Deconstructing Harry, Anything Else, Match Point, You Will Meet a Tall, Dark Stranger, Everyone Says I Love You,* and *Midnight in Paris.* Critics I respect have—incomprehensibly, from my point of view—mined his "Bergman" films and his German-Jewish expressionist experiment, *Shadows and Fog,* for depth and significance, but they just aren't there. "Watching those films is like having a stone on your chest," the film critic Phillip Lopate told me. The critics who take those films seriously are among the ones to whom Allen often grants his most confiding and open interviews: Richard Schickel, Stig Björkman, and Eric Lax, his first biographer. Yet Allen clearly admires and respects writers critical of his work, John Simon and Pauline Kael among them.

"Any kind of dependence is dangerous," John Simon related. "And to be too over dependent is certainly dangerous. I think that admiration for Bergman and a kind of conscious, or even unconscious, imitation is a perilous position. Because you can't imitate a genius. You can imitate lesser men. But with a genius either you become too subservient or you try very hard not to show that you're imitating. That pushes you in a questionable direction." Woody nailed it himself, perhaps unwittingly, when he was asked by Eric Lax about the reaction of some critics that the dialogue of *Interiors* was too stiff, and he made the startling admission that he may inadvertently have been writing *subtitles* instead of live dialogue:

> *After* Interiors, *months later, I was sitting home and suddenly thought to myself, Gee, did I make this mistake? Because of my exposure to foreign films, in my ear for dialogue, was I really writing subtitles to foreign films? When you see, say, a Bergman film, you're reading it because you're following the subtitles. And when you read it, the dialogue has a certain cadence. My ear was picking up on subtitle-style dialogue and I was creating that for my characters. I worried about that. It's something I never really resolved clearly. I don't know.*

What is clear is that Allen is often hung up on doom and gloom, on the lugubrious, when he tackles serious work that does not reflect his own life experience. Not only has he not experienced it but he may not have even *read* the work of writers he name-drops, impressing the legions of people who haven't read them either. This is hot stuff to him, this is what the big guys are into—and he feels like a lonely outsider with his paltry jokes. The absence of his sense of humor harms those films irretrievably.

But don't be surprised if Allen brings it all together yet in a successful merging of drama and comedy, that the influences of Bergman and Fellini do not drown him but somehow conjoin and blend with his magical touch. For Woody never ceases to surprise.

This is what even his critics say about him—John Simon commented: "How can you debate whether the Eiffel Tower adds to or detracts from Paris? He's part of the landscape, and we would be poorer without him. His productivity is admirable. It proves he has energy, ideas, creative spirit. I'm fascinated by these women he picks up the moment they are good-looking and a little bit famous. He lobs them into his next movie.

"When you come to think of it," Simon continued, "he's really the only independent filmmaker who worked for decades, made some very good movies, some not so good movies, some bad movies—like *Interiors*, which is terrible. But he kept going. And he became internationally loved. It's amazing that this Jewish schlemiel became the most universally loved figure in film. Now, who else did that? I can't think of anyone else. Warren Beatty to some extent perhaps. So that's something right there. He is not ashamed to be himself, including his looks. And the fact that he does appeal to foreign markets and that he's not a curiosity like the French being in love with Jerry Lewis. He's not that kind of celebrity. And he has survived his comical looks fairly well. Especially since he casts these comical figures as lovers, which is daring. And he manages to get away with it. He was witty. He still is.

"There's no independent filmmaker in America who has his fame. His humor is always not exactly black, but kind of dark gray. Which gives it a kind of profundity it wouldn't have otherwise. There's always the sense of the fragility of relationships, unpredictability of life. Which is not a cheerful thing, but he makes something out of it. And he doesn't go too far with his magic realism. He knows where to stop. That's a good thing to know.

"Makes fun of himself. Makes fun of other people. That works. In the thirties there was a period when American movies had wit. But that's about it. Preston Sturges, Groucho. A few directors. *His Gal Friday.* But not anymore. There's very little cleverness around. Woody still has it in his films to some extent, which is commendable. He does manage to amuse people, and yet at the same time it's not total frivolity either. He is aware of the world. He does pay attention to what's going on in the world.

"He is someone to reckon with. I hope Woody makes one great film before he quits. It's always been sort of on the verge of something wonderful. But not quite. But that's still better than what most people do."

A harsher critic, the late Stanley Kauffmann, said, "Like Jules Feiffer, he dramatized modern urban Jewish neuroses. One of the reasons for his critical success is that people recognize his contribution to America's understanding of itself. That's an achievement. Probably the future will think more highly of him than we do."


In *Manhattan*, following in the footsteps of *Annie Hall*, he continued to emerge as a real artist. The film not only had artistry; it had audacity. What was it about? A man in love with a girl twenty-five years his junior—and underage as well. A man dating a girl "who did homework." He won an Academy Award for it, and world renown. This was in 1979. He went on to other works in which the theme of a man's love for a much younger woman was prominent, and he's still doing them. And he acted out that theme in real life, and got away with it. He has had a stable, enduring marriage that has already lasted more than eighteen years. He has spent a lifetime writing for himself and about himself—despite his denials. And he has arguably made some of the best American movies of our time—and at least five that are terrible. In the process he has become the most influential filmmaker in American life.

Enchantment was the reason.

In his memoir *Final Cut*, Steven Bach, an executive at United Artists, which produced Allen's films for many years, seemed to regard *Manhattan* as justification for three difficult years at the company. Bach, who hailed from Montana, saw the film at a private screening and wrote of his epiphanic feelings with a Thomas Wolfe–like intensity. He saw the film on a beautiful April day in Manhattan, "one of those spring days songs are written about, the sky a perfect blue, the air balmy, soothing my jet-lagged nerves and smoothing the edges of an often-jangled city." He wrote that "if there are two hours in my three years and three days at United Artists that remain in memory as pure, unambiguous pleasure, they are these two. . . . What I found in those two hours seemed something I'd grown too cynical to expect anymore: some kind of enchantment. . . . I left the screening room . . . and walked slowly, glowing in the continuing spell of the movie. The sky-scraping piles of steel and glass that in daylight seemed so forbidding and faceless now glinted with city lights. I could hear Gershwin playing somewhere—or thought I could—and as I grinned at my own pleasure and at the empty street and at the purple sky, I remembered all the reasons I had always wanted to live in New York and all the reasons I had wanted to be in the movie business."

"Allen comes from an era where you worked and didn't stop," the late screenwriter Ric Menello told me. "His work ethic is not unlike Claude Chabrol or John Ford, although Ford worked within the studio system, unlike Woody. Ford said that the perfect day for him was to get up in the morning, go on the set, direct a picture, solve the problems of making it. 'Then we knock off at whatever time and we all get to have dinner together and then you go to sleep. It's like a work thing. It's like, I gotta get up and go to work.'

"He'll go on for many years," Menello continued. "We have that kind of tradition in the United States like George Abbott, the theater director. He was still directing plays when he was 102. Woody sold jokes very early. He had to work to do this. Thirteen, fourteen, fifteen. Then he became a writer for television. He slowly moved up. He's not that nine-to-five thing. When he's writing, he gets up, it's no big deal, he does this whole thing. He has breakfast, he writes a little. He has lunch and goes back to work. When he's directing he knocks off at six at night, no matter what's going on. You can find bits for the movies in his early stand-up. His books also have little routines and bits that he uses later. Why shouldn't he? That's an old tradition. Howard Hawks used to cannibalize from himself constantly. It's the work ethic. He happens to be an artist too, but he doesn't always have to be an artist. He's always a craftsman. He's always making these things, and once in a while one of them's a work of art. And that's the best you can hope for.

"Ben Hecht, the kind of tough Jew Woody likes," Menello said, "was primarily a screenwriter. Earlier he'd been a newspaperman, novelist, short-story writer, playwright. So this is a tradition where Woody may actually be the last of a breed. He did a play, he did jokes, short stories, essays. All this makes him what he is and connects him to the early guys. He may be the last who went from being an outside writer with a reputation to writing screenplays to directing, becoming a filmmaker. Ben Hecht did that. Hecht comes from a perspective of writing and screenwriting first. Woody is also a writer first and a director second. He directs to protect and express his screenplays. It's not typical anymore for a writer who's not a screenwriter first to move into movies. It's common for playwrights, but they don't direct."

Allen has been nominated twenty-four times for Academy Awards. He has earned more screenwriting Academy Award nominations than any other writer in the Best Original Screenplay category. He is tied for third place for most nominated director, with seven Best Director nominations.

*Annie Hall* won four Academy Awards, including Best Picture (Charles Joffe), Best Director, and Best Original Screenplay (shared with cowriter Marshall Brickman), and Best Actress (Diane Keaton).

The triumphs since then have been towering. They include:

- His short story, "The Kugelmass Episode," won the 1978 O. Henry Award in 1977 and was the inspiration for his later movie *The Purple Rose of Cairo*.
- He won the César Award for Best Foreign Film in 1980 for *Manhattan*, and in 1986 for *The Purple Rose of Cairo*. He was nominated seven other times for his films.
- *Manhattan* was nominated for two Academy Awards: Best Supporting Actress (Mariel Hemingway) and Best Writing Written Directly for the Screen (Allen wrote *Midnight in Paris* with Marshall Brickman).
- Allen won the Golden Globe for Best Screenplay for *The Purple Rose of Cairo* in 1986.
- Allen received an Academy Award for Best Original Screenplay for *Hannah and Her Sisters* in 1986. Michael Caine and Dianne Wiest received awards as Best Supporting Actor and Actress. It was nominated in four other categories, including Best Picture and Best Director.
- Allen received a Career Golden Lion for lifetime achievement at the Venice Film Festival in 1995.
- He received a lifetime achievement award from the Directors Guild of America in 1996.

- He won the Prince of Asturias Award in Spain in 2002. The city of Oviedo, Spain, later erected a life-size statue of Allen.
- He received the Palme des Palmes in 2002, a lifetime achievement award from the Cannes Film Festival.
- He was voted the third greatest comedy act of all time in a 2005 poll in England called "The Comedian's Comedian."
- Allen received a PhD Honoris Causa in 2007 from Pompeu Fabra University in Barcelona, Spain.
- He won the Golden Globe for Best Motion Picture for *Vicky Cristina Barcelona* in 2008.
- *Crimes and Misdemeanors* was named in 2010 as one of the one hundred best screenplays of all time by the Writers Guild of America.
- He won an Academy Award for Best Original Screenplay for *Midnight in Paris* (2012). The film was also nominated for Best Motion Picture, Best Director, and Best Actor (Owen Wilson).
- Allen received the 2014 Cecil B. DeMille Award for lifetime achievement at the seventy-first Golden Globe Awards Ceremony on January 12, 2014.

Allen's comeback—or series of comebacks—in the early years of the twenty-first century is one of the most amazing sagas in the history of American film and show business. But even when he was in relative limbo, his productivity never flagged. Following the debacle of his breakup with Mia Farrow in 1992 after she discovered nude pictures of her daughter Soon-Yi in Allen's apartment, there were accusations of sexual abuse with their adopted daughter, Dylan, and a long legal battle that sprang from those accusations. Allen became one of the most controversial figures in American cultural life. In March 1992, a team of investigators at Yale–New Haven Hospital cleared Allen of Farrow's charge that he molested their seven-year-old daughter Dylan. Farrow had first made the molestation charge in August 1992 and Allen filed for sole custody of Dylan, their adopted son Moses A. Farrow, and the couple's biological child, Satchel. Farrow later filed a separate suit in Surrogate Court to void Allen's 1991 adoption of Moses and Dylan. While the story Mia Farrow told of his molesting Dylan was never proved, there were many who believed it was true. Inferring from the ample evidence of his protagonists' fondness for young girls in his films, they overlooked the right of the artist to fantasize in his art and chose unfairly to conclude that he was therefore capable of monstrous acts in his private life. They decided that if the artist was a monster, they didn't want to see his pictures. Allen never expressed apology or regret about any aspect of his behavior with Farrow in the wake of the 1992 scandal; he angrily refuted the charges. *New York Times* critic Janet Maslin told writer Peter Biskind in *Vanity Fair* in 2005, "There are people who'll never forgive Allen for the Farrow scandal, who won't even see his movies anymore."

Others have different views of him. Jennifer Belle is the author of four brilliant, quirky, and very funny novels including *Little Stalker,* the tale of a thirty-three-year-old woman who—pretending to be a thirteen-year-old girl—begins to write letters to her idol, Arthur Weeman, a very famous movie director.

Belle is one of Allen's most devoted fans and tries to see his new movies at the first show on opening day. She has seen *Manhattan* perhaps a hundred times, and she talks the way she writes her fiction. "For years I completely identified with Mariel Hemingway because I was her age," she related. "And now I identify with Diane Keaton. Mariel is now this annoying little girl who comes in the middle of it. And that's amazing. I mean Woody writes me in all my phases. He writes me as a shrew, he writes me as the working girl trying to date and make a buck. He writes me as the disgruntled wife. He writes me as the bored housewife pushing her kids on the swing and going to Chinatown looking for any kind of herb to wake herself up. He writes me as the sixteen-year-old coquette. That's extraordinary for a man to be able to do that. No other man can do that. He understands women. He understands whores. He understands smart women."

She went on to talk of Allen as if she were doing a stand-up routine. "And Woody did the worst thing that any man can do to a woman," she claimed, referring to Allen's relationship with Mia's adopted daughter Soon-Yi. "It was the worst thing I've ever seen. It was like murder. This was just pure rage."

Allen's career went into a tailspin not in 1992, when he was accused of child molestation, but in 1999 when he began to make a series of terrible films (*Small Time Crooks, The Curse of the Jade Scorpion, Hollywood Ending*). He also did an acting stint that year in a poor movie called *Picking Up the Pieces*. In 2005, Peter Biskind wrote that Allen's "American audience has dwindled over the last decade. The Hollywood studios that once treated him like a prince have turned cold, and even New York film critics, heretofore his staunchest allies—the hometown fans—seem to greet each new picture with a collective yawn. It's as if this filmmaker, who in the 1970s and eighties and well into the nineties seemed to connect effortlessly with an influential if rarefied slice of urban America, has slid into irrelevancy." Yet by 2011 he was bigger than he ever was, and today he is more successful than he has ever been in his life. The scandal of 1992 did nothing to diminish his output; in fact some of the films written and produced in the aftermath of the scandal were among his finest: *Husbands and Wives*—largely written before the scandal erupted (1992), *Bullets over Broadway* (1994), *Mighty Aphrodite* (1995), *Everyone Says I Love You* (1996), *Deconstructing Harry* (1997), and *Celebrity* (1998). Characteristically Allen went into a partial slump following these successes. And just as characteristically, he bounced back with some of the best films of his career.

Writing this book over a period of two years, I vicariously experienced the dizzying roller coaster of Allen's life as he alternately turned out one fine film and one near-disaster. The triumph of *Midnight in Paris*—which grossed more than $151 million worldwide—was followed by *To Rome with Love*. His great commercial success, *Blue Jasmine,* grossed $97.5 million worldwide and earned ecstatic notices. David Thomson in the *New Republic* called it a masterpiece and Allen's finest film—notices that were soon practically drowned out by the listless *Magic in the Moonlight,* a film Allen cribbed from his own previous movies without much embellishment or invention.

Mia Farrow's campaign to reignite her and her daughter Dylan's sexual abuse allegations against Allen included a rehash of Maureen Orth's original 1992 *Vanity Fair* article in a 2013 issue of the magazine (also by Orth), an op-ed piece by Farrow's friend Nicholas Kristof in the *New York Times*, and a letter by Dylan Farrow in the *Times*. But Farrow's efforts seemed to run aground in light of the rapturous critical reception of *Blue Jasmine,* followed by Cate Blanchett's Golden Globe and Academy Awards for the film. Then there were Allen's outraged denial in a letter in the *Times*, a defense of Allen by sex-crimes prosecutor Linda Fairstein, a refutation of the charges by Allen and Farrow's son, Moses Farrow (who even raised the specter of Mia as a punitive and manipulative mother), vociferous support of Allen from Diane Keaton, Dick Cavett, Wallace Shawn, Janet

Maslin, and scores of others, as well as a highly persuasive article defending Allen by the director Robert Weide in the *Daily Beast*. Paradoxically, around this time, Mia Farrow's brother John Villiers-Farrow was indicted on charges of sexual abuse of two ten-year-old boys over a period of several years in Maryland. He pled guilty to two counts while maintaining his innocence and was sentenced to ten years in prison.

Cate Blanchett received the Academy Award for Best Actress in *Blue Jasmine*, Sally Hawkins was nominated as Best Supporting Actress, and Allen was nominated for Best Original Screenplay. Blanchett also won the Golden Globe Award despite the orchestrated campaign against Allen by Mia Farrow. It seemed he could do no wrong. But with the appearance of *Magic in the Moonlight* in late 2014 the tide seemed to turn against Allen once again. (The film featured still another instance of an April-October romance.) Compounding matters was the fiasco of Allen's theatrical version of *Bullets over Broadway*, which received dismal reviews and ran briefly on Broadway. The production had cost his sister and business manager, Letty Aronson, and her investors $15 million, and Allen, who had not invested his own money in the show, reportedly refused to even talk with them. According to the *New York Daily News*, "He wasn't counting on dealing with the people who paid for this disaster eventually even if the lead producer is his sister."

The harshest critics of Allen's behavior have always tended to conflate two matters: his behavior with Soon-Yi Previn (with its various components: his brutal manner of informing Mia with the naked pictures of her adopted daughter, his initiation of a sexual relationship with the adopted daughter of his lover, and his overall betrayal of Mia), and his alleged sexual abuse of Dylan. These different events seem to be indistinguishable from one another for those inclined to indict him for a sex crime without evidence. Yet it's not difficult to conclude that society hardly notices and tends to condone affairs between older men and younger women while taking a decidedly harsher view of child sexual abuse—for good reason. If Allen *is* a sex abuser, he is that extremely rare one who has been helpful enough to leave a paper trail in his films, writing, and interviews stretching back to 1966, when he was asked by *Playboy* if he would like to have children: "Eight or twelve little blonde girls," he replied. "I love blonde girls."

And so, once more, the critics turned on a dime almost overnight, and the controversy took center stage once again. No wonder that Allen has insisted (true or not) that he pays no attention to their opinions. The accusations came leaping back—A. O. Scott wrote in the *New York Times* that it was impossible to watch *Magic in the Moonlight* "without thinking about Mr. Allen's personal life—or to avoid arguments afterwards about whether he is a creep, a monster or a misunderstood artist whose behavior has no bearing on his work." Critic Andrew O'Hehir wrote in *Salon* that "It is the obsessive persistence of the April-October love affair as the apex of Eros in Allen's work, from at least *Manhattan* in 1979 right through the present, which feels pathological." Writer Kate Aurthur in *BuzzFeed* ludicrously brought it all back to the scandal: "On a symbolic level, though, I was interested that the screenplay, which was written and shot before Dylan Farrow told the world in February that her father's fame is a source of continuous pain for her, is basically about an older man trying to prove that a younger woman is a liar." The film enabled critics to return to the theme they'd abandoned for a while: that Allen was obsolescent, washed up—O'Hehir wrote that the film was "an artist's yearning for the Prospero-like magical powers he once had, the powers he keeps on trying to conjure up again out of nothingness."

The death knells for Allen have been rung many times before—as in 2000 in Marion Meade's *The Unruly Life of Woody Allen*, the most recent biography. "Increasingly, he seemed insulated from reality," Meade wrote. Referring to his role in the animated feature *Antz*, she reflected that "modern audiences like Woody Allen better as a bug than as a human being on the screen." She wrote of how old Allen looked for his age (in 2013 Sam Tanenhaus would write in the *Daily Beast* of how young he looked). She thought the end was near: "When exactly will the subject draw his final breath? Will he leave in a rush or float away? What, if any, secrets will a death certificate or an autopsy report spew forth as a mischievous finale?"

Even Richard Schickel, a profound critic and ardent supporter of Allen, whose interviews with Allen are among the most insightful, could not in 2003 foresee much of a future for him. He noted that Allen made a group of films in the eighties and early nineties that constituted "one of the great runs of movies ever made by any director in a relatively short span of time": *Zelig, The Purple Rose of Cairo, Radio Days, Crimes and Misdemeanors, Broadway Danny Rose, Husbands and Wives, Bullets over Broadway,* and

*Hannah and Her Sisters* among them. Yet, he wrote, "Woody Allen is now, as far as the United States of America is concerned, an almost fully marginalized filmmaker." He referred to "the dubious regard in which many Americans now hold him as an individual." Writing of the impact of the 1992 scandal, he observed, "His audience has been drifting away for a long time." He conceded that "It is entirely possible that Woody, before he is finished, will have another domestic hit. But I don't think it is highly likely."

Many years of incredible triumphs have followed Meade's book and Schickel's observations. Allen has bounced back with a vengeance. Two of his recent films have made infinitely more money than any he released previously. Allen remains what he has been all along: the most prolific and productive American filmmaker of his time. His pattern remains the same: If he makes a good film, he isn't really due for another outstanding one for at least two or three more. He still ranges from the sublime to the wretched and back again. At least twenty-five of his enormous output (forty-seven films to date) are really good, and that's a high average. Claude Chabrol, Elia Kazan, and Sidney Lumet are dead. Today only Spielberg, Scorsese, and Allen remain productive. Among young directors Kevin Smith tries to be Woody, but he isn't. Rob Reiner tried. *When Harry Met Sally* was not Woody. With the advent of independent films, Edward Burns tried to be Woody in *The Brothers McMullen*. No contest. Allen has reshaped the landscape, but not by having mega-hits. His films have not achieved the commercial success of *Pulp Fiction* or even *The Graduate*. In the end he does what no one else can do: He makes bright intellectual films that aren't cerebral talkfests. His films appear to have more dialogue than they actually do. And he makes quirky films that aren't one-liner machines. He creates extraordinary female characters without revering women.

In Woody's first e-mail to me, he wrote the following:

*September 10, 2013*

*Dear Mr. Evanier:*

*Here is the problem and please don't in any way take this personally. While I have great respect for authors and journalists in general I have had too many experiences with ones I never should have trusted and there is no way for me to feel any security about your project. You can understand that I have but your description of your intentions and while they [may] be 100% honorable there is no way I can verify that. I have no doubts about your qualifications and your resume but beyond that there is no guarantee that yet another book about me would serve any constructive purpose. All the facts about my life have been written about and rewritten about and my work has been dissected in books and articles all over the world for years.*

*Just a few bits of information in your letter make me wonder. For example . . . Jack Rollins who is in his mid 90s and I know from talking to him myself, extremely shaky on events. His daughter Susan was a very young child in the years that Jack and I were working so closely together. I never heard of or at least can't remember Sid Weedman. Cynthia Sayer I know only passingly as for a time she played in our jazz band where I had no personal contact with her whatsoever and John Simon who I can respect has never liked my work at all— and this is just the little sampling you included in your note. Richard Schickel and Annette Insdorf on the other hand have been very supportive but Schickel has written about me and done a television special on my work and has said it all before. In addition to this your project was undertaken without ever asking if it is something that I wanted done and you can imagine that would make one quite suspicious. Don't get me wrong, I'm not suggesting anything wrong here, only explaining to you why one might feel reluctant to participate. These are my feelings on the matter at the moment but I am open minded and if you had an argument that made more sense than mine I am certainly willing to hear it. I don't mean in any way to be difficult or obstructionist but decades of experience have made me very wary. I might also add your notion that* Crimes and Misdemeanors *and* Zelig *are my two masterpieces when neither is a masterpiece nor are either even the best films I have done worries me. It makes me wonder if I would consider, even if flattering, your takes on my films to just be more wrong-headed appraisals and would not add anything to the cultural landscape. If I am wrong about all of the above tell me what I am missing?*

*Sincerely,*
*Woody Allen*

I answered Allen's letter on September 17.

*Dear Woody Allen,*

*I'm asking you to take a gamble on this. . . . I want this book, which will come out just about the same time as your birthday, to be an accurate and insightful portrait of the filmmaker I most admire. I can't and won't pigeonhole your creativity. I won't attempt to reduce your story to specific events or moments. An artistic gift is inexplicable, as I believe you have said yourself in different ways. I understand that trying to connect the dots of biographical facts about you is pointless. . . .*

I haven't done that. I walk the streets of his old neighborhood in Brooklyn, still partly an Orthodox shtetl, on Avenue J in Flatbush. I pass the Talmud Torah school on Coney Island Avenue where Allen spent tedious hours, the moldy but functioning Kent Theater, now chiseled into a dwarflike multiplex. Allen filmed scenes from *The Purple Rose of Cairo* there, changing its name to the Jewel, because he had hung out there as a boy and had seen *Gone With the Wind* fourteen times there in one week, and the Essen Delicatessen. I go into Hecht's C. & S. Skull Cap Co., an ancient, lively store that carries Judaica, books about Israel, Israeli flags, yarmulkes, and books, with a special section called "Books About Great Jewish Men." (I wouldn't even think of asking the pleasant proprietor, a woman who has been there for fifty-two years, whether there was a shelf for "Great Jewish Women.")

Here time stands still, as much as it can. One is transported back to Eastern European shtetls in the nineteenth century or pre–Holocaust Europe not only by the black frocks of the Hasidim and the Orthodox Jews—the huge boxlike hats, the sideburns, beards, and tefillin—but also by the "*ch*" cadences of the voices of young and old (satirized by Larry David in a memorable sequence of *Curb Your Enthusiasm*). What is most apparent is the rigidity, a way of life cast in stone. I view it as I always do, with mingled feelings of alarm, sadness, wonder, and respect for the stubborn determination of those who continue to believe. I see Hebrew and Yiddish everywhere on stores, homes, medical offices. I feel a resonant connection from somewhere in my past. And I remember my father in his final days in the nursing home when he was nearly blind, telling me that he'd been seeing Hebrew lettering on the walls of his room and wondering if he was dreaming.

And I understand better Woody Allen's total rejection of this world, a world he'd grown up in and out of. Allen specializes in an art form, a tradition of thinking the thoughts that you're not supposed to think. This way of life would have hobbled his art from the start. Strange and exhilarating, then, that while rarely presenting any overt Jewish themes in his work, he sprinkles occasional Yiddishisms throughout his films and prose, that he is a messenger to the world insistently reminding it of the Holocaust, and that he is the most identifiable, brazen, and forthright Jewish film artist in the world.

This is the world in which Allan Konigsberg lived (even though his father was a secular, happy-go-lucky, gun-toting rascal), hanging out in his basement room, doing his magic tricks, and reading his comic books. I stare at the two-story homes and tenements and watch the kids, many with their yarmulkes, sprint out into the street and the summer sunshine.

One of those kids was once Allan Stewart Konigsberg, and how he came to be and who he really is are mysteries I try to unravel in this book.

## 2. "Writing Saved His Life"

*Where I grew up in Brooklyn, nobody committed suicide. Everyone
was too unhappy.*

WOODY ALLEN BECAME a comedy star at a time when every precon-
ception about American life came into question. His arrival and triumph were emblematic of the sea change in American society in the
sixties; a rejection of a multitude of prejudices—sexual, ethnic, racial, and
class—in the spirit of the civil rights movement. The flood had opened up,
releasing a new flexibility, open-mindedness, acceptance of differences—
differences that accorded society a wealth of new insights, ways to live, ways
to explore culturally and sexually. His material was not interchangeable
with that of other comedians. The earlier generation of comics could
steal from one another because their jokes were so similar, and not directly related to their personalities. With Allen there was a presumption,

whether it was true or not, that he was telling you something a little more personal and autobiographical.

Richard Schickel wrote that Allen was "a walking compendium of a generation's concerns, comically stated," that left audiences with the feeling "that our own interior monologues have been tapped and are being broadcast." "He came along exactly at the moment, in the sixties, when everything was being questioned about masculinity," John Simon told me. "And he was extremely heterosexual, desperately heterosexual. Worshipped women."

And he was a loner. "He wasn't a guy who seemed a part of the fraternity," Mark Evanier told me. "Every time you saw Jack Benny he would be with Berle, and Berle would be with Jack Benny, and Bob Hope would be with Benny. Bing Crosby would be with Hope and Berle. And of course everybody knew that George Burns and Jack Benny were best friends. They frequently appeared together in a kind of clubby atmosphere. Very rarely did one of these guys do a TV special without one or two of the others showing up in it. People didn't know who Woody's buddies were, who he hung out with. He seemed to be a guy who was alone, not part of a mob. And his jokes were unique to him."

By the late sixties Jews were one of the first groups to emerge from hiding their identities on-screen. Jews didn't run the world as the anti-Semites thought, but they had played a pivotal role in Hollywood essentially from its founding: Among the leading film producers, all of whom had grown up in destitution, were Samuel Goldwyn (né Gelbfisz); Marcus Loew; Louis B. Mayer; Irving Thalberg; Adolph Zukor; Harry Cohn; Carl Laemmle; Joseph and Nicholas Schenck; and Harry, Jack, Albert, and Sam Warner. Among the companies they formed and ran were MGM, Warner Bros., Universal, 20th Century Fox, Columbia, and Paramount.

Even though they ran the Hollywood studios, the old elite were a product of Eastern Europe, the Great Depression, and the Holocaust, of entrenched layers of anti-Semitism throughout American society that found expression in groups like America First and in nativist and neo-Nazi movements led by men like Father Charles Coughlin and Gerald L. K. Smith. Moguls like Goldwyn and Mayer were very conscious of the anti-Semitic view that Jews controlled Hollywood and were wary of too much exposure. F. Scott Fitzgerald had called Hollywood "A Jewish holiday, a gentiles [*sic*] tragedy."

Dorothy Parker echoed that view in her interview with *The Paris Review* in 1956:

> *I can't talk about Hollywood. It was a horror to me when I was there and it's a horror to look back on it. I can't imagine how I did it. When I got away from it I couldn't even refer to the place by name. "Out there," I called it. You want to know what "Out there" means to me? Once I was coming down a street in Beverly Hills and I saw a Cadillac about a block long, and out of the side window was a wonderfully slinky mink, and an arm, and at the end of the arm a hand in a white suede glove wrinkled around the wrist, and in the hand was a bagel with a bite out of it.*

Pauline Kael commented: "But that bagel with the bite out of it should have cheered [Parker]. Imagine that arm without the bagel and you have cold money. Didn't it tell her that the woman in the mink in the Cadillac didn't quite believe in the mink or the Cadillac? Didn't it tell her that movies, like musical comedies, were made by gypsies who didn't know how to act as masters, because they were still on the road being chased? Couldn't Miss Parker, split down the middle herself—a Jewish father and a Gentile mother—see that that bagel was a piece of the raft, a comic holy water?"

Before our own Gypsies, Allen and Streisand, appeared in the late 1960s, Jews were rarely presented as stars even though film producers were mostly Jewish. Films produced by companies led by Jews "almost totally ignored one of America's most prominent minorities," wrote David Desser and Lester Friedman in *American Jewish Filmmakers*. These pictures "limited almost all references to the cultural and religious heritage of the industry's leaders."

A self-enforced Jewish invisibility also extended to many of the other art forms. Even playwrights like Arthur Miller, less forthright than Clifford Odets in *Awake and Sing*, hid the Jewishness of his protagonists in *Death of a Salesman* and *All My Sons*. *Death of a Salesman*, Samuel G. Freedman wrote in the *New York Times*, had "indisputably Jewish origins. Miller based Willy Loman on his uncle, Manny Newman, a salesman brought low by the Depression. He tried out earlier versions of the character in short stories he wrote in his teens and twenties about salesmen with apparently Jewish surnames—Schoenzeit and Schleiffer."

Neal Gabler wrote in *An Empire of Their Own* that the American film industry "was founded and for more than thirty years operated by East-ern European Jews. . . . Their dominance became a target for wave after wave of vicious anti-Semites. . . . Ducking from these assaults, the Jews became the phantoms of the film history they had created, haunting it but never really able to inhabit it." As a result, Jewish actors "were to be seen and not heard."

Mayer, Goldwyn, and company cast the gleaming blond or dark Anglo-Saxon men in the foreground. Jewish executives, wrote Gabler, "felt that no one . . . wanted to see a movie about a Jew. . . . The ones who were hardest hit . . . were the Jewish actors. 'There was very definitely the feeling that a Jewish personality would not work,' said screenwriter Mau-rice Rapf."

Jewish actors changed their names. Julius Garfinkle became John Gar-field; Emmanuel Goldenberg became Edward G. Robinson; Meshilem Meier "Moony" Weisenfreund became Paul Muni. If an actor looked Jewish, his Jewishness was hidden. Jewish actors were cast as Italian (John Garfield, Paul Muni, and Edward G. Robinson were paisanos in many films; Paul Muni was the original Scarface). Muni's career, Gabler wrote, "became a paradigm for the tortured identity of the actor Jew in Hollywood—always dressed in someone else's ethnicity." The director Richard Quine had queried Harry Cohn of Columbia about casting a well-known actor in a film. Cohn replied, "He looks too Jewish. Around this studio the only Jews we put into pictures play Indians!" (Cohn was referring to the casting of the premier actor of the Yiddish stage, Maurice Schwartz, as an Indian—Geronimo!—in a Western.) Louis B. Mayer in-formed the young Danny Kaye that "I would put you under contract right now but you look too Jewish. Get some surgery to straighten out your nose and then we'll talk."

"These Jewish immigrants," Norman Podhoretz told me, "all of them uneducated, sort of created the American small-town myth: the picket fence. There probably was no such America. It was their fantasy. I knew [director] Robert Rossen. In the last years of his life we were very close friends. He was very Jewish in his personal life but not in the work he did on-screen. You would never know. His name of course was Rosen. He loved to tell Jewish jokes. There was a whole colony of these guys. But the idea was to appeal to a mass audience. Woody Allen didn't need to. He broke that taboo and became an international figure."

Jewish and black characters appeared mainly in "social message" pictures—*Gentleman's Agreement, Pinky, Lost Boundaries*—and usually as victims. Jewish actors who were identified as Jewish in their roles in the forties and fifties included John Garfield as the ex-GI and Sam Jaffe in *Gentleman's Agreement*; George Tobias in *Sergeant York*; Sam Levene, who was murdered by a psychopathic anti-Semite in *Crossfire*; Mort Sahl, who played a Jewish soldier who gets killed in battle in *In Love and War*; and Joey Bishop, who was a Jewish soldier goaded by his sergeant (Aldo Ray) for cowardice and winds up leaping to his death in *The Naked and the Dead* (1958). In these World War II movies there were "comic sidekick" Jews, wisecracking fellows sometimes hooked up with a wisecracking Italian. In *Sergeant York* Gary Cooper's sidekick George Tobias died heroically during the big battle. He has a great monologue about being a subway conductor with the job of getting passengers on and off the train. In *A Walk in the Sun* the Jewish and Italian soldiers, all from New York City, operate the machine guns and wisecrack their way through World War II. These were all positive if stereotypical characters, but it didn't do them much good: They were usually victims, and most of them were killed. This attitude prevailed until the end of the studio system in the late 1950s.

Woody Allen would be the very brash recipient of the new freedom. So would the directors Paul Mazursky and Sidney Lumet. (Muni did present a positive portrayal of a Jewish doctor as early as 1959 in *The Last Angry Man*.)

Allen, whose precursor in the 1950s was Jules Feiffer, with his *Village Voice* cartoons of Jewish bohemians and neurotics, would debut with *What's New Pussycat?* in 1965 (followed by *What's Up, Tiger Lily?*, and *Casino Royale*). Films with Jewish content and/or Jewish stars had emerged in 1967 with *The Graduate* starring Dustin Hoffman (although his character, Benjamin Braddock, was never clearly defined by ethnicity); Sidney Lumet's *The Pawnbroker*, a Holocaust-related film; Lumet's comedy *Bye Bye Braverman*, starring a new Jewish leading man, George Segal; Mel Brooks's *The Producers*, with Brooks and Zero Mostel; Paul Mazursky's *I Love You, Alice B. Toklas*, starring Peter Sellers; and *Funny Girl*, starring Barbra Streisand (all 1968); *Goodbye, Columbus* (1969); *Where's Poppa?*, starring George Segal (1970); and Jules Feiffer's *Little Murders*, starring Elliott Gould (1971). This explosion continued with Neil Simon's *The Heartbreak Kid* (1972)—based on a story by yet another gifted Jewish writer, Bruce Jay

Friedman and directed by Elaine May—starring Charles Grodin; and Barbra Streisand's starring role in *The Way We Were* in 1973. Allen cowrote (with Mickey Rose), directed, and starred in his first autonomous picture, *Take the Money and Run*, in 1969. Referring to this breakthrough as Hollywood's "Jewish New Wave," J. Hoberman and Jeffrey Shandler wrote that the Jewish comic actors (Hoffman, Brooks, George Segal, Peter Sellers, Charles Grodin, Zero Mostel, Richard Benjamin) "were predicated on the spectacle of nice boys acting out, fooling around, and even going berserk." They list a dozen movies "all characterized by their insolent black humor and social satire . . . that featured (mainly) young, (sometimes) neurotic, and (by and large) not altogether admirable Jewish male protagonists cut off from their roots but disdainful of a white-bread America. Self-hatred merged with self-absorption, narcissism seemed indistinguishable from personal liberation, and alienation was a function of identity." They identified the "new wave" as occurring "roughly between Israel's Six-Day War and Yom Kippur wars" and Streisand's performance in *The Way We Were*. "These seven years not only brought Streisand's apotheosis as an openly ethnic, unreconstructed Jewish diva, but also saw the appearance of several male counterparts—including Dustin Hoffman, Elliott Gould, George Segal, and Richard Benjamin—as well as the emergence of the comic auteurs Woody Allen and Mel Brooks." There was, of course, no closer correlative in literature than Philip Roth's novel, *Portnoy's Complaint*, which exploded on the literary scene in 1969 and was turned into a very tepid movie with Richard Benjamin in the lead role in 1972.

The Jew, Albert Goldman wrote in his essay, "Boy-Man Shlemiel: The Jewish Element in American Humor" (1971), was now the representative modern man. By the midsixties "The Jew was raised from his traditional role of underdog or invisible man to the glory of being the most fascinating authority in America. Benefiting from universal guilt over the murders by the Nazis, stiffening with fresh pride over the achievements of the State of Israel, reaping the harvest in America of generations of hard work and sacrifice for the sake of the children, the Jews burst suddenly into prominence in a dozen different areas of national life. The more 'Jewish' Jews appeared, the more universal they became."

Allen got to the heart of Jewish insecurity. He put his Jewishness onstage and screen so brazenly (as did Barbra Streisand, his counterpart) that Jewish Hollywood embraced both of them. He was one of the first Jewish stars of the late sixties and the seventies. "But he didn't do dialects," Mark Evanier pointed out. "He didn't do characters, really. He didn't have another voice. He didn't do impressions." His popularity signaled the real breakthrough for Jews on-screen as film stars and directors. What occurred in American society in the sixties extended to the film industry and its younger Jewish executives, free of memories of Hitler, the shtetl, the ghetto, pogroms, and Eastern Europe. Individuality was now valued over sameness, rebelliousness over conformity. The "exotic," what was different, was now appealing and desirable; Jews and Italians benefited from that love first. Blacks and gays would follow later. Fiercely wanting to belong to their adopted country, wanting to reject their pasts, the earlier generation of Jewish producers had invented a sentimentalized America filled with upright heroes and heroines, stable families, resourceful, optimistic characters who always came out right in the end—the small-town America of one of Woody Allen's favorite American musicals, *Meet Me in St. Louis*.

That saccharine view of America was tossed aside in favor of reality and authenticity. Ironically Woody himself was drawn to the old vision of America but was the embodiment of the new.

American comedy was ready for him. The age of the Borscht Belt comic, the Milton Berles and Buddy Hacketts, was also fading. Just before Allen, Mel Brooks and Carl Reiner created "The 2000 Year Old Man" sketches. Allen arrived in the wake of that totally new breed of New York–centric Jewish comics, including Mike Nichols and Elaine May, Lenny Bruce, Shelley Berman, Paul Krassner, Allan Sherman, and Mort Sahl—mirrors of a new cultural revolution emerging from the coffeehouses of Macdougal and Bleecker Streets in Greenwich Village and San Francisco that departed from tried and true versions of comedy. This was a free-form delivery and stream of consciousness and free association that looked within psychologically and without politically (Sahl dealt with the politics, Allen the psychoanalysis). But he struck a social upheaval that linked him indisputably to the looming sixties and seventies. Max Liebman, the producer of the Sid Caesar–Imogene Coca classic TV program, *Your Show of Shows*, recalled seeing Allen as a young stand-up comic: "This was the period when we were beginning to be affected by the generation gap," Liebman said. "When the young were coming out against old people they believed had led the world into a mess. They felt at a loss as to where they were going or where they came from. And Woody was one of those who had a message they could understand. They created a gulf between themselves and the establishment. Because that was who they blamed for sending them abroad to fight unpopular wars, as cannon fodder for causes they didn't believe in. Woody came from that background. He started out as a cult entertainer. And those young uncertain people were the cult." (It is commonly thought that Allen performed on *Your Show of Shows,* but he never appeared on that program or on its successor, *Caesar's Hour.*)

And so he entered a milieu that somehow was waiting for and anticipating him.

"As a Jewish comic," Mark Evanier told me, "he was the first who didn't seem to try to be superior to his audience. For one thing, he didn't look better than the members of that audience. He couldn't help that part. But he was the antithesis of the traditional male hero: small, unhandsome— the seemingly archetypal schlemiel with a squeaky, whining high voice. His humor was self-deprecating; it wasn't *Gee, my wife's ugly.* He wasn't interested in impressing with how elegant he was and what a fabulous dresser he was. He came out without a tie and looking a little wrinkled at all times. His hair was not exactly coiffed. And he wore horn-rimmed glasses. He really did not look slick in the manner of many of his predecessors onstage. He looked even shorter than he actually was [five feet five]. For many of his television appearances, directors purposely elevated the camera a little so that it looked down on him. And he didn't sing; he didn't dance. He wasn't an all-around entertainer; he was solely a stand-up comic.

"He didn't care what you thought of him," Evanier continued. "He was telling you his worst flaws. Childish and cowardly things he did. From the fifties to the seventies, there were only three really prolific stand-up female comedians: Totie Fields, Joan Rivers, and Phyllis Diller. All three of them had this in common: They had acts about how ugly they were. They all talked about how they couldn't get laid. Rivers had a joke about 'My husband wouldn't touch me. If he didn't toss and turn in his sleep, we would never have had a kid.' She had jokes about being unattractive, sexless. Men didn't do that then. Milton Berle didn't come out and tell jokes about how he couldn't get a girl. Alan King came out as an attack dog. No male comedian prior to Woody had spent a lot of time onstage telling you how he couldn't get girls. He was the only guy doing it at the time. He shook up a lot of people who hired comedians, like Jack Paar, who didn't like Woody's self-deprecation. So that was very refreshing and different. His connectivity to the audience was that he seemed so honest."

Allen's humor was very personal and unique, not interchangeable with that of other comedians. Even when comedians complained that their wives were ugly or fat, they weren't really asking you to believe they had a fat wife at home. It was just a joke. With Allen there was a presumption, whether it was true or not, that he was telling you something more personal and autobiographical about himself and his experiences. It was that very autobiographical quality, one he encouraged his audiences to believe, that has made it so difficult for them to accept his insistent denials that he was really talking about his own life. He was and he wasn't. But he had the capacity to see himself objectively from a distance, to stand outside himself, to make fun of himself. He had that self-knowledge. He saw the nerdy part and exploited that aspect of himself mercilessly and hilariously. It was as if he were perched on the bow of a boat—confronting his miseries, his incapacities and failures with women, with life—and about to jump, and suddenly thinking: Fuck it, this is not so terrible; it's actually funny. Only a person with enormous inner strength and resilience would be capable of doing that.

Paradoxically Allen has often said that his favorite comic role models were Mort Sahl and Bob Hope—but especially Hope, on the right of the political spectrum, who came on as a businessman with a gold watch and who always seemed to be reading his jokes from a teleprompter. Hope was also one of the few major comedians who was clearly not Jewish.

"Everybody was very amazed," Mark Evanier told me. "I remember how people were stunned by the revelation that Woody considered Bob Hope a hero. Because he seemed so unlike Hope. He didn't project that kind of brash confidence. He wasn't a tap dancer or a singer. Hope played the coward, but he got the girl on-screen. But he didn't play the coward when he was on a talk show or doing stand-up. He was a coward only when he was in a movie, about to be killed. Onstage or on TV he presented a very confident, cocky attitude. So Woody was a contrast to that. He didn't come out onstage that way. Woody kind of looked like one of the stage-hands.

"Woody's jokes sounded like he wrote them. Nobody ever thought that Bob Hope was writing his own jokes. He didn't even try to disguise that he was using cue cards. And he came off like a mogul. I think that Woody envied him, because Hope had a lot of attributes that Woody didn't. He got the girl. And also he was a man of importance."

It almost strains credulity that a Jewish film star and comedian who placed his Jewishness front and center and audaciously proclaimed it—utilizing constant references to his Jewish identity, his preoccupation with anti-Semitism and the Holocaust, and his ambivalent and satiric ways of defining gentiles (white bread and mayonnaise was the most popular)—could capture the imagination and even beguile a wide audience as Allen has done. Of course he worshipped gentiles, and especially beautiful gentile women; that may have been a factor in his popularity. "In so many movies," Donna Brodie, writer and executive director of the Writers Room, told me, "through the choice of leading ladies like Diane Keaton and Mia Farrow or the creation of fictional lovers, Woody Allen mirrored the wonderful romantic and erotic synergy between Jewish men and gentile women, for each other the exotics next door. To be a young Catholic Manhattanite watching a Woody movie in the seventies and eighties was to be validated as an object of desire. In every Jewish boy who courted you there was a little bit of Woody's desire."

He was, in fact, quite disdainful of some aspects of Jewish life, making it clear that he preferred the neatness, "gentility," safety, calm, and order—not to mention the *wealth*—of the gentiles of the Upper East Side to the sweaty messiness, insecurity, crowdedness, disorder, and noisiness that he found in Jewish life, obsessed as the lower-middle-class Jews of his childhood, haunted by memories of their families caught in pogroms or the Holocaust, were with mere survival. Allen was especially derisive of Orthodox Jews; his early caricatures of them are raw and steeped in malice. The origin of that distaste might reside with his contentious relationship with his mother, the Orthodox half of his parents. Allen wrote me that he read the Old Testament in Hebrew as a boy and admired the rebelliousness of Job's wife toward God and toward the unquestioning, weaker males around her. (His attitudes toward the Orthodox Jewish environment of his youth are finally moderated in his finest film, *Crimes and Misdemeanors*.)

Ralph Rosenblum, Woody's great film editor for *Take the Money and Run* and *Annie Hall,* grew up in Woody's neighborhood a few years before Allen; he wrote of its ambience in his memoir, *When the Shooting Stops*: "Its lessons and ways were those of impoverished immigrants hanging on desperately to the niche they had made for themselves. Thrift, self-improvement and a thudding practicality ruled everything, a heavy-spirited regime that was molded into permanence by the weight of the Depression. Ten years later when Woody Allen was growing up in the same milieu, its values and oppressive conformity would still prevail."

That contrast of Jew vs. gentile is apparent in the parallel scenes of Annie Hall's family (based on Diane Keaton's) and Alvy Singer's in the film of the same name; and Jewish messiness, vulgarity, and overeating (the fatso uncle played by Josh Mostel holding up his adored catch of fish for the family to gaze at) are a focus of *Radio Days*, Allen's nostalgic look at his childhood in the Rockaways with his family. (Mia Farrow writes in her memoir, *What Falls Away*, that Allen admired William F. Buckley, Jr., to him the quintessential brilliant, wealthy, unflappable, erudite, elegant gentile—not politically but personally—and would stand across from his townhouse on East Seventy-third Street with Mia to savor the magic of Buckley's aura from afar. In Farrow's version of events, Allen exploded with rage when she got the address of Buckley's house wrong. Allen also displayed his respect and affection for Buckley when the two had a friendly "debate" on television on *Firing Line* in 1981.)

Jack Benny, George Burns, George Jessel, Eddie Cantor, and Groucho Marx preceded him, but they did not advertise their Jewishness in the most brash and aggressive way; it was implicit and polite. Borscht Belt comics were open about their Jewish ethnicities by the 1950s, but they entertained largely Jewish audiences. Allen was a national comic from the start.

On-screen he is the only comedian in Hollywood history to insert the same unchanging comic persona into every genre of his filmmaking: comedy, satire, melodrama—and yet work himself effectively into the plot. It is always the same character/persona, but it somehow seamlessly blends into many of the films he does. No one else has ever succeeded at this. He always manages to be Woody: Jewish, horny, a touch paranoid, and a wry schlemiel—yet he hasn't done stand-up comedy in his films since some scenes in *Annie Hall*. (Though he has certainly continued to utilize shticks from those comic routines in films up to the present day.) Woody Allen is Woody Allen with slight variations in films as disparate as *Take the Money and Run, Bananas, Sleeper* (he's the only robot wearing glasses, horn-rimmed, no less), *Annie Hall, Crimes and Misdemeanors, Everyone Says I Love You, Manhattan, Hannah and Her Sisters, Oedipus Wrecks,* and *Broadway Danny Rose.* His stand-ins—Kenneth Branagh in *Celebrity,* John Cusack in *Bullets over Broadway,* and Larry David in *Whatever Works*—are also Woody Allen, if to a somewhat lesser degree. His alter egos include Cheech (Chazz Palmintieri), the mafioso in *Bullets over Broadway,* who represents Allen's fantasy persona. Cheech is wild creativity, raw talent. Like Allen, he speaks and writes from the heart, unlike the overcerebral David (John Cusack), the typical brainy intellectual type out of touch with reality (and lacking the ability to write real dialogue) that Allen makes fun of. In *Hannah and Her Sisters* it is Michael Caine; in *Small Time Crooks* it is Hugh Grant; in *Anything Else* it is David Dobel (Allen). His other alter egos include the holy fool or klutz (*Bananas, Crimes and Misdemeanors, Hannah and Her Sisters, Annie Hall, Love and Death, Broadway Danny Rose*) and the criminal (*Match Point, Small Time Crooks, Crimes and Misdemeanors, Cassandra's Dream*). He is permanent, unchanging, iconic, fixed in our consciousness. And so every film without Woody in it often seems to have something missing.

Only Charlie Chaplin comes close to this kind of omnipresence, and Chaplin, too, endures, having had an astounding nearly thirty-year run of global popularity. Yet even Chaplin ditched the Tramp in later years. When he did, his popularity waned. Woody never ditches Woody.

Allen is not only a Jewish comic or a Jewish artist. He is an artist. He came into adulthood with the sudden flourishing of an independent film sensibility that rendered the old Hollywood films less important than what was being achieved in Europe. In the forties the Thalia Theater on West Ninety-fifth Street and the Apollo Theater on West Forty-second introduced audiences to a wide spectrum of European classics. They offered double bills of Rossellini's *Paisan* and De Sica's *Bitter Rice,* Kurosawa's *Rashomon* and De Sica's *Bicycle Thieves.* One could spend four hours in these theaters and walk out into the hurly-burly and sunshine of Times Square or the Upper West Side stunned by the greatness of what one had just witnessed. By the time Allen was in his twenties, the golden age of independent cinemas hit. The rise of art film houses (and, soon, an American independent cinema) stretched across New York City, expanding into theaters that Allen would often record for posterity in some of his films: such as the New Yorker, the Regency, the Carnegie Hall Cinema, the Bleecker Street Cinema (utilized in two Allen films), and scores more. These houses influenced an entire generation to look at film as an art form that had the potential to equal the greatness of the best novels and plays. Allen first experienced the filmmakers who would inspire (and perhaps intimidate) him in those theaters: Fellini, Bergman, De Sica, Rossellini, Renoir. In their wake would soon come the great independent American filmmakers and an entirely new vision of what American film could be.

Allen's reach with small-scale, nuanced films was sometimes thought to be confined to an urban audience in more sophisticated areas of the country (New York and Los Angeles above all) and, of course, in Europe. (The French discovered him only after Groucho Marx praised him highly in the early days when he visited France. When asked about Jerry Lewis, Groucho said that Lewis was okay but the real comic genius for him and the inheritor of the Marx Brothers' legacy in movies was Woody. Groucho talked up Woody everywhere.)

Woody's work encompassed all of the major media forms, including television, nightclubs, films, theater, and concert halls. His prose appeared in *The New Yorker* and the *New York Times*. And his popularity broadened with the wide success of *Annie Hall*, *Manhattan*, and *Hannah and Her Sisters*. More recently, he reached still another level with the triumphs of *Midnight in Paris* and *Blue Jasmine*.

There were good times, good food, and a warm bed in Allen's childhood, as he has written, but since Allen's boyhood was spent in the shadow of the Holocaust, he has continued to be obsessed with it as an ineradicable nightmare of the twentieth century.

Yet most of his childhood friends do not recall that they or Woody himself were preoccupied with the Holocaust as boys. It may have been a subliminal more than a conscious reality for them, or it may have been denial or repression. The facts about the concentration camps were barely known, and unless one had been personally affected by the fate of family members in Europe, the war seemed far away. Elliott Mills could not recall any anti-Semitism in his childhood, or any awareness of the Holo-caust. "I do remember vividly sitting in the Midwood theater and seeing a Pathé newsreel in which there was this bulldozer—this was after the camps were opened—shoveling these piles and piles of corpses into a trench. It stayed embedded in our heads. Some refugees moved onto our block. I remember one of them came screaming into our street periodically. But I was ten years old; how do I make a connection to the Holocaust? There's a bunch of bodies there and they're shoveling them into a grave. I didn't connect that up with a mass extermination of the Jews. It took a while before we realized what that was about, unless you had immediate family. I don't recall ever talking to Woody about the Holocaust when we were kids. I never remember hearing him say anything about the Holo-caust at all. It's a retrospective thing."

In *Radio Days* the possibility of a Nazi submarine surfacing off Rocka-way affects Woody's alter ego, Joe, and the other boys, and trying to spot the submarines becomes a game for them. In reality the German navy was active off the coast of the United States, and Long Island had advance-warning towers and anti-ship guns. In a similar context the refugee running into the street whom Elliott Mills recalled is transformed by Allen in *Radio Days* into Mr. Zipsky, a lunatic adult suddenly running, screaming, into the street in his underwear holding a meat cleaver—yet the viewer does not know anything about him, does not know that he is a refugee, or why he has lost his mind. The effect is comical and deracinated of any causal meaning.

Jack Victor recalled that "I'm first generation; all the rest of the guys in our group were second generation. I was beaten up several times because I was Jewish. My father's brother was killed in Auschwitz, and my mother's family in Poland were all shot. We talked about that in the family, and about our cousins who had hid from the Nazis and now lived in Israel. But I don't remember talking much about the Holocaust with Woody."

Allan Lapidus, who was at Midwood High School but not close to Woody, told Tim Carroll, author of *Woody and His Women*, "Everything in that movie was so real it was painful. There really were submarines off Long Island. . . . For a nickel you could take the Coney Island trolley down to the beach, so we would go down there and sit on the boardwalk looking intently for Nazi subs. The blackouts in *Radio Days* were because of ships in the straits, which would be silhouetted by New York's lights. And we were all issued spotter cards so that we could identify enemy aircraft.

"But I'm surprised at how Woody has downplayed the impact of Nazism on our youth. We were all acutely conscious of it, and at the onset of the war it looked likely Germany would win. You could sense that people were looking at us as if we were the losers. And we were bullied—not just because of the normal course of schoolyard bullying, but because we were Jewish. I remember being tackled by some boys who demanded to know my name, and I just couldn't think quickly enough of a gentile one. So they beat me. It was an awful time."

While *Annie Hall* has significant references to anti-Semitism and several strong mentions of Marcel Ophuls's documentary about the Nazi occupation of a French town, *The Sorrow and the Pity,* one of the most pungent references to Nazism was later removed from the film—one that underscores Allen's frequent assertions that he would be a coward if confronted by the Nazis. There was supposed to be a fantasy scene in which Alvy is a resistance fighter interrogated by the SS. When he won't answer their questions, they pull out guns and threaten to shoot him. Woody pulls out a puppet and says, "Because of my moral convictions I cannot name names. But he can." And the puppet speaks. The film did retain the scene where Alvy puts the onus on Annie: "If the Gestapo would take away your Bloomingdale's charge card, you'd tell them everything."

Allen's reticence about examining the impact of the Holocaust in *Radio Days* might be understood as an aspect of his conflict about maintaining the right proportions between comedy and tragedy so that comedy—especially cartoonish comedy or, conversely, dark drama—does not diminish the artistic effect and truthfulness of his work. He is caught between being an entertainer or an artist, a Neil Simon or a Tennessee Williams. He doubts that he will ever surmount that conflict successfully.

Still, there are references to Nazis in the film, and the war looms over everything. The Holocaust is understated, but it is very much there, hovering in the shadows. Joe's mother ( Julie Kavner) fearfully asks, "Do you think Hitler is going to win?" The children collect scrap iron for the war effort, and a news report over the radio mentions Nazi bombings. The Japanese bombing of Pearl Harbor is a major moment in *Radio Days.* Nazism and Communism are identified as twin evils menacing the world. There is no doubt that the war looms over everything.

*Radio Days* is portrayed partially through the eyes of children, particularly Joe, for whom the Holocaust was thankfully unknown. With the reluctance of major publications such as the *New York Times* to acknowledge it in depth, it would remain almost incomprehensible to adults then too. (Laurel Leff's book, *Buried by the Times*, explores this matter exhaustively.)

In fairness, *Radio Days* is not primarily about the war years but about the radio years. It deliciously explores the time when radio was king and the private lives of the actors who starred in it were a prime subject of interest for the tabloids. Actors playing supermen and glamorous action heroes are seen in reality as often to be runts, baldies, and fatties. Allen had begun the film by deciding he wanted to re-create the songs of his childhood and the memories they evoked, and he does so lovingly. The layered, intricate plot is skillfully done, and the film is funny, evocative, melancholy, and finally very moving. Perhaps he did not achieve the balance between humor and drama that he was seeking, but he was getting closer and closer.

Phillip Lopate, who hails from Jewish neighborhoods in Brooklyn somewhat like Allen's ( Jewish Williamsburg and Fort Greene in the pregentrification days), told me that when he watched *Radio Days,* he missed a deeper or grittier reality: "I thought that Allen was making a myth of his childhood, that he was both nostalgic and distanced. That's perfectly okay. It's just that I had actually lived it. And so for me his making a myth of it was very distorting. Like if I had lived during the 1950s with the tough kids who had the high pompadours and then to see all that become *Happy Days,* kind of denatured, just seemed to me like, No, that wasn't what the experience was like."

Allen has always been caught in a wrestling match with his own Jewishness. His persona is the classic Jewish loser filled with lust, a lust undermined by his inadequacy with women. The Jews are a metaphor for his own feelings of anxiety.


Allan Stewart Konigsberg was ostensibly born on December 1, 1935, in the Bronx. That's the official version. Jerry Epstein relates that Woody told him that he was actually born on November 30, 1935. Epstein's interpretation is that Woody always wanted to be number one. The family relocated to Flatbush, Brooklyn, and lived at several homes before settling at 1215 East Fifteenth Street when Woody was nine years old. Woody's closest pals were Jerry Epstein, Jack Victor, and Elliott Mills.

"We had a very close, intense relationship from the time we met at twelve," Jerry Epstein recalled. "He was psychic. He could see what people were all about. We were interested in magic, hypnosis, extrasensory perception, psychic phenomena. From the first day we immediately became very close friends. First we talked to each other about boxing and baseball. And he was also a Giants fan. So when Bobby Thompson hit the home run off Ralph Branca, he went nuts. So we hit it off; we were on the same wavelength. I lived on Avenue J; he on East Fifteenth Street between K and L. And then he moved to K and Fourteenth, the corner apartment building. I told him not too long after that he would be very famous, that he was the funniest person I ever knew. I think he's the funniest person alive; I feel that way to this day. There's no one that reaches his level. He always had that quality, even much funnier offstage than onstage. I was depressed as a teenager, and his humor lifted me. He had me roaring and took me through my adolescence and out of my depressed state. He was my antidepressant. I would literally be on the floor all the time because he was so funny.

"We would meet almost every day. He got involved in a crooked dice game. He went in with loaded dice he'd gotten from the Circle Magic Shop on Fifty-first Street and Broadway. So he came into this game but they cleaned him out. He had great sleight of hand with cards. He could deal. In poker he could deal hands to himself. We cheated a friend out of money playing gin rummy. We had signals. So this kind of pilfering would go on with us. Woody always took the position of having to get away with something. There's the trickster element in him. Like he tricked me with a girl at a movie theater. All the girls I would bring around, he wanted. With him there was never a feeling of guilt; it was always you who was at fault, you were always wrong."

In the May 1952 copy of *Genii, The Conjurors' Magazine*, there is a suggestion on the "Teen Topics" page from one "Allan Konigsberg, Brooklyn, N.Y." for "an effect which will find much interest from some magicians but, on the other hand, will, no doubt, find criticism from others." Woody speculates authoritatively on the use of "stooges":

*Effect: Performer hands a slate to one assistant and asks him to think of any card in the deck and write it on slate and not to let anyone see the name of the card he has written.*

*Performer then has second assistant select a card from a well shuffled deck. With absolutely no trickery performer takes card and slate, backs to audience, holding them high in the air. He then asks second assistant to name the card. As assistant does so he turns the card face to audience and they see it is the card named.*

*Now he asks first assistant to name the card he wrote on the slate. As assistant names the card performer turns slate face to audience and, sure enough, the same card is written there. You'll agree the effect is startling to say the least.*

*Now, the solution lies in the stooge and a fake deck of all alike cards. Stooge selects the right card of course and writes it on slate. The other assistant takes the same card in the deck, all being alike. Of course a regular deck could be used and the card forced, if you can force a card.*

*The use of a stooge is a most controversial subject. There are stooge haters and stooge users. Some of the great magicians of our time have used stooges. I suppose, if the effect warrants, the stooge is just as permissible as apparatus. There are those who will disagree.*

Woody developed his love for New Orleans jazz when he was fourteen. "He began to take clarinet lessons from this guy Sammy Stein upstairs on the corner of Kings Highway and Coney Island Avenue," Elliott Mills said. "And then he negotiated two-dollar clarinet lessons from Gene Sedric, one of Fats Waller's sidemen, who agreed to come to his house. We formed a band, Woody Allen and the Franklin Street Stompers."

"Our biggest bond as a group was traditional jazz," Jack Victor remembered. "We'd go to each other's houses and play records; that was our big kick in life. We went to Stuyvesant Casino. Sidney Bechet was our hero, a stimulus for Woody's going into jazz. That's why he played the clarinet and soprano sax. One of the greatest thrills that Woody and I ever had was meeting him in person and talking to him. He came to New York and played at two clubs, and we saw him both times: Child's Paramount and a little club called the Bandbox. And we also played George Lewis records like crazy, especially 'Burgundy Street Blues.'"

Woody holed up in the basement, eating his dinner alone, reading his comic books (Superman, Batman, and Mickey Mouse), practicing his clarinet and his card and coin tricks. He stayed away from his mother's critical remarks, the tension between his parents. "His parents were the oddest couple," Jack Victor told me. "They had nothing whatsoever to say to each other. I never heard them exchange a single word." His parents would actually not speak to each other for many months at a time. "It was like oil and water between mother and father," Jerry Epstein said. "Marty had no religious feeling at all, while Woody's mother came from an Orthodox background." Allen was alienated from his parents. "I always ate alone—lunch, breakfast, all meals," he told John Lahr. "There were no books. There was no piano. I was never taken to a Broadway show or a museum in my entire childhood. Never." It was a cultural barrenness and a total lack of emotional connection. His parents did not know what to make of him. His talent would remain invisible to them until the end, as is evident in the scene of Allen's visit (with Soon-Yi) to his parents' home in *Wild Man Blues* in their geriatric years. In effect they throw up their hands; their son could have been a pharmacist, he could have made a successful career. Look what happened to him.

The origins of both families were in Europe, Nettie's from Vienna and Marty's from Russia. Both families had fled the oppression and pogroms of shtetl life in the diaspora. Nettie's parents, Sarah and Leon Cherry, spoke Yiddish and German. Nettie was born on November 6, 1908; she had six older brothers and sisters. The family lived in the heart of the Jewish Lower East Side on East Fourth Street near Second Avenue, near the Hebrew Actors Union and the lively Yiddish theaters and cafés that lined the avenue. Her parents ran a small luncheonette in the neighborhood. Leon and Sarah kept an Orthodox kosher home and went to synagogue on the Sabbath.

Martin Konigsberg was born on December 25, 1900, and at first was the beneficiary of his parents' wealth and success. Sarah and Isaac Konigsberg were on a higher economic plane than the Cherrys. They were also observant, and their primary language was Yiddish.

Isaac was a natty, sophisticated character. A traveling salesman in Europe for a coffee company, he dressed elegantly and had a box at the Metropolitan Opera. He'd been known to travel to Europe just to go to the horse races. Marty was the mascot of the Brooklyn Dodgers when he was a boy. When he enlisted in the navy and was stationed in England after

World War I, Isaac gave him a four-thousand-dollar Kissel roadster. Marty absorbed his father's modern ways and interest in gambling and expensive clothes. Isaac owned a number of elegant movie theaters in Brooklyn (including the Midwood, around the corner from Woody's home on East Fourteenth Street) and a fleet of taxicabs.

The stock market crash of 1929 brought about the collapse of Isaac's fortune. He lost the Midwood Theater, his taxi fleet, and his sales position. He kept the opera box. He was reduced to working in the butter-and-egg market (in *Radio Days* Joe asks his parents what his father does for a living and among their vague responses, his mother says he's a "big butter-and-egg man") and Marty worked with him. Soon the Konigsbergs had to leave their luxurious home and live in a small dark apartment in the back of a building on Coney Island Avenue.

Woody's parents in fact found each other at the butter-and-egg market on Greenwich Street in Brooklyn during the Depression. Nettie was a bookkeeper for a company there, and she came to know Isaac. She was impressed with his sophisticated manner, the way he dressed, and the fact that he had the opera box. Isaac introduced her to Marty. He still dressed well and took her to nice restaurants, and she looked upon him as a "high stepper."

Woody saw his first film, *Snow White and the Seven Dwarfs,* when he was five, and, in a foreshadowing of a film he would create many years later, *The Purple Rose of Cairo* (in which a cast member walks out of the screen and participates in real life and later returns to the movie), the young Woody ran up to touch the screen. Like Cecilia in *The Purple Rose,* he figured out early that life was a hell of a lot better on the screen than in real life. He traveled to Manhattan for the first time at six. He was hooked by Manhattan and by the movies: *Beau Geste, Pinocchio, Bambi,* the Bob Hope and Bing Crosby Road pictures, Roddy McDowall in *The White Cliffs of Dover,* and Tyrone Power in *The Black Swan.* He saw the nonsensical surrealism of the Marx Brothers and Charlie Chaplin on-screen for the first time in 1944 at the Vogue Theater in Coney Island.

He was fascinated with comedians and joke telling as well, and would watch the old troupers perform onstage at the Flatbush Theater during the dying days of vaudeville, an art form he was drawn to. He went on Saturdays, copying their jokes onto candy boxes and memorizing them.

Woody entered P.S. 99 in the fall of 1940. His sister, Letty, was born in 1943. By ten, Woody was high-strung like his red-haired mother, moody and prickly. He paid no attention at school and was frequently in trouble. His mother hit him constantly; she was the ultimate nag. Woody's withdrawal from people and his coldness, his ability to keep his emotions in check, his tendency to use silence as a weapon of intimidation can probably be traced to his relationship with her. He saw at an early age from his mother's example that uncontrolled emotion and anger were signs of weakness and helplessness. Yet his mother probably deserves some credit for his goal-oriented persistence, his tenacious work ethic, his enormous drive, his ability to work and never be distracted. She constantly reminded him, "Don't waste time!"

His friends, Jerry, Jack, Mickey, and Elliott, got together with Woody and talked for hours about girls, about their innermost feelings, about what motivated people and how psyches worked. Woody was their leader. And uppermost on their minds were girls. "It was rough for Woody," Jerry Epstein told me. "There was a girl he had a crush on, Nancy Kreisman. She didn't know from him. She lived on Fourteenth Street between Avenue I and Avenue J. She had a dog named Woody. And that's how he derived that name. That was spooky. He never made an advance on her. He was awkward and introverted with girls. He wasn't comfortable. He was concerned about his looks. He was a nerdy type of person, growing up. In those days there was a lot of talk about his being a nerd.

"When I met him at twelve, he was as funny then as he is now. He wanted me to write comedy with him when we were seventeen. And I turned it down. In hindsight I really wanted to. But I was pressured by my family to go into medicine.

"He always had this concern about death, death looming. And pessimism. The bottle is always half empty. Concerned with the underworld—death, ghosts, phantoms, cemeteries, graves. And hypochondriacal. On top of that, people with a great deal of money become more and more frightened of death, believing money is a hedge against it."

Allen has often said that his personality seemed to change at the age of five. "My mother always said I was a happy kid for my early years, and that when I was around five, something happened, she always felt, that made me turn sour," he told Eric Lax. If one was to look for an answer to this mystery in his films, it would seem to be forthcoming. In *Annie Hall,* for example, Alvy's mother takes her little boy to a doctor because he has become so depressed. Alvy announces that he has learned that the universe is expanding and will one day explode. "Someday it will break apart," Alvy says, "and that would be the end of everything." He then asks, "What's the point?" In other words, death looms, as it does over all Allen's films, plays, and the interviews Allen has given over the years: Life and art are meaningless. In the long run everything dies and nothing lasts. As he tells Stig Björkman, "I've made the joke before, that I'm not interested in living on in the hearts of my countrymen, I'd rather live on in my apartment!" Speaking of his character Renata, a poet in *Interiors,* he says that art is not going to save her, "that really what we're all talking about is the tragedy of perishing. Aging and perishing. It's such a horrible, horrible thing for humans to contemplate, that they don't contemplate it. . . . There is no other fear of significant consequence . . . perishing is what it's all about."

The powerful counterforces to these fears and anxieties that Allen found for himself were writing, comedy, and music. Allen embraced them with overriding passion, and he does so to this day. It is only when he stops working that they return. But he always keeps working.

Another counterforce was sex, but getting any was hard work for teenagers in the 1950s. Both Woody and Jack Victor were too shy to call girls on the phone. Woody would get abdominal pains and freeze up with fear. Pursuing girls was nerve-racking and unbearably frustrating. Woody's dilemma was compounded by the fact he would chase the most desirable girls, the ones that were sure to reject him. But he could overcome his fear of phoning girls if it was on behalf of his friends. "I would shake and be unable to speak," Jack Victor recalled. "There was a girl I had wanted to date who had turned me down, so we did this prank. Woody made a prerecorded tape at Jerry's apartment which was hilarious. We used the name of another student, both the name and address of this poor guy. Woody dialed her number. When she answered, the tape with Woody's voice started. Woody said, 'I'm Jesse Roth.' He gave her a romantic spiel, and there was no response on the other end, so she seemed to be listening seriously. At the end of the routine he said, 'Don't just sit there, say something!' She did. She said, 'Good-bye.' It was actually the girl's mother on the phone."

"He was timorous," Elliott Mills remembered. "He was small. He was redheaded. He was conspicuous. And he didn't want to get beat up. He didn't want to be targeted. It's all a matter of physical size and appearance, which made him vulnerable. And easy to pick on.

"We double-dated quite a few times. One time we went to the movies, and it was late. There was a trolley car on Ocean Avenue but we didn't know if it was running. So we're standing on the corner. These hoods came up and they started making fun of him, because he was little and redheaded and he was wearing this trench coat. So they were picking on him. And he hailed a cab and took off, leaving us there, me and the two girls. The two hoods cracked up."

Woody may have been shy and timid with girls, but he was a mischievous plotter. He has said that as a teenager, his thoughts on sex centered on its availability and how fast you could get it: quantity and accessibility. To that end, he was what Jerry Epstein called a "bird-dogger": "I was taking a girl to a movie," Jerry told me. "We had ideas about scoring with girls that were akin to roofies today. If you put aspirin in a Coca-Cola, the girl was supposed to lose her inhibitions. Woody said to me, 'Look, I'll stand outside the movie theater in a disguise. And you bring the girl to the movie house. When you go inside, you go to the back where the candy counter is and you get a Coke.' So we went to the theater—I really liked this girl a lot—Woody was standing in front of the theater wearing a broad-brimmed hat, sunglasses—this was at night—a trench coat with the collar turned up, and a Band-Aid on his cheek. My brother, Sandy, came by while he was waiting out there, and he said, 'Hi, Woody.' He saw immediately who it was; there was no question.

"This was the plan: Woody told me, 'I'll go to the back of the theater by the candy counter. When you come back, you get the Coke and I'll drop the aspirin in.' Of course, when you stop to think of it, why do I need another guy to drop the aspirin into the Coke, which I can do on my own? So anyway he put the aspirin in the Coca-Cola. Needless to say it had no effect whatsoever. And Woody ended up going with this girl soon after. He called her right away. So he bird-dogged this girl whose name and telephone number I gave him. He wangled himself into a way of meeting these girls that I was bringing around, and then he bird-dogged them. That was his MO.

"Woody has the temperament of the trickster," Epstein continued. "That's his natural way. Criminality played a tragic role in his family's life. His first cousin was Arnold Schuster. Willie Sutton, the bank robber, escaped from prison. They were looking for him for a long time. Arnold was riding home on the subway. And Willie Sutton was in the car. Arnold saw him and called the police. Sutton was captured. Unfortunately they gave out Arnold's name. Albert Anastasia was watching the news, and he ordered his murder. Arnold was murdered at a subway station in Borough Park in Brooklyn.

"We practiced hypnosis together, ESP," Jerry continued. "He was always blaming his parents for everything, particularly his mother. He would come into a room and turn the pictures around on the wall, to goad her and to be provocative. She was a thin, redheaded woman. You could easily annoy the hell out of her if you found something. And she would overreact. He found it funny, and he was always provoking her. But later he was quite generous toward his parents and his sister.

"He had very quick perceptions, and he immediately found the flaws in people. He felt very inferior as a boy. So you had to always walk on eggshells when you talked to him."

"The big thing in Brooklyn was to be funny," Elliott Mills told me. "There was a lot of Jewish talent in that neighborhood. It was a golden age. Nobody had money but everybody had brains, and everybody was funny. Our heroes were the Dodgers and jazz musicians. Nobody got laid until they got married. It was an idyllic childhood. But Woody needed, wanted to be noticed. He did magic in the schoolyard during recess. He would try to figure out ways to make money off the kids. He would guess cards. You could buy tricks at the Circle Magic shop in Manhattan. There was a cigarette producer that you could stuff in your belt. You dropped your hand down near your jacket, and you could suddenly produce a cigarette in your hand. That kind of stuff. He was into that completely. He felt power that way. Trying to shill the Italians out of their money. He could do these tricks better than anybody. But he needed to be in a confident position like that. He would never put himself in a situation of being what we called a *fumferer*—someone who stumbles and doesn't do things well. He would never put himself in a position where he might *fumfer*. He would prepare. That's the essence. His comedy is prepared, figured out. Practiced in front of the mirror for seven hours a day."

Woody came from the land of tummlers (professional pranksters). Norman Podhoretz, who grew up in Flatbush, told me, "On virtually every street corner in Brooklyn where Jews lived, there was a comic, a tummler.

We had one on my corner. And they were very funny, these guys. Of course not all of them became professional comics, but many of them did: Alan King and Lenny Bruce among them." There are various but related definitions of tummlers. Mark Evanier defined them as "the life of the party, the person who led games and kept things happy by entertaining. Catskill resorts hired tummlers to keep things active for the guests."

"We all watched Milton Berle and all those shows," Elliott Mills said. "Next day we'd get together: 'Did you hear that line?'" To come up with a good line was a big deal.

But, according to Mills, Woody was neither a spritzer nor a tummler. "He could sit down; he was a writer! He would write it. From early on he was doing scenarios in his head. If you watch his stand-up, all he does is recite jokes. You can see he's written out this wonderful series of jokes, and he's trying to deliver them. And he has a lot of these actions and expressions which are sort of constructed. He really wasn't that natural as a stand-up. He prepared it carefully. The gestures were prepared. I'm sure he would practice a lot in front of the mirror, like he practiced magic in front of the mirror. Sleight of hand. I mean if somebody insulted him from the audience, I don't know what he would do. That wasn't his thing. Later on he and the insult comic Jack E. Leonard [a predecessor of Don Rickles] were on a show together. Leonard called him America's oldest living dart—so small and thin. Woody didn't have a comeback. He was not a wisecracking kind of guy. There was a general pervasive atmosphere in Flatbush that being funny was a lot of points. That's where Woody came in."

Woody's mother was unintentionally funny, never understanding what was funny about her. She cracked Woody up every day. "Woody's mother was like a cartoon character," Mills told me. "She was a hysteric, and Woody drove her to greater heights of hysteria. The angrier she got, the funnier she got. Woody would tell her that she looked like Groucho Marx, and she was both flustered and flattered. 'Well, so what?' she said. 'He's a handsome man!' Woody said, 'But, Ma, you're a woman.' We roared, but she did not see what was so funny."

Allen's unsmiling, laconic detachment, his seeming coldness, his quiet (he rarely raises his voice), and his clearheaded rationality seem to be related to his experience of his mother. He learned early on that silence and coolness were superior tools in controlling social situations, in contrast to his hysterical mother, who—at the mercy of her anger—seemed to fall apart at the seams and lose her self-control and ability to maintain a rational balance.

"His mother was not in favor of what he did at all. Not at all," said Jerry Epstein. "She called me and asked me to plead with him to give it all up, the show-business thing, and become a pharmacist. A steady profession; you could always make money that way. He was already making thousands, but it didn't matter to her. To her that kind of career was not for a Jewish boy. She just never felt anything gratifying about whatever he would achieve. It was the Al Jolson syndrome, like in *The Jazz Singer.* [In that film the protagonist leaves behind his Orthodox family and "betrays" his father, a cantor, by going into show business and becoming a popular singing star. The film actually mirrored Jolson's experience with his own Orthodox family—his father was also a cantor—and upbringing.] What kind of a business do you have going into something like that with all the sluts and whores?"

The family was right out of *Radio Days,* with uncles, aunts, and cousins sharing the apartment or living in the same house on different floors. Relatives ran in and out of rooms. The father's name in the film is Martin, he drives a cab, and he wants to be a jewelry engraver, just like Woody's. "I always said to Woody that he lived in a *mir* culture, that's like a Russian collective," Jack Victor told me. "Always the family was together."

Jerry and Woody went to camp together as counselors in 1952, but things did not work out. "Woody would take the kids to the mess hall for lunch," Epstein told me. "But when he was finished eating, he just left. The kids were still eating. He was supposed to be taking care of them. This caught the attention of the owners. So eventually he got fired.

"So he was fired, and I didn't want to stay there anymore. I wanted to spend the summer with him; we were very close. So he called his father and said, 'Get me out of here! Come get me!' His father came up with a couple of goons, with guns! They came on the grounds, and his father shouted 'Where's my son?!'" He thought Woody was in danger.

"The reality is that Woody had been picked on unfairly by the other counselors at that camp. That was one reason he wanted to get out. He wasn't and isn't the most sociable of people; he's an uncomfortable person in his skin. And if you're a psychic like Woody is, you want to be very careful about the energies that you're around. So when we left, there was one guy he really hated for picking on him. So we short-sheeted his bed and urinated either on or under the blanket.

"I was very influential in Woody's life, introducing him to jazz at age twelve, for example, as he was in mine," Epstein continued. "So we had a very close symbiosis. I gave him a lot, and he gave me a lot. Through his psychic ability he helped me connect to girls. We were sitting in a diner on Fifteenth Street and Avenue J in Flatbush having a sandwich. Up on the wall was an ad for Coca-Cola. And there was a silhouette of a girl, a cardboard ad. This was 1956; I was twenty. It was nearing the end of the school year, and I was going to go to camp as a counselor. He said, 'When you go to camp you're going to meet a girl who looks like that. Her favorite song is going to be 'Moonglow,' and her favorite color will be South Sea island blue.'

"So when I went to camp, this girl was sitting in front of me at a meeting. And she was the exact replica of that silhouette. So we made a connection. In camp we became closer. I would write to Woody about what was happening. And he would write me back, 'You'll be walking with her on a country road,' and he described just what the setting would look like. And he told me how I should pursue the relationship and how it would turn out. And it happened. And I asked her during the course of our connection what was her favorite song and what was her favorite color. And her answers were exactly what Woody had told me. Later I married her."

Woody was the mischief maker. "In 1948 they had blue cans from the Jewish National Fund—*pushkes*—to collect money for Palestine," Elliott Mills said. "Israel had just been born. Woody comes up to me one day—he's thirteen now. He says, 'Here's what we're gonna do. I've got these cans. We're gonna cut out the bottom.' So we did this in front of the Midwood Theater. We collected money with these cans that had the bottom cut off. The canister was sitting on top of the bottom, which was metal. People dropped money into it and you heard the sound of the coin hitting the bottom: *ping, ping, ping*. Then we just lifted the thing up and took the money. The money went into our pockets.

"Another time we were on this street that went past the back of a bakery that had an exhaust fan. And across the street was a little triangle of land that had one of the last farms left in Brooklyn. There were horses there and horseshit in the street. So as we went past it, Woody said, 'I wonder what happens if the shit hits the fan.' And he took a piece of cardboard that was lying on the ground, and he picked up some horseshit and threw it at the fan. We all had to run because we were spattered with horseshit.

"He was not a schlemiel. If anything, he was a go-getter. He was a hustler. He was very goal-oriented. He had a great hustle in mind but if we had tried it we would have all gotten killed. He decided we were going to predict the score of the NCAA basketball game. Woody taught me how to use this device called a nail writer or a Swami Gimmick. It concealed a small piece of pencil lead. All these guys from school were going to get together and listen to the game on the radio while Woody held an envelope with the winner's name on the sheet of paper inside. He was going to write down the score, and I was going to hold the envelope. Me, I would have on my finger the little pencil. And when the game was over I would open the envelope and say, 'Oh my God, he got it right!' while using the nail writer to put in the right team. And I said to him, If we do this I'll get killed. So we didn't do it."

"Here's an example of how he would think up a scenario," Mills continued. "He was not a wisecracker. This was long before he played James Bond's nephew, Little Jimmy Bond, in *Casino Royale*. We were talking about the first James Bond. And Woody developed a riff on it. You know how Bond didn't like martinis that were too dry or too wet? Woody wondered what would happen if somebody went into a candy store and asked for an egg cream like that? We were passing by a little mom-and-pop candy store on Ocean Avenue. He said, 'I'm going to do this bit.' So we walked in there. There was this old Jewish couple. Woody walks up to the guy and he says with a British accent, snapping his fingers, 'An egg cream, my good man. Vanilla. Not too sweet, not too dry.' He actually pulled this. So the old guy threw him out of the place. That's what he was really good at, creating these scenarios in his head."

"He was the biggest rebel," Jack Victor recalled. "In high school I wanted to introduce him to the faculty adviser of the school paper. She was this old Irishwoman. She starts like fingering Woody's shirt while talking to him. So he starts fingering her shirt. She got upset and ran out of the office. He could make fun of his tormentors and make fun of himself as being tormented. He could go out of himself and see himself. He's an objective being, which is very hard to do. He was always like that."

As much as he hated school, there were teachers who appreciated his writing talent from the start. They would read his compositions aloud to the class in the fifth grade and even bring other teachers into the room and read them together and point at Allen.

"The admirable thing about Woody in growing up and getting to meet him at twelve," Jerry Epstein mentioned, "was that he never wavered for a moment in what his intention was in life. His intention was comedy and to write comedy and to be in the world of comedy. The influence and the pressures of his family did not matter. He followed his own star. He never wavered a moment. I wavered. Everybody that I knew wavered. He did not. And that was a great quality. Take his desire to be a jazz musician. He went heaven and earth to get these different teachers to teach him. And he practiced all the time, because he has this great capacity to drive himself in this passionate way to achieve something. And he does it. He was at Michael's Pub and now the Carlyle Hotel every Monday night over the years with his jazz band without fail, no matter what.

"And Woody found in humor a great avenue for the tragedy, the *mishegoss* [the craziness] of what we call the manmade world. This world around us. Because with humor your immune system goes up, and it's a force of life."

And, of course, he loved movies from the start. He led his flock (Elliott, Jack, Jerry, and Mickey) to the multitude of theaters in the neighborhood almost every day. There was a revival of *Gone With the Wind* at the Kent in Brooklyn, and he had some of his friends go with him (for two showings) the entire seven days of its run. The grand Midwood Theater (which his grandfather Isaac had owned in palmier days) was around the corner on Avenue J. In summer he went to the movies every day with popcorn and Milk Duds.

For Allen, movies were an escape throughout his childhood. He saw *Casablanca, Yankee Doodle Dandy,* the films of Preston Sturges, the Marx Brothers, and Frank Capra at an impressionable age, and they transported him into a different world. "You would leave your poor house behind and all your problems with school and family," he told Stig Björkman, "and you would go into the cinema, and they would have penthouses and white telephones and the women were lovely and the men always had an appropriate witticism to say and things were funny, but they always turned out well and the heroes were genuine heroes." He has often spoken of the contrast between the grim reality of life and the luminous fantasies of the movies. This contrast is a constant leitmotif in his work, most especially in *The Purple Rose of Cairo, Alice,* and *Play It Again, Sam.*

Allen feels that those early experiences in the movie houses had a crushing influence on him and on many of his friends well into late middle age because they made it so difficult to adjust to the harsh and often brutal realities of real life. The reality they felt was true was an illusion, and one that was impossible to surmount. "When you sat in those movie theaters," he said, "you thought it was real." The impulse of the writer was to reshape reality and make sure that things came out well in the end—as Alvy Singer does in *Annie Hall* when, in his first play, he rewrites reality so that Annie does not reject him and decides to marry him and return to New York from Los Angeles—which Allen loathes above all cities and regards as the snakepit of the world.

Allen's little-known and imperfect—but moving—Broadway play, *The Floating Light Bulb,* dealt with the desire to escape from life through the fantasy of magic. Produced by the Lincoln Center Theater Company, it debuted on April 27, 1981, at the Vivian Beaumont Theater in New York City. It is his finest play, a great leap from the dreadful *Don't Drink the Water* and some steps ahead of the charming *Play It Again, Sam.* Its obscurity is unjustified. The play starred Beatrice Arthur and Danny Aiello and was directed by Ulu Grosbard. It was named one of the outstanding plays of the 1981–82 Broadway season and was included in the notable Otis Guernsey's *Best Plays* series. It is a key to the young Allen and to a road not taken in his life. The play depicts a young Allen stand-in, Paul, as a stammerer who escapes from the reality around him with magic tricks and the dream that success in magic will bring him power and social acceptance. This is clearly not the feisty Woody who surmounted his environment and escaped Brooklyn at such an early age. Allen's childhood friends told me that Allen never had a stammer and was basically in charge of his life from the start. It could be interpreted as the Woody who might have been, or Woody at an earlier stage, or lingering depressive strands of the inner Woody's darker memories of his childhood.

In the play Allen created a deracinated Brooklyn Jewish milieu devoid of the raucous festivity of *Radio Days,* with its happy tumult of an extended family bursting the seams of the household. The aunts, cousins, uncles, and neighbors are absent, and we are left with Paul, a little-seen brother, and the festering, disintegrating relationship between mother and father. There is also a "gentleman caller." And lest there be any doubt that this is Allen talking, the overriding subject is magic, the same subject that reappears over and over again in his films—as recently as his 2014 *Magic in the Moonlight*. And where does Paul escape to when he gets out of the house? New York, the Automat, the magic shops—Woody's usual destinations as a young man.

The play, set in 1945, is painful, somber, and intimate. Its atmosphere is one of despair, futility, and depression. This is a world, the playwright is telling us, you either escape from or die. Allen wrote in the stage directions that the Pollacks live in "an apartment reeking of hopelessness and neglect" that "looks out on the bleak brick courtyard in the back and rear of the surrounding buildings, giving one the feeling of being at the bottom of a well." The raffish father, Max, who never finds a niche in life, is reminiscent of Woody Allen's real father but devoid of his wastrel charm. He goes from job to job. He is a consummate loser pursued by loan sharks, and cheats on his wife. Enid, the mother, has a muted affection for her son; she says of him, "He's one of those people . . . that goes his whole life drifting, dreaming, dependent—in his own private world—with someone always having to take care of him." She cannot overcome her own feelings of desperation, working as a clerk selling hosiery and grasping at straws: get-rich quick schemes such as selling "personalized matchbooks" or tropical fish, and asking her sister for money. She laments lost catches like Herb Glass, "a crackerjack foot specialist [who] worshipped me" and a wild boy she calls "the Kissing Bandit."

Allen has never ceased talking about his hatred of public school, which is expressed by Paul in the play to Enid:

**PAUL:** I can't go to school. I'm n-not going back.
**ENID:** You're not?
**PAUL:** I can't do it. There are so many faces. I can't breathe. I get confused in the halls . . . everything's closing in.
**ENID:** Don't give me that nonsense! What's wrong with you? Where do you run off to when you don't go to school?
**PAUL:** Out.
**ENID:** Out where? Where?
**PAUL:** S-sometimes I j-just w-walk around and sit and r-read the

p-paper at th-the Automat and th-then w-walk t-to the m-magic shop and l-look around.

**ENID:** Naturally. The magic shop. I should have known.

His mother accuses Paul of being "different," that he is vulnerable and shielding himself from reality with floating light bulb tricks. She fears he will not make it in life: "You're different because you live in your world of Chinese boxes and silk handkerchiefs and marvelous effects. Unfortunately that is not the real world, as you will learn soon enough."

She goes on to voice the same objections to a show-business career for Paul that Woody's mother expressed over and over again: You couldn't count on show business. Millions tried and most failed. He would need something to fall back on—a real job. A profession.

Paul tries to escape from her hectoring and says he needs to "practice." She replies: "Good, Paul. Practice. . . . Learn magic. That's exactly what we need around here—more tricks and illusions." There are traces of Woody's real mother in the way Enid tries to pressure the men in the family to be productive, to work hard, and to succeed.

In the most poignant scene (somewhat reminiscent but not at all imitative of the scene in *The Glass Menagerie* when the mother tries to find a savior for her daughter, Laura), Enid arranges to have Jerry Wexler, a small-time talent agent whom she mistakenly thinks is an important producer, "audition" Paul in the apartment. Wexler boasts about his obscure clients the way Broadway Danny Rose talks up his one-legged tap dancer and hopeless ventriloquist, Barney Dunn. Wexler mentions a talking dog who sings "Little Sir Echo" (Allen, in one of the many charming instances of his cribbing from his own work, actually sang "Little Sir Echo" to a talking dog on a television show in 1965; he also boxed with a giraffe) and two Armenian boxers who performed "Ave Maria" while fighting. Paul, as "The Great Pollack," begins to do his magic act: "I h-have here this o-ordinary p-piece of n-newspaper, which I f-fold into the sh-shape of a c-cone. And an ordinary p-pitcher of m-milk. I p-pour the milk into the c-cone, thusly." He sets the pitcher back on the table. "Presto!" When he takes a corner of the newspaper and with a flourish opens up the cone, the milk has vanished.

Paul proceeds to do several more magic tricks successfully, but then he begins to fall apart: He apologizes for his stuttering, he begins to tremble, he loses his nerve and is unable to continue. He runs into his room, slams the door, and locks it.

The scene is naked and painful, and it could conceivably stem directly from Allen's childhood memories, perhaps a hidden recollection of one of his most humiliating early experiences. Allen, sometimes eager to deflect biographers from scavenging around in his life, told Diane Jacobs in . . . *But We Need the Eggs* that a model for Paul was a boy in his childhood: "I would pass by this particular house, and there was a seventeen-year-old kid who would sit by the window and shuffle cards constantly. He was his mother's cross to bear—there's no question about it." Jacobs bought this explanation and wrote that "autobiographical comparisons" ended with Paul's obsession with magic. She accurately wrote that Allen was totally unlike "the painfully shy, stuttering Paul [who] hasn't the stamina or drive to envision a real-life application for his art behind 'prrracticing.'" It's certainly true that Allen's father was affectionate and loving, and the father in the play is distant and self-absorbed. Paul is sixteen in the play, and Allen, at that age, was an aggressive, assertive young man on the make.

The Paul of the play could have been written as a much younger man, and might contain within his character aspects of a younger Allen. Perhaps significantly Allen was really ten in 1945. Allen has always been churlish about any attempts to link his real life to his art, and resents any suggestions of vulnerability unless he admits to them himself. Who of us does not share that need for self-protectiveness? But some of *The Floating Light Bulb* seems to ring too true and too close to aspects of his own experience to let us take his denials entirely at face value. The character of Paul may have been Allen's innermost fear. Allen as a boy was bullied yet aggressive; he was ambitious and determined yet a mediocre student and scoreless with chicks. It is possible that Paul was what Allen feared lurked inside him: a loser, oppressed by his mother—someone who would never live out his dreams.

Allen follows the scene in which Paul fails at magic with a lovely one that seems more a matter of invention than of experience. Jerry Wexler, with a few drinks in him, begins to find Enid beautiful, and she in turn is drawn to him. The scene comes to a sad denouement when Jerry announces that he is leaving Brooklyn to join his ailing mother in Phoenix. Enid is shattered. In the evening Max tells Enid he is leaving for good. Enid in her fury strikes him with Paul's magic cane, and a bouquet of paper flowers flutters out. Magic has betrayed Paul and Enid and, like Cecilia in *The Purple Rose of Cairo*, they are left as dreamers coping with the compromises of reality.

Walter Kerr perceptively wrote of the play in the *New York Times* that while Paul is depicted as a "born loser":

> *I did not know Mr. Allen himself as a lad of 15. . . . But I will lay you bets that anyone on the block . . . knew perfectly well that he was a comer. Shyness is nothing if there's quality inside it. It finds its way out. But Mr. Allen was so determined to Chekhovize the boy—and, for that matter, everyone else in his play—that he won't give the kid a chance. And I think that's the beginning of what's wrong with the play.*

Kerr went on to write that the play had "an honestly detailed background" and "shrewdly observed, affectionately written characters," but regrets that Paul is written as a "boy who won't fight back. He lapses into silence, retreats to his room, leaves his mother banging her fists purposelessly against his locked door." He found the play's hopelessness too predetermined and arbitrary, Paul's audition breakdown unbelievable: "We know that the boy is a capable enough magician. Why, then, must he make such a mess that he breaks down entirely, fleeing for his sealed-off room for good?" He noted that "it is all so arbitrary; failure has been forced on these likeable people by Mr. Allen." He wrote that Allen's writing "suddenly leapt to such funny responsive, touching life" in the "lovely" scene between the mother and Wexler (Jack Weston) "because he is at last dealing with a character—perhaps two characters—he has observed at a little distance rather than intimately lived with. . . . The moment Mr. Weston enters in the second half . . . Mr. Allen's imagination takes off, does a zany and original little dance of its own."

The play is somber and grim (these are certainly aspects of Allen's own personality; he has said that in forty years of analysis he never told a joke), but it is affecting and it is not, as some have suggested, a replication of *The Glass Menagerie*. Tennessee Williams may well have been an inspiration, but artists are entitled to be inspired by, without imitating, fellow artists. The play is wholly serious—a dangerous road for Allen when he tried it in *Interiors, Another Woman, September,* and *Shadows and Fog.* (Another play apparently born of his life experience, *A Second-Hand Memory*, was produced off-Broadway by the Atlantic Theater Company in 2004 and was really pummeled by the critics. That play, unlike any other Allen has written, was never published, and I have not been able to locate a copy.) But here he knows his world and his characters, and he is working out of his life experience. In those almost unwatchable, lugubrious films he imagined what his WASP characters were like, but did not really know them at all. They turned into abstractions, deadly boring ones at that. Here he is at home, and if the play does not entirely work, as Kerr indicated, it has many fine moments and is yet another instance of Allen's expansive gifts.

We also learn some significant things from *The Floating Light Bulb* about Allen's childhood and, in retrospect, how he escaped that world. (In *The Floating Light Bulb* only the father escapes.) His is a gigantic success story against the odds, but genius always has an element of the inexplicable. "When you talk about genius," Jerry Epstein said, "Woody sang 'The Star-Spangled Banner' when he was six months old. Really sang it. He had locution when he was eight months old. He could have a conversation at that age."

Many of us have crippling, devastating childhoods, but few of us find ways of transmuting that pain into art. Retreating to the basement of his parents' home, eating his meals alone, practicing his magic, his coin and card tricks, practicing the clarinet, he achieved a unique comic perspective—a comedic talent that is so instinctive he cannot fully understand it himself—a talent that from the beginning would bring him great financial success. He was absolutely certain of his gifts. And he was a whirlwind. His story is one of limitless ambition, success, and triumph, interlaced with the sorrows and pain of someone who cannot fully outrun a childhood that had some desolation and sorrow. But if he does try to have it both ways—to insist on both his normality and his endless phobias and fears—he doesn't mind letting us in on the latter as long as he is the one telling the story, in control, shifting the gears, writing the scenarios. We know he was scorched by the early years despite the "warm food, milk and cookies," and, as he freely admits, he still lives in a condition he has defined as "anhedonia"—his original title for *Annie Hall*—an inability to experience joy in life. "Writing saved his life," says Woody Allen as Harry Block at the end of *Deconstructing Harry*.

# 3. The Real Broadway Danny Rose

WOODY ALLEN BEGAN his performing career at thirteen, singing Al Jolson songs at his bar mitzvah. At sixteen he was doing his magic act at Young Israel of Brooklyn, the East Midwood Jewish Center, and Weinstein's Majestic Bungalow Colony in the Catskills. He was writing comedy while still in high school, using his pen name and selling jokes to the columnists Earl Wilson, Walter Winchell, and Leonard Lyons. Jack Victor recalls Allen proudly showing him his first published joke in Earl Wilson's column on November 25, 1952: "It's the fallen women who are usually picked up, says Woody Allen." The jokes soon appeared in all the columns; "Woody Allen says he ate at a restaurant that had OPS prices—over people's salaries." He placed many in Earl Wilson's column "Earl's Pearls": "Taffy Tuttle heard of a man who was a six-footer, and told Woody Allen: 'Gee, it must take him a long time to put his shoes on.'"

"I was sixteen years old when I got my first job," Allen told *The Paris Review*. "It was as a comedy writer for an advertising agency in New York [David Alber]. I would come into the agency every single day after school and I would write jokes for them. They would attribute these jokes to their clients and put them in the newspaper columns. I would get on the subway— the train quite crowded—and, strap-hanging, I'd take out a pencil and by the time I'd gotten out I'd have written forty or fifty jokes . . . fifty jokes a day for years. . . . Believe me, it was no big deal." He quickly became a comedy writer, first for the TV personality Herb Shriner. After leaving Shriner, he got a job as a staff writer at NBC. He was enrolled in the NBC Writers' Development Program, which was formed to find writers for the *Colgate Comedy Hour*.

He virtually abandoned Midwood High School, where he participated in no activities and detested his teachers. He recalled later "getting up in the morning, having my big piece of chocolate cake and milk for break- fast, my parents still asleep, going out, presumably to Midwood High School but not going [there]." He took the subway to Times Square and the Paramount Theatre.

Allen told Eric Lax that when he was six years old, he had first seen Times Square with his father. "It was during World War II . . . He would take me from the train station on Avenue J in Brooklyn and we'd ride into New York. [We'd] go to the Automat. [We'd] go to the Circle Magic Shop, which had a big arcade downstairs. We'd go to the arcades on Forty- second Street—my father loved to shoot the rifles. It was *dazzling*."

The Times Square Allen encountered was not the metallic Times Square of today, nor was it the snakepit of crime and prostitution it be- came in the 1970s. It had the show-business innocence of *Broadway Danny Rose*; it was a world of live stage shows and vaudevillians and hoofers get- ting by at the many small hotels on the side streets, of record shops and sheet music stores. It was a Damon Runyon and Billy Rose world. The Metropole was not the stripper's palace it became later; it was the home of great New Orleans jazz, with Max Kaminsky, Wild Bill Davison, and Pee Wee Russell playing on the bar, the doors wide open, and the music drift- ing sweetly into the street.

The Laff Movie, where Woody's father took him, played the Marx Brothers, Laurel and Hardy, and the Three Stooges twenty-four hours a day; beside it was the all-night Horn & Hardart Automat, where aspiring performers, varied eccentrics, and socialist proselytizers gathered with their newspapers in their back pockets (New York had eight major newspapers then). The RKO Palace, once the beacon of vaudeville, revived eight acts along with headliners Judy Garland, Danny Kaye, Betty Hutton, Belle Baker, Smith and Dale, Buddy Hackett, and Eddie Fisher. Lindy's, where show-business royalty mingled with the wannabes and Winchell wrote his column, was the heart of the area, its cheesecake legendary. Jack Dempsey's restaurant was nearby, Dempsey often sitting at a table by the front window. The resplendent Winter Garden Theatre, Jolson's home base, still stood, as did Toffenetti's, with its giant strawberry cheesecake in the window. The Paramount Theatre at Forty-third Street starred Sinatra and Tony Bennett and was the apex of theaters in New York City. The Colony Record Shop was a center of the music industry, as was the Brill Building with its songwriters and song pluggers several streets away. Nightclubs were still in their glory: the Copacabana and the Latin Quarter were the meccas, but there were also Billy Rose's Diamond Horseshoe; the Old Roumanian, starring Sadie Banks; Monte Proser's La Vie en Rose (where Dorothy Dandridge and scores of others got their starts). Forty-second Street movie theaters stayed open all night. Hanson's drugstore with its soda fountain was also open all night, and Broadway denizens, song pluggers, and singers like Bobby Darin hung out there for hours. So it was good to be alive in those days—not least of all because there was absolutely no fear: New Yorkers often stayed up all night there when they could.

This was the vibrant show-business world that Woody Allen imbibed as a young man, and—as the Gershwin, Porter, and Berlin soundtracks of his films, the ambience of *Broadway Danny Rose*, and the Times Square rooftop scenes of *Radio Days* attest—it is still embedded in his heart.

This was only one aspect of the beauty and intensity of New York that captivated him, but what hovered about all of it was a quality of innocence that cannot fully be recaptured.


What he continued to hate was traditional education. He enrolled at New York University as a film major and took three courses: Spanish, English, and motion picture production. He almost never went to class. At the end of the first semester he flunked Spanish and English and barely passed motion picture production. New York University expelled him. He tried a night course in motion picture production at City College in 1954 and was expelled again. He tried a course in dramatic writing; he enrolled in a photography class and never attended it.

"I got him into psychoanalysis when he was twenty," Jerry Epstein told me. "I was waiting to be an analyst myself, and I eventually became a student and graduate at the New York Psychoanalytical Institute. I referred him to the clinic there. He was suffering. A lot. Woody had a lot of anxiety. We're talking about five-times-a-week analysis. He was seen for fifty cents a session: two dollars and fifty cents a week."

Allen was related to the noted, highly successful comedy writer and playwright Abe Burrows; his uncle had married Burrows's aunt. Burrows had cowritten some of the great Broadway hits of the fifties, including *Guys and Dolls, How to Succeed in Business Without Really Trying*, and *Can-Can*. Allen went to Burrows in 1956 for advice and told him he wanted to be a television writer. Burrows urged him to think beyond that, to consider writing for the theater. In his 1980 memoir, *Honest, Abe*, Burrows recalled his first meeting with Allen. He was bowled over by his talent. "One day he phoned me," Burrows wrote, "told me he was Nettie's son, and asked if we could meet. The next day he came to my house. A wispy little fellow, very innocent look, but there was an interesting gleam in his eyes. . . .

"Woody asked me if I would like to see some of his work. It can be very painful to read a bunch of jokes by a new, inexperienced comedy writer, but in this case I had no choice. Woody handed me two pages of jokes. I politely started to read them, and wow! His stuff was dazzling." Burrows observed that none of the thirty jokes were ones he could ever have thought of.

> *Frequently I hear a good crack somebody makes and I laugh and give him a polite note. What I'm thinking is that given the same setup, I would have thought of the same punch line. But Woody's jokes seemed to come from a different world.*

Burrows cited one of the thirty jokes Woody had given him, about his wife sinking his boats. It would soon be one of Woody's biggest jokes in his stand-up routine as he rose to stardom, and it's indicative of just how fully ready Woody was in 1956 at the age of twenty-one.

Burrows wrote letters of recommendation for Woody to Sid Caesar, Phil Silvers, and Peter Lind Hayes, a well-known comedian with his own radio program. Caesar turned him down (but would later hire him). Woody then went to see Hayes, who hired him. Burrows noted that comedy writers start out imitating well-known writers who are successful, often stealing their jokes. "But Woody is inimitable," he wrote. "The comics and the comedy writers who try to copy his stuff never come close because Woody's wit and style are part of Woody himself. He writes like Woody Allen, he acts like Woody Allen, and he looks like Woody Allen. He's a tough act to copy."

At NBC he found a mentor—the first of many who took an intense interest in him—in the comedy writer Danny Simon, brother of Neil Simon. He said of Simon, "Danny is one of the most important people to my career . . . for teaching me the fundamentals of how to construct sketches and, even more, for the psychological boost of having someone that accomplished believe in me." Allen has often said, "Everything I learned about comedy writing I learned from Danny Simon." Woody told Eric Lax, "He turned my professional career around completely." Simon gave him a sense of certainty about his own judgment of his own work and that of others. "One of the many things he instilled in me, because *he* had it, was an unyielding self-confidence, an unyielding sense in your own convictions, and I've never lost it. So everyone in town could be saying that the sketches on a particular show were funny, but if he said they weren't funny, he couldn't be swayed. And when he thought something *was* funny and somebody screwed it up he would not lose confidence but show you how to do it so it worked. He'd say, 'Of course it's not funny. But if you do it *this* way, acting it out, it is funny.'" Simon helped Allen find work in Hollywood, and he was soon, by the age of nineteen, writing comedy for Bob Hope, Garry Moore, Ed Sullivan, *Candid Camera*, and *The Tonight Show*. Allen said, "I was seventeen years old and I was earning more money than my parents put together had ever earned in their life. . . . The kids in my neighborhood were earning I don't know what—the minimum wage was like 55 cents an hour or something and I was earning like sixteen hundred dollars a week." In 1953 he left New York University to become a gag writer for Garry Moore and Sid Caesar. His salary then was $1,500 a week, but to his parents, especially his mother, he was a failure.

Woody met Harlene Rosen in 1953. He was eighteen and Harlene was fifteen. She played the piano in Woody's jazz band along with Jack Victor, Elliott Mills, and Jerry Epstein. "Woody wasn't that terrible with girls," Jack Victor recalled. "He was average. None of us dated a lot. But there was no one special until Harlene. He had no real relationship until he met her. She was soft, nice. She was quiet and all that, but you couldn't push her around. When we played the East Midwood Jewish Center, we needed a piano player. That's where we met Harlene. Her mother had been a professional singer and was a difficult person, kind of cold. She did not care for Woody, a college dropout. Harlene's father, Julius Rosen, had a shoe store on Kings Highway."

"The thing at the East Midwood Jewish Center was hysterical," Elliott Mills remembered. "Harlene got all panicked because she was playing in public for the first time. She blew up to about three hundred notes a minute, an incredible tempo. We couldn't keep up with that."

"After that, we played music at Harlene's house," Jack Victor said. "Elliott or Mickey Rose [another friend of Woody's, who collaborated on writing *Take the Money and Run* and *Bananas* with him and died in 2013] played the drums. Harlene's father had been a trumpet player and once in a while he played with us.

"Harlene had a wry sense of humor. She took Woody with a grain of salt. She would laugh at his things. He felt at ease with her, I think. A lot of Jewish girls at that time were pretty bitchy. And Harlene wasn't."

Woody first proposed marriage to Harlene, a lovely petite brunette, in 1955, the same year he lost his job with David Alber. They were still virgins. He began working for $169 a week as part of the NBC Writers' Development Program. He was then offered the chance to write comedy in Hollywood for the *Colgate Comedy Hour*. He would be one of eight writers on the show. Woody flew to Hollywood on his own and lived a lonely existence at the Hollywood Hawaiian Motel on Yucca and Grace Streets, sharing a suite with another writer, Milt Rosen. He wrote Harlene twenty-page letters every day.

Jack Victor shared with me some of the letters Woody wrote him in 1956 from Hollywood. The letters disclosed his loneliness, his yearning to be back in Brooklyn with his constant friends Jerry, Jack, and Elliott, his ambivalent attitude toward Harlene, his centeredness and seriousness of purpose, including his immersion in New Orleans jazz, about which he shows considerable knowledge and love—especially for George Lewis, Sidney Bechet, Kid Ory, and Muggsy Spanier—and his warmth, affection, and support for his friend Jack, whom he keeps urging to have the courage to approach and date girls. He seemed especially close to Jack because of their mutual idealism and interest in literature and art. Woody urged Jack to join a local synagogue in Brooklyn to meet girls as he had done. Apparently he had not changed his name yet, as he signed off "Alan" or "Al" and, once, "the Woodster."

He had already written a sketch for Bob Hope and Kathryn Grayson. He noted that Los Angeles was sunny and warm, houses pink against white streets, but he soon got tired and bored with it. He ate at the Brown Derby every day and was running all over town. The other writers on the program—Danny Simon (head writer on the program), Arnie Rosen, and Coleman Jacoby—all of whom he described as TV big shots, were staying at his motel. He suddenly announced that he was married to Harlene Rosen. He had kept urging her to join him and get married. The couple were married in Los Angeles by a rabbi on March 15, 1956. Allen's and Harlene's parents were not present. He was clearly quickly bored with marriage and eager to resume his walks and talks and listening to jazz with Jack.

The marriage was on the rocks nearly from the start. "Woody wrote me regularly from California," Jack Victor told me, "but especially during the honeymoon. I could see it wasn't a honeymoon anymore. There were problems. It just didn't work out, really."

On April 28 Woody told Jack he and Harlene were leaving Hollywood on May 8, but would see Kid Ory play at a joint in Beverly Hills the day before. He was going to Las Vegas to gamble for two days, then to New Orleans for two days to hear jazz, visit George Lewis on St. Philip Street, and in general case the town. He would return to New York and live in Harlene's parents' den for a month, and then they would rent an apartment near Central Park.

The Colgate program had been canceled after a month due to poor ratings, and Woody and Harlene were forced to live with Harlene's parents for a while in Manhattan. They soon moved into a one-room apartment at 110 East Sixty-first Street. Shortly afterward they relocated to a brownstone at 311 West Seventy-fifth Street. Harlene resumed her studies in philosophy at Hunter College, and Woody resumed his psychoanalysis. He was writing jokes for TV programs; again his state of disenchantment was mirrored in his attitude toward these programs in *Annie Hall*. Woody and Harlene played their recorders together, and Harlene tried unsuccessfully to cook. "I visited them at West Seventy-fifth Street," Elliott Mills recalled. "It was a divided crazy apartment. It had a monster chandelier that must have [once] been at the center of somebody's living room. In their apartment it was right on the edge of the wall.

"A huge water bug came up in the bathroom," Elliott added. "Woody was terrified of those things. And he had this huge insecticide can. He was furiously spraying it, jumping around. He was waltzing around with this spray gun trying to get this bug. Harlene was making fun of him. She went into the bathroom and smashed the bug with a broom. Later, in *Annie Hall*, he transformed the bug into a lobster, then a spider 'the size of a Buick.'" He always does riffs on what actually happened."

Harlene wanted Woody to take up more serious writing. She was really not into show business, jazz, movies, or gambling at all. Woody, who read only comic books, was angry and competitive with her and began to read the classics and philosophy. Based on his later sardonic satires of philosophical writing, he could not have been enamored of them in the first place. But he embarked on a course of self-improvement, keeping a list of new words to build his vocabulary, assiduously followed her courses, and read the books that she was assigned to read. He even hired a tutor to assist him in studying philosophy and spent an hour a day with his friend Len Maxwell at an art show, followed by a discussion about it on the way home.

It was a marriage mired in stumbling inexperience. "I think Woody was bored," Jerry Epstein said. Considering his rocky and ambivalent relationship with his own mother, it's not surprising that Woody's first venture into an intimate relationship with a woman faltered badly.

Allen was writing jokes for many of Danny Simon's shows, and in 1957 Simon recommended him for a job at Tamiment, the resort near Stroudsburg, Pennsylvania, that served as a training ground for writers. Founded by the socialist Rand School of Social Science, Tamiment had a 1,200-seat theater, dance hall, boating lake, and golf course. Simon had urged Allen to venture beyond writing jokes into creating characters and sketches, and thought that Tamiment would be the right place to develop those skills. Moe Hack had succeeded Max Liebman (the producer of *Your Show of Shows*) as producer of Tamiment's famous Saturday-night shows. The lodge was a hotbed of talent: Danny Kaye, Sid Caesar, Imogene Coca, Carl Reiner, and Mel Brooks had performed there; Neil and Danny Simon wrote sketches. An entirely new show was written, not improvised, by the writers in residence every single week. It was a very valuable experience for a young writer. Tamiment also served as a showcase for Broadway and TV producers, who would come in to see the shows and recruit new talent. One book musical was done each year. *Once Upon a Mattress* was written there. Both Carol Burnett and Larry Kert, who would go on to play the role of Tony in *West Side Story*, were at Tamiment in 1955. The atmosphere of old show business and of the "stage door" world was congenial to Woody, and his strenuous work ethic was entirely suited to the Tamiment experience. He jumped in with alacrity. Marshall Brickman, collaborator with Allen on *Manhattan, Sleeper*, and *Annie Hall*, would say of the pressure of writing for such a strenuous deadline: "You knew the train was leaving the station, and you had to be on it."

Allen became an actor almost by accident. A member of the company at Tamiment, lyricist Marshall Barer, said in *Writers' Theater* that "Woody certainly did not come to Tamiment to be a performer, but performing was almost imposed upon him by the other writers." He recalled sitting at a writers' conference at Tamiment listening to Allen read one of his sketches and discuss who should be in it. Suddenly an idea struck everyone at once: "Woody, do it yourself!" they all shouted. "You can perform it better than anyone we have here." Allen reluctantly agreed. He moved into sketch writing and directing in much the same way. In the second season he began creating sketches in rehearsal through cast improvisations. In the process he moved from being a joke writer to a writer of comedy sketches. He also directed and acted for the first time. "The directing was purely out of self-preservation," Allen would say later, "and was not the fulfillment of some long-time desire to direct." Dissatisfied with the way the resident director worked out sketches, Allen insisted during the second season that he be allowed to direct his own work. He would demonstrate to the actors how characters and situations should be played.

Allen, Barer recalled, "would select the cast, set the scene, throw out a premise and invite everyone to contribute suggestions."

Sid Weedman, who was at Tamiment for three seasons starting in 1956, told me that "Everybody lived in long wooden barracks. Woody and Harlene lived in one room with a bath. I almost never saw Harlene. Woody performed a sketch called 'Opening Night.' It had four theater seats facing the audience. Woody, his 'mother,' and two 'aunts' sat there. The women were talking about everybody in the imaginary audience. 'This is my son. He wrote this movie. He's such a talent.' They were just raving about him, telling the audience what a genius their son and nephew is. Then the sketch starts, and one of them says, 'That's not me, is it? Why, I never said anything like that!' So they're watching themselves being portrayed. By the end of the sketch they're berating him, and one of them beats him over the head with her pocketbook.

"We passed each other backstage, but he was not an outgoing person, and I was. To me he was just kind of a bump on a log. Actually he was a nervous wreck. He had confidence when he wrote, but he had a lack of confidence in a lot of things in life, I think. He didn't socialize; he was just by himself a lot. The other writers would interact, hanging out at lunchtime. But the sketch was a bitch and the biggest hit of the season." Other sketches by Allen were equally hilarious, including a convicts' stage show. The convicts present annual awards for Best Murder, Best Assault with a Deadly Weapon, and Best Robbery. Another sketch, "The Mad Baker," was about a giant chocolate cake that terrorized the countryside. "Psychological Warfare," clearly inspired by Allen's psychoanalysis, was set on a battleground. A group of men enter dressed like American GIs but without conventional weaponry. The sergeant discusses their plan of attack: "Hit them in the ego, hit them in the id, hit them in their inferiority complexes, and if that doesn't work, hit them below the belt and we'll go back to the old way!" Then the "enemy" enters and begins to battle with the sergeant:

SERGEANT: You're too short! You're too short and your mother never loved you!

ENEMY: You're a nail biter and you still have to sleep with a light in your room!

SERGEANT: You're a failure in life! You buy all your clothes at Klein's!

ENEMY: You're a failure! You live in Westport with your own wife!

Willis Hall and Keith Waterhouse, authors of *Writers' Theater*, wrote:

> *Allen bemoaned the fact that he was not able to sell any of his Tamiment material, yet many of the ideas and themes formulated at Tamiment were seminal in terms of his later work. The idea of a gigantic chocolate cake assuming a life of its own and assaulting humans was a classic piece of tomfoolery in* Sleeper. *The entire "Mad Baker" sketch, in fact, was recreated by Allen in one segment of* Everything You Always Wanted to Know About Sex, *where he used the same plot and character development but changed the focus of the story from food to sex. . . . In the movie, the chocolate cake became a giant female breast.*

Tamiment was ideal for Woody, but Harlene was uncomfortable and ill at ease. The young, inexperienced couple played duets on their recorders in the evenings on the veranda while Tamiment seethed with sexual activity. Allen felt deprived and frustrated. One time the folksinger Dick Davy wanted to talk to him, and Allen asked him, "Well, where shall we talk?" Davy played the guitar by the lake and suggested chatting there. "It was the first time all summer he'd been out there," Davy told the writer Phil Berger. "And that's the main thing they did at resorts. Lie around on those chaise longues with their music and their gin and watermelon and make out. And Woody looks at it like it's a scene from a strange movie. And he got all excited. 'Is this what goes on here all day? All these naked women? Wow, you must have a ball. Wow.' And he's looking at all those girls. And he was like very uncomfortable . . . a fish out of water, looking around. 'Cause he was always writing. He had stacks of spearmint gum. You know, for the nervousness and writing." He talked openly about his marital problems with the other writers. He'd tell them, "Well, I got to go back to the cabin and do the husband bit." He told them in front of Harlene that they had gone to a rabbi for counseling and the rabbi had told him, "All you have to do is mount her like a young bull." Moe Hack told the writer Gerald McKnight that Harlene "could take a lot of punishment."

Back in the city, Allen began to move up in television comedy. Danny Simon continued to mentor him and make connections for him. Allen was hired by the producer Max Liebman to write *Stanley*, a sitcom starring comedian Buddy Hackett. His cowriters were Larry Gelbart, Danny Simon, and Lucille Kallen, a writer for Sid Caesar's *Your Show of Shows*. The show was a hapless failure, not at all because of him. Allen moved on to work on Pat Boone's program. In 1958 Sid Caesar hired him for *Sid Caesar's Chevy Show* with cowriters Gelbart and Mel Brooks. (Brooks, first spotting Allen, described him as "a little red-haired rat.") Allen and Gelbart won the Sylvania Award for the best TV comedy of the year.

It was not an easy assignment. Caesar was a raging, alcoholic megalomaniac (as well as a comic genius) who threw furniture around. Allen referred later to Caesar's programs as a "mass of hostilities and jealousies." In his memoir, *Laughing Matters*, Gelbart recalled his first impressions of Allen at a writers' conference for the Caesar program:

> *Woody looked to be all of six years old. . . . Then, as now, he is not very impressive physically, . . . he seemed so fragile, so unformed, a tadpole in horn-rims. Then he started pitching jokes. Magically, he became instantly handsome, growing a foot taller with each fresh and funny punch line. This frog was a prince of comedy. For the next two weeks of writing sessions with Sid and me, Woody did more than pull his own weight: he was capable of lifting us both.*

Gelbart went on to describe Allen's attitude toward male nakedness and the country, attitudes that have been documented endlessly over the years:

> *In mid-afternoon, Sid, in predictably unpredictable Caesarean fashion, announced that he was going to take a steam bath and suggested the three of us continue working in his sauna. . . . Woody wouldn't hear of it. When Sid and I entered the sauna, Woody stayed outside, refusing to get undressed, saying he couldn't be funny naked.*
>
> *A year or two later, Woody and I . . . wrote a TV revue for . . . David Susskind . . . at a small farm I owned in upstate New York. I remember picking up Woody and his then wife, Harlene, at the train station the first time they came to visit for a working weekend. . . . In his three-piece suit (at least), button-down shirts, and black tie, Woody got off the train looking like a rabbi in mid-elopement. Harlene, resembling his bride and widow all in one, wore a black dress, a veiled hat, and elbow-length gloves. I'm sure Woody brought their passports. . . .*

*He hated flies: feared them really, not so much that one might bite him but rather possibly carry him off. He never went near, let alone into, the swimming pool. There are "things" in there, he said. To him, the sparkling blue water was a black lagoon.*

Allen went on to become a top writer on the Garry Moore TV show, but his hatred of the work was becoming unbearable. He showed up late, needled the other writers, and made no secret of his disgust for what he was doing. He had come to realize TV writing was a blind alley. His contempt for its sterility, hollowness, and plasticity is expressed in *Manhattan*, where Isaac walks off a ridiculous program he cowrites in disgust while the other writers sit around stoned, and in *Annie Hall*, where Alvy is appalled at the phony laugh track his pal Rob (Tony Roberts) utilizes for his Los Angeles TV sitcom. Speaking of his experience with the *Colgate Comedy Hour* he told Larry Wilde, "There is no future in being a TV writer. You hack around from show to show and you're always worried— is the comedian you're writing for going to be dropped because of bad ratings? And if he is dropped you may find yourself moving three thousand miles to the other coast to write for a new comedian. It's a rough business."

At the same time Neil Simon was establishing himself as a playwright, and other comedy writers were earning reputations for performing comedy acts they'd created and written themselves: Mel Brooks and Carl Reiner ("The 2000 Year Old Man"), Mike Nichols and Elaine May, Allan Sherman ("Hello Muddah, Hello Fadduh"). They were no longer invisible, and their newfound visibility was due to their originality and freshness. This was a different kind of comedy: not a string of one-liners and punch lines, but character-driven, fully realized sketches, often improvised at the start but later refined and developed into perennial favorites. Mort Sahl and Lenny Bruce were political rebels poised at the center of the new political currents that would soon sweep the country in the sixties. All this was fanned by the proliferation of jazz clubs and bohemian coffee shops and the rise of the hippies in Greenwich Village, North Beach, San Francisco, Berkeley, and Los Angeles. Allen first saw Sahl at the Blue Angel in New York City in 1954. Allen was stunned: "Seeing Sahl," he said, "I felt I had two options, to kill myself or quit the business. There was nowhere to go after that. He cut a great figure in those days. He had a canine intelligence, he was witty and attractive. He wasn't a comedian in the old mode—some cuff-shooting tuxedoed guy who'd come out and lapse into comfy purchased material." (Allen's scathing portrait of the comedian in the old mode appeared in *Annie Hall*, where a pathetic comic parades his routine in front of Alvy, asking him to write similar routines for him.) Sahl hardly returned the compliment when he dismissed Allen and just about every other comic in his 1976 memoir *Heartland*. "To go from John Garfield to Woody Allen is putting in a lot of Clorox. . . . Woody Allen is funny, but he is dated." While Sahl did inspire one of Allen's hilarious routines in *Take the Money and Run*, by telling about a bank robber who slips a note to the bank teller that says "Act Normal," and the teller returns it with a note that reads, "Define normal," it is Sahl who has dated. Allen, who told exactly two political jokes in his entire career—one about reading the "nonfiction" version of the Warren Report and one about David Greenglass—has never lost his relevance.

A number of mentors played an important role in Woody Allen's success besides Danny Simon and Arthur Krim, the former head of United Artists and Orion Pictures, but none played a more pivotal role than Jack Rollins. It was Rollins who urged Woody to try stand-up, and it was Rollins (along with partner Charles Joffe) who stood by him, holding his hand, for the years it took for Woody to gain self-confidence and poise onstage. "Woody trusted him," Carol Joffe, Charles Joffe's widow and a set designer on many of Woody's films, told me. "Woody listened to him. And that was so gratifying to Jack. Because he worshipped Woody. It was mutual."

Rollins was the inspiration for *Broadway Danny Rose*. He certainly embodies some of the qualities that Allen placed in the character of Danny: selflessness, passion, integrity, idealism, and a total commitment to his clients. When he accepted an Academy Award for *Good Will Hunting* in 1998, the late Robin Williams, at the conclusion of his speech, said: "And I want to thank Jack Rollins, the most ethical man in show business." The one quality that Rollins did not have in common with Danny Rose was failure. He became a top agent with some of the most important acts in show business: Williams, David Letterman, Nichols and May, Billy Crystal, Dick Cavett, Tony Bennett, Robert Klein, and Harry Belafonte among them. But no client crowned his success and returned his loyalty and love with as much devotion as Woody Allen. Long after Rollins had retired,

Allen gave him prominent credit on every film and refused to stop paying him. His name was prominently displayed as a producer of every Woody Allen film. Allen visited him, ailing and confined to his home, with other friends and clients like Crystal and Cavett, and generally kept tabs on his health and well-being. "That's a great step for Woody," Carol Joffe told me. "Because he doesn't like old age, illness, and death. And those visits must make Jack very, very happy." (Rollins died at the age of a hundred in 2015.)

Allen's devotion and loyalty were more than justified. Jack Rollins (and Charles Joffe) were instrumental in persuading Allen, one of the shyest people in the universe, to go onstage as a stand-up comic.

It was a father-and-son relationship from the start: Rollins was the loving father who, unlike Marty Konigsberg, actually understood what Allen was about, recognized his incredible potential, and hadn't the slightest doubt that he would become one of the foremost stars of stage and screen. Allen, in order to practice his new craft, went from earning $1,700 a week to earning $100 a week. Jack Rollins, like Broadway Danny Rose in the film, offered to cover the losses of club owners if Allen bombed (which he did, again and again). Rollins and Joffe would see no real money for a long time, until Allen began to work in movies.

Rollins really wanted to be a personal manager; he was essentially the first of the breed, and is considered the grandfather of the profession. Before him there were business managers and agents. Rollins had a hard struggle, starting from nothing. He filled his pockets with dimes and walked the Manhattan streets, making cold calls from phone booths because he couldn't afford an office. Then he graduated first to a tiny room atop the Lyceum Theater, and then to another cubicle, a former maid's room atop the Plaza Hotel.

When Allen met him, Rollins was ensconced in a new office on West Fifty-seventh Street with his new partner, Joffe. Allen initially offered to sell him some of his jokes. "It was a beautiful office with wonderful antique furniture," Howard Storm, a comic and client of Rollins and Joffe, told me. "And we would all hang out and talk to Jack. Cavett hung out there, Milt Kamen, Tom Poston. It was a very special time, and being a part of it was just amazing. Rollins and Joffe were the premier managers. They were the cream of the crop.

"You would spend hours with them sitting in the car talking about your act and dissecting it. Talking about comedy and why things are funny. You did that until the sun came up. This was almost an everyday occurrence. We'd do a show somewhere. Then we'd go up to the Stage Delicatessen. We'd sit there and talk forever about our acts and comedy. I never heard of any other managers doing this. When you opened out of town, either Jack or Charlie would go with you. They'd be there for the first night and see if everything was okay. I saw Woody's first stand-up. Jack and Charlie would just push him on the stage."

Rollins's first client had been Harry Belafonte. Rollins never had a contract with any client after Belafonte, only a handshake. He was urged to draw up contracts for his own self-protection, but he said no; it was counterintuitive, he conceded, but it was the right thing. The relationship between a manager and a client could work only if both of them wanted to be there and wanted it to be mutual. "The second it's not mutual," he said, "it's over. I don't want a contract tying me to someone, and I don't want to tie a client to me. They can walk any day of the week. They can say goodbye."

By the time Allen met Rollins, he was representing Nichols and May. That must have been very important to Allen, who recognized their brilliance. Rollins had been devastated by his experience with Harry Belafonte, whose betrayal of him resembled the behavior of Lou Canova (Nick Apollo Forte), the has-been singer in *Broadway Danny Rose*. Rollins had literally created Belafonte when he was penniless and working as a short-order cook in Greenwich Village, devoting all his time to developing Belafonte's career.

Rollins was poor himself and trying to support his wife and two daughters. Belafonte slept on the couch in Rollins's five-flight walk-up apartment for a time while Rollins devised strategies to promote him. He advised Belafonte not to try to be a pop or a jazz singer. "Stop trying to do all those things," he told him. "Do what you do which is unique, that nobody else has done." Rollins came up with the idea of having Belafonte sing calypso music, and it was this that really launched Belafonte's career. Rollins and Belafonte went out to Los Angeles together so that Rollins could promote him there.

Max Gordon, the proprietor of the legendary Village Vanguard and

Blue Angel nightclubs in Manhattan, recalled in his memoir how Rollins pleaded with him to book Belafonte:

> *When Jack began to sell me Harry Belafonte, he kept telling me how handsome Harry was.*
>
> *"The women go crazy," said Jack. "I'm not saying he's handsome because he can't sing. He sings like a sonofabitch." . . .*
>
> *Jack stage-managed everything, told the porter to stop sweeping, asked me where to turn out the lights and turn on the spot. He got up on a chair and inserted a piece of amber gelatin in the spot. . . .*
>
> *Once Harry Belafonte became a star he dumped Jack Rollins—contract or no contract. It was always happening to Jack. He'd bring me an act, and when the act became famous, they'd dump him. . . . I asked Jack whether he felt any bitterness, and he told me, "When an act is unhappy, when it sulks . . . let 'em go. I'm not sore. I got no time for grudges."*

One reason Rollins had no time for grudges was that he had just discovered Woody Allen. Allen would eventually make up to Rollins in extraordinary measure for what Belafonte and, to a lesser degree, others had done to him.

The actor Frank Buxton was a client of Jack Rollins at the same time as Woody. "I think Jack's experience with Belafonte shaped part of his attitude toward everybody else he ever worked with," Buxton told me. "I think he held that in his heart. When he found somebody like Woody, like Tom Poston, like me, he was delighted that he could trust us. He felt that's the way it should be. He was like a father figure to all of us."

I met with Jack Rollins and his daughter Susan in 2013 at his home in New York City. Frail and ailing, Rollins fired up at the mention of Woody. "Woody was one of a kind," he said. "He was an individual. And there was a universal touch to him. He was making the rounds as a gag writer, going from office to office trying to sell his material to other comics. I was the first to suggest that he perform his own material. I said to him, Why aren't you doing this stuff yourself?

"We became very close. For me it was a great pleasure. He needed a push. He was shy, very shy, the shyest person I ever knew. And I had a great deal of fun working with him because he was so utterly wonderful.

A delight. He was a grateful person. He never took advantage. He was not a know-it-all; he wasn't arrogant."

"I remember a lot of long late-night conversations on the phone," Susan Rollins said to her father. "And you'd say, 'Hey, Wood!' You were the person he came to if he had decisions to make or worries on his mind."

"We were just right for one another," Jack said. "And because of that, he grew as a person. We, Charlie Joffe and I, would have to be in the wings and push him out onstage, literally. That's the way he reached the center of the stage. He was terrified. Terrified. And I knew how gifted he was. What a pleasure it was for me to push him out on the stage. And he did the rest. At first he would walk like a small caged lion, up and back, up and back. Filled with nervous tics. Nervous, nervous. It was a sight. But once he found himself out there, he was okay.

"And what he had in store, in his soul! I knew he had that; he was a great comedian. Little by little he got more confident. He was one of the seven wonders of the world."

"Did you ever dream that he would become as successful as he became?" I asked Rollins.

"I did! Yes. I knew it from the start, but I felt, you gotta find the button to press. His father, 'Mister K,' worked for me later. He had nothing to do. He supported Woody, but he and Woody were from different worlds. He was very proud of his son and pleased with his success. But he wished he had a 'secure career.'

"It's very hard to talk about Woody. There was nobody I ever knew that was like him. He had a drive that was unstoppable. He had the goods: as a human being and as a comedy figure. And amazing self-discipline. He worked all the time. He never really enjoyed anything else. He came up to our place in the country once for the weekend and he went crazy. Two days with us, and it was like, What am I supposed to do with all this fresh air?

"Comics like Mort Sahl had a shrill brilliance. But when they were gone, that was it. But with Woody, audiences saw a person behind it, a human being they could identify with."

Rollins, who accepted the Oscar for Woody for *Annie Hall*, told me that he didn't think Woody had made a great film yet. "He still stands a chance of doing it. Because he's now totally involved and focused, with no personal appearances. I think he may very well achieve it. He really knows how good and how not good his stuff is. He does not kid himself. Doesn't listen to the critics."

I told Jack that Woody had said, "Jack pushed me to always be deeper, more complex, more human, more dramatic. And not to rest comfortably."

"That's the first time I heard that," Jack replied.

"And Belafonte?"

"I'll just say he's the lowest and let it go at that."

"And Woody was the opposite?"

"Oh! Woody is such a decent person, such an understanding person. I have nothing but respect and love for him."

On another day I met with all three of Jack's daughters. We talked about their own relationship to Woody when they were children. Francesca told me that Woody had taught her to walk. "He was shy and awkward and gawky and uncomfortable among adults," Hillary said, "but as soon as there was a kid in the room, he could relate to us. I think he was comfortable with little ones. Because you could bop them on the head with a balloon. He kept doing this shtick with us. He'd take balloons and hit us on the head with them. We giggled. He turned away like it hadn't happened. Every time we walked by he bopped us. We used to love when he came over; he was small, not imposing, not like an adult."

"I have Woody's first clarinet," Hillary said. "It's a long-term loan. There are different fingering systems, and he plays a different system. But he had this standard fingering system back in the day. I was in junior high school and assigned to the clarinet as my instrument. So he gave it to me. My mother had told him that I was taking it in school. And I had a terrible school clarinet to begin with. I wanted my parents to buy me one, and they wouldn't. And my mother said to him, 'Oh, we were thinking of getting Hillary a clarinet. Can we get one wholesale?' And Woody said, 'Well, why buy one? I have an extra one and I don't play it anymore.' And she said, 'Well you're not going to just give us your clarinet.' He said, 'Fine, I won't give it to you. Tell you what: I'll loan it to you open-endedly.' Like she can have it forever. He basically gave it to me."

We talked about the Belafonte episode. "The Belafonte thing is critical to understanding my father's relationship with Woody," Francesca Rollins said. "Because in Belafonte's case the boundaries were crossed. Mom would cook him dinner. I know that Woody was aware of the story; it was classic, a 'Broadway Danny Rose' story. As soon as Belafonte hit, became a household name, he was gone.

"In 2011 Belafonte wrote his autobiography. He was so insulting. He called my father a coward. Said that he was over his head when he went to make a deal for him in Vegas. That he couldn't handle the negotiations, that he was scared of the folks out there. He talked about their trip to California. This was the early fifties. Didn't know a soul. In New York, Dad didn't know a soul either, but he understood that world. Dad had no car. Everybody in LA was so casual, all smiles and nonsense. And he's in a suit, he's in some cheap motel on Sunset. He was cold-calling people, desperately trying to get in, trying to get Belafonte seen, trying to set him up in clubs. It was two of them against the world. They were going to fight the good fight. They were both lefties. It was a disaster. He was miserable and depressed. And what happened to the two of them against the world?"

Belafonte—while writing glowingly about himself and wrapping a halo of progressive politics around his behavior in his memoir, *My Song*—wrote deprecatingly of Rollins, "a small-time theater producer . . . a fairly anxious, uptight guy . . . pretty humorless." After the split "Rollins was furious . . . he began spewing an angry story of treachery and betrayal on my part." Belafonte also wrote that at the start of his career, Rollins had been a great help and a great comfort to him. "He believed in me and gave me good advice."

"Because of his experience with Belafonte," Francesca Rollins said, "my father vowed that he would never let a client get as close again. But then Woody came along. He knocked on the door, selling jokes. Charles Joffe was there, just hanging out with my dad. Woody had a good job at the time, writing for Jack Paar. But he was selling jokes on the side, looking to make some extra cash. My father told him, 'I don't buy jokes, but tell me what you have; maybe somebody wants something or I can direct you to somebody.' So Woody said, 'Okay, can I just read them to you?' My father said, 'Sure, go ahead.'

"So Woody took out his pieces of paper and read the jokes. Dad and Charlie were falling off the couch. They just thought he was original and hilarious, and so odd and bizarre. It was his personality and delivery and his wacky mind! They'd never seen anybody like him. And my father said to him, 'I don't know a comic who is going to buy this stuff. Nobody can do this material but you. This is fantastic material, but you have to do it. Are you interested? Have you ever been onstage?'

"Woody replied resolutely, 'No! I'm not interested in being a performer.'

"So that was that," Francesca said. "But a year later Woody returned. He knocked on the door again and said, 'Well, all right, I'll give it a try.' My father got to work. Woody made the rounds of all the coffeehouses and clubs in the city: the Blue Angel, the Duplex, Cafe Wha?—wherever they would have him. And at first he was terrible."

"He was going to the clubs every night," Susan Rollins said, "and not getting one laugh! For a year! Torture. The people were completely confused about what the hell this strange being was doing. Who could get onstage every night *and not get a single laugh*? The audience response was zero! And he'd do it again the next night!" One danger was that in his awkwardness and terror, Allen wrapped the cord around his neck so tightly that he might strangle himself. He was also humiliated by the fact that he had a solid standing as a comedy writer who commanded thousands a week and here he was, stumbling around, for a hundred bucks a night. "Onstage," Larry Wilde wrote, "he is a little less slender than the microphone, which he frequently seems to lean on for support. Sometimes he wraps his arm around his head as if to fend off drafts—or blows—and his fingers dribble nervously over his hair. It seems an effort for him to hold up his glasses."

Wherever he appeared, there were the young girls in black stockings and low-cut blouses who drove him into a frenzy. "Woody was a friend of mine then," the designer Vicky Tiel said. "I was a waitress at the Fat Black Pussycat on Macdougal Street. I passed the hat for all the guys who sang: Steve DeNaut, Dave Van Ronk, and Bobby Zimmerman [Dylan]. I was called Peaches La Tour. I had this lace or chiffon thing and [it] was totally see-through on the top, and I had a little black leather skirt. So I was this babe, and Woody was like just one of the guys. This was the beginning of the sexual revolution. Everybody slept with everybody. Except Woody. And Bobby Zimmerman. Nobody. Nothing. Could not get arrested. Neither of them. Woody was a nerd. We were friends. He didn't make a move on anybody."

"We rode in a cab to one of his gigs," Elliott Mills told me. "This is like 1960. It was Cafe Wha?, down near Washington Square, in an alleyway. Woody had bitten through all his nails in the taxicab. He had no nails left. These gigs were really horrors for him. This was when he was starting up. He was out of his mind. He was trembling. You have to admire this. It was a real battle for him to get up there. We went to eat something before the show. He got sick and threw up. He was never a traditional Borscht Belt comedian. He couldn't *spritz*. All he could do was tell stories. He said to me emphatically, 'I'm not a hippie.' He was never into that. Never. I remember going into the club with him and maybe there were two other people there."

"At one point," Jack Rollins recalled, "Woody came to me and was ready to give up. He said to us: 'Listen, fellas, do you really think I should continue this? You know, I make a very good living as a writer. And I'm making nothing here . . . does it make sense?' Remember, this is the shyest guy that ever lived. I said to him, 'Woody, you can become a performer. I know you can. And at a very good level. Woody, Charlie and I see something that we can't explain. . . . But we're not up on that floor suffering every night. You are. And if it's so difficult you certainly should not continue it. Look, give it one more try. I know it's easy for me to say this, but I do believe you can do it.'"

Allen replied, "I'll think about it," Rollins recalled. "Then he came to us. It had to be Woody's last shot if it was going to work. And he had to *want* to do it. Woody told us, 'If you fellas think I haven't given it enough time, and that I still have the potential to be a performer, then I'm going to try it a bit longer. I'll give it another month.'

"That was it," Rollins said. "We knew he meant it. Amazingly, in that month it really began to take shape. Not at any one particular moment, but slowly, over a period, things began to change. And Woody started to relax. He knew now that if it went on as badly as before he only had those final four weeks to last out. So he stopped worrying so much. The change came just in time."

One reason for Woody's determination to make it work was that he detested writing for television. "Writing for other comedians as a lifetime pursuit is a blind alley," he told Larry Wilde in 1968. "I never had any intention of continuing writing for other comedians before I started performing. At that time, I was just writing for them to earn a living. . . . It occurred to me [performing] might be a good avenue of expression. So I decided to try it."

While all this was going on Woody, in his Broadway debut, contributed to a new revue, *From Z to Z*, starring the eccentric English actress Hermione Gingold, which tried out at the Long Wharf Theater in New Haven. It opened at the Plymouth Theater and closed after twenty-one performances. Allen provided two sketches he had written at Tamiment, "Psychological Warfare," and a skit about Groucho Marx. "Woody wrote me letters about it from New Haven," Jack Victor remembered. "He said it wouldn't go anywhere. And of course it didn't."

Max Gordon wrote in his book of his first encounter with Allen due to the efforts of Jack Rollins. (Rollins makes a plea to Gordon that is very similar to the one Broadway Danny Rose makes to Phil Chomsky, a theatrical booker, on behalf of his client, a lady who plays water glasses: "I'll let you have her now at the old price, okay? Which is—which is anything you want to give me. Anything at all, Philly.")

Gordon wrote:

> *The kid got up as Jack introduced us. He was a short, frightened kid with a weak handshake.*
>
> *"Meet Woody Allen," said Jack.*
>
> *We all sat down. "This kid is a writer," Jack began, "he writes the most brilliant comedy material in New York. But what does he do with it? Gives it away. That is he sells it for peanuts to other comedians who are making a fortune out of it. . . . So he goes around with his toes sticking out of his shoes while others get rich on his material. I've said to him, "Woody, why don't you get up and do this material yourself. Then you'll be rich and not the schlep that you are."*
>
> *Woody lifted his eyes gravely at this buildup.*
>
> *"The salary isn't important," said Jack. "Pay him what you want. I want a place where he can stay awhile. I'll give you all the options you want. If he loses you any money, I'll pay his salary myself. . . ."*

So Woody opened at the Blue Angel in the summer of 1960. He bombed, and would bomb again and again for a long time. "I always thought the material alone mattered," Allen would recall. "But I was wrong. I thought of myself as a writer and when I was onstage all I could think about was wanting to get through the performance and go home. I wasn't liking the audience; I was petrified. Yet there was no reason the audience wouldn't like me; they had paid to see me. . . . But then I went onstage with a better attitude and I learned that until you want to be there and luxuriate in the performance and want to stay on longer you won't do a good show." Charles Joffe said that Allen "was arrogant and hostile [at first]. If the audience didn't get it, he had no patience . . . the pain in those first years was terrible." Allen recalled, "It was the worst year of my life. I'd feel this fear in my stomach every morning, the minute I woke up, and it'd be there until eleven o'clock at night."

"Jack used to stand at the back every night, listening to Woody's show," Gordon recalled. "During the intermission he'd walk Woody up to one of the dressing rooms. I could hear Jack through the door. He'd call me in to add my voice to his.

" 'Tell him, tell Woody he's doing okay,' Jack would beg. 'He thinks he's terrible. He's ready to quit. You're doing terrific, do you hear? Terrific. Tell him.'

"Woody wasn't doing *that* terrific, a fact I didn't think it right to bring up at that particular moment. Woody hadn't yet learned how to deliver. Only sophisticates who were tired of being assaulted by nightclub comics welcomed his low-keyed delivery. But he was learning. We kept him three months."

It went on for two years, at $100 a week. To go from a successful career (although an unsatisfying one) and $1,700 a week to an unknown one, experiencing rejection night after night, was torture. He spent the days worrying about the night's performance, walking about the city and writing. He could not eat at all until after the performance. It was purely an act of faith and determination in the face of self-doubt and fear that he stuck it out. And there was also an underlying steely self-confidence. He began psychoanalysis during this time, at Jerry Epstein's insistence.

It was during this time of intense struggle that he made a lifetime friend in Dick Cavett. Cavett was working for Jack Paar, and Paar had sent him to check out this new comic he'd heard about. "The minute I walked in that night," he told Eric Lax, "the sound of the material was so high; I couldn't believe that he could go on so well for twenty minutes with this level of wonderful stuff." Allen took Cavett with him to the billiard clubs he hung at evenings after his shows. "A certain number of mug-types would come over and say, 'Hey, Woody, out playing games, ain't you?'" Allen

also took part in poker games. "I went to a couple of games," Cavett recalled. "They were very serious. No fooling around. It was very frightening
to me." Cavett saw Allen perform again two years later in Los Angeles.
The audience sat silently without laughing, and Allen soon stopped talking. Then he said, "If I were giving prizes for the worst audience I've ever
seen, you'd win it." On another occasion, at the hungry i in San Francisco,
Allen turned his back on a crowd and talked to the brick wall.

Larry Gelbart was at the Blue Angel on opening night. He wrote, "After the performance, I joined him in his dressing room. The cabaret critic
for the *Daily News* had been in the dressing room moments earlier to type
his review of Woody's act, and had thrown the carbon paper into the
wastebasket. Reading it, Woody was crushed. The critic had characterized him as an intellectual Menasha Skulnik, an actor-comedian of the
period famous for his thick Yiddish accent, but certainly not for his intellect. Woody had worked so hard to come off as hip and sophisticated (which
he was) and here he was being compared to a shticky immigrant comic
(which he definitely was not)."

And then, suddenly, it turned around.

Audiences turned toward him and embraced him as their own. The
critic Vivian Gornick saw him at the Bitter End in 1964: "Anxiety was
the juice that electrified him, that set him going and kept him running.
And thousands of us drank in his anxiety like adrenaline, because it was
the same for us. Half in the culture, half out, we too were anxious." His
anxiety, Gornick wrote, "meshed so perfectly with the deepest undercurrent of feeling in the national life that it made outsiders of us all."

Several years later Gelbart saw Allen perform again at a Democratic
rally in Washington, D.C.:

> *The transformation was total. He'd become a performer who exuded confi-
> dence and authority, doing joke after joke about how little he had of either of
> those qualities. . . . After a good deal of practice and acceptance, he was no lon-
> ger a male Elaine [May], or a young me, or an anything anyone else. He was
> Woody Allen. And Woody, the writer, was supplying Woody, the comic, with
> absolutely stunning material, material that showcased his gift for defying and
> deflating that which disturbs him the most: like sex, no sex, not enough sex, too
> much sex, and of course, that old standby, death. It is a gift that has allowed*

*him to deal with those fears that have dogged him throughout his life, triumph-*
*ing over them one laugh at a time.*

Succeeding—triumphing—as a stand-up comedian was the key turning point in Allen's life. He had already succeeded as a writer who
could turn out brilliant material for other performers. In that guise he
remained invisible, a servant to others. Now he stood exposed to the
world, and instead of pretending to be something he wasn't—a tough guy,
a macho lover, a winner—he pretended to be something that he really
wasn't either: a loser, a nebbish, the guy who fails at everything. True, he
*looked* like a loser; he *sounded* like a loser, and he plucked those characteristics from a secluded place within himself. But it wasn't really him. It
never had been. He was strong, and his greatest strength was his ability
to look at himself, recognize those things within and without him that
seemed to define him, and he figured, Fuck it, why not go with that if it
was so funny, if it made audiences happy? As people laughed, he made
millions, got the girls, maintained a self-discipline that enabled him to
churn out an endless stream of work, and forged an amazing career that
would withstand any setback—in fact, one of the most successful careers
in American show-business history. In *Manhattan,* lying on his couch, he
thinks of his idols, those who made life worth living: Louis Armstrong,
Frank Sinatra, Groucho Marx, Willie Mays, and Marlon Brando—that
list of immortals must now, without a doubt, include Woody Allen.

That triumph had a lot to do with Jack Rollins, Broadway Danny Rose
himself. Woody would never forget it. Robert Weide, producer of the
documentary on his life, said to him, "Jack Rollins hasn't been near any
film you've done in ten years. He doesn't do anything for you anymore.
Why do you still pay him as a producer?" Woody replied, "Because
without him, I wouldn't be here."

In April 2013 I came across a brief reminiscence in a blog by Jonathan D. Cohen, who had interned with Rollins in 1989. Cohen referred to
Rollins's stormy experience with Harry Belafonte and his gratifying work
with a string of illustrious clients. Then he wrote:

*This brings me to his relationship with Allen, one of the most longstanding
loyal relationships between talent and management. As producers and managers,*

*Mr. Rollins and his partner, Charles Joffe, shared in the movies' gross receipts. There was a time when Rollins and Joffe went to Woody and suggested that they take a smaller percentage, and Woody said absolutely not. He reasoned that he wouldn't have had a career if Jack and Charlie didn't convince him to try reading some of his work on stage as a stand-up. Apparently, tears were shed; the relationship was that deep.*

I wrote to Allen asking if this account was accurate. Had he insisted that Rollins and Joffe share the income from his films at the same percentage that they always had?

He replied, "The story is true; money in any way has never been an issue with me. Jack, when I was starting, never took a commission from me. Best, Woody."

## 4. "Woody, C'est Moi"

CAROL JOFFE, A COSTUME DESIGNER on Allen's films for ten years and the widow of Charles Joffe, recalled Woody's early years of stand-up. "My first date with Charlie was going down to the Bitter End and watching Woody work," she told me. "I saw Woody from the very beginning get up onstage and utter his first trembling words. The very first times. He was a nervous wreck, of course, but he was so brilliant. And it was a thrill for me to watch his evolution and growth. My husband, at that point, was Woody's buddy. Because Woody was really terrified of going places alone, entering rooms full of people. And Charlie was kind of brash and confident, and he would lead the way. Woody was very frightened of people. I mean he was very sure of himself in certain ways. But in social situations he was awkward. And it was hard for him to connect with people in groups. But he was such a pleasure to be around because he was such a unique person and a brilliant mind and a talent."

Howard Storm also remembers the early days. "I remember when Charlie and Jack would just push him on the stage," Storm recalls. "He really didn't want to do it. He was kind of doing Mort Sahl early on. But it was just a matter of his getting comfortable enough to play his own character. Jack and Charlie were also my agents. They were the cream of the crop; they were just the best. There was no one like them really.

"In those days it was Cavett and Woody. They were both very high-line guys. Woody was just starting. But he was really cooking, and I knew there was a genius there. It happened fast for him. Within maybe five months he was doing the Carson show."

By the early sixties he was starting to draw crowds in Greenwich Village. Dick Cavett and Jack Benny enthusiastically endorsed him. Benny said, "He's one of the most amazing men I've ever known. It's very tough to use the word genius. . . . But I don't know anyone who is as clever and funny and has the knowledge of what to do in his writing. No one compares with him."

William K. Zinsser wrote the first long piece about Allen, for *Time*, after seeing him perform in 1961. He recalled later, "A frail and seemingly terrified young man of 27, blinking out at the audience through black-framed glasses. . . . Allen's monologue consisted of telling the story of his life. It was the life of a chaotic loser, told in a rapid salvo of jokes. The jokes, though simple, were unfailingly funny, and beneath the humor they were doing serious work as autobiography. This was a champion nebbish, one that every underdog in America could—and soon would—identify with. Allen had invented a perfect formula for an anxious new age: therapy made hilarious."

It was while performing at the Duplex in Greenwich Village that Allen, twenty-four, met a fan: a petite well-endowed twenty-one-year-old strawberry blond actress named Louise Lasser, who was studying at Brandeis. She was the wild, "crazy" type of woman Allen has always insisted in his films that he is drawn to, prone to depression and swinging moods. She was hip, razor-sharp funny, and well read, and the kind of intellectual and sexual challenge that Woody enjoyed. She grew up in New York as the pampered daughter of prominent tax authority S. Jay Lasser. Her parents divorced, and her mother would later commit suicide. She had gone to Brandeis for three years and then took a "psychological leave of absence." She told a reporter in 1976 that "I called my father and said, 'You can come and get me now. I've finished here.'" Lasser returned to Manhattan and studied acting with Sanford Meisner, landing roles in an Elaine May skit and replacing Barbra Streisand as Miss Marmelstein on Broadway in *I Can Get It for You Wholesale*.

Allen has said that he "became a human being when I met Louise." He began to see her secretly for months, meeting her at the Metropolitan Museum and taking carriage rides through Central Park. Harlene was completely unaware of the relationship. Lasser told *Newsweek* in 1978: "We were very smitten with each other . . . I invited them [Woody and Harlene] to a New Year's Eve party and Harlene was very hostile toward me so I guess she must have known something. But our relationship didn't start until some time later. . . . He asked me to go with him downtown once to go shopping which we did, running through the streets. . . . Then, after a few months, he asked me out on a date. . . . So we went out together and he took me in a hansom buggy through Central Park where he turned around and tried to kiss me. And I *did* say, 'But you're married.' But he explained everything. He said it was over between him and Harlene and they would be splitting up after she had finished college. . . . But they were still living in the same apartment and once I needed some bed linen and called Woody to borrow some. Harlene answered the phone and I went around to pick the sheets up. She said to me after they split up, 'I knew you had your eyes on my husband from the moment you came around to my house for those sheets.'"

She found work as a waitress at the Bitter End, where Woody was doing his stand-up routine. Woody was distracted by her presence and also bewildered that she had taken the job, since her family was wealthy. "He tried to persuade me to stop but I liked the job," Louise told Tim Carroll. "So he said, 'Why don't you be my maid instead?' [Woody had moved into his own apartment.] In the end I agreed, and for 50 dollars a week I became his maid but only on the understanding that I couldn't work for him when we were going out. One night . . . I arrived at his apartment to do my 'maidenly' duties and found stickers everywhere saying, 'Don't do the washing-up,' 'Don't move the books,' 'Don't do this,' 'Don't do that.'"

Thirty-six years later, in 2014, Lasser gave an interview to *The Point* and talked about Woody:

*I was twenty-one. . . . In those last few years of college I'd started to fill up with the dark side. I'd wake up in the morning and I didn't know what was wrong. I didn't know what the word depression was. . . . I didn't make that connection.*

*When we met . . . we immediately, immediately, just were meant to be in the same playpen. . . . So I met him, and it was so clear the whole night the four of us were there, and neither of us are talking to anyone else, do you know what I mean? We know what's going on and it's like you feel nervous about it because it's like you can get into trouble for this. . . . So he would call me and he would say do you want to buy some music . . . and we would go in his car and we just got along really great.*

*We really understood what the other was saying. Like I'd barely heard the word "existentialism," but when he and I talked it was like I already knew about it. . . . We'd go downtown, and we'd go jumping over benches, what people do, you just do it because you seem so free.*

*He would show me everything he knew. We'd go to the theater, these little out-of-the-way joints, and we'd have a drink, and by the second drink I was drunk, but he was that way too. He was a really bad drinker. . . . I didn't want to go as fast as he did. He was sure from the beginning and I was afraid I'd feel closed in. . . .*

*We'd break up. We lived right around the corner from each other . . . then within a very short period of time we'd bump into each other on the street, and I'd start to cry, like why did we do that, break up.*

Harlene flew to Mexico for a divorce in November 1962. As part of the divorce agreement he agreed to pay her a lump sum of $1,750, and $75 a week in alimony for the rest of her life or until she remarried. If Woody was steadily employed, she would get $175. Jack Victor told me, "Leaving when she did, just as Woody was about to make it, she got a bad deal out of the whole thing. The settlement was peanuts. The marriage had lasted five years.

"I felt very close to Harlene," he continued. "She was soft, nice. We became very close—platonic, though. There was a time she even regretted the divorce. She said, 'Maybe I should have stuck it out.' She didn't know about Louise. Because I said to her, what was Woody going to do with Louise? And she gave me this look. I thought, Oh my God, I felt like hiding under the table. I had always thought that Louise was the reason why they divorced. Apparently it was something else. Harlene was quiet and all that, but you couldn't push her around."

Just after the breakup, Woody began working as a writer on *The Tonight Show* hosted by Jack Paar, and soon became the most talked-about comedian in show business.

Allen appeared on *The Ed Sullivan Show* in 1962 and narrowly avoided a fracas with Sullivan. In a seeming foreshadow of his divorce, he used his joke about orgasm at rehearsal: "If her husband fails to satisfy her sexually, Mutual of Omaha has to pay her every month." Sullivan, who ran what was then called a clean, family show, screamed at Woody, "Attitudes like yours are why kids are burning their draft cards!" Woody apologized.

He was earning five thousand dollars a week by 1964 for his nightclub act. He was a popular and frequent guest on Johnny Carson's and Steve Allen's shows. He performed at Mister Kelly's, the Purple Onion, and the hungry i in San Francisco. His first comedy album, *Woody Allen*, was released by Colpix records in July 1964. The album was nominated for a Grammy but lost to Bill Cosby's *I Started Out as a Child*. Allen appeared on *Candid Camera* and *That Was the Week That Was*—one of the most sophisticated satirical programs—along with Steve Allen, Tom Lehrer, and Mort Sahl.

As soon as the divorce was finalized, Allen began ridiculing a generic comic "wife" in his act, both in nightclubs and on television. He called her "Quasimodo." He held up a picture of a house with her and said she was the one who had the shingles. He said that on her birthday he gave her an electric chair, pretending it was a hair dryer. He said on NBC television: "My first wife lives on the Upper West Side and I read in the papers the other day that she was violated on her way home. Knowing my first wife, it was not a moving violation." He was relentless in his putdowns and received huge laughs.

Allen's hilarious delivery deflected any anger on the audience's part toward him. He could get away with anything on that subject. And he was also hard on himself, making fun of his immaturity: He would complain that he would be in the bathtub and his wife would come in and sink his boats. To this day, while I have encountered some anger or even fury toward him about his treatment of Mia Farrow and the entire Soon-Yi affair—and also, among some people, for his alleged sexual abuse of Dylan Farrow—almost no one has ever raised the issue of his public humiliation of Harlene. If the subject is mentioned at all, it is because someone is quoting his remarks as examples of his hilarity—even fifty-two years later.

He is forgiven—even by Harlene.

Another reason, I suspect, is that Allen appears to feel guiltless about his behavior toward women. He seems to feel no sense of responsibility. There is something so guileless, so childish, in his denial—he's still the young rascal who is impossible to resist—and it is accompanied by such funny jokes—that we are swept away by laughter and forget about the person who is the object of the joke. And of course, the other object of most of the jokes is Allen himself.

Allen has never acknowledged the pain he caused Mia by letting her discover the nude pictures of Soon-Yi in his office—in fact he acts indifferent and blind to the issue. A scene in *Deconstructing Harry* suggests that he is far more aware than he admits. He really knows what he's doing but prefers to feign innocence, to act as if it is the woman's problem and as if he can't figure out what the fuss is all about. The scene between Harry and his wife (played by Kirstie Alley) is illustrative of this. The scene recalls ways in which Allen would taunt and tease his mother, driving her to bouts of hysteria.

In the scene—one of Allen's great ones—his wife confronts him with his infidelity with her patient, a lovely young woman. Here Allen paints a picture of a total lack of empathy on his stand-in protagonist's (Harry Block) part. Allen had tried to cast Elliott Gould in the part rather than play it himself, in order to avoid the audience's identifying Block with Allen, but Gould was unavailable. Harry is madly opaque about and oblivious to his wife's pain. Allen paints a sharp satiric picture of Harry's seeming inability to see what he has done. But Harry is playing dumb. Allen has a total *awareness* of Harry's seeming unawareness. The scene is hilarious precisely because of the pointed portrait he draws of Harry's denials and the ways in which he incites and baits his wife. Just as Woody acted calmer the more his mother erupted in fury at his taunts, Harry acts as if he is the reasonable and judicious one.

When Harry's wife, a psychiatrist, accuses him of seducing her female patient he explains patiently that he has no choice because of his lack of access to other women. He says, "I was merely explaining why my choice of necessity is confined to your practice." He "innocently" pleads: "You think getting a blow job by a big-bosomed twenty-six-year-old is pleasurable for me?" His wife, of course, explodes. The soul of reason, he says innocently, "I cannot understand why the most sophisticated of women can't tell the difference between a meaningless, hot, passionate sexual affair and a nice, solid, tranquil routine marriage."

He keeps going, twisting the knife in: "You're always [working]. We never socialize." She responds: "So now you're blaming me because we don't go out enough places where you can meet strangers to fuck?" She screams: "I knew you were mentally ill before we were married but I thought, as a trained professional, I could help you." He replies with mock concern: "Now, please don't get down on yourself as a therapist."

She has abandoned a patient lying on the couch during this entire scene, and the patient can hear everything that is going on.

Elliott Mills recalled that "Woody drove his mother nuts. He provoked her. She would make him a whole duck, and he would sit there eating it, picking it apart, and then criticize her cooking. She was funny-hysterical. He found it funny, and he would do it more. He knew what set her off. So he would do it."

Allen's Harry Block seems to observe no boundaries and to have no remorse. And yet in his films, Allen himself has sometimes demonstrated a self-knowledge that is centered and humane, especially in his love stories, which make clear that he has destroyed his own relationships: *Annie Hall* and *Manhattan*.

He has always denied that he is the person he portrays onstage and screen. As I listen now to Allen's classic early stand-up routines from 1962, a period when he was already an established figure, it is not difficult to understand why audiences confused—and would continue to confuse—his antihero, public schlemiel persona with its canny creator. From the beginning Allen sprinkled bits, pieces, and sizable chunks of his real-life personality and experience into a wild narrative filled with farce, whimsy, surrealism, metaphorical fantasy, and a careening set of invented comic incidents. Clearly audiences needed to identify with him, to project their lives onto his. There was enough leavening—enough reality—in Allen's act to encourage that response in his audience. He injected real aspects of his life often enough to offer what appeared to be road maps to his actual life story.

Playing the schlemiel was the route to fame and fortune, and yet there *were* traces of that character within him. He mined it brilliantly. He was the original antihero. Antiheroes never got the girl. But here was one— short, skinny, redheaded, big nose, glasses—who did get her. He outwitted everybody. He was so smart and charming that instead of hanging him, the Ku Klux Klan contributed two thousand dollars to Israel Bonds. He validated an entire spectrum of society that had been written off. He gave them a voice. The schlemiel who got up there and said smart, insightful, hilarious things. The schlemiel who won the girl. It was innovative, inherently revolutionary. He gave voice to the funny-looking Jewish guys, but, he also gave voice to the tall blond gentile football players who secretly felt like the short Jewish guys inside. He spoke for everyone; it was universal.

Who *was* this creature who captivated a broad segment of the public? "Woody, *ç'est moi*," wrote Richard Schickel.

Reflecting on the audience's identifying him with the comic character he portrayed, Allen has said, "Just talking as myself to the audience was the most comfortable for me and the most enjoyable for the audience. I never consciously did any of it. I just went out onstage and tried to get laughs. The only sense of a persona is that one exaggerates for the sake of humor. If I come out for forty minutes and regale you with one harrowing tale after another, tales of childhood and relationships—and they were all reasonably funny because I had spent a lot of time getting the most out of them—I guess after a while a character emerges; it is me in a way and it's not me." He has also observed accurately that his persona "was assigned to me by the audience." He would test what worked with an audience, and when it did, he merely stretched, accentuated, and exaggerated it for effect. The schlemiel character worked.

He would begin his act as if he were talking to his therapist or to other participants in group therapy: "Since I was here last, a lot of significant things have occurred in my private life that I thought we could go over tonight and evaluate. And then we'll have a question-and-answer period. Let me start at the beginning. I lived in Manhattan, uptown east, in a brownstone building. But I was constantly getting mugged and assaulted.

Sadistically beaten about the face and neck. So I moved into a doorman apartment house on Park Avenue that's rich and secure and expensive and great, and I lived there two weeks, and my doorman attacked me."

He often started his sentences by stating, as a pedantic academic might when addressing a class, "I'm paraphrasing, of course." The audience recognized the lingo of their classes or of their own therapy sessions and never dreamed of encountering it in a nightclub. And it was bold and very funny. If there was a relationship with a girl: "We were involved," he said, investing that last word with the exact suggestion of intimacy. Nothing was off-limits: sexual and personal failure, social awkwardness, phobias, neuroses ("I am at two with myself"), and traumatic family histories. And it was all hilarious.

There were the claustrophobia of Brooklyn, his hatred of high school, many rabbis, an unhappy marriage, a father who held many low-level jobs, studying at New York University, and being bounced out of college. There were his early years in Greenwich Village witnessing the hippie scene and, of course, his endless experience of psychoanalysis. Any indication of verisimilitude or reality in Allen's narrative was probably sufficient for audiences to give credence to the bulk of his comic routines that bore less resemblance—or none whatsoever—to his actual experiences.

His comic routines bristled and sparkled with intelligence, metaphor, and invention mixed with little doses of reality. He said he had consulted his rabbi about doing a vodka ad with Monique van Vooren, a popular Belgian-born film and TV actress, for fifty thousand dollars and was told by the rabbi that to do so was immoral. He turns down the ad and then sees a TV commercial of van Vooren posing on the beach. Next to her, holding a "cool glass of vodka," is his rabbi, who has snagged the job. Then he speaks of a bunch of topless rabbis: "They had no skullcaps." Allen says of a gambling habit: "Mine is the only horse in the race with training wheels."

He spoke of his refusal to take "consciousness-expanding" drugs, also a true reference to his own life. Yet he went on to say that he took a puff and "broke two teeth trying to give a hickey to the Statue of Liberty." His idea of a swinging time, he said, was to go to the grocery and watch the chickens swinging on a rotisserie. He spoke of going to Hollywood, where they wanted to make "a musical comedy out of the Dewey Decimal System." He said that his father was fired and replaced with a tiny gadget that "did everything my father does but better. The depressing thing is that my mother ran out and bought one."

Many of his monologues were parables of social exclusion. The ultimate surreal Allen monologue was the story of the moose. Allen said he'd shot a moose, strapped it on his car, and to his dismay discovered that the moose was still alive and had woken up in the Holland Tunnel and was signaling for a turn. He took the moose to a costume party, hoping to ditch it. Another couple, the Berkowitzes, were also dressed as a moose. Leaving the party, he intended to take the moose on his fender, "but got the Berkowitzes" by mistake. Woody dumps them in the woods, and the next morning, waking up in their moose suit the Berkowitzes are shot. The upshot was that the Berkowitzes were stuffed and mounted at the WASPS-only New York Athletic Club. "The joke is on them [the Athletic Club]," Allen said. "The place is restricted."

The jokes continued in the same vein, often with Allen as victim. He was kidnapped and "my parents snapped into action. They rented my room." His abductors were sentenced to a chain gang, but escaped chained together, "getting by the guards posing as an immense charm bracelet." (A variation of this tale would wind up in *Take the Money and Run*.) His father, he said, tried to play "Flight of the Bumblebee" on the tuba and "blew his liver out through the horn."

He spoke of spending two weeks at an interfaith camp where he was "beaten sadistically by boys of all races and creeds." Every story had embedded within it a sense of cynicism and despair. The twentieth century was a period of catastrophe and unspeakable cruelty. Life was brutal and a snakepit; hatred and racism were endemic; human growth and change for the better were a myth. The human condition was immutable, and political and social movements would alter nothing. Religion— Orthodox Judaism, all religions in fact—was straitjackets and mythologies. Similarly philosophical constructs were a crock, and their purveyors, the intellectuals, were phonies. (He takes courses in Truth, Beauty, Advanced Truth and Beauty, and Intermediate Truth.) There is no security to be found in art or intellect. Even worse are the cults. Hippies in a commune who play records of the mime Marcel Marceau and make opium out of paper Veterans Day poppies, New Age prophets, psychics, *est*, revolutionaries—these fads and panaceas will pass, and mankind will be stuck in the same morass.

Yet the messenger was devastatingly funny. There is oppression, and there is comic relief from it.

Another sketch, "The Lost Generation," presaged his Academy Award–winning film *Midnight in Paris* by some forty-five years and was surely its genesis. Allen might have found a moldering scrap of paper with a sketch of the plot in the drawer in his bedroom where he keeps all the ideas he has ever had over the years. Allen speaks of a trip to Europe with Ernest Hemingway, Gertrude Stein, Picasso, and Scott and Zelda Fitzgerald. Hemingway, Allen said, had written his first novel. "I told him it was a good novel but not a great novel, and he punched me in the nose."

There were always the scraps of real life that served as anchors for an audience hungering for the "real" Woody. It was true he went to New York University, but in his act he took a philosophy course called Death 101, and cheated on his metaphysics final: "I looked within the soul of the boy sitting next to me." He said he was thrown out of New York University, which was true, but that his "mother, as as a result, took an overdose of mahjong tiles." It was true that he was endlessly in analysis, but not, of course, that he was "captain of the latent paranoid softball team of nail biters against the bed wetters," or that he would "steal second base, feel guilty and go back." In another routine he said that he was not in the army, but in the "canine corps—me and eleven dogs." He said that he wanted a dog at home, but that his parents couldn't afford one. They went to a "damaged pet shop" and told him they'd gotten him a dog. But instead "they got me an ant" and he didn't know the difference. He said that he and his wife were married by a "reformed rabbi . . . a very reformed rabbi . . . a Nazi."

He was invited to a costume party, he related, and went dressed as a ghost with a white sheet over his head. On his way to the party, three men in a car drive up to him wearing white sheets and tell him, "Get in. We have to go pick up the Grand Dragon." He sits with the three Klansmen "trying to pass—I said 'You all' and 'Grits.'" The men throw a rope about his neck and Allen "saw my life before me: frying up a mess of catfish . . . going to the general store . . . getting gingham for Emmy Louise. . . . And I realized it's not my life. . . ."

Allen proceeds to beguile the Neanderthals with his wit, and "The Klansmen were so moved by what I said that night I sold them two thousand dollars' worth of Israel Bonds." The story echoes the moose tale in which Allen the cunning Jew triumphs over the gentiles. In both cases the underlying message is a cynical and despairing one: In real life the New York Athletic Club would not have abandoned its anti-Semitism and the Klansmen would not have been transported by Allen into apostles of brotherhood—in fact, they would have lynched him on the spot. Laughter overcomes grim reality, but not for long.

And there was the final closing zinger, the showstopper: the account of his beautiful watch. "My grandfather . . . [pause] . . . on his deathbed . . . [pause] . . . sold me this watch."

What bonded Allen so strongly with his audience were these depictions of himself as deeply flawed, vulnerable, lovable, and an overall screwup whom they could relate to. It was only in his later films, beginning with *Annie Hall*, that his comic shtick, that cascade of comic incidents, would be replaced by a more realistic and structured connection to Allen's real-life experience. And then audiences bonded even more deeply with him.

He struck a resonant chord, a chord that echoed in many other areas of the culture: the arrival of the film auteurs (Scorsese, Coppola, Cassavetes, Altman, Spike Lee, and Spielberg, among others), the singer-songwriters (Carly Simon, Paul Simon, James Taylor, Bob Dylan, Peter Allen, Joni Mitchell, all writing out of their own life experiences), and the "New Journalism" of Tom Wolfe, Hunter S. Thompson, and Norman Mailer, these authors often becoming their own favorite subjects. Allen's closest literary counterpart, Philip Roth, was also writing out of his own life. Roth, in fact, began to find his writing voice by performing stand-up comedy routines about his family at his friends' parties—routines that eventually led to *Portnoy's Complaint*.

Allen's shyness didn't preclude a capacity to deal with and manipulate the press and exploit publicity. John Corry wrote that "In his calculated disdain for publicity and carefully cultivated eccentricity he [Allen] makes it absolutely certain that he will receive as much publicity as any man possibly can." John McPhee, who wrote a piece about Allen for *Time*, recently recalled a visit from Woody to his cubicle at the magazine in 1962, when Allen was twenty-seven. Some of the people McPhee interviewed as a beginning reporter, he wrote, "were a great deal more difficult to manage than others, [but] none [were] simpler or more agreeable than Woody Allen":

*[Allen] volunteered that he was a "latent hetereosexual." He said he strongly wanted to return to the womb—"anybody's." I described him in the piece as "a flatheaded, redheaded lemur with closely bitten fingernails and a sports jacket." He spoke of people who "perspire audibly." . . . At the time of the interview, Woody Allen was working standup in a Greenwich Village nightclub. As a writer for TV comedians, he said, he had written twenty-five thousand gags in two years. The fact that he was telling some of them to me did not concern either of us.*

Allen made a number of hilarious guest appearances on Allen Funt's *Candid Camera* TV show in 1963. The program featured pranks played on unknowing participants (or victims) who were being filmed. The highlight was one in which, dressed in a dark suit, he pretended to be a very serious, fastidious businessman dictating a love letter to a public stenographer. He dictated deadpan, "Dearest beloved darling, comma, I cannot live without you anymore; semicolon. I need you more than I have ever needed anybody (parenthesis: And when I say anybody, I *mean anybody*. Close parenthesis). Quote: 'You walk in beauty like the night,' comma, quotation mark, wrote the poet, colon: And he must have—dash, been thinking of you. Period. New paragraph."

Allen ended: "Until we meet again my love, know this: colon, I love you! Exclamation point. I must have you!! Two exclamation points. You are everything to me!!! Three exclamation points. The world revolves around you? Question mark."

The bewildered secretary asked, "After 'revolves around you'?"

"Yes," Allen answered. "I love you. I love you. What should I remain?"

"*You're* writing the letter," she protested. She said, "I'm sorry, I never expected to take a letter like this."

Allen asked, "Do you think it's a funny letter?"

She replied, "It's not funny if that's the way you feel about someone, but I would think you would sit down and write a letter like this yourself."

"But I composed it."

"But you're not going to typewrite a love letter, are you? If it's not a love letter what is it?"

"It *is* a love letter."

"You're going to typewrite a love letter to someone?"

"It's an electric typewriter."

And so on. As with almost all Allen comedy, it's incredibly funny to watch every time, and one never grows tired of it. On the other hand, watching it many years later, Allen thought it was "degrading" (to him) and "shit." Now he was trying to do Dostoyevsky.

In 1964 he was earning $250,000 a year. His world extended, as it does today, from East Ninety-sixth Street, along Fifth Avenue, Madison for shopping, and Central Park, and he might drift over to Central Park West if he could hurry back quickly to his twin penthouse on Fifth (now it's to a townhouse on the upper East Side). He was a guest at a state dinner honoring the president of Costa Rica, at which he danced with Lady Bird Johnson and shook hands with LBJ. He was invited to entertain at Johnson's inauguration six months later.

He had formed a close connection with former model and future TV and film producer Jean Doumanian, an enigmatic figure and one of the women he seemed to need for protection. He had met her at Mister Kelly's in Chicago. She became his closest confidante and sounding board. They spoke on the phone daily and had dinner frequently. He told *Rolling Stone* that she was his "closest friend in the world, . . . the person you want to be with you when you're waiting for the results of your biopsy." He arranged a job for her booking celebrities on Dick Cavett's television program. No one could figure out this relationship or could predict how it would crash.

Despite his frenetic schedule, Allen would often take time to befriend aspiring comics or writers, as he had done with Jerry Epstein's brother, Sandy, Jack Victor, and Mickey Rose, a writer he met in Flatbush in his twenties. Craig Modderno, a Hollywood writer, meticulous interviewer, and the coauthor of *I'll Be in My Trailer: The Creative Wars Between Directors & Actors,* was fifteen when he met Woody in 1966. It was a life-changing event for him because of Woody's generosity. "He was performing at the hungry i in San Francisco," Modderno told me, "the crown jewel of clubs, where Cosby, the Smothers Brothers, and Belafonte got their start. Tim Hardin was his opening act. I had become an instant fan of Woody's after seeing him on *The Tonight Show.*" Modderno had found out that Woody was performing near his home in Walnut Creek, California. He called the local paper, the *Contra Costa Times,* and asked if he could interview Allen for their "Green Sheet," which was part of the newspaper actually printed in green. They agreed to print the story if it was good enough. He went to the school library and borrowed a reel-to-reel tape recorder, which weighed about eighty pounds. "But I was too young to have a driver's license," he said. "I called the hungry i and said I wanted to interview him for the *New York Times*, which wasn't exactly true, of course.

"So I had my father come with me, and he drove. In a *Look* magazine article, Woody had a line about loving chocolate milkshakes. So I had my father stop and let me buy Woody a milkshake. We got there," Modderno continued, "and Tim Hardin's performing. I'm supposed to talk to Woody between the end of Hardin's act and his appearance. So I see Woody, and I'm giving him his milkshake and telling him I'd read he liked them. And he was very appreciative of that. He's looking at this milkshake, which is three hours past its best moment. He treated me as an adult from the start. The tape recorder, of course, doesn't work. So now he's seen I've lugged it in and it probably weighed half as much as I did at that point. And the milkshake.

"But I brought a notebook, and we did the interview. Then he was about to go on. Enrico Banducci, the club owner, came over to us. And I said, 'Oh my God, can I still buy a couple of tickets?' They laughed and said, 'We've got you a seat.' And I said, 'Can I bring my dad?' Woody cracked up beyond belief at this. Banducci laughed and said, 'Sure—uh—where is he?' I said, 'Well, he's probably up front.' Banducci laughed and said, 'Oh, you mean the man who's been at the bar drinking for three hours? I think we can find him.'

"So they knew I wasn't from the *New York Times*. But Woody liked me instantly. He sipped his milkshake. My dad and I had ended up sitting down on the side of the stage. Now Woody goes onstage, and my dad whispers to me in a voice that stretches to San Francisco. Now remember, Woody back then looked like the very funny Woody, wild red hair. And my dad says to me so that the whole world can hear: 'That guy has to be hysterical because he's the funniest-looking guy I've ever seen.'

"And Woody did something absolutely brilliant. He turned to me and my dad, and he saw that it was my dad. And he smiled, and he played off of it in a benign, almost benevolent way. He could have said something nasty. Instead he turned to the audience and said, 'I was not a pretty child.' Now, Woody hadn't done his first real joke yet, and he's already gotten a huge laugh, courtesy of my father. Now remember, his opening line was usually 'I was an ugly child,' and then something about this was the result of being breast-fed on falsies. But what he said was, 'I was not a pretty child.' So he played off my father's line. In two seconds he improvised his opening and got two enormous laughs before he got to the punch line! But he showed me something brilliant as a comedian. He wasn't nasty, he wasn't abusive, he wasn't combative. He was just kind of, Let's have fun with it."

Modderno also believes that Woody hated doing stand-up, that he cared only about the writing. "He always thought it was too private, too intimate," Modderno said. "He didn't like being in front of people. And from my conversations with him, he was never somebody who got off on the applause. I think that what he thought was—and he was absolutely correct—that if he performed, people would recognize what a good writer he was. He's always loved that part of it. But once he's tested the material on the audience, he can edit the thing, really like an editor—and that's why I think he also likes directing."

Modderno saw him again two years later at King's Castle Casino in Tahoe. Rollins and Joffe owned part of the casino, and Woody had a piece of that action. Modderno called Woody from Walnut Creek. "Two minutes later, I got Woody on the phone. I said, 'Hi, Mister Woody,' and told him who I was, and he remembered me. He said he was performing there and why didn't I come out. He said he didn't know if he could get me a room because they were sold out, but he could get me dinner and into the show. I'm seventeen now. So I got there and was brought to his dressing room, and he told me that his girlfriend was going to be there and to come by and get whatever I would need, a free ticket to the show. And he said he was going out to dinner with this girl, but that I should come back later and it was going to be just the two of us. So first I go to meet him and his girlfriend. I'm a gangly kid, he's incredibly shy even though he likes me, and she is shyer than him. So for a moment it's like three people not even saying anything! The girl was Diane Keaton, and they looked adorable together. This was after they'd done *Play It Again, Sam* onstage but before the movie. I was introspective enough to realize that this was their time to be together. So I went out and saw the show."

The rest of the evening haunts Modderno. "So what happened was after he'd done the first show, after we'd had our conversation, I'll never forget this: We're walking through the back of a kitchen area; mind you, it's three o'clock in the morning. The guy's mopping, putting his mop away. But Woody's got a second show to do. I'm walking Woody to the stage for his second show. It was just the two of us; there was nobody back there. He looked back at me, and he said, 'The only reason I came here is because my managers asked me to do it since we own some small part of this club.' In other words, I'm performing for the money and to help them out. And he said, 'But I just had a great time tonight. A romantic dinner with my girlfriend. And you were very much fun to talk to.' And he said, 'And right now, if I could give you all the money I own in order for you to go up to do my stand-up, I would do it. It's three in the morning, and I've had this good time with her and with you, and I just don't want to be funny anymore. I don't want to do this tonight.'

"And he showed me a trick of the trade that same night regarding his gold watch routine and his grandfather. He showed me the watch. 'You know the reason I use this in the routine, don't you?' he said. 'To get the great laugh?' He said, 'Yeah, that's part of it. But when I open the watch, before I do the punch line, I can see how much time I still have left onstage.' Dependent on when he checked the watch, if he was two minutes short, he did other gags before he did that great punch line. That punch line was his exit line. If he'd been on too short a time when he checked it, then he just closed it, did a couple more jokes, and opened it again. That may be another example of his reluctance to perform. But he did all that with me. And I remember that I didn't have to push him. But that night, I was nudging him to go back on that stage. I said, 'You'll be fine.' Like you do to a boxer. He didn't want to. And while he had a young Diane Keaton up in the hotel room, that wasn't the reason. He was really doing it for Jack and Charlie, without doubt.

"Well, I would see him again soon. But during that very first night, when I interviewed him at the hungry i, I had said to him, 'Is there anybody in history that you would have liked to have been?' He put his head down, and he put his hands together like he's praying. He said, 'Give me a moment.' Then he popped his head up like the Pillsbury Doughboy, which was very popular then. And then he nailed it in terms of the delivery. He said, 'Judas. Because I like to lie a lot.' I thought that was one of the funniest lines I've ever heard.

"All I knew was that for a guy who'd never written a professional story,

I had my ending. Later on I thought, That was gold. He gave me gold at the end."

It would not be Modderno's last encounter with Woody.

"Woody was always psychic," Jerry Epstein related. "I had gone to see him perform in Washington, D.C., when he was twenty-eight. And we talked. He said to me, 'Your life-changing career will be centered on the investigation of death.' Which it has been. My new book is titled *Love Trumps Death*. I've had this intense investigation of the life process, the death process.

"Afterward Woody said to me, 'I've been invited to go to a hotel to meet an astrologer. Come along with me." I did, and I sat in the room when the astrologer said to him, 'Your chart shows that you will be in the movies. And that you will be a movie director. And that you'll be making a name in films.' It was amazing to him, because at that point he had no idea. Never. He was only a stand-up comedian and pursuing his comedy career. And shortly after that, just months later, he got the call for *Pussycat*."

In 1964 Warren Beatty and a businessman and producer named Charles K. Feldman sat ringside at the Blue Angel watching Woody's set. Feldman had been a very powerful agent in Hollywood, handling Howard Hawks, John Wayne, Charles Boyer, Lauren Bacall, and George Stevens, and had gone on to produce *The Glass Menagerie* (1950), *A Streetcar Named Desire* (1951), and *The Seven Year Itch* (1955) but was burning out by the time he encountered Woody in 1964. Feldman was looking for a writer to work on a movie about a Don Juan character much like Beatty, who would actually answer the phone by asking any woman on the line, "What's new, pussycat?"

On the following day Feldman sent the photographer Sam Shaw to ask Charles Joffe if Woody would be interested in writing a film script. Woody saw it as an escape from stand-up and was overjoyed at the offer. He accepted the offer and went to London in July of 1964. His disastrous experience with commercial filmmaking on *Pussycat* would shape many of his key decisions about making films in the coming years. They were decisions that he would never regret; they became essential to his psychic and artistic survival. He had assumed that his script would be preserved as he wrote it, and as it turned out, he felt a total loss of control. His insistence on his complete independence as director, writer, and filmmaker were all the result of the traumatic experience of working on *Pussycat* and *Casino Royale*. "They didn't know what to do with it [the script]," Allen told Stig Björkman. "I didn't like it at all. And I vowed at that time that I would never write another film script unless I could be the director of the film."

Allen's plot featured Peter O'Toole as the editor of a fashion magazine, seeking help from a psychiatrist, Peter Sellers, about his sex addiction. Woody played O'Toole's friend Victor Shakapopolis, who dresses and undresses strippers at the Crazy Horse Saloon. What ensued was really a romp, a farce, pure anarchy. It's more like a Marx Brothers film, and calls to mind Georges Feydeau farces with their slamming doors, the chaos of Mack Sennett films, or the TV series *Laugh-In*.

There is a lot of slapstick, mainly on the part of Sellers. Allen is already the nerd, the nebbish here. He's admitted his character is slight, based on Bob Hope's personae in his 1940s films *Monsieur Beaucaire, Casanova's Big Night*, and *My Favorite Blonde*. Allen has said that his cowardly wise-cracking is also derived from Hope. In Hope's films he is always trying to get the girl. While he eventually succeeds, he's always inept; he always thinks he's better than he is.

The concept was funny, but by the time Feldman, Sellers, and company got through with it, there was little plot to hold it together; it was a kind of a circus, a cabaret, a joyful bacchanalia—and a chaotic mess. The visual style recalls an animated cartoon. And it just wasn't very funny. Sellers took over the movie with Clive Donner, an underrated British director from the sixties, and changed it, switching dialogue and reworking the story. Free-form and rarely amusing, it is structurally inchoate. Woody (Victor) decides to kill Peter O'Toole in several scenes so he can get O'Toole's girlfriend, but this story line is just abandoned about halfway through the film and never resurfaces. Woody's story was butchered, and his objections were shouted down or ignored. He was a cog in a moneymaking machine, treated with contempt. He had absolutely no control or creative input after writing the script. "They just killed it completely," Allen said. "They didn't know what to do with it. They didn't know how to make it . . . the producers I turned it over to were the quintessential Hollywood machine. They undertook to execute this project with everything that everyone hates about Hollywood films. [It was] the worst nightmare one could think of. And just about every creative decision made was incorrect. The producers never understood the script, not any of it at any point. And, of course, I had no say over anything."

The friction between Allen and Feldman was intense. "Charlie Feldman ran that thing with an iron hand," Allen related to Eric Lax. "And I kept thinking, Just get out of my way and let me show you how to do this. . . . He just had a block, some kind of psychological block, which prevented him telling the truth. So it was hard to work with him."

The film was a critical disaster and a huge commercial success, grossing $17.2 million and becoming the fifth-biggest-grossing film of the year. Allen made a fortune from it. The title song, by Burt Bacharach and Hal David, and recorded by Tom Jones, was also a hit.

One can see the beginnings of the Woody Allen prototype in this first film, and it makes an interesting bookend to *Midnight in Paris*. It initiates the Allen format in which the main character is not totally the central character—many other characters interact. The comic lines are reminiscent of Groucho Marx and Jerry Lewis, early Woody idols. His best line is about his job dressing strippers for twenty dollars: "That's all I can afford." In the Jerry Lewis film *The Errand Boy*, Lewis is asked if he wants a job in the studio. He asks, "How much?" They answer, "Fifty dollars a week." Lewis replies, "I can't afford it."

"My husband, Charlie, went to Paris with Woody," Carol Joffe told me. "I think they chased women together. They were in a great position, both of them. They enjoyed Paris, and they enjoyed all the things that came their way. He was the bad guy to Woody's good guy. I know they spent time at the Crazy Horse Saloon in Paris, where they did those partially nude shows. Charlie would be the first one to jump up and give somebody a hug and a squeeze and a grab. Of course I don't think Woody would ever do that. Woody would naturally be in there with it—I think. He needed Charlie to go with in different social situations. But Woody seemed to make very intense connections with the female actresses in the early days. He was comfortable with that, in context. When he was in his own comfort zone he would be fine. He had the power, and people came to him in droves. He didn't have to do the reaching out. You know, if he didn't have this gift I don't know what he would be, actually! He needs to work to survive. I mean, that's him. That's who he is. I think he's trying to live up to his idols. And meanwhile everybody's trying to live up to him."

Allen came to love Paris, but he still lived his hermetic existence, working constantly, practicing the clarinet every day, eating fillet of sole every night in a little restaurant. "I have a regret, or a kind of semi-regret that I didn't stay there," he told Lax. "Two of the girls who did the costumes [Vicky Tiel and Mia Fonssagrives] liked Paris so much they stayed and lived and worked there. I didn't have their independence of spirit or originality."

"When I got to Paris," Vicky Tiel recalls, "Woody was doing *Pussycat.* I went there with Irving Penn's [step]daughter, Mia. The two of us became Mia-Vicky, the originators of the miniskirt. The producer of *Pussycat* was looking for an idea for the film and hadn't hired a designer yet. *Life* magazine did a story on us: The mini has come to town. I was also see-through. I was the first woman in the world to have lace blouses on where you saw my breasts completely. The producer said, 'Let's get these New York girls who are wild and sexy looking to become the costume designers for the film.' I was hired for the film; it was my first job and his first movie; we got to be together in the same movie by coincidence.

"So Woody goes down the hallway. It's his first job, it's my first job, and there's trashy Peaches: 'Peaches, what are you doing in Paris?' So I told him 'I'm the costume designer for your movie, Woody.' We hadn't seen each other since Greenwich Village. He was the same shy Woody.

"I had a boyfriend in Germany, I had a boyfriend in England, and a boyfriend in New York, but I didn't have anybody in Paris. The director wanted me, and Woody wanted me. The guys on the crew said we should have a contest to see who won me. The art director said he would judge. Both guys would buy me a birthday present, and whoever gave me the better present got to sleep with me. So we had this amazing party on the night of my twenty-first birthday. And Woody won. He got me a pinball machine and hired two guys to schlep it up the five flights to my apartment.

"The next day," Tiel continued, "I was supposed to sleep with him. He was lying in the bed at the George V Hotel waiting for me. We had a plan. I was supposed to come in, take a shower, and jump in bed with him. And I didn't show up. What happened was this: The makeup man who also worked for Elizabeth Taylor had come to work on the film that day; he had just arrived from LA. His name was Ron, and he came into the studio cafeteria that day at lunchtime. He came in with the Burtons and came over to my table to talk with Paula Prentiss. Afterward she said, 'He's the stud at MGM.' Then he came back to our table, and he asked me for my phone number, and I gave it to him.

"He called me later that night when I got back from work, and he said, 'Can I come by and see you?' I was supposed to go to Woody at the hotel at eight o'clock. And Ron came over to my apartment. He never left.

"The next day was terrible. I see Woody in the hallway. He said, 'What happened? You didn't show up.' Those were his exact words. I said, 'I met the man I'm going to marry, Woody.'

"He said, '*What? What are you talking about?*'

"And I said, 'I met the man I'm going to marry at lunch.'

"He said, 'At lunch?'

"I said, 'Lunch.' I put my head down, and I walked away. It was devastating for him.

"And then later, I saw *Manhattan*. Isaac says to Tracy in effect that she's going to meet somebody in London and fall in love at lunch. I was shocked.

"Woody and I have always stayed friends in spite of everything. He would come to Paris all the time and visit me in my shop.

"Woody intellectualized with women. He intellectualized the romance. It would be talking. It wasn't like, I'm going to throw you down and screw you. It's not a Warren, you know? The other person who was intellectual like that was Richard Burton. Richard had the talk like Woody, and then he'd throw you down on the bed like Warren. Woody is a thinker. He's writing the script of all these experiences. Most people are not living on all the levels that Woody's living on. He's all about having an intellectual exchange, and then if you go into the relationship where you end up with him as his woman, then it's sweet and tender. Just like his movies. He trusts you and you talk about everything, you share everything."

To compound Allen's woes that year, he was astonished to learn that Harlene had brought a $1 million lawsuit against him, NBC, and its affiliates charging him with defamation of character. She compiled examples of his comments, including his jokes about rape and a moving violation. She also charged that Allen owed her eight thousand dollars in back alimony. Allen, characteristically, was flummoxed at the notion that he had done anything wrong. (Remember the scene in *Deconstructing Harry* when Harry cannot conceive why his wife is angry at him.) He maintained that it was all a joke and Harlene was oversensitive.

Harlene raised the amount to $2 million. He settled out of court years later in 1970. Included in the settlement was an agreement that he would stop telling jokes about her if she promised not to talk about the marriage or the terms of the settlement.

Allen had courted Louise Lasser in Central Park and by going to movies together: the simple, basic things that constitute Allen's life outside his writing. Soon after he returned from Paris, Allen and Lasser went down to City Hall to get their marriage license. According to Louise, he fainted at the blood test. He married Louise on February 2, 1966, in the living room of her father and stepmother's apartment at 155 East Fiftieth Street. Mickey and Judy Rose and Jean Doumanian were the only other friends present. On the same night Woody performed two shows at the Royal Box of the Loews Americana Hotel (today the Sheraton).

They rented a six-room, nine-hundred-dollar-a-month duplex apartment on the top floor of a town house at 100 East Seventy-ninth Street. Much of the apartment would remain essentially unfurnished, but with a jukebox and Hammond organ. The dining room had French antiques and a billiard table.

Allen hired a cook and a Filipino valet. On New Year's Eve 1966 they invited 150 guests to a disco party. Five hundred gate-crashers converged on the building. At the sight of them Louise cried. She and Woody decided to get out and went to the corner drugstore and ate a sandwich while the festivities raged on.

The marriage was shaky from the start, with Louise's depression, pill-popping, and cyclical moods, sleeping all day, and overall erraticism wearing down any hope of a stable future for them. Above all, it was not an organized work environment for Allen, who held on to a second apartment (just as Alvy does in *Annie Hall*). They genuinely loved each other; Allen treated her with tenderness. They were on the same high intellectual level; they were soulmates. Lasser was very funny—a perfect match for Allen—odd, quick witted, and eccentric and a genuine talent; she soon costarred in 1967 in a Broadway musical titled *Henry Sweet Henry*. Later her title role in the sweetly goofy and strange TV series *Mary Hartman, Mary Hartman* would fit her perfectly. When Allen would depict his propensity for "crazy" women, a constant in his films—from Nancy in *Bananas* (Louise Lasser) and Annie in *Annie Hall* (Diane Keaton) to Mary (Keaton) in *Manhattan* to Dorrie (Charlotte Rampling) in *Stardust Memories* to Rain in *Husbands and*

*Wives* (Juliette Lewis) to the character of Holly (Dianne Wiest) in *Hannah and Her Sisters* and Amanda Chase (Christina Ricci) in *Anything Else,* he often seemed to have Louise in mind. But it was not a putdown of her or of the screen women he created; he always acknowledged that he was drawn to this type of woman and that they moved and challenged him and turned him on. It was his problem as much as theirs. And Lasser was far more than "crazy"; she was authentic and original—one of a kind, like Allen.

"Louise was a big part of our lives," Carol Joffe recalled. "She was an amazingly funny woman. Very offbeat, kind of flaky. Very loving; a very affectionate warm person and quite uninhibited. She was a little nutsy in a good way. Together she and Woody were really funny. Sometimes she'd disappear. She had a birthday. There were about eight of us around the coffee table. Somebody brought in this scrumptious cake. And Louise blew out the candle, we sang Happy Birthday, and then she put her hand into the cake and took a load of it and just smashed it into her mouth. And she said, 'I've always wanted to do this.' I mean, that's Louise. She was a nut. She was wild and wonderful and funny. And very sweet with my children and babysat with them. They adored her."

Right before the marriage Woody wrote dialogue for a Japanese film that he dubbed into English, *What's Up, Tiger Lily?* He worked with Louise, Mickey Rose, Frank Buxton, and Len Maxwell. He also created voices for two of the characters. Woody rented a room at the Stanhope Hotel, set up a projector, and ran the film several times. Everyone said whatever came into their minds while the images played. If Woody liked their dialogue, he inserted it. Allen thought the film was dreadful. He tried to sue to keep the film from coming out, but it opened to good reviews and he gave up. Again he had good commercial luck almost against his will, but it wasn't the kind he really wanted.

Allen's prodigious output now included, in addition to acting in films he'd written, TV specials, short stories, and plays. He had completed his first play, *Don't Drink the Water,* about an unsophisticated Jewish family accused of spying while vacationing behind the Iron Curtain. It opened on Broadway in the fall of 1966 with Lou Jacobi and Kay Medford as the American couple and Tony Roberts as the ambassador's son who falls in love with their daughter, Anita Gilette. Allen has said it was a "terrible play." He is right. It is Neil Simon–lite—if that is possible—a humorless, coarse slapstick filled with stereotypical characters. Except for *The*

*Floating Light Bulb*, *Play It Again, Sam*, and his one-acters *Death* and *Death Knocks*, Allen has never brought his best game to drama; in this play he reverted to Borscht Belt humor and cartoonlike characters. And, as in some of his lesser films, he seems to have tossed them off without real effort, although he is said to have worked hard on the play. But *Don't Drink the Water* is his nadir; it would have been a big hit in the Catskills, and it is still a success at dinner theaters. My first reaction was: Could this have actually been written by Allen? But it was. Early reviews were negative. Walter Kerr wrote in the *New York Times*: "The legend that a show of this sort can have too many jokes for its own good is just that, a legend. Aristophanes would surely have clouted the man who suggested such a thing. What actually happens is that the theatrical current stops flowing, the stage doesn't fill to the watermark. The one-liners are coming thick and fast, and the reservoir is emptying steadily. Comedy, like any other kind of theater, needs an interior impulse. The impulse comes from the story line and bubbles up into situations that would be funny even if the lines were as straight as can be. . . . It's the set-up that counts, not the spangles." Nevertheless, the play went on to great commercial success, running eighteen months. It was purchased for the screen by Joseph E. Levine and released as a film starring Jackie Gleason in 1969. The film is even worse than the play, and in its second incarnation it finally flopped.

Allen had also begun writing prose and aiming short, S. J. Perelman–like humor pieces at the most prestigious magazine in America, *The New Yorker*. *New Yorker* editor Roger Angell found his initial submissions too closely modeled on Perelman's. He told Allen, "This is very funny but we already have one of these." As is customary for Allen, he took the criticism to heart and immediately corrected himself, writing originals that have stood the test of time. "The Gossage-Vardebedian Papers" was his first publication in *The New Yorker*, on January 20, 1966. Allen was elated. The story consisted of a series of increasingly hostile letters from two men playing a game of chess by mail. Each man thinks that the other is crazy. He went on to publish "A Little Louder, Please" and "Yes, But Can the Steam Engine Do This?," an account of the invention of the sandwich. He would contribute some fifty stories to magazines, mainly *The New Yorker*, from 1965 to 1980 (at the time he said he was tired of writing "little souffles"), and has written for the magazine intermittently since then. Many are memorable, but the pattern of the meshing of the real with the absurd, the surreal, and the paradoxical became somewhat repetitive, as Allen himself came to realize. Unlike the constant surprises and innovations of his films, which have managed to veer off in startling new directions, his prose continued to be recognizably centered on a predictable cleverness and parody, and cut from a certain similar cloth. They did not always call for a second reading, but, as always, Allen was never predictable. He managed to surprise once again when one least expected it. The difference may be more that parody and satire, following a certain pattern, can go only so far, because character is not at the center and parody is not an emotional genre but by nature critical. The films, in contrast, have often been not only entirely different from one another, with an infinite variety of styles and storytelling methods, but far more steeped in characterization and driven by feeling, passion, and personal experience. But still, many of the stories are superb. "A Look at Organized Crime" tells the reader of the structure of the Cosa Nostra: "At the top is the capo di tutti capi, or boss of all bosses. Meetings are held at his house, and he is responsible for supplying cold cuts and ice cubes. Failure to do so means instant death. (Death, incidentally, is one of the worst things that can happen to a Cosa Nostra member, and many prefer simply to pay a fine.)"

Allen was the scourge of every contemporary fad: New Age thinking; *est*; psychic phenomena; clairvoyance; extrasensory perception; Uri Geller, a spoon-bending illusionist; the supernatural; every form of radical chic—the panaceas that inflame his hatred of Hollywood, where he thinks so many of them seem to originate and flourish. (In *Annie Hall* at Paul Simon's chic party, the camera passes among the crowd as Jeff Goldblum calls his guru and says, "I forgot my mantra.") Allen always chooses common sense, the practical, the real. (In *Hannah and Her Sisters*, Mickey's father replies to his son's question: "How the hell do I know why there were Nazis? I don't know how the can opener works!") In a story in *Without Feathers* (1975), "Examining Psychic Phenomena," he imitates the turgid language and mind-set of this genre while simultaneously mocking it: "There is no question that there is an unseen world. The problem is how far is it from midtown and how late is it open? . . . and after death is it still possible to take showers? Fortunately these questions about psychic phenomena are answered in a soon-to-be-published book, *Boo!* by Dr. Osgood Mulford Twelge, the noted parapsychologist and professor of ectoplasm at Columbia University." Allen writes that Twelge has gathered a history of bizarre supernatural incidents, including the experience of two brothers "on opposite parts of the globe, one of whom took a bath while the other suddenly got clean." The punch line always hurls a rarefied abstraction to earth, ridiculing it by comparing it to the trivial practical matters that really engage us most of the time. Allen demonstrates the absurdity of what he is parodying. And he does so in a language that captures the vernacular, the style and cadence, of the genre of writing he is imitating. Allen sounds like a vaudevillian's version of Kafka in his takeoff of the writer in "The Diet" (*Side Effects*, 1986). In this clever parody, the subject is "F.'s" overeating problem, his conflict with his boss, Schnabel. He's done something wrong, but he doesn't know what it is. The boss has taken away his chair and given it to his coworker, Richter, who now has two chairs. He seeks justice from the mysterious minister. Meanwhile, his father (reminiscent of the father in Kafka's *The Judgment*) rejects him mercilessly (The minister, he tells his son, "has no time for weak failures") and, as in that story, condemns him to death. The story has a lot of bug imagery (think *Metamorphosis*): "F." states that he is "a wretched, abysmal insect, fit for universal loathing."

Allen deals with his favorite, most dreaded subject in the delightful story structured as a one-act play, "Death Knocks" (*Getting Even*). (Echoes of this sketch reappear in *Deconstructing Harry*.) A hooded figure dressed in skin-tight black clothes tries to make a grand entrance through Nat Ackerman's window and almost breaks his neck. Ackerman, a dress manufacturer, is not ready to go, and Death, on his very first assignment, is annoyed: "Don't make a production," he whines. Death sounds as much like a dress manufacturer as Ackerman does. He's thirsty and hungry and asks for a Fresca and potato chips or pretzels, maybe: "Put out something." Nat proposes a game of gin rummy. If he wins, he gets a day's reprieve. He asks what death is like. "What should it be like? You lie there," Death replies. The casual banter is, as usual, very Jewish/Yiddish-inflected. In the end Ackerman wins the game; Death has to come back the next day. He's broke and has to hang out in a down-and-out cafeteria, Bickford's, for the night. Ackerman is tougher than the indecisive Death, and there's the likelihood he will keep winning at gin and hold Death, who is broke and a kind of schlump, at bay. Allen had always said that the writer creates in his art the wished-for outcome he cannot achieve in life (as does Alvy with his play at the end of *Annie Hall*, when Annie leaves Los Angeles, comes back to him, and tells him she loves him). Allen achieves his fond-est wish in this play: He outwits death.

In his comic masterpiece "The Whore of Mensa," Allen created a take-off of pseudo-tough-talking detective-style prose, imitating the cadences of that genre in telling of cracking a ring of prostitutes who turn men on intellectually. The story begins like any Raymond Chandler narrative. Here is the "tough guy" narrator: "A quivery pat of butter named Word Babcock walked into my office and laid his cards on the table. . . . He was shaking like the lead singer in a rhumba band. I pushed a glass across the desktop and a bottle of rye I keep handy." Word had been blackmailed for patronizing mentally stimulating women who could talk about litera-ture: "Sure, a guy can meet all the bimbos he wants. But the really brainy women—they're not so easy to find on short notice." These women "will come over and discuss any subject—Proust, Yeats, anthropology, exchange of ideas. . . . I mean, my wife is great, don't get me wrong. But she won't discuss Pound with me. Or Eliot. I didn't know that when I married her. See, I need a woman who's mentally stimulating . . . and I'm willing to pay for it. I don't want an involvement—I want a quick intellectual expe-rience, then I want the girl to leave."

In "Fine Times: An Oral Memoir," he creates the memoirs of a Mae West–type of speakeasy owner, capturing the character and inverting the clichés of a century of such books: "Originally I danced at the Jewel Club in Chicago for Ned Small. . . . He was famous for breaking both your legs if you disagreed with him. And he could do it, too, boys. . . . I danced at Ned's club. I was his best dancer, boys, a dancer-*actress*. The other girls just hoofed, but I danced a little story. Like Venus emerging from her bath, only on Broadway and Forty-second Street, and she goes to a nightclub and dances till dawn and then has a massive coronary and loses control of the facial muscles on the left side. Sad stuff, boys; that's why I got re-spect." Just the insertion of "boys" throughout the passage conjures up Mae West and a whole vanished chapter of show business.

And in "If the Impressionists Had Been Dentists (A Fantasy Exploring the Transposition of Temperament)," the first letter from Vincent van Gogh to his brother begins: "Dear Theo, Will life ever treat me decently? I am wracked by despair! My head is pounding! Mrs. Sol Schimmer is suing me because I made her bridge as I felt it and not to fit her ridiculous mouth!"

One can hear vintage Allen in every line. The stories bristle with energy, humor, surrealistic imagery, and all kinds of wordplay. If he has wearied of these "soufflés," and if they do not resonate nearly so much as his better films, they still have great merit and wit. "He's not one of the great short story writers," Phillip Lopate told me. "And partly because he never got beyond the pastiche. In a way he never got beyond S. J. Perelman. So his early love of Bob Hope and Perelman carried him a long way, but it didn't carry him into substance. He could do a kind of Borscht Belt postmodernism like the Emma Bovary piece, 'The Kugelmass Episode.' And it was fun. It really is the kind of thing you can do in *The New Yorker*. You're just doing a kind of satirical pastiche."

In a later interview with Michiko Kakutani in 1987 in *The Paris Review*, Allen spoke of his experience writing for *The New Yorker* and his lack of confidence in writing prose as opposed to his certainty in writing comedy:

> *When I brought something into* The New Yorker, *I didn't know what I was standing there with. Their reactions could have been, Oh, this is nothing. You've written a lot of words, but this isn't really anything, or, Young man, this thing is really wonderful. I was happy to accept their judgment of it. . . . I would have thrown the stuff away and never batted an eyelash. . . . There are only one or two areas where I feel that kind of security, where I feel my judgment is as good and maybe even better than most people's judgment. Comedy is one. I feel confident when I'm dealing with things that are funny, whatever the medium.*

Allen is often mistakenly perceived as the liberating "freethinker" who champions the very thought and cultural patterns he makes fun of. Whatever his audience thinks is desirable, they project onto him. His neuroses may persist, but there is a bedrock reality that he clings to, the same reality that anchors his relentless work ethic, that makes him eat early, watch a movie or a football game, and go to sleep. He may be frenetic on film and stage, but he is seemingly calm, self-disciplined, and rational in person.

Three months into his new marriage, at the behest of Charles Feldman, Allen flew to London with Charles Joffe for the filming of *Casino Royale*. It would be this last, despised film over which he again had no control that sealed his determination to have complete autonomy over what he wrote in the future.

*Casino Royale* would conclude his education in how not to make a movie and how not to survive as a writer in the movies. The results were desperate, forced, phony, hysterical, and hollow. He was disgusted by the whole process of making a film by committee, by the endless time wasting, people spending their lives "taking" lunch, the insane expense, extravagance, bloatedness, impersonality, grandiosity, gimmickry, and sheer stupidity—the insanity—of what he had witnessed while being involved with three vacuous and meaningless films. The experiences of working on *Pussycat* and *Casino Royale* must have been on his mind when he wrote the Hollywood party scene in *Annie Hall*. As Alvy wanders around the party he hears this:

1st MAN: Well, you take a meeting with him, I'll take a meeting with you if you'll take a meeting with Freddy.

2ND MAN: I took a meeting with Freddy. Freddy took a meeting with Charlie. You take a meeting with him.

1ST MAN: All the good meetings are taken.

Then Alvy overhears this conversation about the art of creation Hollywood-style: A man stands talking to a group. He says, "Right now it's only a notion, but I think I can get money to make it into a concept . . . and later turn it into an idea."

*Casino Royale*, supposedly based on a James Bond novel by Ian Fleming, was produced by Charles K. Feldman and Jerry Bresler at Columbia in 1967. The stellar cast included Allen, Peter Sellers, Ursula Andress, David Niven, Orson Welles, Deborah Kerr, Peter O'Toole (in a cameo appearance), Charles Boyer, and George Raft.

Feldman ceremoniously flew Woody to London and set him up at a luxurious hotel. There Woody waited—and waited—for six months before acting in the film, while the three writers and the directors and producers tried to figure out what they were doing. He gambled, worked on his plays and prose, and wandered around London. Later Woody told Stig Björkman that it was "a moronic enterprise from start to finish; everything about it was a stupidity and a waste of celluloid and money. It was another dreadful film experience."

"Woody told the producers he wanted me to work with him on his portion of *Casino Royale*," Frank Buxton told me, "so he and I wrote together the things that Woody did in the film. We would play cards at night. We would show each other magic tricks. Many adult performers started with magic. We all got magic kits when we were kids, with balls and cups, cards, coins in them. I could still do some reasonably good card passes."

Feldman was attempting a spoof like *Pussycat*, but this one was worse, far worse, if that was possible. The central character, Sir James Bond (Niven) was a retired secret service agent. An impostor was imitating him, maligning the sacred family name and using it as a way of seducing women. Bond decided to kill the enemy agents, the leader among them being Le Chiffre (Orson Welles). Ultimately Bond finds out that the real brains behind the enemy camp is his sniveling, tiny neurotic nephew, Little Jimmy Bond (Woody). The character of Jimmy is not unlike other Woody personae: He is frustrated by his incompetence at trying to live up to his hero, James Bond. Frustrated, he gives in and becomes a villain instead, and insane.

No one escaped with honor in the film except Allen, whose scenes are its only highlights. The themes accompanying his appearance are already familiar to us: An obsession with beautiful women and his failure to attract them drives him to hatch a plot to make all women beautiful and to kill all men taller than he is. His ineptness with mechanical objects, a player piano or a mechanical horse, also provide the only genuine moments of laughter in the film.

The critics had a field day with this one. *Time* called it "an incoherent and vulgar vaudeville." Howard Junker in *Newsweek* wrote that it "burbled like a hyperthyroid idiot with disconnected skits and gags."

Unlike *Pussycat*, *Casino* was a box-office disaster, though Woody emerged richer and professionally unscathed. He would not forget what he'd experienced, and he would soon forge a path free of all the foolishness and stupidity he had seen.

It was a sobering experience. John Simon caught a glimpse of him in London that winter: "I remember him in London," Simon told me. "I was involved with Patricia Marx [syndicated radio host for public radio], who married Daniel Ellsberg, and we were in London for a time. She knew that Woody was there, and she knew that he was depressed. So she invited him and a few other people to a quite-nice restaurant, and I sat next to him. He was enormously downcast. We were all trying to cheer him up. We had a bit of a conversation. He was very much hangdoggish on this occasion. It was very sad because he was sitting in a corner and not very communicative. He was the morose, silent one."

# 5. Bathing in Honey

WHEN ALLEN RETURNED TO AMERICA, he joined the cast of Frank Buxton's NBC TV show *Hot Dog*. It would be his only television series. "It was a program about stuff," Buxton related. "Where do things come from? Lead pencils, baseball, and plywood; how do they make a hot dog? Jonathan Winters, Tommy Smothers, and Woody did comic responses to questions in the pilot. I would ask Woody who invented the hot dog. His response was 'The Earl of Hot Dog, 1643.' It was all ad lib. Everything I did with Woody we shot in one day. Because we just sat down and talked. One take. At one point he was trying to get a comic response, and he looked at me and said, 'Let's keep going until we strike joke.'" (While the pilot featured Allen, Winters, and Smothers, most episodes would include Jo Anne Worley [later featured on *Laugh-In*] along with Winters and Allen.)

Within months Rollins and Joffe completed a deal with Palomar Pictures to produce Allen's first autonomous film, *Take the Money and Run*. Palomar put up about $2 million for Allen to write, direct, and act in the film—this on the basis of one screenwriting credit and no directing or extensive acting experience. Allen enlisted his childhood friend Mickey Rose to cowrite the film. He approached Jerry Lewis to direct, but Lewis backed off, telling Allen he should do it himself. Allen also met once with the director Arthur Penn, who provided him with "practical information." (Penn's film *Bonnie and Clyde,* also on the subject of bank robbers, would precede Allen's by a few months.) "The smart thing Woody did," Howard Storm relates, "and Jack and Charlie agreed with it, was that he took less money so that he would have control of his work. Right from the beginning he had final cut on the film. It was almost unheard of."

Allen was supremely confident that he could do the film. Asked by Stig Björkman in 2000 if he'd consulted more experienced filmmakers for advice to prepare himself to direct, Allen replied, "Well, to tell you the truth, it never occurred to me for a second that I wouldn't know what to do. I was guided by the fact that I knew what I wanted to see, so it seemed to me elementary how to get to see it. There was no trick at all. I know that a man has to come into a room, he pulls a gun out, etc. And it doesn't require any great brilliance to know how to do that. . . . I just thought it would be funny."

And it was—riotously funny. A pseudodocumentary about a bumbling petty criminal, Virgil Starkwell, *Take the Money and Run* is as fresh today as it was in 1969. A parody of documentary crime stories such as *Naked City* and *The Untouchables,* the film is a collection of rapid-fire comic sketches and sight gags in the guise of a biography, with a portentous narration provided by Jackson Beck, who'd narrated scores of Paramount newsreels as well as the *Superman* radio show. Virgil's greatest disappointment is that he cannot make the Ten Most Wanted list. As his wife, Louise, laments, "It's who you know."

When we first glimpse Virgil as a shoeshine boy, instead of spitting on the leather of his customer's shoe to give it a high gloss, he misses and hits the customer's pant leg. In one of the cleverest biographical scenes, Virgil plays the bass in a marching band and has to keep moving his chair to keep up with the other members. Virgil's early years are marked by a series of inept attempts at robberies; he tries a pet shop but is chased out by a gorilla; he winds up with veal chops when he tries to rob a butcher shop. He gets his hand caught in a gumball machine, and it's a little heavy to carry as the cops pursue him. His eyesight is poor, and people constantly break his glasses and stomp on them. (Once he stomps on them himself to prevent this.) He always gets caught. He is a misfit whatever he does. The robberies in the film were based on Warner Bros. crime dramas, just as the chain-gang scenes are derived from *I Am a Fugitive from a Chain Gang.*

In the most memorable scene, he tries to hold up a bank, but the teller cannot make out his handwriting. Virgil has thrust the note at him and insists that his note does not say, "I have a gub," but, of course, a gun. The note also intends to say, "Act natural," but the teller thinks it says, "Abt natural." The teller consults the other tellers while Virgil waits helplessly. The teller requests to see Virgil's gun, and Virgil dutifully shows it to him. Then the note has to be countersigned by a manager.

Virgil confides that he has a tendency to dribble with women, that he is too "sensitive" and shy and nervous when he is in love, and becomes nauseous. He has fallen in love with Louise, a beautiful laundress (Janet Margolin), who becomes his wife and waits for him when he goes to prison. In the prison visiting room, the prisoners speak to their visitors through metal mesh. In a fine lunatic touch, near Virgil two dummies are seated across from each other, one a prisoner, one a visitor. They are seated on the laps of their ventriloquists, chatting with each other.

In prison Virgil cannot make a shirt-folding machine work; instead, it attacks him. We see him attempting to escape from prison with a pistol carved out of soap, but the rain melts it. Sentenced to a chain gang, when the sadistic warden speaks menacingly to the prisoners and then asks if there are any questions, Virgil raises his hand and asks, "Do you believe in petting on the first date?"

Jewish touches abound. Virgil shouts from his cell to the guard that he is sick and has to go to the infirmary. "What's wrong?" the guard asks. "Don't ask," Virgil replies plaintively.

The warden asks for volunteers for a vaccine experiment in order to earn a parole. Virgil steps up, and a side effect briefly turns him into a rabbi. (Later Alvy Singer will turn into a Hasidic Jew when visiting Annie's family in *Annie Hall.*) He intones in a sonorous voice the meaning of Passover, and a hora (Jewish dancing music) plays joyously.

Virgil's teachers, probation officer, and parents are interviewed in a long battle. To Woody's bewilderment, early screenings of the film were disastrous. It didn't help that there were no titles, sound effects, or music. Audiences didn't laugh. A group of soldiers watched it at the USO in Manhattan and left bewildered, shaking their heads.

Rollins and Joffe turned in desperation to Ralph Rosenblum, a film editor, who had rescued William Friedkin's *The Night They Raided Minsky's* in 1967 when it was in dire trouble. (Rosenblum was also the editor of *The Producers* and was credited by some with saving Mel Brooks's first directorial effort.) When they screened it for him, Rosenblum diagnosed the problem. The fragmentary nature of the material meant that it needed a total restructuring. In addition, the maudlin ending stemmed from that other side of Allen, the dark, grim, extremely unfunny side: It featured Virgil's bullet-riddled body. Rosenblum would write in his memoir that the film "seemed to be flying all over the place, with highs as high as the Marx Brothers and lows as low as a slapped-together home movie. . . . Most of [the] incidents were delightfully surrealistic." Rollins and Joffe told Rosenblum that a huge amount of footage had been discarded by the ultracritical Allen. Rosenblum perked up at this news; it held out hope for a work he already found "packed with funny material" and written by a "very fresh mind."

Rosenblum recalled, "The attitude of Woody's managers seemed to be that their young ward was a delicate orchid who might wither if approached incautiously." He met with Allen over lunch and found him very serious and soft-spoken. Allen, who has never let ego get in the way of learning from criticism, was amenable to Rosenblum's suggestions. Rosenblum was impressed with Allen's "Prussian discipline." They agreed that Rosenblum would look at the discarded footage and see what could be done. Two hundred boxes of film were delivered to his cutting room the following day.

Rosenblum viewed the outakes for two weeks, "one of the most pleasable [experiences] in all my years of editing." He set to work reconstructing the film. He restored many scenes Allen had thrown out, including all of those with Virgil's parents, which he used as a bridge between segments of the action that did not connect in a natural way. There three devices used for transitional material: the parents, Woody's er narration, and Jackson Beck's interviews with Virgil. Some-was simply a matter of inserting the right background music. Vir-

documentary-style (a device later employed extensively in *Zelig*). Ashamed of their son, his parents wear Groucho Marx–style glasses. Virgil's father says he "tried to beat God" into his son, but nothing worked.

Woody was insouciant about his inexperience in making the film. He told the writer Bob Thomas, "I am operating on the principle that the less you know about directing the better off you are." He enjoyed improvisation on the set: "We have a script, but use it only as a guideline. . . . In lots of cases we'll shoot alternatives—as many as three different jokes for the same spot . . . but there's a lot of improvisation in the dialogue scenes."

Filming began at San Quentin in San Francisco on June 17, 1968. Woody invited some of his childhood pals to the set. "They were doing the bank robbery scene in an actual bank," Elliott Mills recalls. "Mickey Rose and his wife, Judy, were there, and I and my wife. Each of us tried to do the scene for Woody where a citizen comes into the bank. All you had to do was come through the doors from outside into the bank, hit the line, and say, 'Hey, what's going on?' Nobody could do it. It's really hard to do that professionally. It's a difficult thing to do. So I did it, Mickey did it, my wife, Mickey's wife. Woody let everybody try. He waved everybody off because we were no good. Then we went out and ate pizza."

Craig Modderno, who was still in high school, found out that Allen was shooting the film both at San Quentin and at Stockton for the chain-gang scenes. "I called up Allen's office," Modderno told me, "and got a call back that if I wanted to come see him in Stockton, I could.

"We got a chance to talk a lot on the set the first day. At the end of the day Woody gave me money! I said 'You don't need to do this.' Woody said, 'You got tolls. And gas and stuff. You're still in high school, for Christ sake.' I went back to school, but he gave me a number and somebody to call so I could come back. He gave me full instructions on how to get him. I went back in a few days, and he made me assistant for the day. He said, 'That's how you earn your toll bridge money.'

"I didn't do much," Modderno continued. "Mainly it was just talking to him. Or holding his notebook while he did a scene. At one point I told him that my father had died a few months back. Woody said, 'I remember him. He gave me my first laugh in a nightclub [that I didn't create].' Woody's always had a terrific memory like that.

"and Janet Margolin were really in sync. But the crew of *Take the*

*Money and Run* didn't know him and didn't particularly trust him. Most of them didn't have a clue what Woody was doing on the film. They liked him personally, but they just didn't get the way he was working. He didn't even have an assistant on the movie. The good thing was that Palomar wasn't putting pressures on him. They wanted to get into the business. It was a cheap movie and a funny script. But nobody thought anything of this film or of him. So they were not very nice to him. The cast, especially Janet, were very warm. But that reclusive quality he's had for decades back then looked like rudeness or arrogance. Because he hadn't done anything yet."

During the filming at San Quentin, Woody and his cast were constantly mistaken for actual guards or prisoners. Woody himself mistook actors for guards. "We shot at San Quentin for two weeks," Howard Storm told me. "Every morning we would all go into the prison. The whole crew, the grips, the young guys, were wearing tie-dye shirts, jeans, hair down to their shoulders. We would hear kisses from the windows above us: 'Hey, sweet buns'—I mean it was scary. The warden told us, 'If you are taken hostage we can't be responsible for you. You're not to ever leave the group without one other person and a prison guard.'

"So Woody and I," Storm continued, "are breaking for lunch, and we're walking with a prison guard across the football field where the prisoners are playing. I glance over, and the prison guard is wearing an emblem on his shoulder that doesn't say 'San Quentin'—it says 'Rahway State Prison, New Jersey [the supposed location of the film].' So I know he's really an extra. They just put him in a uniform. He wanted to hang out with Woody, so he followed us. I said to Woody, 'This guy isn't a real guard. He's an extra.' Woody said, 'You're kidding!' So Woody turned to him and said, 'Act like a guard. Act like a guard.'

"Then we shot a riot scene. Woody decided he wanted to use the actual prisoners. So we're doing a rehearsal, and they don't know from rehearsals. They're killing each other, beating the shit out of each other. Woody says to me, '*They're hitting! What are they doing?*'

"But they liked Woody; they were fine. They were excited by the project. But he was saddened that they were so young."

While the film was in process, Allen also took the time in August 1968 to appear at a San Francisco rally for Democratic presidential hopeful Eugene McCarthy, who was running on an antiwar platform.

Craig Modderno would have his last encounter with Woody at the conclusion of the shooting of *Take the Money and Run*, the final stage of the early, sensitive mentorship Woody gave him—a mentorship that made him become a writer. "Woody was about to go home," Modderno remembered. "I'd written a play for class. I told Woody about it, and he was amazed at its adult theme. I asked him if he would look at it. And he said something so amazing: 'Here's my address. Send it to me in six months. I will by then have forgotten the really good relationship we've had. So I won't read it with any prejudice, any partiality. But send me a photo of you so I'll remember it's you. We had such a good time together that I'll read the script.'

"That was Woody in 1968," Modderno said. "He wanted to be fair. First off he didn't want to break my heart, but he didn't want to deceive me.

"Four or five months pass. I'm having a miserable time. My father had died a few months before. I'm an only child. I'm eighteen years old. I'm up for the draft. In the Bay Area where I lived, so many people fled the draft or refused to go that they increased the eligibility pool from 150 to 250. It's a miserable day outside. I'm working in a movie theater. That part is okay. We were showing John Frankenheimer's *Grand Prix* for about the ninetieth time. Thanksgiving is coming in two days, and my dad is gon[e]. My writing teacher had gone out of his way to tell me I'd never be a wri[ter].

"So my mom calls me up and tells me that she's got a letter for me [that] I might want to see. A brown envelope and in the back it had Woo[dy Al]len printed on it. She drove down and gave me the letter. And it wa[s] But it was from Woody. A couple of paragraphs. He told me how [he] liked the script. And that I should pursue a career in writing. A[nd he] wrote a line that I must have read five hundred times just t[o be]cause I thought he'd made a mistake. And then about the [ninth] and tenth, I got it. And what he wrote was, 'You should [have it] done somewhere just to see how your work plays.' And [I thought it a] typo that he meant to say, 'How your play works.' He m[eant see how] your work plays in front of an audience. The other thi[ng was that] he'd done one play, he'd done one unreleased film, [one he had no] control over, and I'm an eighteen-year-old kid. So [he was treat]ing me as an adult and giving me serious guid[ance, a side of him] you never see printed about him. I wanted no[thing from him,] no benefit for him."

When *Take the Money and Run* completed

gil's Bowery-like hotel room, where he hoped to romance Louise, where he had to pull the toilet flusher to get his shower to run, had to be the most depressing dump the director could have conjured up. Rosenblum replaced the mournful music accompanying the scene with ragtime musician Eubie Blake's compositions. "The sequence [had been] heavy and oppressive and unfunny," said Woody. "And without changing a frame, just changing the music, the thing became funny." Allen rehired composer Marvin Hamlisch, who furnished a magical score that enlivened the film at every turn.

The biggest problem was the ending. There were six versions, "all of them sentimental, weakly amusing, or sad," Rosenblum wrote. Now Woody created a hilarious new scene with Louise Lasser, mainly improvised by her, playing a neighbor who is astonished that her schlemiel-like neighbor was a criminal: "I actually believed that he was an idiot. I mean I really believed it. . . . Like, everybody thought so. . . . To think that idiot was a criminal! I just can't believe it. . . . You've never met such a nothing. I can't believe it! That there was a mind working in there that could rob banks! It's phenomenal! Phenomenal!" The final scene now showed Virgil back in prison, interviewed by Jackson Beck. He's reflecting on his life of crime and—yet again—carving a bar of soap. His final line is "Do you know if it's raining out?"

The film opened to rave reviews in New York on August 18, 1969. Vincent Canby wrote in the *New York Times*: "It has the texture of a collage—blackout sketches, sight gags, fake cinéma vérité interviews, old newsreel footage, parodies of all sorts of other movies . . . and the kind of pacing—or maybe it's just momentum—that carries the viewer over the bad gags to the good ones."

Woody's character was indelibly etched on the mind of the audience: the nebbish, the neurotic, the schlemiel. It was a character suited to modern times even as Chaplin's tramp and Keaton's great stone face—perhaps partly because they were so identified with what was by now a remote era of silent films—receded from the audience's memory.

The audience hungered for more Woody, and would continue to do so for the next forty-five years—and counting.

Woody is dismissive of *Take the Money and Run* as a primitive collection of gags, but I rate it among his twenty-five best. It is so fresh, so startling, so unendingly funny—even at the twentieth viewing. Woody fully emerged in it as a landmark talent, a character the audience waited to see on-screen. And it was the same Woody, essentially the same character that Allen would utilize for fifty—or sixty—more years: sex-starved, lecherous, romantic, put-upon, wisecracking, a mechanical dunce, Jewish and brazen about it, employing a humor based on paradox, absurdity, incongruity, and audacity. The novelist Jennifer Belle's grandmother saw it and pronounced Woody "the eighth wonder of the world," the same phrase Jack Rollins used about him.

They were right.

Kevin Thomas wrote of Virgil in the *Los Angeles Times* that "Starkwell is so appealingly hapless you don't think of him as a criminal at all but rather as a kind of everyman in [whom] we can all recognize our sense of frustrated helplessness at being at the mercy of a toweringly indifferent universe. It is, in a very true sense, a film of the absurd."

There are those who continue to see Woody's films as a veiled autobiography, but whether they are any more so than any artist's creative expression is a matter for conjecture. I do not view them solely that way, particularly since there is such a tremendous range of subject matter and a vast variety of themes, styles, characters, and settings. They do not stray far from his main thematic and personal obsessions, but that is true of many artists.

Louise Lasser would tell Robert Higgins, "There is a great deal of fury in Woody, an attraction to the element of danger, the unpredictability of the situation. And crime is a rebellion against the Establishment—like robbing banks, it's rebellious—and Woody's a rebel."

Jerry Epstein recalls that he and Woody were attracted to crime and criminals when they were growing up. "Remember, the epigraph of *Take the Money and Run* is 'Crime Lives.' Woody and I used to pore over an encyclopedia of criminology. Think of his other movies that deal with crime [the Mafia family in *Broadway Danny Rose*; Cheech and Nick Valenti in *Bullets over Broadway*; the murderer who threatens Sally White in *Radio Days*; the murderous brothers in *Cassandra's Dream*; the murdering social climber in *Match Point*; the pimp in *Mighty Aphrodite*; the congenial murderer, Paul House, in *Manhattan Murder Mystery*; Charles Ferry, the ex-convict in *Everyone Says I Love You*; the assassin in *Stardust Memories*; and Judah Rosenthal in *Crimes and Misdemeanors*].

"My practice for a time was at East Ninety-sixth Street in Manhattan.

The street's called the 'mental block' because it has the highest proportion of psychiatrists in the city. I used to meet Lou Lynd, another psychoanalyst I sent Woody to, on the street, and we would schmooze. He was practicing in an office down the street from me. We would commonly get around to talking about Woody. Lou said to me, 'Woody did so well with me. But the one thing I missed—I'm taking responsibility for it—I didn't seek to socialize him.'

"The thing about Woody," Dr. Epstein explained, "he lives in the instant, jumping from one sensory impression, or experience, to the next. The things he does, says, writes, have to be short. Everything has to be quick because he's governed by the moment. He's not governed by time. In sum, he lives in the 'empire of the instant.'

"So analysis was the wrong treatment for Woody. Because analysis makes you reflect on your past. And that's very painful for a person like him. It would take the form of: 'Please don't draw me back to the instant before. Because I'm done with that. I've extracted everything I need to get from it. And I don't want to be drawn back to it. Governed by the moment. Moment to moment to moment.' Over the many years he was in analytic treatment he told me he never once told a joke while on the couch."

Reflecting on Allen's development in later years, Epstein remembered that "Woody has always taken the position of having to get away with something. Like he would do with Mia and Soon-Yi. He had to get away with something, and he was caught. There's no feeling of guilt in him, nor of conscience. It's always your fault and it's always your responsibility. He doesn't feel he has any complicity in the mutual process that's going on. The onus is always on you. So you always have to live up to the standard that he sets for people to abide by, what he deems to be the ideal, and, incidentally, to his advantage. In relationships he adheres to the mantra of dominant relationships. Me real, you shadow. Nevertheless he experiences constant anxiety, as for him catastrophe is always around the corner.

"As Woody became richer and richer," Epstein related, "the themes of his films have turned from the middle class to the upper middle class or the upper rich class he identifies with. It's all about the money and safety it brings for him. When you're in that higher echelon of privileged society, you become more and more frightened of death and buy into the belief that money can act as a hedge against it.

"As to relationships, he now has an enduring one with Soon-Yi of a certain sort. Because as he said to me, 'She's not interested in my work.' It's understandable. Her work has been with special-needs children. So she has, to my mind, a special-needs child that she's taking care of.

"He's had ways of being good to people. He called me after many years of silence in 2000 when I had a heart attack, and we walked in Central Park together. Then when my brother, Sandy, died in 1991, Woody called me to express his condolences. And he said to me that Sandy was the greatest influence on his humor of any person. Then he shocked me by saying that he and Sandy had a relationship, that they spoke a lot. My brother had never told me of this.

"Sandy was incredibly funny. Woody had offered to write for Sandy in the seventies. Sandy was a lawyer by then. He said to Sandy, 'Go out to Las Vegas and do a stand-up comedy act and I'll write for you for free.' He thought so much of his talent. But Sandy turned it down. He said to Woody, 'I have three children. I'm married. How am I going to earn a living? I don't know if I'll make enough money. There's no fixed income to count on.' So he had the opportunity to go and believe in himself and just do it. And he would have the funniest guy in America writing for him. How could he fail? My brother was such a great comedian himself, he couldn't fail. I couldn't understand why he wouldn't do that. But he couldn't be faulted. It would take an act of faith to take such a leap that most people do not ever risk. It was a generous act on Woody's part. But it was hurtful to tell me in that way that they'd had a secret relationship."

In 1968, just before making *Take the Money and Run*, Allen reflected on the nature of being a comedian in an interview with Larry Wilde for a book called *The Great Comedians Talk About Comedy*. Allen had already arrived; other contributors to the book included Milton Berle, Jack Benny, Jimmy Durante, Danny Thomas, and George Burns. Allen's writing habits were formed: He said he wrote on matchbooks and napkins and threw his ideas in a drawer at home. When the time came he laid them out in his room and went over them. This was the very process Allen would describe in the 2012 *Woody Allen: A Documentary*, produced by Robert Weide.

Allen said he didn't think one could learn to write jokes, that it was "purely inborn." The key thing wasn't the jokes, "It's the individual himself. When I first started . . . the same jokes I did at that time that got nothing for me, now will get roars, and not because I am more known. It's the funny-character emergence that does it." He stated he did not know why people laughed at him. "The only thing I can surmise is that there is something about me they are responding to, above and beyond the material, something in myself that I don't see. I don't believe the performer knows what's funny about himself, or can see it. . . . They can never stand outside themselves enough to know what it is."

Asked what was most difficult about being a comedian, he responded (one is reminded of the 3:00 a.m. scene at Lake Tahoe between Allen and Craig Modderno, when Allen was so reluctant to go onstage for a second show), "The pressure. It's very hard to constantly have to go before the public and get laughs. . . . If they are not roaring, you're in trouble. You have to be great all the time. . . . You've got that pressure of facing an audience—get them laughing for forty minutes. You go to your dressing room, and in an hour you have to do it again for the second show that night or the third, and the next night you have to do it all over again, and this goes on year after year."

Asked what counsel he could give new comedians, he said, "When I first became a comedian, I thought, gee, I write funny material, I bet I could get up and just read this to people and they would laugh. I tried that. I took the sheets of paper out in the nightclub and it meant nothing to the audience. They wanted something else entirely. What they want is an intimacy with the person. They want to like the person and find the person funny as a human being."

Wilde wondered if there was anything else a comedian could do to advance his career. Allen offered advice that was really a statement of principle and a foreshadowing of the paths he would take for the next forty-eight years: He envisioned "the chap who really will discipline himself and develop. I mean really hard work. Writing material for yourself, not believing your press notices whether they are good or bad, constantly doing new things, constantly moving into new areas—movies, Broadway— studying new projects, constantly risking everything without ever thinking about the money or how it will hurt or build your career. Just thinking about work."

Wilde asked if this meant taking risks and not caring about failing. Allen replied, "Right! Once you start to think about do the newspapers like me, or did the audience like me, or am I making enough money, or should I be doing this? The only important thoughts are: *Am I being as funny as possible in as many different ways.* Once you view the rewards too tantalizingly, you're dead. Then you start accepting and turning down jobs on the basis of how it affects your income tax. Then you might as well be working in Macy's, except that the money is better in this business."

Woody began production on his second stage play, *Play It Again, Sam*, in 1969. He was soon secretly entangled with Diane Keaton, who had auditioned for the play and been cast. Keaton hailed from Santa Ana, south of Los Angeles. Her father was a civil engineer; her mother had been a Mrs. Los Angeles. Keaton had come to study acting at the Neighborhood Playhouse, and her first important role on Broadway had been in the musical *Hair*. She was the only member of the cast who refused to take her clothes off. Louise was aware of the romantic connection between them, and she moved out of their apartment in June 1969. The marriage was over.

After ten years of trying to make the marriage work, Woody and Louise traveled to Mexico for a divorce in the spring of 1970. They held hands while appearing in court, which was emblematic of the affection and tenderness they still felt for each other and which had kept them together against the odds for a long time. "We had a good time," Lasser said of the trip. "We stayed together that night in the same hotel room. We had a lot of what now appear contradictions like that. Because at the time we were still drawn together." Lasser may have been much more drawn to Woody than he was to her at that point. His infatuation with Diane Keaton had begun. Lasser suffered a nervous breakdown soon afterward. He would continue to have both a personal and professional connection with Louise. In May 1970 Allen cast Lasser to star opposite him in *Bananas*.

Lasser has warm and good memories of Woody. She told Eric Lax in *On Being Funny: Woody Allen and Comedy* (1975), "The worst thing in the world could happen to him and he could go in that room and write. . . . Considering how obsessed he is, he was really terrific to live with. There was never anything fragile about his work. He gets up and goes in and writes, but you can disturb him at any time. He's not moody. He is demanding in that you pretty much have to do something when he wants. He's very specific. . . . He's ritualistic about a lot of things, like the food he eats and the time he eats."

Allen spoke of both Diane Keaton and Lasser in an interview in the *New York Times*, with writer Natalie Gittelson in 1979. He said, "They both had more to give me than I had to give them. I couldn't have accomplished half of what I accomplished without Louise. . . . [She] is a great woman, a great companion. Her comprehension of life is very great."

In a 2014 interview Lasser said that "The relationship didn't fully dissipate until a couple of years after we got divorced." Asked if they were still in touch, she said, "We speak not that often, but he usually invites me to come at Thanksgiving. They live a block away. And I've gone a few times. But it's all different. And your life goes different ways. It was such a strong part of my life, so public, in a sense, that you don't just put it away, like 'oh, when I went out with so-and-so.' I think he talks about this relationship as the crazy relationship too. . . . It's very strange when you're that close to someone and then you're not. But you speak, but you don't know which part of you is having that conversation. And yet you do have an affection for that person."

In another interview that year with *Interview Magazine,* she said, "It's so great when people meet someone they can stretch with, that you want to be better than you are and they can stretch you. . . . I'll forever be influenced by his work. A lot of my best work comes from his work."

Allen was enamored of Keaton from the time he met her (at her audition for *Play It Again, Sam*), and very intimidated. His initial behavior with her seems an echo of the way Vicky Tiel described his behavior with women. "Outside of rehearsal, I was frightened to talk to her," he told Jonathan Moor, author of *Diane Keaton,* "and she was frightened to talk to me, and we'd go home separately every night, and nothing ever happened." This situation prevailed during out-of-town tryouts, but they became lovers by the time the play reached Broadway. Soon after, Lasser moved out of Allen's apartment and Keaton moved in. Author and film critic Foster Hirsch wrote of Keaton's appeal to Allen in his book about Allen:

> *Like many Jewish romantics he is drawn to shiksas whose pretty blonde blandness represents both forbidden fruit and the incarnation of the American dream. . . . Now Keaton is as deeply and intensely goyische as Woody is Jewish. Tall, lanky, with even features and a bland voice, Keaton is the real thing: a dyed-in-the-wool Californian Gentile.*

*Play It Again, Sam* premiered at the Broadhurst Theater on February 12, 1969, and was an immediate hit, running 453 performances on Broadway. Allen added "Broadway actor and star" to his list of credentials. And he was becoming a good playwright: The play is a huge step ahead of *Don't Drink the Water*. But that would be faint praise. *Play It Again, Sam*, despite Allen's stated indifference to it, is a very good play. He knows his character (himself) well, and, unlike *Don't Drink the Water*, which is saturated with his contempt for the individuals and the shallow Jewish milieu, here, of course, he loves him. Allen is once again the sex-starved writer, nervous, shy, insecure, a movie critic and nerd who fantasizes that Humphrey Bogart appears in his life to counsel him on how to win a woman and to become a man of courage and honor. The play begins with the voice of Bogart from a scene in *The Maltese Falcon*.

Allan Felix has just been divorced by his wife and is trying to put his life together again with the help of his best friends, Dick Christie (Tony Roberts), a slick Wall Street executive, and his neurotic wife, Linda (Diane Keaton). They try to set him up with a girl, and in one of the funniest scenes veering on slapstick Allen had ever done to that point, he completely screws up the opportunity and drives the befuddled girl away. (The scene is expanded and enhanced in the film version.) Linda, who shares many of his anxieties and fears, deeply identifies with him and is drawn to him, especially while Dick is away on business. Allan invites Linda over in the evening and is at a loss as to whether he should try to seduce her, and if so, how to do it. Bogart materializes at key moments, advising him on the moves he should make.

*Play It Again, Sam* is charming and adroit and holds up well. Allen's dialogue is continuously fresh and funny: He sidles up to a cute girl at the museum looking at a Franz Kline painting and tries to engage her in conversation.

**ALLAN:** What does it say to you?

**GIRL:** It restates the negativeness of the universe. The hideous, lonely emptiness of existence—nothingness—the predicament of man, forced to live in a barren, Godless eternity, like a tiny flame flickering in an immense void—with nothing but waste, horror and degradation—forming a useless, bleak straitjacket in a black, absurd cosmos.

**ALLAN:** What are you doing Saturday night?

**GIRL:** Committing suicide.

**ALLAN:** What about Friday night?

Beneath the wisecracks, the one-liners, the hilarity, there is emotional resonance in the sense of utter frustration and unrequited lust that Allen depicts so well, tapping into an experience he went through at an earlier time in his life. Has anyone in film or the theater written about heterosexual lust and yearning so palpably, so desperately as Allen has? Has any male character practically frothed at the mouth (okay, "dribbled," as Allen puts it) over women in public like this?

Allen may have contempt for his comic gift, but it is utterly unique.

During the rehearsals for *Play It Again, Sam*, "I fell for Allan [Allan Felix, Woody's character in the play] as scripted, but for Woody as well," Keaton wrote in her memoir, *Then Again*. "How could I not? I was in love with him before I knew him. . . . Our entire family used to gather around the TV set and watch him on Johnny Carson. . . . He was even better-looking in real life. He had a great body, and he was physically very graceful.

"As in the play, we became friends. I was a good audience. I laughed in between the jokes. I think he liked that, even though he would always remind me I wouldn't know a joke if it hit me in the face."

Aspects of their relationship sound right out of *Annie Hall*, including Keaton's arriving late to the Baronet Theater to see *The Sorrow and the Pity*, and Keaton's self-derision, partly due to her bulimia: "I used to think of myself as an attractive victim, a sort of sweet, misunderstood casualty. No one mistook me for the fat woman in the freak show. But I was. And I got away with it. I became a master, as well as a fraud.

"On the surface," she wrote, "all was going well. Woody slowly began to see me as something more than a gal pal. Our relationship wasn't off and on, but it wasn't exactly committed either. Even then Woody was the most disciplined, hardworking, dedicated, organized, and—ironically—resilient person I'd ever met. On a daily basis, he practiced his clarinet, appeared in the play, read all the works of Tolstoy, and wrote new jokes. . . . Woody does a lot of let's just say unusual things onstage, things you wouldn't think a person of his stature would do. Last night in the middle of a scene he suddenly started impersonating James Earl Jones in *The Great White Hope*. I tried not to laugh but it was impossible."

Remember how Woody wanted Annie to keep her apartment while living with him? "I moved a few things into his new penthouse apartment," she relates, "but I kept my studio on 82nd." In fact, the character

of Annie Hall is all over Keaton's memoir. In the initial days of their relationship, Keaton wrote her mother on February 18, 1969: "I think I had a
date with him [Woody]. We went to Frankie and Johnnie's famous steak-
house. Everything was going well until I scraped my fork against the plate
and made a normal, I stress normal, cutting noise. It must have driven
him nuts, 'cause he yelped out loud. I couldn't figure out how to cut my
steak without making the same mistake, so I stopped eating and started
talking about women and the arts, like I know anything about women
and the arts. What an idiot. The whole thing was humiliating. I doubt we'll
be having dinner together anytime soon."

Their self-deprecation seemed to be the glue that held them together.
While filming *Love and Death*, Woody wrote to Keaton that she was his
"endearing oaf"; he was her "White Thing." She suffered from bulimia; he
was an alarmist. "Although his body was fit and well proportioned," she
recalled, "he treated it like it was a strange assortment of disembodied
appendages. His feet never touched the ground. He was constantly in the
care of one doctor or another. We were quite a couple, one more hidden
than the other. We both wore hats in public, and he always held my hand
or, rather, gripped it without letting go. People were to be avoided. I had
him pegged as a cross between a 'White Thing' and a cockroach you
couldn't kill. We shared a love of torturing each other with our failures.
He could sling out the insults, but so could I. We thrived on demeaning
each other. His insights into my character were dead on and—duh!—
hilarious. This bond remains the core of our friendship and, for me, love."

Anticipating the scenes he would create about her Chippewa Falls family in *Annie Hall*, he wrote her, "I have decided to let your family make me
rich! It turns out they are wonderful material for a film. A quite serious
one. . . ."

The relationship would last three years (the friendship endures until
today). Woody seemed to like Diane as much for her limitations as for her
virtues. Allen was perhaps thinking of her, not only as Annie the jittery,
inarticulate dingbat (which is how Keaton characterized her in 2014), but
as she appeared as Mary in *Manhattan*. He wrote a story, "Retribution,"
in the 1970s for the *Kenyon Review* about falling in love with Connie Chasen,
a shiksa goddess: "Tall, blond, high-cheek-boned, an actress, a scholar, a
charmer, irrevocably alienated, with a hostile and perceptive wit only challenged in its power to attract by the lewd, humid eroticism her every

curve suggested. . . . That she would settle on me, Harold Cohen, scrawny, long-nosed, twenty-four-year-old, budding dramatist and whiner, was a *non-sequitur* on a par with octuplets." Allen's fascination with breaking taboos is also manifest in the story: His character Harold develops a passionate obsession with Connie's fifty-five-year-old mother, an obsession that supersedes his lust for Connie herself. Connie is only able to rekindle her lust for Harold when he marries her mother and symbolically becomes her father.

Allen's dissatisfaction with Keaton's limitations—he once said that when he met her, her mind was completely blank; another time he called her "a real hayseed, the kind who would chew eight sticks of gum at a time"—led her, at Allen's urging, just as in *Annie Hall,* into psychotherapy, serious reading, studying photography, and ultimately to moving beyond him. Their relationship was winding down by the time *Play It Again, Sam* ended its Broadway run in March 1970. Keaton moved on to Warren Beatty and Al Pacino (whom she had known before meeting Woody). The course of the relationship is fully delineated in *Annie Hall,* including the reasons for the breakup: Annie uses the word "neat" too often. She tells Alvy, "You don't think I'm smart enough." He insists she keep her own apartment, and she says, "You don't want to live with me." She starts dating her teacher, and Alvy confronts her about it. "You're the one who never wanted to make a real commitment," she reminds him. In a split-screen scene in which we see Alvy and Annie simultaneously talking to their therapists, Alvy whines to his that he's paying for Annie's therapy "and I'm the one getting screwed." Annie tells her therapist: "I'm entitled to my feelings." When they are splitting up, Annie says, "I feel a great weight is off my back." The LA / New York conflict acts as a trigger for the final breakup. But Annie tells Woody/Alvy the underlying problem: "You're incapable of enjoying life. . . . You're an island unto yourself." How could this not be Woody?

And so it ended, perhaps as it did in life.

It would seem that that there were actually few sexual sparks between Allen and Keaton—at least, according to Louise Lasser, though her opinion may be that of an aggrieved ex-wife. Lasser did seem to be the wild crazy woman that Allen was most attracted to, the "Harriet Harmon" nutcase he celebrates in *Husbands and Wives,* and as Dorrie (Charlotte Rampling) in *Stardust Memories,* both women, Allen tells us, winding up in psycho wards. As Lasser said, "There's disturbed disturbed, and there's cheerfully disturbed. I was always disturbed disturbed, whereas Keaton was cheerfully disturbed for him." Keaton—both as Annie Hall and in life—is a sweet shiksa neurotic, not in any way certifiable, a dingbat enough for Allen to both feel superior to and identify with, and to exert control over. "Diane was a great friend of Woody's," Lasser said, "but he was not greatly attracted to her in a sexual sense. He'd feel for her, and it wasn't as if he didn't do stuff with her, but it wasn't like with me. He has a great sexual appetite, and she had one too, but for some reason he didn't have it for her." That may be one reason Keaton and Allen have managed to remain friends over the years.

Two years later, in 1971, *Play It Again, Sam* was made into a movie with Allen and Keaton—but not with Allen as director. It was the only time he let that happen. Peter Bart, the former editor of *Variety*, was vice president in charge of production at Paramount Studios in 1971. "I had always liked *Play It Again, Sam*," he told me. "This was the only time I interacted professionally with Woody. *Play It Again, Sam* had been stalled at 20th Century Fox, where it was supposed to be produced as a film. Meanwhile I had developed a very good script, *Emperor of the North Pole*, and I couldn't put it together the right way with the people I'd hoped would get interested in it. I thought that Fox had really missed an opportunity with *Sam*; it was a wonderful property. So I talked with David Brown, who was at Fox, and he helped me engineer this. Bob Evans and I had both gotten very fond of a director named Herbert Ross. I was youthful at the time. I thought that Woody was making pictures for a relatively small audience, and Herb Ross was making them for a much wider audience. So I thought if you married the sensibilities of Herb Ross and Woody Allen, you might end up with a picture that would reach a much broader audience. Which we did. So it was a pretty good strategy, but not one that Woody loved. So what happened was that because of my relationship with David, we worked out something that was unusual in Hollywood: We basically traded projects. I gave him *Emperor* and he gave me *Sam*. No money; it was just a trade.

"Woody was thrilled that it was going to go to Paramount and that [they] wanted to make it. Then he found out that I wanted Herb Ross to direct it and not him, and of course that was the end of my relationship with Woody Allen. He never deigned to speak to me again. Which was all right, because we ended up with this terrific movie. I had done the unthinkable: I had made a Woody Allen picture without Woody Allen. He wanted control, and he was outraged he wasn't director."

In 1968 Allen had purchased an eleven-room top-floor duplex in a building on Fifth Avenue and Seventy-ninth Street overlooking Central Park, and began an extensive renovation. He bought a Rolls-Royce and hired a driver for it. In his unsympathetic biography, John Baxter reads many motives into what he construes as Allen's transformation from the image of a "modern wised-up Manhattanite," "snappy, confident, well-dressed, urbane," into what he terms "New York's most famous recluse," and accuses Allen of letting him down by not being the neurotic loser in life that he pretended to be on-screen:

> He calculatedly embarked on a long-term strategy to build a new persona, and with it a more marketable character . . . in truth, Allen wanted both fame and obscurity. . . . In an audacious act of self-abnegation, he abandoned the [reality of ] the well-heeled, intellectual comedy writer successful with women. Replacing it was the image of a nebbish. . . . On screen, "Woody" was a hang-dog, whining victim, pill-popping, indecisive, impotent, unattractive, physically and socially maladroit, occupying himself with the most trivial of tasks.

The "transformation" that Baxter perceives is hard to square with the fact that Allen's image has always been composed of these multiple, complex, contradictory images: The boastful confident lover is really an inept loser; the sad-sack romantic manfully captures the girl in the end. Artifice is the prerogative, indeed a virtue and obligation of the artist. What appears to be calculated and somewhat nefarious in Baxter's view can also be seen as simply the multiple layers of the human condition: neither angel nor saint.

Instead of the overidentification with the invented Allen persona that has bedeviled some of his disillusioned fans, in Baxter we have the opposite disillusionment: that the artist is nothing like his persona. He is foisting a trick on us. But implicit in this view is that the scope of the artistic achievement, the incredible hard work that has gone into a lifetime of achievement, is not important. What is important is that we are being deceived. What we see is not the *real* Woody.

What is also resented here is both Allen's enormous success and the self-protectiveness of the artist, Allen's shielding himself from rapacious public view. There is no question that Allen is an inordinately shy man. That shyness has accompanied him throughout his life, as has a preternatural set of fears and phobias. According to this view, Allen has secretly overcome his shyness and is foisting a false image upon his unsuspecting public. What a colossal nerve. The question is: Why must an artist be exactly like the fictional characters he created? Baxter goes on to bolster his view by citing Mia Farrow's memoir, in which she writes, "Woody the actor had long ago invented his screen persona: a loveable *nebbish*, endlessly and hilariously whining and quacking, questioning moral and philosophical issues great and small. He was a guy with his heart and his conscience on his sleeve, whose talk was peppered with quotes of Kierkegaard and Kant; an insightful and unthreatening mascot of the intelligentsia. A guy who is nothing like the real Woody Allen."

But Allen has never denied he is not a nebbish; in fact he practically shouts it. He told *Esquire* in 1987: "I've never been the nebbish. . . . It's an appellation for the unimaginative to hang on me. . . . I really wasn't a scared and lonely child at all. I played at all sorts of games and was good at quite a lot of them. I wasn't poor or hungry or neglected. We were a well-fed middle-class family. We wore good clothes and lived in a comfortable house. . . .

"People always associated me with Greenwich Village and sweaters with holes in them and things like that. And I've never been that kind of person. Never. I never lived in the Village. I always lived on the Upper East Side of Manhattan. I always ate at good restaurants." Allen took the same stance with Sam Tanenhaus in 2005: "People always have the mistaken impression that I was an intellectual when in fact I'm not. I first started to read because the women that I liked when I was a teenager were always culture vultures and bluestockings. And I tried my best, and they had no time for me. I read so I could hold my own in conversations with them and not get written off." He told Natalie Gittelson in 1979: "I'm not holed up in my apartment every night poring over Russian literature and certain Danish philosophers. I'm really hardly a recluse. . . . I do go out all the time—to movies, to shop, to walk around in the street, to those parties I think I'll enjoy, to Elaine's [which closed in 2012]." His neuroses may persist, but there is a bedrock reality that he clings to, the same reality that anchors his relentless work ethic, that makes him eat early, watch a movie or a football game, and go to sleep. He is frenetic on film and stage and seemingly calm, self-disciplined, and rational in person.

*Play It Again, Sam* is itself a clear refutation of Baxter's theory, in that the Woody character is exactly the same lovable schlemiel, the same lecherous loser with women, that audiences had seen in his stand-up routines since the late fifties. There is no transformation whatsoever.

Allen traveled with Diane Keaton to the New Orleans Jazz and Heritage Festival in 1971 and regarded the trip as one of the high points of his life. He soon began what would become an enormously life-enhancing ritual: his Monday-night gigs leading the New Orleans Funeral and Ragtime Orchestra. There is probably not a single Monday night since 1974 that Allen has not performed except when he was on tour with the band or filming abroad. Nothing has kept him from it, not even the Academy Awards when he was the winner.

Allen's passionate attachment to New Orleans, Dixieland, and traditional jazz is often detached from portraits of him. Yet he cannot be fully understood without recognizing his passion for the music. That passion is a key to the joyous side of Allen lurking beneath his morose, somber exterior, the side that bursts forth in so many of his films. You can track it all the way back to his childhood, when he and Jerry, Elliott, and Jack read Mezz Mezzrow's *Really the Blues* and haunted the Stuyvesant Casino, Central Plaza, and Child's Paramount, the Dixieland hangouts of the time, to watch the great figures of Dixieland—even meeting Sidney Bechet in person when he visited New York. For forty-five years he has put aside every single Monday night—first at Michael's Pub and now at the Carlyle Hotel—to play clarinet with his band. The music, as both the late Jerry Wexler of Atlantic Records and the composer Johnny Mandel mentioned to me, is still the most joyous in the world, and Allen worships its great practitioners: Sidney Bechet, George Lewis—"Burgundy Street Blues" is perhaps his favorite record—Bunk Johnson, Johnny Dodds, Albert Burbank, Kid Thomas, Muggsy Spanier, Turk Murphy—it all fills him with joy. The 1998 Barbara Kopple documentary, *Wild Man Blues*, tracks Allen's trip with banjoist Eddy Davis and the band to Europe for a tour.

Allen's concentration, scarcely glancing up from playing, both in the film and at the Carlyle, is solely on the music. He has said that playing the music is for him like "bathing in honey." When he starts to play, it's almost as if he throws off all his clothes and stands naked, like *Aahhh!* He is totally exposed.

He told the *Village Voice* in 2010: "To be as bad as I am, you do have to practice every day. I'm a strict hobby musician. I don't have a particularly good ear for music. I'm a very poor musician, like a Sunday tennis player. . . . I certainly like modern jazz as well, but my favorite kind is New Orleans jazz. Something about the primitive quality, the simplicity of it, the directness. It is the one style of jazz that stays with me the most. Jazz has a mythological feeling to it—time has done that. And early jazz especially, since it was the birth of the art form. I just love it." "The more primitive the better for me," he elaborated to John Lahr. "The enjoyment is more direct. The feeling is completely uncomplicated by any kind of cerebration. . . . Sometimes it's three chords. The guys who play it, who can really do it, make it so beautiful that it's astonishing."

Allen's comedy style—its untrammeled, unalloyed joyousness—has an emotional affinity with the music. Like Dixieland, it is blunt, heartfelt, and spontaneous. The music forms the backdrop of scores of his films, among them *Bananas, Zelig, The Purple Rose of Cairo, Alice, Sleeper, Bullets over Broadway*, and *Sweet and Lowdown*. Allen uses the great original artists' recordings of James P. Johnson ("Charleston"), Bix Beiderbecke ("Singin' the Blues"), Jelly Roll Morton ("Wolverine Blues"), Django Reinhardt, the contemporary Preservation Hall Jazz Band (*Sleeper*), as well as his own band and the great contemporary pianist Dick Hyman, who frequently composes and arranges the scores for Allen's films. "Woody is a very musical fellow, really a very knowledgeable musician," says Hyman. "He consciously, deliberately uses jazz, and understands how it works with the kinds of scenarios he writes." It says something about Allen's tenacity and integrity, his refusal to follow anyone's vision but his own, that he persists in playing and championing this music in his films and in his life very much against the fashions of the time (just as he champions the Gershwins and Cole Porter, the Great American Songbook). As he said, "I don't think New Orleans means much to anybody, but to a small few of us, it's great."

Cynthia Sayer was a founding member of Allen's current jazz band.

She has performed with him on and off for more than twenty-five years as a banjoist, pianist, and vocalist, and appears in *Wild Man Blues.*

"I was advised before the first time I met him to be assertively friendly," Sayer related. "They said you can't wait for him to turn around and say hello. Because you might sit there for five years without him ever saying anything. So I did, and he was like 'Oh, hi.' He's had moments of being truly friendly and most of the time he's distant from everybody. But I also felt supported in his band."

Allen's focus on early jazz has come to be synonymous with the New Orleans style based on the music of Bunk Johnson and George Lewis. According to Sayer, this style has a special ensemble overlap than contributes to a rawer sound than the more familiar music and style of clarinetists like Benny Goodman. "Woody was yearning to play this George Lewis–Bunk Johnson style of music when I met him," she told me. "This is what he loves. He is extremely knowledgeable about this genre, and his own playing pays direct homage to George Lewis's distinctive clarinet sound and style. Woody's connection to this music is real, heartfelt and profound, and his love for it comes through every time you hear his clarinet wail. By putting it in his films and performing it with his band, he helps to keep it out there and alive.

"This music has a rich, uplifting feel to it," Sayer continued, "a kind of inherent spirituality. And it's both raw and sweet. To me it feels like joyousness mixed with a big splash of wildness when everything clicks musically, like riding on the crest of a wave and being carried right along in the grip of this powerful, natural movement. I felt it most often when we were on tour. The heightened energy of an excited audience in a major concert hall really helps the band—including Woody—sizzle.

"In *Wild Man Blues,* the film of our band's first European tour, you can see Woody being very open and acknowledging of the audience, but that's not his usual way. Normally he just walks across the stage, sits down, calls a tune to the band, and starts playing, without even a glance at the audience. It's clearly a choice he's making to be there as a musician and for the music, not as Woody Allen the movie star. He jumps in and plays with such emotional abandon and openness that the audience can't help but be swept up.

"On our tour we'd arrive at major concert halls in Europe with crowds waiting outside, chanting his name in the local accent, 'Woo-dee, Woo-dee.' You could hear their excitement swell with anticipation and then their deflated sigh as we, the band without Woody himself, filed out and into the stage door. But all that star-struck mania disappeared once everyone was in their seats and Woody came onstage and started to play. You could feel the audience's energy shift and evolve into something else entirely as they became engrossed in having a real musical experience despite whatever preconceptions they may have had before the show."

In John Lahr's transcendent profile of Allen in *The New Yorker* in 1996, he wrote of Allen practicing in the early morning hours at home, playing along with a Bunk Johnson record. "In music, in film—in fact in everything he does—Allen has created a fantasy world so potent that some of his most far-fetched dreams have come true. Willie Mays has flied out to him in a softball game at Dodger Stadium; he has played clarinet marching in New Orleans parades and at Preservation Hall; he has supped with Groucho and with S. J. Perelman. . . . he has certainly seized life with passion and with gratitude. 'As you watch comedians with joy, or watch films with joy, it becomes metabolized and you pay it out,' he says. 'You're eating this food endlessly, endlessly. Then you look up and it's part of you.' There is something poignant in Allen's avidity for delight. 'If I were to close my eyes and imagine Woody,' Diane Keaton says, 'something I would keep with me is just the image of him watching *Cries and Whispers* . . . being swept away. I've seen it on his face. I've seen it. It's moved me. It makes me love him.'"

It was while working on *Sleeper* that one of Allen's dreams would be fulfilled. He traveled to Preservation Hall, the legendary, authentic home of New Orleans jazz, to create the soundtrack for the film with the members of the Preservation Hall Jazz Band. The ancient hall is forty-five feet long and half as wide, with worn wooden floors. Several rows of benches are situated three feet away from the band, and the balance of the crowd stands up in back.

Allen played clarinet with the band. By now most of the famous players with Preservation Hall have passed away, but then some of the great musicians were still alive, vital in their seventies and eighties: trombone player Jim Robinson, banjoist Emanuel Sayles, pianist Sing Miller, bassist Chester Zardis, drummer Cie Frazier, and the leader of the band, trumpet player Percy Humphrey. Allen entered the hall and sat down beside Humphrey, and they sprang into "Little Liza Jane." Percy said later of Allen, "He has a wonderful ear. He did what you should do when you sit with another man's band. He played along with what we played. He didn't try to be a celebrity."

In what was surely the capper for Allen, at the last session, Jim Robinson stood over Allen and asked him, "Did anyone ever tell you you sound like my old friend George Lewis? What's your name again?"

"Woody."

"Willard? You're real good, Willard."

In 1971 Allen starred in, wrote, and directed a TV drama, *Men in Crisis: The Harvey Wallinger Story,* for WNET, the Public Broadcasting System affiliate in New York City. Written during the peak of Richard Nixon's malevolent years, it was a satire about the relationship between Nixon and Henry Kissinger (Harvey Wallinger). It was unusually political for him. Wallinger is portrayed as a lawyer who originally served as an errand boy to Nixon, became prominent in his administration, and is known as a playboy. One of his girlfriends, Sister Mary Elizabeth Smith, says that Wallinger "is an unbelievable swinger, a freak." Allen wrote, "Attorney John Mitchell has many ideas for strengthening the country's law enforcement methods and is hampered only by lack of funds and the Constitution." PBS was worried about the character of Sister Mary; a picture of Hubert Humphrey making a suggestive gesture with his finger; and Wallinger boasting that Pat Nixon would invite him over when Nixon was traveling. Allen refused to remove these jokes. In addition, CREEP (the Campaign to Re-Elect the President) learned of the production and had obtained a copy of the script. Nixon, paranoid about all media including PBS, had earlier sent word through Clay Whitehead, of the White House Telecommunications Policy office, that if criticism of Nixon continued, PBS funding cuts might be initiated. The program was screened for the PBS legal department, and its lawyers suggested only that a real news clip with Hubert Humphrey be deleted. In spite of the mild recommendation, WNET president Ethan Hitchcock, after viewing the program, issued a memo stating that "under no account must the [program] be shown." Allen would later state that the program was "in enormously bad taste . . . [but] it was hard to do anything about the administration that wouldn't be in bad taste." PBS would contend that the program was canceled because presidential candidates were mentioned who could have demanded equal time. No one believed that explanation.

It was during this period that Allen ended his stand-up work and writing for television. He abandoned talk, game, and variety shows; his disgust with his formulaic TV work (and with TV in general) would constitute an important theme in both *Annie Hall* and *Manhattan*.

Allen also ceased working on other people's films. Though the old studio film system was long gone, Allen would soon manage to re-create his own exclusive studio film system—an even better one—with roughly the same setup that screenwriters enjoyed in the 1930s and 1940s, at United Artists.

After Allen's success with *Take the Money and Run*, Jack Rollins and Charles Joffe negotiated a three-year contract for him at UA that would give him $350,000 for writing, directing, and acting, $150,000 to Rollins and Joffe as producers and a $2 million budget for each film. David Picker, head of production, gave Woody creative freedom to write and direct a film of his choosing. UA would give Allen the wherewithal to make pictures without having to scramble for funds. And he would avoid the most negative aspect of that obsolete system: the power of the studio heads to dictate what a writer created. He inherited only the best part, the kind of powerful support that the old-time studio heads provided when they liked someone—someone, however, they could dictate to. Allen found patrons who left him alone yet provided the same support.

United Artists was the most prestigious independent movie studio in the United States in the early seventies. Founded in 1919 by four of the most famous stars in Hollywood—Mary Pickford, Douglas Fairbanks, Charles Chaplin, and D. W. Griffith, the company was sold by its surviving owners, Chaplin and Pickford, to Arthur Krim and Robert Benjamin in 1951. "Arthur Krim and Robert Benjamin," Steven Bach, former senior vice president of United Artists, wrote, "were not furriers, junk dealers or glove salesmen. They were lawyers, smart and respected ones, and they knew something about the movie business." The company thrived under their direction, with such quality films as *Some Like It Hot*, *Marty*, *The African Queen*, *The Apartment*, *Elmer Gantry*, *West Side Story*, and *High Noon*.

Based in New York City, UA was the only film company that did not have a physical studio. It functioned as a financing and distribution company, leasing its features from producers for seven years. Located far from Hollywood, it lacked some of Hollywood's baser values and commercial standards. By 1970 Krim was chairman of a company that included Eric Pleskow; Bob Benjamin; William Bernstein, senior vice president for business affairs; and Mike Medavoy, senior vice president of production, who took over UA with Krim in 1951. These were cultured and literate men not governed solely by mercenary motives. An American entertainment lawyer, Krim was the former chairman of Eagle-Lion Films, the former finance chairman for the Democratic Party, and an adviser to presidents Lyndon Johnson and John F. Kennedy on issues involving arms control, civil rights, and the Middle East. Pleskow and his family in Vienna fled the Nazis in 1938 and emigrated to the United States. He served in the army and after the war returned to Austria and conducted interrogations during denazifications. He began working for United Artists in 1951 and would become its president in 1973. United Artists won Best Picture Academy Awards three years in a row, for *One Flew Over the Cuckoo's Nest* in 1976; *Rocky* in 1977; and *Annie Hall*.

It was the perfect place for Woody Allen. And Arthur Krim would become one of his most supportive mentors. But not at first. Woody's first try, *The Jazz Baby,* was met with bewilderment by the UA staff, and Allen promptly withdrew it. Then he (with his collaborator Mickey Rose) came up with *El Weirdo*, which would eventually be retitled *Bananas*. Woody played Fielding Mellish, the sex-starved, schnook persona he had cultivated so carefully, who falls in love with Nancy (Louise Lasser), a pretty Marxist activist who initially rejects him because he is not radical or manly enough for her. To prove himself to her and win her love, he flies to San Marcos, a banana republic, where he becomes the pawn in a plan by the military dictator Vargas (Carlos Montalban) to kill Fielding and pin his murder on the socialist rebels as a way of currying support from the United States. Fielding escapes, joins the rebels, and helps their leader overthrow Vargas. He becomes president and returns to New York wearing a hapless red beard as a disguise and seeks to promote foreign trade, offering locusts at popular prices. Nancy is taken with his assumed alter ego, but when he reveals his true identity to her, she says, "I knew that something was missing." He is arrested and pardoned. The movie concludes with the couple's wedding night, which is televised with

Howard Cosell (who had earlier given a play-by-play account for TV of Vargas's assassination) now supplying a play-by-play commentary on Fielding and Nancy's sexual performance in bed. As with almost all of Allen's films, the happy couple's reunion seems like a compromise. It is not all that happy, especially on Nancy's part. She does not seem very impressed with Fielding's sexuality. "Something is missing," she says.

I met with Eric Pleskow in 2014, the year of his ninetieth birthday. He told me that Arthur Krim was bewildered by the movie. "When we looked at *Bananas*, Arthur was perplexed. He was troubled by its irreverence about religion, about the United Jewish Appeal," Pleskow said. "It was a generational thing. And he was image conscious. He said, 'We can't release this picture.' I said of course we would release it. He just didn't understand it at that point; he didn't get it. But he got it later, a hundred percent. I'm not saying this to criticize Arthur. I understand. Woody admired Arthur very much. Because Krim was a special person. He also arranged the party in Madison Square Garden for JFK with Marilyn Monroe: 'Happy Birthday, Mister President.' That was Arthur Krim. He was close to LBJ and, I think, even closer to Kennedy.

"So at the beginning," Pleskow continued, "Woody had Jack Rollins and Charlie Joffe [in his corner]. Not Arthur Krim. And he had David Picker, who brought him to us. The credit goes to David. David left the company and did his own thing. I took it over and took it further. And Arthur was out of it the first few films. I think Arthur did recognize Woody's qualities from the first and was probably very glad to have social contact with this great star. I think Woody perhaps had a complex because of his lack of size. There's also a certain affectation about him too. If you didn't want to be recognized, which he claimed, then you didn't wear a [fisherman's] cap like that. You don't walk down Madison Avenue with that. You can't do that. But I wasn't going to tell him how to live.

"Woody was a very talented man, basically a very modest human being, very nice to work with. Of course I didn't interfere with him. I very often felt like a Medici, his patron. I let him make one of his films, *September*, twice. There's nobody else in the industry who would do that. We weren't going to destroy our relationship with him over one film. It wasn't me alone who felt that way. He was able to get the most expensive talent for comparably modest fees to work for him. And everybody soon wanted to work for him. Whether he had a film that was extraordinarily success-ful or not, they were there for him if he wanted them.

"In those early days," Pleskow continued, "south of Forty-second Street started Mexico for him; north of Ninety-sixth Street was Canada. He never left Manhattan. There was no way I could have gotten him to go somewhere else. I didn't try. Time stands still for Woody. The way we operated, I and Arthur would get a script from him, and we would be able to read it overnight. It was picked up the next day. Which was fine. What was I going to tell him? There's very little that I knew that he wouldn't know. I say this modestly: I think he was fortunate to be working with us. We recognized who he was. I couldn't have dealt with everybody like that. I would have been out of business. I took chances with him. I'm glad we did; I have no regrets."

The deeper relationship for Woody was the one that gradually devel-oped between him and Arthur Krim. Woody had found another father figure—Krim had no children of his own, and seemed to regard Woody as a long-lost son—who was as devoted to him as Jack Rollins was. For both Rollins and Krim, it turned out to be a very good investment. In the long run Woody brought them both a great return—financially, prestige-wise, emotionally—on their initial investment and support of him.

Thanks to Krim and Pleskow, Woody's deal was that he could make any film he wanted to; it was an unbelievable blank check with no strings whatsoever. He had carte blanche; he was family. "I have absolute con-trol," Woody told *Cinema* magazine. "They don't have approval of the script. They don't have casting approval; they have absolutely nothing." On another occasion he elaborated: "I always try and give them the cour-tesy of listening and talking with them. It never comes to anything. They always ask for permission just to come to the set." That cold, curt, arro-gant way of putting it was characteristic of Allen; this was the reality, he was not exaggerating, and he would have had it no other way. Sentimen-tality was not his style, nor was it needed: He knew he could deliver on the basis of his talent, and he did. He'd been burned with his first films, when he had absolutely no control over their development, and he wasn't going to let it happen again. And he never has. He would walk away in-stead.

What endeared him to these men was not only his talent but also his integrity. He always kept his word to them, and he was not disdainful of their commercial concerns. And there was another, perhaps unspoken factor. Woody was the first to put his Jewishness on-screen so forthrightly. Jewish Hollywood, with its many refugees from Hitler—from Billy Wilder to Eric Pleskow to Otto Preminger and hundreds more—with its years of concealing the identity of its Jewish stars, embraced him, the first Jewish star of the seventies, from the start. Allen was, indeed, family, and not least to the cultivated Jewish figures who ran United Artists. It is not a stretch to connect Allen's emergence as forthright, cheeky Jew to the emergence of the state of Israel, born in 1948 and arising out of the ashes of the Holocaust into an unapologetic, proud, determined country.

Steven Bach confirmed Woody's version of events in his memoir, *Final Cut*. The deal "was unique in the business. Contractually his pictures could be made virtually without approvals. If they could be made below a specified budget figure. . . . Woody submitted a script to Arthur Krim . . . with a copy to Lehman Katz, UA's formidable one-man production and budget-estimating department, and if Krim liked the script and Katz vetted the budget at a figure Krim agreed to, that was it. There were no readers' reports, no committees, no creative meetings, no casting approvals (unless informal, from Krim), no dailies, nothing but Woody and his script and his budget and Arthur Krim's blessing."

A reason the agreement worked was that Woody's films always came in on budget, on schedule, and he kept his word about everything. And the budgets were relatively small. "Woody had an old-fashioned, deeply ingrained sense of honor about his commitments," Bach wrote. Woody was not required to seek approval but adhered to his own code of a gentleman's agreement. "As he explained to me later," Bach recalled, "'I wouldn't want the company to spend money on something it didn't believe in,' and he meant it in both commercial and thematic senses." Commenting on the relationship between Allen and Krim, Bach told Marion Meade, "Had there been no Arthur Krim and UA, Woody's structure could not have evolved any other place in the world."

Allen has never let his ambition cloud his need for artistic autonomy, and he is absolutely alone among the major directors in achieving his goals over a half century. Film artists have collapsed all around him in the course of fifty years; he is a sole survivor.

While Woody ascended the ladder, his quirks and phobias never left him. "We were in Puerto Rico doing *Bananas*," Howard Storm remembered. "Woody said, 'There's a mouse in one of my suitcases.' And he's like freaking out. So I got up, and it was a dead mouse. The suitcase was open and the dead mouse was lying there. So I got a piece of Kleenex and I grabbed the tail of the mouse and picked it up. When I walked toward him, Woody went nuts; he ran away from me. He's standing there, like waiting for me to take it out to the garbage. He didn't want to go near it. He said to me, 'Throw the suitcase out.' 'What? It's a good suitcase.' 'I'll buy another one.' So I took it out."

Stories about Woody's minor neuroses are legion. The film producer Vincent Giordano recalled for me that he was in an elevator with Allen in the 1980s: "When I was young I worked in the editing and production houses to pay my way through college and to get a real education in filmmaking. When I worked in editing, it was on the same floor as Woody Allen. I used to get on the elevator with him. Every time I got on, he would turn and face the back wall of the elevator. I felt badly for him because it looked like he was scared or something. The other thing is, he would wait for you to leave the elevator first before he would leave. One day I decided I was going to wait for him to leave first, and I held the door open for him. He panicked, waited, waited, then turned and bolted out the door."

Yet for every neurosis, there is a joke, a sketch, a movie that comes out of it. Remember the elevator that talks to Woody in his stand-up routine, intimidates him by "speaking better" than he does, and which "makes an anti-Semitic remark"? It can be found on the recent album *Woody Allen: The Stand-Up Years* (Razor & Tie, 2014).

The oddities and neuroses of artists are nothing new. I recall the late Julie Hayden, a writer at *The New Yorker* in the eighties, telling me of some of the writers and staffers, including herself, who would not use the elevator at the magazine (or anywhere else). In fact, the stairway was a problem for some of them too: There were those who descended the stairs backwards.

Frank Buxton remembers filming the hilarious deadpan trailer for *Bananas* with Woody. "It was just a straight out-and-out interview, totally unprepared, totally improv," Buxton told me. "We were very comfortable with each other. I think Woody trusted me, and of course I knew what to ask, the path to take, to get him to something that would be usable, to get the comedy out of it. Like *Zelig* and *Take the Money and Run*. That's kind of the essence of comedy. You do comedy seriously. You don't make jokes. That's what made the interview funny. It was dead serious."

In an excerpt from the trailer, Buxton asks Woody what the film is about:

> **WOODY:** It's about propagation of snails, and the emotional crises that snails go through, meeting, relating to, and breaking off with other snails.
>
> **BUXTON:** Is it in color or black and white?
>
> **WOODY:** The dream sequences are in color, and the picture itself is in a kind of brown tone which was because of something that happened to the camera. . . .
>
> **BUXTON:** Is it a silent film?
>
> **WOODY:** Yes, but not intentionally . . . when we screened the film the first time irate viewers ran off with the sound track and heaved it into the sea. . . .
>
> **BUXTON:** How long does the picture run?
>
> **WOODY:** With the intermission? Five minutes.
>
> **BUXTON:** How long is the intermission?
>
> **WOODY:** The intermission is about three and a half minutes. The second half is longer than the first half. Most people have more trouble sitting through the second half. . . .
>
> **BUXTON:** How do you think it's going to do at the box office?
>
> **WOODY:** Well, we have a very interesting plan. We're going to let the people in all over the country for nothing and then charge them to get out.

*Bananas* had the same surreal, rapid-fire comic intensity of *Take the Money and Run*. It reflected Allen's cynicism, skepticism, and rejection of all utopian social and political movements, and it was commonly thought he had Fidel Castro's Cuba in mind. Fielding and Virgil were interchangeable characters—it was all Woody all the time—and the audiences responded with delight to the barrage of wild humor. Paul D. Zimmerman wrote in *Newsweek* that the film was "the wildest piece of comic insanity since Harpo, Groucho and Chico climbed Mount Dumont. Allen shares their anarchic impulse to subordinate everything—plot, plausibility and people—to the imperatives of a good joke."

Woody had found his home at UA. They were family. Unlike his basement living arrangement in Flatbush with parents who understood nothing about his work—his father would comment with a kind of venom about Woody's films that he "never watched that crap," and his mother to the end of her days wished he'd change his mind about his career and become a pharmacist—there were unconditional love, support, and admiration from the sensitive and savvy Jewish men who led United Artists from triumph to triumph in the 1970s. Woody returned the favor. Among UA's greatest triumphs would be the films of Woody Allen.

## 6. "As Tough and Romantic as the City He Loved"

ALLEN HAD HIS first major box-office success with his next film, *Everything You Always Wanted to Know About Sex* (1972), which was one of the top-ten moneymakers of the year. The producer Jack Brodsky had purchased the screen rights to the bestselling book as a vehicle for Elliott Gould at Paramount, but Gould dropped out of the project. "My late ex-partner Jack Brodsky knew Dr. David Reuben, who wrote the book," Gould told me. "I was told there were two young new filmmakers who were interested in the project. One was Rob Reiner, and one was Woody. Woody was my favorite, so we gave it to him. It was Rollins, Joffe, Brodsky and Gould, but it was all Woody. I had known Woody a little. Louise Lasser was my first wife's [Barbra Streisand] understudy in *I Can Get It for You Wholesale* on Broadway. I remember Barbra and I were walking through Central

Park and seeing Woody and Louise there, being Woody and Louise. And I had seen Woody doing stand-up at the inauguration of Lyndon Johnson. So I recognized Woody as a brilliant satirist then, never even dreaming the great filmmaker he would become.

"Years later," Gould said, mentioning the downside of celebrity for Woody, "I was crossing Fifty-seventh Street right off of Fifth Avenue on the west side. And I saw Woody, but he didn't see me at first. And I put my arm under his in the middle of the street. And he sort of jumped. I think I scared him; that he was a little frightened. My gesture was affectionate but I guess it was a little aggressive, a little assumptive to put my arm under his. It was a little frightening to him. He was all the way out in the open."

*Everything You Always Wanted to Know About Sex* was based *very* loosely on the self-help pop manual by the sexologist David Reuben. Allen made the film without ever reading the book. He jettisoned all of it except for the highly commercial title and the silly questions that introduced each chapter. He used them for the titles of the seven separate sketches intended as film and media parodies.

It's an erratic film, with long unfunny sequences, but Allen elicits a wonderful performance from Gene Wilder in the sketch "What Is Sodomy?," as a doctor who falls in love with a sheep and ruins his life, and he does a funny subtitled parody of Antonioni films with Louise Lasser ("Why Do Some Women Have Trouble Reaching an Orgasm?"), in which he plays an aristocrat whose wife can be turned on only by having sex in public places. Allen plays his Marcello Mastroianni part well and rather suavely: It is the rare instance when you forget about Woody the schlemiel.

In "What Happens During Ejaculation?" Allen illustrates what occurs in the male body during orgasm. Allen portrays a neurotic sperm who is anxious about what will happen to him. "Do Aphrodisiacs Work?" is the best sketch: Allen plays a medieval court jester who tries to seduce the queen (Vanessa Redgrave). The sketch is shot like a classic costume picture, and it features Allen's standard nebbish persona and his wiseacre stand-up comic routines as he pursues the unattainable beauty and tries unsuccessfully to unlock her chastity belt, mechanical dolt that he is.

Two of the sketches have Jewish targets and are not only unfunny but rather repugnant. In one of them, "What Are Sex Perverts?" Allen vents his rage against Jewish Orthodoxy in the person of a giggling rabbi who gets off on the fantasy of being bound and whipped by a young gentile woman while his wife is forced to eat pork at his feet. During this period Woody targeted rabbis and Hasids frequently for humor, first in his stand-up routines (the rabbi who did the vodka ad; the rabbis who were topless—they didn't wear their skullcaps) and in his films. Framed as a parody of the TV game show *What's My Line?*, the sketch reminded me of Louise Lasser's comments about Allen's feelings of rage during the period of their marriage. The sketch is extreme and malevolent, but even worse: It's not funny. In another segment, "Are Transvestites Homosexuals?" Allen cast his favorite example of the fat, vulgar Jew, Lou Jacobi (*Don't Drink the Water*), in another broad burlesque as a businessman who secretly dresses in women's clothes. These sketches are bottom-of-the-barrel Allen, devoid of laughs, not effective as a media or film parody, really relevant only as a clue to the volatile inner conflicts Allen was still carrying from his childhood. This is where the phrase "self-hating Jew" usually gets injected, a rather loose appellation that can be applied to any treatments of Jewish characters that are not approved by the critics. Allen and Philip Roth are the most frequent targets of this criticism. Allen has defined his own condition differently. He admits to self-hate, but contends it has nothing to do with his Judaism: "The reasons lie in totally other areas—like the way I look when I get up in the morning. Or that I can never read a road map." If the pattern of Allen's depiction of Jews had persisted in the direction of the two sketches in *Everything You Always Wanted . . .* I might have conceded that the detractors have a point. But there is no other trace of this kind of malevolence in Allen's other forty-two films. There is certainly comedy and ambivalence about Jews in all of Allen's work, but, as the noted author Hillel Halkin has written, the main point is that the jokester has a deep identification with the group being joked about. Allen has expressed just how passionately he identifies with Israel and how central the Holocaust is to his deepest concerns. According to Morley T. Feinstein, "The single most important fact in Woody Allen's Jewish identity is the Holocaust. It's his philosophical touchstone, his constant reference point, his favorite metaphor." "Jokes aimed at God," Rabbi Joseph Telushkin wrote, "tend to be the gentlest in the Jewish tradition—ironic digs, rather than belly laughs. More than any other contemporary comedian, Woody Allen is the master of this genre."

Jews laughing at themselves occurred in the work of Sholem Aleichem and are an honorable tradition in Yiddish literature as well as American Jewish literature, from Bruce Jay Friedman's *Stern*, Stanley Elkin's *Criers & Kibitzers, Kibitzers & Criers*, and the work of Isaac Bashevis Singer, Stephen Dixon, and Philip Roth to Wallace Markfield's *To an Early Grave* (the source of the film, *Bye Bye Braverman*), and Daniel Fuchs's *Williamsburg Trilogy*. Freud wrote in *Wit and Its Relation to the Unconscious* that "a number of the most excellent jokes . . . have sprung into existence from the soil of Jewish national life. . . . I do not know whether one often finds a people that makes merry so unreservedly over its own shortcomings." "Jewish humor," Sarah Blacher Cohen has written, "is not only based on the masochistic characteristics of the Jews expressed in their self-critical jokes. It has also been a principal source of salvation. By laughing at their dire circumstances, Jews have been able to liberate themselves from them. Their humor has been a balance to counter external adversity and internal sadness."

*Everything You Always Wanted to Know About Sex* was a hit with audiences but not with critics. "This is one of those rare films that is funnier to write about than to watch," Paul D. Zimmerman wrote in *Newsweek*. "In the end, the movie fails because it cannot survive the leap from pen to screen." *Everything* scored a domestic gross of $18 million (estimated gross today $86.9 million), making it Allen's eleventh-highest-grossing film.

In *Sleeper*, which Allen cowrote with Marshall Brickman in 1973, Allen successfully executed a comic science fiction film. Miles Monroe (Allen) is a former clarinet player and the Jewish owner of the Happy Carrot Health Food Store in Greenwich Village, who has an unsuccessful operation and is wrapped in aluminum foil by the doctors and frozen. He awakens to find himself transplanted from 1973 into the dystopic future of 2173. The totalitarian state views him as a foreign, dangerous force who threatens to contaminate the population. Monroe/Woody typically finds solace "in the two things that come once in life—sex and death." He has been reprogrammed into a new identity by the state and needs to be deprogrammed by the rebellion. He disguises himself as a robot to hide from the state police and begins working for Luna (Keaton), a socialite poet. Erno the muscleman and Luna try to accomplish this by re-creating a scene from Miles's childhood. A seder is enacted, and they play Miles's parents, who speak with a Yiddish dialect. It doesn't quite work, for Miles is transformed not into his previous self but, in a brilliant tour de force that stands out as a highlight of the film, he turns into Blanche DuBois, Southern accent and all, and Keaton turns into Stanley Kowalski in a deliriously funny take on *A Streetcar Named Desire*. Earlier, in another cross-dressing scene, Allen takes part in a Miss America contest as Miss Montana.

*Sleeper* opened at Radio City Music Hall on December 18, 1973, and was a great commercial and critical success. The film ranks ninth economically among all of Allen's films, grossing $18,344,729. Allen really arrived as a movie star/director with the movie, and shortly after its release United Artists extended his contract to seven years. He caught the attention of Vincent Canby, the *New York Times* film critic, who would become his most devoted, if not most talented, champion. An acolyte of Allen's, Penelope Gilliatt, in a *New Yorker* profile of Allen expressed adoration.

The two most important and gifted critics, the ones who really mattered to Allen, Pauline Kael and John Simon, now became more aware of and more respectful toward him. Kael wrote that Allen's last two films, *Bananas* and *Everything*, "had wild highs that suggested an erratic comic genius." She found *Sleeper* "the most stable and most sustained of his films. . . . It's a small classic." But she went on to write that it didn't "have the loose, manic highs" of the two previous films. "I had a wonderful time at *Sleeper*, and I laughed all the way through, but it wasn't exhilarating." She correctly observed that she could not "completely explain" the contradiction in her thinking. But that was typical Kael. She also conceded that Allen was "improving as a physical comedian and gaining infinitely greater skill as a director."

Simon was, for the first time, more unequivocal in his praise: *Sleeper* was Allen's best film to date. "Suffice it to say that in this movie Allen makes less of his sexual fears and social ineptitudes . . . the visual elements are more carefully worked out than in Allen's slapdash yesteryears."

Simon divined Allen's own intention of moving in the direction of a more coherent and sustained dramatic narrative: "Allen," he wrote, "is slowly getting away from a comedy based chiefly on one-liners and throw-away gags, and tending toward a more structured and disciplined dramatic whole. At the same time, he stresses visual comedy more than before, with mixed results. Nevertheless, the script by Allen and Marshall Brickman manages to be more often funny than not, and funny more often uproariously than mildly. Allen also composed and plays some of the jolly jazz score, and acts and directs with greater poise than ever. Above all, he adds to our cinematic repertoire political and cultural satire, almost as sorely needed as a change in our politics and culture themselves."

In a 1973 interview with writer Stephen Banker, Allen spoke, as he has often done, about the inexplicable nature of talent and how it was linked to instinct, chance, and luck. He was at a loss to explain his gift for comedy: "I don't think you can analyze humor," he said. "It's always a surprise to me. When I'm writing jokes, they come as a big surprise to me. When I'm in the room alone and I'm looking for a joke, and I'm thinking and thinking and suddenly I hear myself say the joke. I'm hearing it for the first time just like anyone else, and it's funny. You don't think of the joke and then say it. You say it, and then you write down what you said."

Asked if he felt like a loser, Allen returned to his characteristic preoccupations with mortality and death: "I have a feeling that everybody feels like a loser. Automatically. And if they don't, they're wrong. Because everyone is a loser. It's just impossible not to be a loser. Just the very facts of life make you one."

Banker requested that Allen give a sample fact of life. "Well, we know that we're mortal," Allen said. "People find themselves living here, and they don't know why they are. And they can't get their human relations straightened out, and before they know it they die and they never knew what anything was all about. And so, you're automatically a loser. There's no question about it. In fact, I don't like people who aren't self-effacing. I take an instant loathing to them. You know, I just can't help it. I just don't like people that are confident, and I don't trust them, and I never have. And I'm always attracted to people, men and women, who are self-effacing."

Allen continued to publish his literary parodies of classic literature, scholarly biographies, theological histories, and philosophical treatises in *The New Yorker*, the *New Republic*, and other journals. They were usually a mixture of the metaphysical, the mundane, and the colloquial, the paradoxical clash between classical form and funny, outrageous content. They were often Jewish in subject matter and irreverent in their attitude toward Judaism and the Bible. Allen wrote me that he grew up reading the Old Testament in Hebrew, especially the Book of Job. His doubts about the existence of God permeate many of these tales, with their parodies of biblical stories and Jewish religious traditions, and their ridicule of rabbis. Yet he is always looking for some proof of God; failing to find it, he keeps spritzing about it, hocking a *chainik* (complaining, making a big fuss), somehow hoping against hope that God will surface somewhere, somehow. In "Hasidic Tales," a woman questions a rabbi about why Jews were not permitted to eat pork. The rabbi replies, "We're not? Uh oh." In his version of the story of Job, "The Scrolls," which Allen published in the *New Republic* on August 31, 1974, he wrestles with the problem of continuing to believe that God is just despite the reality of the Holocaust. Allen writes of the discovery by a shepherd of six parchment scrolls (as well as two tickets to the Ice Capades) inside large clay jars. The authenticity of the scrolls seems in doubt since "the word Oldsmobile appears several times in the text." Allen quotes from the scrolls that the Lord sent six plagues, and that Job's wife was angry, rent her garment, "and then raised the rent but refused to paint." Allen rewrites Abraham's command to sacrifice Isaac. God tells him that he was only joking and tweaks Abraham for being so gullible. "It proves that some men will follow any order no matter how asinine as long as it comes from a resonant, well-modulated voice."

Then there is the case of the shirt salesman "smitten by hard times. Neither did any of his merchandise move nor did he prosper." He beseeches the Lord: "I have kept thy commandments. Why can I not earn a living when mine younger brother cleans up in children's ready-to-wear?"

> *And the Lord heard the man and said, "About thy shirts . . ."*
> *"Yes, Lord," the man said, falling to his knees.*
> *"Put an alligator over the pocket."*
> *"Pardon me, Lord?"*
> *"Just do what I'm telling you. You won't be sorry."*
> *And the man sewed on to all his shirts a small alligator symbol, and lo and behold, suddenly his merchandise moved like gangbusters and there was much rejoicing while amongst his enemies there was wailing and gnashing of teeth. . . .*

There are many accounts that dispel the image of Allen as being remote and aloof with people; these accounts come from people who were just starting out in life, who were not his peers. Craig Modderno told me one, and Steve Stoliar told me another. Stoliar is the author of the best book about Groucho Marx, *Raised Eyebrows: My Years in Groucho's House.* When he was in his twenties he was Marx's personal secretary and archivist, living in his home from 1974 to 1977. During that time he made two other friends: Dick Cavett and Woody Allen. Groucho had handed him Cavett's autobiography and said, "Here, read this. You'll like it." Stoliar did like it very much, and wrote Cavett. They began corresponding, and when Marx died, they stayed in touch. One day Cavett wrote him, "By the way, I hope you don't mind, but I've shown some of your letters to Woody and he says they're very well-written." In 1982, when Stoliar was thirty, Cavett hired him to write for him at HBO and Stoliar moved from Hollywood to New York City.

"One day Cavett called," Stoliar told me, "and said he noticed that Woody was shooting his latest film in the building around the corner from his apartment. He thought if we just sort of happened to walk in together, I could meet Woody. And I said, 'He wouldn't mind?' And Cavett said, 'Oh, I didn't say that. I would fully expect him to say, "Really, Dickie, I wish you hadn't."' So I was already afraid of meeting Woody. We went into this medical office where they were filming. There was a long hallway, and at the end of it there was a door that was open with a brilliant white light coming out of it, emanating from it; it was like the Wizard of Oz. Then the light went out, and I saw Woody and Mia Farrow come out of the office and talk with Cavett. And I'm just standing there, thinking it's Cavett and Woody Allen and Mia Farrow. Then I saw Cavett say something and then point to me, and all three of them turned and looked at me. And I did the standard pantomine of 'Me?,' looking behind me, and then I walked down what seemed like a very long hallway and I met them. And Woody said, 'I'm Woody Allen and this is Miss Farrow and we're here on the set of our latest motion picture.' As though this was *Entertainment Tonight* or something.

"And what followed," Stoliar continued, "was remarkable for its lack of remarkableness. It was just the four of us talking very comfortably. I was not snubbed; I mean, he knew who I was. And Cavett had said I'm okay. It meant that I was not only a drooling fan, even though I was. Woody mentioned he had tried to contact Greta Garbo when he was working on *Zelig* and he never heard from her. And Cavett said, 'Well, did you send it to 132 East Fifty-eighth Street?' Woody said yes. And I said, 'You probably put the wrong apartment number on it.' And Woody nodded seriously and said, 'That was probably my mistake.' Like yeah, you put Greta Garbo at 1A and she's at 2A so it never got to her.

"So what they were filming was a scene in *Hannah and Her Sisters,* a flashback where Woody and Mia go to a doctor who informs them they can't have children. And now whenever I see that scene, I know that's the day I met him. And it was very comfortable.

"Cavett's show was canceled, and I moved back to LA in 1985. And my correspondence with Woody began. When I started to think about writing a book about my Groucho years, I wrote to tell him. He wrote back that he thought it was a great idea, and there'd never really been a great one. When I finished I sent the manuscript to Woody, and he sent me back a letter that remains one of the proudest moments of my life. Because it was this effusive handwritten letter saying it's one of the best books about a show-business icon he'd ever read. I asked him if we could use what he said on the dust jacket, and he wrote back and said it's okay to use it, but just make sure your name is bigger than mine and include my comments with others. My book came out and did okay. I wrote to Woody about the lack of TV promotion for it, and he wrote back that can you imagine if Dickens or Tolstoy had to worry about going on television to promote their book? He said your book is a fine one and welcome to the club of people who try to do decent honest work and find it's hard getting a big audience.

"I have only seen Woody in the flesh one time since New York. He came out here very briefly to shoot scenes for *Scenes from a Mall* [a rare instance of Woody acting in someone else's film] and sent me a letter saying feel free to drop by the set, we can chat a little. So my wife, Angelique, and I went to the Beverly Center. Finally he came out of his dressing room, He said, 'I'll be glad when this is over,' and his voice was slurry and weird. And I thought to myself, Oh God, it's happened; he's become old, he's had a stroke, this is terrible. And then I looked and I saw the half-eaten Snickers bar in his hand. The other half was stuck in his cheek. He told me he had gone with Cavett to see Sid Caesar and Imogene Coca at a nightclub, and how Coca was quite old and frail. But as soon as they came out and started to perform, all the years melted away. So Woody and I talked about how there's something about those troupers, those people who went through vaudeville, the rough times, who don't let old age and illness get them down. They're able to hit their mark when they have to.

"And then, in 2008, my wife died suddenly. And Cavett informed him of that. So I've gotten periodic letters in my grief recovery from Woody that have meant a whole lot to me. Because part of him is very nuts-and-bolts realistic about things, and certainly not saccharine or sentimental. But he'll say things like 'I know like it will never get better, but somehow we're hardwired to deal with things like that. And it will get better even if it doesn't seem like it ever will.' And then in a later letter, saying something like 'I can tell you're doing better by the tone.' It's like, gee, you remember the tone of the letter I wrote you six months ago.

"I told him I was going to be writing a book about my life with Angelique, and the difficulty of going it alone after the sudden death of my spouse. And he wrote me, and he said he couldn't believe I felt up to writing about this. He would stick his head in the sand ostrich-like until the worst of it passed over. It meant the world to me that he was essentially saying, 'You're doing something that I don't think I could do.' Because I have so much admiration for him, for all that he has accomplished and continues to accomplish.

"So between all those years, there've just been these wonderful, conversational letters—over forty of them—where he'd fill me in on what he was working on, something in the news that caught his attention, film reviews, jokes—and invariably he would end up with, Keep in touch, let me know how you're doing. Especially in the depths of my depression over my wife's death, to see that New York postmark brightened up my day. Once I was talking to Cavett on the phone and he said, 'Well, Woody and I went for a walk in Central Park and I said, "Stoliar made an interesting observation."' And I had the feeling, Wow, Dick Cavett is talking about me with Woody Allen. Cavett continued, 'Stoliar said that you and I are now older than Spencer Tracy was in *Judgment at Nuremberg*. And Woody stopped and stared at the ground and said, "Do you mind if we sit down for a minute?" And we both sat down on a bench in Central Park and Woody just kind of stared at the ground for a minute, taking that in.'"

*Love and Death*, released in 1975, was Allen's parody of the works of the Russian artists he loved—Dostoyevsky and the Tolstoy of *War and Peace*—with references to Sergei Eisenstein's *Alexander Nevsky* and *Battleship Potemkin*. Allen plays Boris, a coward (with touches of Bob Hope and Groucho) who doesn't want to participate in the war against Napoleon but becomes an inadvertent hero. Boris gains the love of his cousin Sonia (Keaton), who decides that she and Boris will assassinate Napoleon. Still, it's the same old Woody in his horn-rims (which also appear in *Sleeper)* and squeaky voice: schlemiel and stud, coward and hero. The references, as always, are often Jewish and/or contemporary: insurance salesmen as tormentors or "My Uncle Sasha picking up a check," and with Yiddishisms thrown in for good measure (*meeskite*). And there are cheerleaders at the battle scenes. Allen superimposes his usual sexual frustrations and longings: On their wedding bed, when he tries to touch his wife, she says, "Don't; not here." In a childhood scene, Boris meets Death and asks him, "What happens after we die? Heaven? Hell? God? Are there girls?"

"By incorporating aspects of diverse (even antithetical) comic approaches [Chaplin, Buster Keaton, Hope, and Groucho] into his own unique comic outlook," film critic Douglas Brode wrote, "Allen establishes himself as the end-product of the various styles that preceded him, all yoked together in one movie and one man."

Like many of Allen's films, *Love and Death* was panned by Stanley Kauffmann, the movie critic for the *New Republic*. Paul D. Zimmerman in *Newsweek* wrote that "we catch him at his best—more nervous, desperate and inspired than ever before. If there is a jittery edge to our laughter, it is because Allen, in this comic response to the angst of death, is treating something of a common problem. . . . [The film] bristles with Allen's private terrors, which connect with our own."

John Simon found the film a step backward from *Sleeper*: "a curious olio of night-club patter, revue sketches, and one-liners, most of them quite funny but uneasily stitched together. What comes out resembles a movie only as something midway between a crazy quilt and a potato sack resembles a suit of clothes. . . . There is a grave problem with *Love and Death*, hilarious as much of it may be. This sort of film wears thin too easily; laughter that is largely pointless becomes in the end exhausting. . . . We could have gotten roughly the same effect from laughing gas, sneezing powder or a mutual tickling session with a friendly prankster."

Nevertheless, in spite of his criticism, Simon added a significant paragraph that, despite his negative reaction to the film, expressed appreciation of Allen and held out hopes for his future development. He wrote that his response to the film was "particularly saddening because Woody Allen is more than merely funny; at his best, he exhibits a penetrating intelligence—indeed, intellect—well beyond the mental means of our run-of-the-mill farceurs. Such intelligence can uncover, ridicule, and perhaps laugh out of existence genuine evils, and a little, a very little, of this elixir survives even in the anomic laugh-fest of *Love and Death*. But the movie stoops far too often to such things as a facile sight gag about a convention of village idiots that, when you come right down to it, yields laughter that leaves you with a bad taste in the soul."

The film was yet another big moneymaker, grossing $20.1 million, the equivalent of $80.8 million today, and still ranks sixth among all of Allen's films. These early films—*Everything, Sleeper,* and *Love and Death*—still outpace most of Allen's more recent films, even *Match Point, Bullets over Broadway,* and *Vicky Christina Barcelona.*

*Death,* Allen's one-act play, was published in 1975. Allen may have been influenced by Friedrich Dürrenmatt's *The Visit* and Eugène Ionesco's *The Killer,* but as with almost all of his work, the result is an autonomous one that stands on its own. Both Dürrenmatt and Ionesco dealt with the ominous visit of murderous strangers and the outbreak of madness in their wake. Allen's play can be seen as an allegory of Nazism or of revolutionary movements that wind up like the murderous regimes they have initially opposed. His play is much more successful than its later incarnation as a film in 1990, *Shadows and Fog,* with its Brechtian overtones, underscored by its Kurt Weill / *Threepenny Opera* music, and burdened by its contradictory tones of drama and occasional comedy, with Allen sometimes injecting his "Woody" shtick into it.

In *Death,* a maniacal murderer is loose in an anonymous town. Kleinman (Allen) is the nebbish whom the townspeople wake from a warm bed and insist he take part in the vigilantes' hunt for the killer. Since he is an Allen stand-in, Kleinman is ashamed of his own cowardice and wants to be left alone. Instead he finds himself in the middle of the manhunt, but no one seems to be able to tell him what the plan of action is. All of Kleinman's questions are rebuffed, and he is treated with suspicion. He is the outsider, slightly comical, and we know we are never far from Woody, for Kleinman tells us, "I have a great fear of death! I'd rather do almost anything else than die!" When one of the men, Hacker, is murdered, the tension increases, and then the doctor is mortally shot as well. It turns out that Hacker was shot because he is a member of a "rival faction." This is news to Kleinman, who knows nothing of factions. One of the men asks him, "You know about the rival faction, don't you?" Kleinman replies, "I don't know anything! I'm lost in the night."

The play treats life as without rhyme or reason. What is certain is the constancy of human madness, of history's chaos as it is shaped by irrational men. Faction upon faction forms, and they plan to kill one another. The anti-Hacker faction threatens Kleinman: Whose side is he on? In the tinderbox of violent revolutionary movements, one cannot remain neutral. Whichever side he joins, he will be killed by the other side. Allen's deeply cynical feelings about political and social movements inform the play: The allegiances drown in blood and become indistinguishable from one another. While searching for the murderer, the townspeople turn into murderers and have no compunction about it. Whoever ultimately wins will write the version of events that suits their side (which is the theme of the dinner-table discussion, as articulated by the anarchist aunt in Judah Rosenthal's Orthodox Jewish family in *Crimes and Misdemeanors*).

The atmosphere is one of utter confusion and chaos, and Allen renders it convincingly. The men challenge Kleinman: "Choose now, Kleinman, the moment is here!" Kleinman, the voice of reason, replies, "We'll kill each other and the maniac'll remain loose. Don't you see? . . ." The men reject Kleinman's neutrality and discuss killing him. One man tells Kleinman, "I've got a good mind to cut your throat, the way you shilly-shally." No one objects. Earlier we hear echoes of anti-Semitism in the men and the policeman addressing Kleinman as "You stupid vermin" and "You worm."

The townspeople find a solution in Spiro, the telepath. A clairvoyant, he will solve the case by sniffing around. Spiro sniffs Kleinman and declares that he is the murderer. The men and Gina, the town prostitute, gang up on Kleinman and decide to hang him. At the last minute the real murderer is discovered in the act of trying to strangle someone else. They all run off, and Kleinman, alone, is suddenly confronted by the real killer, who closely resembles him. Kleinman asks him why he kills. He replies, "I'm a screwball. You think I know?"

The maniac kills Kleinman. As he lies dying, the other men come upon him and ask if he's afraid to die. In true Woodyesque fashion, Kleinman replies, "It's not that I'm afraid to die. I just don't want to be there when it happens."

Soon after that the killer is spotted by the railroad tracks.

The men run off, leaving Kleinman to die.

*Death* is a successful one-acter. Like most of Allen's plays, except *Play It Again, Sam* and *The Floating Light Bulb,* it doesn't blaze with some of the originality and intensity of his best films. The play is not exactly derivative, but its Kafkaesque echoes and Kleinman's characterization, yet another version of the Woody persona, keep it in a minor key. As a parable of twentieth-century madness, however, the play does resonate.

In 1976 Allen agreed to star in a film which he had not written and would not direct, *The Front.* The film dealt with the blacklist of Hollywood writers and artists that began in the late 1940s as a result of growing panic about the postwar international threat of Communism posed by the Soviet Union's aggression in Eastern Europe and North Korea's invasion of the South. Right-wingers in charge of the House Un-American Activities Committee saw a growing internal threat posed by the American Communist Party's allegiance to Stalin and the USSR. They thought that Communist screenwriters would seek to impose their ideology on the films they were involved in. Hundreds of actors and writers were told they could clear their names only by becoming informers on their friends and families. If they didn't, they could not work in the film industry.

The film was a labor of love for its director, Martin Ritt; its screenwriter, Walter Bernstein; and its cast, many of whom—like its star, Zero Mostel—had themselves been victims of the Hollywood blacklist. It had devastated the lives and careers of many figures in show business. Philip Loeb, who played Gertrude Berg's husband on the TV program *The Goldbergs* between 1949 and 1950, committed suicide; John Garfield's death at an early age may have been precipitated by the blacklist; and scores of others had seen their lives broken and careers crippled. Allen undertook the project for both moral and personal reasons: Abe Burrows, the relative who had befriended him when he sought help in getting started in the business, had been a target of the blacklist. Burrows had been selected to be the recipient of the Pulitzer Prize in Letters for *Guys and Dolls* in

1951, but the prize was withheld that year. In addition, as Allen told the interviewer Ken Kelley in 1976 in *Rolling Stone*, "I remember hearing about blacklisting when I was in public school, not really understanding the implications of it all. But in retrospect, what I know now historically, it was a horrible time. The script expresses me politically even though I didn't write it."

"When Martin Ritt and I were finally cleared of the blacklist and were able to work again," Walter Bernstein told me, "we had always wanted to do a movie about the blacklist. We wanted to do a straight drama about someone who's been blacklisted, why, and what happened. But we could never get anybody interested. Marty, who had some kind of clout as a director, would take it to a studio, and they would turn it down. Too controversial; they didn't want to touch the subject. Finally we got the idea of coming at it sideways. About a guy who was a front for blacklisted scriptwriters, and doing it as a comedy.

"An ex-agent of ours," Bernstein continued, "David Begelman, had become the head of Columbia. We went to him and got a derisory amount of money. He liked it, he would do it if we got a star. Redford, Jack Nicholson, people like that. The only way he would do it. So we puzzled awhile, and finally one day I was playing tennis with Marty and he stopped and said, 'What about that kid?' I said, 'What kid?' He said, 'That funny kid.' He couldn't think of the name. Finally I said, 'You mean Woody Allen?' 'Yes, that's who.' 'Well, he'd be great.' We called Begelman, and he said yes. So we sent the script to Woody, and he said yes. And that made it possible.

"So we flew to Paris to meet with Woody. He was making *Love and Death*. He was living in a hotel. He had covered up all the windows in his room. He said, 'I like the script and I'd like to do it.' That was it.

"He came on the set. He said, 'Fellas, I'm here as an actor. What do you want me to do?' And that was it. He didn't write anything. His sympathies were liberal. He took direction. He was a gent. We didn't talk much politics. We talked about sports mostly. It was a significant experience for us. Woody contributed to that. He's a good guy. He's an Energizer Bunny. He knows where he's going, know what he has to do. I mean he's found a way to handle his craziness.

"Zero Mostel's character [Hecky Brown, who commits suicide by jumping out of a hotel window] is partly derived from John Garfield and partly from Philip Loeb. Garfield and I were friends. Garfield had a heart condition and was being squeezed. Very much. HUAC was after him. They wouldn't let up. They made it so that there was no way out unless you became an informer, and gave names. He solved it by dying. He didn't want to be a snitch. He didn't want to have to give names. He liked being a movie star."

In a key scene in the film, Woody's character, Howard Prince, drives Hecky up to the Concord Hotel in the Catskills to play an engagement. He expects to get a paltry $500 because he is damaged goods, but receives an even more humiliating $250 from the hotel director. He explodes with rage. The scene was based on Mostel's actual experience, with Bernstein as witness. "I drove Zero up there," Bernstein said. "The guy cut him, and he went on in a rage. Eight hundred people in the audience. Cursed the audience in Yiddish and called them names. The more he did it, the more they loved it. They had no idea what was going on. He came off and drank half a bottle or more of booze and went to bed. I wanted him to do that in the movie, but he wouldn't do the scene. It was still too painful."

As the final credits of the film roll, they identify the producer, director, writer, and cast members—and also list the year in which each was black-listed.

The film's potential for overearnestness, considering the subject and the personal experience of its participants, is somewhat undercut by its comic form. It is, to its credit, not a diatribe. To that extent it benefits from the levity. However, its black-and-white view of characters and events (the progressives are always purely good guys, the committee members are always monsters) keeps complexity and nuance at bay. And paradoxically, because of the humor, it emerges as a hybrid of drama and comedy that don't fully mesh. Woody's Howard Prince is a character portrait of a nebbish, a cashier and small-time bookie in hock who becomes a charlatan, pretending to be a writer, and displays courage at the end. The film doesn't block out the feeling that we are watching Woody Allen; we don't forget who he is. "*The Front*, while ogling Significance, is content to cohabit with Farce," wrote John Simon. "A serious problem can, of course, be treated as comedy, especially as black comedy, if it has been sufficiently dealt with as a serious problem in the past, if we have become tired of it when served up straight. But when its surface has barely been scratched, yukking up the subject seems at best evasive, at worst jejune." Simon added, "To have been a Communist or Communist-sympathizer is not an automatic guarantee of moral and intellectual superiority."

"There is, in the end," Richard Schickel wrote, "something held back about *The Front*, some strange refusal to really dig into and turn over very rich historical and psychological soil. The result is a film unworthy of its excellent intentions." What is held back is the complexity of the deceptive nature of the Communist Party, which controlled its members' thinking to the extent that they believed that Stalin was the "new Moses" (the words of American party leader Elizabeth Gurley Flynn), that the gulag was a workers' health resort, and that, during the Hitler-Stalin Pact, opposing Nazism was giving support to "imperialism." They were capable of striking for milk for poor children in the United States and organizing black workers in the South against the Ku Klux Klan and segregation, while supporting the purges and sadistic murders of millions (many of whom had given their lives to the cause of "progressive humanity") in the Soviet Union.

Nevertheless the authenticity of feeling and atmosphere, the injustice of the blacklist, and the serious historical events that we see unfolding give *The Front* a seriousness of purpose and integrity.


*Annie Hall* was the first of the five pictures to be made when Arthur Krim and Eric Pleskow renewed and extended their UA contract with Allen. "A career that seemed a fluky and limited one," Steven Bach wrote, "full of New York angst and schtick which didn't travel well into mid-America and had almost no foreign passport, had turned into a prodigiously likable series of pictures: *Bananas, Sleeper, Everything You Wanted to Know About Sex,* and *Love and Death.* They were original not only in subject but in their angle of vision and style, evolving from an early awkward jokiness to the seriocomic poignancies and polish of *Annie Hall.* Taking a flyer on Allen had proved to be one of the happiest and smartest gambles in recent movie history." Allen had singlehandedly revitalized UA's reputation for originality and independence. He was in a filmmaker's heaven.

So imagine we're seeing *Annie Hall* for the first time. It is 1977. We've seen Woody as Virgil, Boris, and Fielding, characters caught up in wild, slapstick adventures. We've seen him closer to earth in *Play It Again, Sam* as Allan Felix. But here we are much closer still with Alvy Singer. He stands there facing the camera. No music. Woody's Dixieland scores are absent. He tells two jokes, then tells us he's turning forty. He confides that one of the fates he fears is turning into the old guy with the shopping bag, dribbling at the mouth, hanging out at cafeterias shouting about socialism. (Woody will give us variations of that dreaded image in films to come, like the guy selling comic books in front of Bloomingdale's in *Annie Hall*.) And then he gets down to it: "Annie and I broke up." He doesn't know why.

He tells us he had a normal childhood, but the first flashback contradicts him. He's in Brooklyn on a doctor's couch, and his mother has taken him there because he has grown depressed since realizing that the universe is expanding and will eventually break up. "What is it your business?" shouts his mother, and the doctor tells him it won't happen for billions of years and it's his duty to enjoy himself—and the doctor laughs heartily to show how enjoyable life is. Alvy informs us he's in analysis and that his house was beneath the roller coaster in Coney Island—a brilliant Woody stroke. (He was driving around Brooklyn looking for locations, and his art director, Mel Bourne, and cinematogapher, Gordon Willis, discovered the little solitary apartment actually lodged beneath the roller coaster.) Soon we're back in elementary school, and Alvy at six is stealing kisses from the girls (just as Woody actually did) and being upbraided by the strict, wizened Irish teachers. We immediately segue to an actual scene from a Dick Cavett TV interview with Woody, lest there be any doubt this is Woody's real story, that this is the story of the successful star of stand-up comedy, Johnny Carson, and many other television shows, the Woody who rejects the world of TV comedy writing because it is insipid and sterile—as he will do again in *Manhattan, Hannah and Her Sisters,* and *Crimes and Misdemeanors.* Back to his mother, telling him he was always out of step with the world and distrusted people. And Woody's themes begin to cascade over us: (*1*) Anti-Semitism and the Holocaust. Woody tells Rob (Tony Roberts), the eternally shallow, swinger friend dressed in white, who represents the emptiness of Los Angeles, where he moves (he pops up in several Woody films in the exact same role, even in a cameo in *Hannah and Her Sisters*), of people muttering "Jew" at him or framing innocent-sounding questions so that "Did you" turns into "Djew," or playing Wagner in record stores to torment him. Scenes from the great Ophuls documentary *The Sorrow and the Pity,* about the Nazi occupation of France, are referred to and shown several times.

Now we are at the Beekman Theater, where we will meet Annie for the first time. Alvy is waiting for her to go in to see an Ingmar Bergman film. He is surrounded by three primitive Brooklyn guys, and we are introduced to Allen's second theme, (2) the burdens of being a celebrity. Annie arrives late (the film's events are actually all in flashback, since we know they have broken up), and Allen cannot go into a movie that's already been running for two minutes, which opens up the third theme, (3) Alvy's uncompromising search for truth. They now wind up on line at the New Yorker Theater, where we (and everyone in line) learn that Annie and Alvy have sexual problems and that she is dealing with them in analysis. Alvy is infuriated by the comments of the academic pedant behind him in line, and a fourth theme is introduced, (4) Alvy's judgmental nature. Almost no one lives up to his expectations, including Annie. The film's experimental techniques also begin here, when Alvy conjures up the real Marshall McLuhan to refute the professor's fatuous remarks about him. Another flashback introduces us to Alvy's first wife, Allison (Carol Kane), whom he meets at an Adlai Stevenson rally where he is going to do his stand-up routine. He immediately disparages her while simultaneously flirting with her, guessing at her "New York left-wing Jewish Intellectual" background, going to Brandeis, socialist summer camps, and her father's Ben Shahn drawings on the wall, reducing her to what she calls a "cultural stereotype." As he is about to go onstage, a fifth theme briefly appears, (5) Bob Hope's influence on Allen's comedy. Alvy asks Allison for encouragement, and she says he's cute, causing him to straighten his tie and emit a smug Bob Hope whistle. We see him at the rally with yet more examples of the Woody Allen stand-up comedy routines. In the next scene we see him avoiding sex with Allison by obsessing about the JFK assassination, leading Alvy to face the camera and address the audience (another device Allen employs throughout the film) and repeat the joke that started the film (and this is a sixth theme): (6) "Oh my God! She's right! . . . Is it the old Groucho Marx joke that—that I-I just don't wanna belong to any club that would have someone like me for a member?" The next scene, filmed at a beach house, is iconic: Alvy's struggle with getting live lobsters into a pot. It was the first scene in the movie that Allen and Keaton filmed, and they broke up spontaneously with laughter. The joyousness of the scene is overwhelmingly conveyed by its improvisatory feeling. This couple had lovely moments together, and here was a record of those idyllic times.

And that was only the beginning of the film. Each scene glistens, the story borne forward by Allen's whip-smart comic sense: Alvy and Annie on their first date and Alvy stopping Annie in the street and suggesting they kiss for the first time right then because "We're just gonna go home later, right? There's gonna be all that tension," Alvy reasons. "You know, we never kissed before and I'll never know when to make the right move or anything. So we'll kiss now and we'll get it over with and then we'll eat. Okay?"

"Oh, all right," says Annie.

"And we'll digest our food better," explains Alvy.

They kiss. "So now we can digest our food," he says.

The sexual problems between the couple start early and permeate the film. Annie does not seem to be turned on by Alvy; she needs marijuana to enjoy sex. Alvy is turned off by what he regards as her rejection. He argues quite reasonably that as a comedian, he knows that if an audience is high, their laughter doesn't mean anything because it was artificially induced. In one of the many original scenes that break with naturalism, we see Annie's spirit leaving her body as they are having sex: She crosses over to a chair and watches them having intercourse and chats with them.

Anyone watching the film remembers their own first date, the fumbling and embarrassment, moving one's arm tentatively around the shoulders of the girl, fearing rejection. Allen has encapsulated that entire experience in the most original, fresh, and charming way. Did he actually do this in life? Of course he did.

And so the story is everyone's story of a first love that goes astray, often for reasons that are understood only years later. Alvy is controlling, judgmental, rejecting of everyone else's failings. He is an island of integrity and morality in himself; he feels both superior and inferior to everyone else. Does that sound familiar? He rejects Annie by not wanting her to move in with him. He ridicules her intellect so that she finds solace in the embrace of a college teacher and, ultimately, with the smooth-talking, mantra-spouting Hollywood record producer, Tony Lacey (Paul Simon). Alvy isolates Annie from the world because no one can live up to his high standards, except, inexplicably, his swinger pal Rob, who can't wait to sell out to Hollywood and doesn't seem to have a clue as to what Alvy is talking about—even preferring fake laugh tracks for his TV comedy shows so that he won't have to bother to write funny dialogue.

Alvy supports Annie's aspirations to sing and to "find herself"—he even pays for her therapy—but he rejects Tony Lacey's offer to produce her record and is stunned to discover that Annie's therapy is liberating her from his control. After all, he is paying for it. He has lost Annie by denying her a chance at success in life, and he experiences the results in her rejection of him.

Allen gained the distance to write about his love affair with Keaton very quickly; perhaps that was because the more intense affair had been with Louise Lasser, one which he has never dealt with in his movies except by creating relatively extreme characters like Dorrie and Harriet Harmon—grotesques. Lasser was an exquisitely talented comic actress, as she demonstrated in *Mary Hartman, Mary Hartman*, whose later career was undermined by her own serious emotional problems. (She was arrested for cocaine possession while starring in *Mary Hartman*; this event was turned into a brilliant episode of the program as well as a sketch on *Saturday Night Live*.)

Keaton and Allen had had diametrically different life experiences, were from wildly different ethnic and social classes. (Lasser was also from an upper-class milieu.) Keaton and Allen were sources of exotic fascination for each other. The lifeblood of each other was ingrained in Lasser and Allen; they knew and understood each other even before they met. They were brilliant Jewish comic originals and terrific ad libbers; they were sexual flames to each other and intellectual equals. Louise, like Allison Portchnik, studied at Brandeis. Allen could not patronize Lasser or raise her up to his level: She was *on* his level. They spoke each other's language. She could pick up on Allen's Yiddish expressions; she could do shtick almost as well as he could. Both were secular Jews to the core, but very Jewish all the same. Lasser had a zaftig, fully feminine body, just what Allen craved. What undermined them was Lasser's emotional turmoil; it was impossible for Allen to function in that hothouse. What was initially her psychic withdrawal twice a month turned into twice a week and, finally, almost all the time. Allen was left alone; his companion was gone; his rigorous work schedule threatened.

The story of *Annie Hall* is universal and the first film of Allen's that would be loved by audiences throughout the world. The last scenes, in which Diane Keaton sings a moving, even mesmerizing version of "Seems Like Old Times," and the final montage of moments in the love affair, accompanied by her singing the song, are unforgettable. This is everyone's memory of a first love that has gone astray but remains tenderly enshrined in the memory forever. Even if it was not really Allen's first love—Harlene—or his second—Louise—it was artistically and universally true.

Entwined among the images at the end of the movie is an especially poignant one of Alvy encountering Annie again after the breakup and feeling gratified when he sees her leaving a showing of *The Sorrow and the Pity* at the Thalia with her boyfriend. In *Annie Hall* it appears that Alvy has taken Annie to see the film at least several times and she has resisted; now he sees years later that his deepest feelings about the Holocaust have made a lasting imprint.

Pauline Kael accused Allen of creating a character of "self-love" in Alvy, of a New York chauvinism and contemptuous attitude toward Los Angeles, as well as a self-abnegating, deprecating treatment of his Jewishness. She also wrote in her notes about the film (she didn't review it at the time it was released) that Alvy "only shows you what you see anyway" (by which, I think, she meant that he was a set of attitudes and opinions, that there was a lack of depth to his characterization). Kael's biographer, Brian Kellow, wrote that Kael thought *Annie Hall* "was a promising idea that wasn't developed deeply enough and never quite found its real subject because it veered off into a tale of two cities—New York versus L.A." That was hardly fair; LA was a backdrop, not the center of the picture. But here is Kael at her best: "What made the movie run down and dribble away was that while Woody Allen showed us what a guilt-ridden, self-absorbed killjoy Alvy Singer was, always judging everyone, he (and not just Alvy) seemed bewildered that Annie wearied of Alvy's obsession and preferred to move on and maybe even have some fun. By the end Alvy and the story had disappeared; there was nothing left but Woody Allen's sadness." Except—she was dead wrong. The movie does not dribble away. Allen understood that Alvy had killed the relationship. Alvy understands it himself, if a bit dimly.

On the matter of Allen's relation to his Jewishness, Kael came closer: "What's apparent in all his movies," she wrote in 1980, "is that for him Jewishness means his own kind of schlumpiness, awkwardness, hesitancy.

For Woody Allen, being Jewish is like being a fish on a hook; in *Annie Hall* he twists and squirms. And when Alvy sits in that dull WASP dinner and the screen divides and he sees his own family at dinner, quarrelling and shouting hysterically, the Jews are too heavily overdone for comedy. Here, as almost everywhere else in Woody Allen's films, Jews have no dignity. That's just about how he defines them and why he's humiliated by them."

Phillip Lopate sees the film in a somewhat similar light. "I had a lot of resistance to *Annie Hall*," he told me. "A resistance which I think was typical of a certain native New Yorker. A feeling that it was very blinkered in a way and privileged and not a New York that I particularly knew. This was also true of *Manhattan*. I didn't feel he caught the texture of New York in a way that, say, Sidney Lumet's films did. I felt that *Annie Hall* pulled its punches, in that the relationship fell apart but we never really saw why the relationship fell apart. In other ways, Allen was being gallant in a way. But there was always this kind of elusive quality, where I didn't feel he was getting to the nitty-gritty. He was allowing the audience to romanticize. There are wonderful touches in the film, and I certainly like it more than I did when it first came out.

"I think I was also in rivalry, that we were both taking from the same magic barrel of Jewish humor. It wasn't that I was influenced by Woody Allen. But he was part of a tradition, a common experience, something sardonic and lower middle class. So we were working the same side of the street. But he was doing it in a way that was both more nostalgic and more distanced. *Annie Hall* meant a lot more to people who were not Jewish, who were not New York. It streamlined and mythified elements that were more complicated. It didn't capture the texture; he managed to make a cartoon of it, like that famous shot in the film where he looks like a Hasid at the Halls' dinner table. It was something that the non-Jews could appreciate, that they were in on the joke."

Echoing Kael, Lopate asked: "What was really at stake? What did the Woody Allen character really want? He is often protective of that character, making the Woody character the only one who can deliver aphorisms, who has a shred of self-insight, while the other characters tend to dither on [like Annie]. It was not an even playing field. I still feel that the films [*Annie Hall* and *Manhattan*] were commercial more than artistic. Somehow they had the trappings of the art film, but they were pandering to the audience. They were playing to the audience's prejudices."

I have sometimes wondered if *Annie Hall*, if it were a novel rather than a film, would shine in quite the same way. It is true, as Kael suggests, that Alvy's personality is defined by a set of attitudes and prejudices that do not constitute a whole character. We are meant to completely identify with his point of view and self-righteousness, although Allen does provide some irony by letting Alvy realize his own hypocrisy in encouraging Annie to go to school and then ridiculing her ("Adult education is such junk! The professors are so phony! How can you do it?") for taking educational courses (and a particular professor) seriously. And he suddenly acknowledges to Annie that it was he who suggested she keep her own apartment, not she. There are other instances where he is aware, if dimly, that he is not the wronged one in the relationship. As they were working on the film, Ralph Rosenblum asked Allen if Alvy's constant complaints were completely legitimate, and Allen replied that they were: "The degree to which he obsesses over them in the movie gets to be seen as neurotic, but to me that's not neurotic."

> **ROSENBLUM:** But in the movie you make fun of his obsession, imply that he's carrying it too far.
>
> **ALLEN:** Right. Because I recognize that as the more rational point of view. I just don't happen to hold that.

In a novel more irony and distance, more self-knowledge on the part of the author might be necessary. Here—and perhaps that is one of the magical functions of movies—we are beguiled by scenes of the beauty of Manhattan, by Alvy's wit, his one-liners, his sheer funniness. The comedy and the immediacy sweep us away. We love Alvy/Woody as he loves himself. And we love the almost romance of the story, the yearning, the tactile feeling of the lovemaking, the relationship between Alvy and Annie.

*Annie Hall* is, like so much of Allen's work—and despite all his protestations—partially naked autobiography, a personal history which he parades before us while partly denying it at the same time. Alvy Singer, like Allen, is a stand-up comic and a TV comedy star; his appearances are taken directly from Allen's appearances on the college circuit and on Dick Cavett; he has turned away from the TV comedy he detests to do stand-up; he despises Los Angeles, the heart of that TV scene; he meets and has an affair with Diane Keaton, whose real name is Diane Hall, who had a WASP family somewhat like the one depicted in the film. There was a real Grammy Hall, "a classic Jew-hater," says Alvy, just as anti-Semitic in real life as she was in the film. "You're what Grammy Hall would call 'a real Jew,'" Annie tells Alvy. "She hates Jews." In her memoir, *Then Again*, Keaton wrote that when she told Grammy Hall about the Academy Award nomination, Grammy Hall said, "That Woody Allen is too funny-looking to pull some of that crap he pulls off, but you can't hurt a Jew, can you?"

Even though Allen has been the subject of endless press, his essential integrity as a filmmaker has been hard for many writers to grasp. His opinion of Hollywood is not an idle crank's expression of contempt. It is strongly related to Allen's determination to work unimpeded, and to his clarity about his artistic goals. "I think that in the United States there are only a handful of filmmakers that are really in the serious business of making movies," he told Björkman. "The others are doing what they call 'projects.' It takes them a long time to do them. They are preceded by lots of meetings, lunch meetings, and dinner meetings and meetings with writers, meetings with directors, meetings with actors. Their life centers around the preproduction ceremonies. And finally they make the picture, and it's usually commercial nonsense." Allen captures that lunacy in his account in *Annie Hall* of the Hollywood party at Tony Lacey's house.

In one conversation, a man with two hornlike gadgets attached to his shoulders says to another man: "Right now it's only a notion, but I think I can get money to make it into a concept . . . and later turn it into an idea." The utterly frivolous, mindless attiudes toward history are summed up by the smarmy Tony Lacey's casual comment that Chaplin once owned his house "right before his Un-American thing." Alvy and Annie hear a girl in white refer to Alvy/Woody's favorite, cherished Renoir film: "We saw *Grand Illusion* here last night." In a priceless moment, a man (Daniel Stern) lying on his back on a sofa cheerfully says, giggling, "That's a great film if you're high." Smiling, he looks up at them and offers them a joint. Then they pass a man (Jeff Goldblum) talking earnestly on the phone: "Yeah, yeah, I forgot my mantra."

Allen's disinterest in pleasing his audience can't really be understood without the perspective of distance and history. His remarks are passed over or ignored, or people think he is dissimulating. Perhaps the reason is that they are so unusual that they verge on the incomprehensible in a society in which even the most successful artists struggle to reach—and keep—some degree of acceptance. If they do not, they cannot survive financially, and they lose the celebrity and status that they have worked hard to achieve.

Allen has been entirely consistent about it. He expressed his indifference to critics—even when most of them were positive toward him—as far back as 1975 in *On Being Funny*: "Their value is strictly economic. They can hurt your picture sometimes; sometimes they can do that. They can't do anything for you as an artist, for or against. If they say you're bad, it doesn't mean you're bad. If they say you're good, it doesn't mean you're good. I think if there were no critics there wouldn't be the slightest scintilla of impairment of art. The true artists have no connection with them and do their work. I don't have contempt for critics or anything. It's just that artists do all they know how to do." Allen was insisting, as he has continued to do since, on the right to "fail" while he searched for new ideas, new concepts, deeper modes of expression: "What happens with a more serious artist like Chaplin," he said, "is you try to do other things. You don't go to your strength all the time. And you strike out so people think you're an ass or pretentious, but that's the only thing you can do. You can find your groove and stay in it, and I think you will inevitably fail a little if you don't stay in it."

But Allen can survive no matter what, and almost no one else in filmmaking can. He worked that out from the beginning. Speaking to Björkman of two of his worst bombs, *Interiors* and *September*, he said, "I knew when I was making them that nobody was going to go and see them. Even if I made them artistically and worked hard and they came out good, I *knew* that there wouldn't be an audience for them. You can feel that. . . . I make any film I want. I don't care if the public likes it, the critics like it. I mean, I would like them to. But if they don't, they don't. I make films for my own enjoyment." How could one man have been so smart or so lucky (or both) to achieve this freedom? It's a difficult concept to swallow and easy to attribute arrogance to. Allen is someone who will not accept backing from anyone who would control his vision. This is an independence of *soul*. There is a corollary disbelief about Allen's attitude toward awards, particularly the Academy Awards. He has to be showing off; he has to be pretending that he does not care about such a high honor, they say. (This is the culminating argument between Annie and Alvy when they go their separate ways at the end of *Annie Hall*. Annie just doesn't understand what he is talking about. Alvy mutters to himself as he storms off: "Greatest fascist dictator: Adolf Hitler.") How could he possibly be playing the clarinet with his band when he could be basking in the glory of receiving the most prestigious award of the industry he works in? Keaton writes of the thrill of receiving the Academy Award in 1977. Allen of course was not present. "Woody woke up the morning after and opened *The New York Times*. On the front page he read that *Annie Hall* won best picture and went back to work on his next script. . . . Woody stood by his principles. To him there was not a 'best' in an art form—that included no best director, no best picture, and definitely no best actress. Art was not a Knicks basketball game."

*Annie Hall*, like *Take the Money and Run*, was a hard-won victory for Allen. With all his skills, he had not yet mastered the technique of bringing together a series of vignettes to form a cohesive, unified story. He was not even sure what the story was. It was hidden beneath the vignettes and needed to be clarified, organized. Instead there were a series of brilliant lightning flashes; it was a matter of separating the forest from the trees. One can imagine the dilemma just from the fact that Allen seriously intended to call the film *Anhedonia*. When he first announced it at an early title session, Eric Pleskow was patient with him. "A hundred faces looked at me blankly," Ralph Rosenblum recalled. And Arthur Krim walked over to the window and threatened to jump.

"Anhedonia" was a state of mind. The concept was appealing to Allen because it defined his depressive state. But he was not writing a medical manual or treatise. He was writing a love story in which the protagonist suffered from that condition. At last it became a love story. Allen is quoted in Rosenblum's book: "It was originally a picture about me, exclusively, not about a relationship. It was about me, my life, my thoughts, my ideas, my background, and the relationship was one major part of it." The protagonist also happened to have a fabulous sense of humor, a romantic spirit, a sweet personality. He was not buried by his neuroses. The spellbinding scenes *illustrated* his psychological condition with comic flair, farce, slapstick, poignancy, and depth of feeling. A key to the film's success once

again was the intervention of Ralph Rosenblum, who was able to orga-
nize and piece together the vignettes and scenes into a cohesive whole. Allen needed help, and he has always been able to accept that help graciously
without his ego obstructing his goals.

When Rosenblum was first consulted about the film, he wrote in his
memoir, *When the Shooting Stops*, *Annie Hall*, unlike the early stages of *Take
the Money and Run*, was "an untitled and chaotic collection of bits and pieces
that seemed to defy continuity, bewilder its creators, and, of all Allen's
films, hold the least promise for popular success." The original draft by Allen and Brickman was largely Allen's story (Annie appeared briefly, then
disappeared for long stretches), and according to Rosenblum, "the surrealistic and abstract adventures of a neurotic Jewish comedian who was reliving his life and in the process satirizing much of our culture. . . . The
movie was like a visual monologue . . . Its stream-of-consciousness continuity, rambling commentary, and bizarre gags completely obscured the
skeletal plot." The film was supposed to take place in Allen's mind. "Something that would happen would remind me of a quick childhood flash,
and that would remind me of a surrealistic image," Allen has said. "None
of that worked." The film was undramatic and ran off in a hundred different directions. Rosenblum's task was to locate the plot amid the brilliant vignettes.

Allen began to notice that the film started to move forward and gain
momentum when he and Keaton were together in it. "We sensed immediately where the life was," wrote Rosenblum. The first twenty minutes of
the film were trimmed away to make room for Keaton. "We had to get
back to Annie," said Rosenblum, "because if she was going to be the dramatic focus that would hold this picture together, we could not stray from
her for long." The relationship was taking over the film.

When the time came to decide on an ending, Allen had considerable
difficulty, as he has often had with resolving his films. Then Allen asked
Rosenblum, "What about memory—shouldn't we have them discuss old
times?"

The question clicked with Rosenblum, led inevitably back to the song
Keaton had sung so beautifully, and he came up with an epiphanic ending: "I knew what we needed to do." He told his editor, Susan Morse, to
assemble shots of Alvy and Annie with the lobster, Alvy and Annie at the

beach, Annie and Alvy driving uptown from the tennis courts, Alvy and Annie in bed, Alvy reaching over to kiss her, Annie and Alvy at the pier, Annie arriving at Alvy's apartment with her luggage, Annie holding up the sexy negligee Alvy gave her for her birthday ("This present is for you," Annie said). Morse spliced them together on a single reel, and Rosenblum edited them down to a reprise of Keaton singing "Seems Like Old Times" to form one of the most haunting montages in American cinema.

"I'll never forget," Marshall Brickman told Rosenblum, "suddenly there was an ending there—not only that, but an ending that was cinematic, that was moving, with that simple recapitulation of some of the previous scenes, with that music. . . . The whole film could have gone into the toilet if there hadn't been that last beat on it."

"I really feel [*Annie Hall*] was a major turning point for me," Allen told Stig Björkman. "I had the courage to abandon . . . just clowning around and the safety of complete broad comedy. I said to myself, 'I think I will try and make some deeper film and not be as funny in the same way. And maybe there will be other values that will emerge, that will be interesting or nourishing for the audience.' And it worked out very well."

*Variety* wrote: "In a decade largely devoted to male buddy-buddy films, brutal rape fantasies and impersonal special-effects extravaganzas, Woody Allen has almost singlehandedly kept alive the idea of heterosexual romance in American films." Even Andrew Sarris, usually a harsh critic of Allen, agreed. "One can forgive [Allen] almost anything for the cinematic valentine he has woven for Diane Keaton. I never dreamt that a Woody Allen movie would ever remind me of a [Lorenz] Hart lyric. After *Annie Hall*, it will be hard to argue that romantic heterosexual love is not making a strong comeback."

*Annie Hall* won four top Academy Awards, the National Film Critics Awards, the Directors Guild Award, and four British Academy of Film Awards, including Best Picture and Best Editing.

S. J. Perelman, one of Allen's literary idols, had given a speech presenting Allen and Brickman with the New York Film Critics Award for Best Screenplay for the film.

Allen was not present at any of the award ceremonies. On the night of the Academy Awards he was doing his regular Monday-night stint with his jazz band at Michael's Pub in New York City. A year later he stated, "I know it sounds horrible, but winning that Oscar for *Annie Hall* didn't mean anything to me. I have no regard for that kind of ceremony. I just don't think they know what they're doing. When you see who wins those things—or doesn't win them—you can see how meaningless this Oscar thing is."

He would keep playing at Michael's Pub every time he was nominated by the Academy.

*Annie Hall* had not been a blockbuster before the awards, but after they were announced, it went through the roof. "Middle America responded to Woody's New York anxiety," Steven Bach wrote, "and for the first time a foreign public seemed to get the jokes and rhythms, giving a lift to [the film's] worldwide receipts and making possible foreign reissues of his earlier films, which had performed indifferently, if at all, abroad." But even at this stage United Artists did not value Allen for his economic importance. He made UA seem "as separate as he was from the Hollywood herd," wrote Bach, "as independent, as special. He was New York's very own mensch auteur, UA's 'critics' darling.'" The film, which is Allen's fourth all-time highest grosser, has earned $38,251,425.

Allen, who was forty, had struck up a relationship with seventeen-year-old Stacey Nelkin after meeting her on the set of *Annie Hall*; it would secretly continue for two years. Allen was seen with her at Elaine's, where he carried her schoolbooks—a detail that would surface in Allen's comment about Mariel Hemingway's character, Tracy (who was partially based on Nelkin), in *Manhattan*. Nelkin would go on to have a short-lived film career. She is now a "relationship expert." When I phoned her, she concluded our brief conversation by saying, "Woody never did a fucking thing for me." (She canceled what was to be a subsequent interview on the advice of her lawyer.)

Many years after Allen's first serious drama, *Interiors*, was released in 1978, he would recall the sickly, gentlemanly smile of Eric Pleskow after seeing the film. He knew that Pleskow was too gentle to express his true feelings. Pleskow was not the only one in shock. Everyone who saw *Interiors* felt that way. When I read what some of Allen's sympathetic critics—highly insightful, intelligent writers—have written in praise of the film or have expressed in their conversations with Allen, I find it difficult to understand why they temporarily lost their minds over this film.

Allen originally pitched the idea to Arthur Krim. He was well positioned to present it; *Annie Hall* had consolidated his reputation as UA's resident genius. "In all modesty," Pleskow told me, "Woody was very fortunate to be with us." Steven Bach noted that it was Allen's fundamental respect for "his financiers, his patrons, that won him the right to make *Interiors*, his 'serious' picture (Ingmar Allen, they called him at 729 [UA's address]), in which he did not star and which may be one of the rare instances in modern American movie history in which an artist has been allowed to make a picture because of what it might mean to his creative development, success or failure. That it failed commercially does not diminish the picture or the mutual respect with which it was financed and made. Nor does it diminish the tremendous debt of faith that Arthur Krim incurred with Woody in understanding the importance of *Interiors* to him."

Allen's attitude toward it can be understood from his comments in 1979 to Natalie Gittelson of the *New York Times*. Allen was struggling with what he continued to regard as the limitations of comedy: "Tragedy is a form to which I would ultimately like to aspire," he said. "Comedy is easier for me. There's not the same level of pain in its creation, or the confrontation with issues or with oneself, or the working through of ideas." From his perspective it was better to fail with *Interiors* than to succeed with something of lesser import: "If you try for something and it fails honorably, it's better failing that way than to succeed with something exploitative." Of course there were other alternatives, and Allen would find them. And the "level of pain" he was striving for was experienced mainly by the audiences watching the film.

*Interiors* is practically unwatchable. It is dead on arrival. *Interiors* bears no relation to the rich multilayered originals that Allen's best films are. It is a pale replica of an Ingmar Bergman film, divested of life, real characters, drama, tension, immediacy. These are people Allen does not know, has not experienced, doesn't have a clue about. The stiffness is claustrophobic. I have quoted earlier how he considered the possibility that he'd been influenced by watching the subtitles for foreign films and had unconsciously imitated them. And *Interiors* would not be a one-time anomaly. More were to come—and soon: *Another Woman*, *September*, and *Shadows and Fog*.

Arthur (E. G. Marshall) is a lawyer married to Eve (Geraldine Page), who is hung up on interior decoration. Their daughters are in bad shape. Eve's not a good mother. Renata (Diane Keaton) is a poet who writes for *The New Yorker*, but it's impossible to believe that this is true. Her husband,

Frederick (Richard Jordan), is an author and an alcoholic. Joey (Mary Beth Hurt) drifts from job to job with no real talent, and her husband, Mike (Sam Waterston), is a documentary filmmaker and do-gooder. Flynn (Kristin Griffith) is young, acts in TV soap operas, and snorts coke.

Are you with me? None of these characters has any sign of original life. They are lifeless prototypes. Arthur is leaving home. Eve is in shock. Arthur turns up with Pearl (Maureen Stapleton), who is dressed in red against the grayness of everyone else because she is supposed to be a life force who dances, laughs, stirs things up with her sensual, down-to-earth personality. Except that she's a caricature and a bore. Eve goes right out and drowns herself. Joey tries to rescue her, and Pearl saves Joey (because Pearl's a life force). Pearl takes over the family, supposedly a hell of a lot more fun than droopy Eve, and Joey thinks she may find something to do.

The wooden, numbing dialogue of *Interiors* is something to hear. It is the kind of long-winded cerebration Allen would ordinarily make fun of. Here's a sample:

> **EVE:** I think I found a very nice vase for the foyer. . . . (*taking out a box from the shopping bag and opening it*) You'll probably think it's an extravagance, but it's not, all things considered. These pieces are becoming increasingly rare. (*holding up a delicate blue vase*) Isn't that exquisite? (*Mike, filling a kettle of water at the sink; looks up at Eve; she walks toward the foyer*) I hope you like it, because it's perfect for what I have in mind for the foyer.
> **MIKE:** (*placing the kettle on the range*) We already have a vase in the foyer, Eve.
> **EVE:** (*speaking from the foyer*) Yes, but this will never look right when we redo the floors.
> **MIKE:** (*preparing a tray with jar of instant coffee and sugar bowl*) I never understood why the floors have to be redone. . . .

But then there's the issue of the lamp in the bedroom:

> **EVE:** (*glancing at a lamp sitting on a cabinet in the dining area*) You didn't like that in the bedroom?
> **MIKE:** (*looking at the lamp*) I knew you were gonna say something. I get better use out of it here.

Eve: *(walking over to the lamp)* Well, if you utilized it in here, that's
   fine. It's meant to be used. It's just that it's part of what we were
   trying to do in the bedroom. *(pointing at the lampshade)* It's the
   shade and the bedspread. They set each off so nicely, I thought.

I have struggled to give some idea of the film's plot, since I did not care
about anyone in it and would have given anything to stop watching it.
There are lots of reflections of winter trees on misty windows, gray waves
on the beach. It's all Bergman without Bergman's touch—and more important without Allen's touch. How could he be capable of making this?

Three days before filming began, Guy Flatley of the *New York Times*
asked Allen if the film would be "bathed in Bergmanesque misery." Allen
denied it, but did say, "Right now, I'm faced with the pitfalls of half-baked
ideas and derivative techniques. I'm feeling my way."

A private preview screening was held in December 1978. The *New York
Post* reported: "The ever-so-chic private screening audience sat in stunned
silence." The film did not open until August of that year. Louise Lasser
complained to Allen that the film was about her family and her mother's
suicide. Actually, if it had been, it might have been a better film. The family in *Interiors* was a family that Allen knew nothing about.

"*Interiors* has that dour severity of his other early Bergmanesque films,"
Phillip Lopate told me. "It feels too derivative and doesn't feel like he
really knows these people. You just feel Allen's ambition to be Chekho-
vian. But his weaknesses as a playwright start to harm that. But there's
this 'Once-over-lightly' quality to Woody Allen. A lot of times when I see
an Allen film I think, this would have been a good movie with one more
draft. This is funny to say, but his lack of a sense of humor harms *Interiors*
as well as *September* and *Another Woman*. It's almost as though Allen's polar-
ized. He's either doing humor or he's doing nonhumor.

"Ingmar Bergman always had a kind of quality of irony," Lopate continued. "The kind of sardonic quality to the way that people go at each
other. Their zest in taking each other to pieces. Woody Allen has done
some remarkable work. But *that* Woody Allen can't do. Because Woody
Allen is still an arriviste in that WASP world. And there's a part of him that
wants to have decorum. So every time he tries to show people who are in
that kind of bourgeois WASP world, he shows their repressiveness but he
doesn't know how to show what Bergman shows when they really take the

gloves off. He stiffens. That's part of the problem with the social-class as-pirations of Allen.

"Woody's contempt for comedy—I think it's something that he's learned to discipline. He can crank it out, he can put his mind in that place. But I feel like his vision isn't essentially comic. At the heart of com-edy is the idea that you don't take yourself so seriously. You have an ap-propriate sense of your own unimportance. I feel in some ways he's too narcissistic to have that perspective. This may really be unfair to say, but it does account for the fact that his films tend to divide between those that are comic and those that are absolutely not comic.

"These characters are unbearable, but partly because I don't think he really understands these people or is not amused by them the way Chekhov is by his characters. It's a world he wants to get into, and he's disappointed that these people are so unhappy."

*Interiors,* wrote Pauline Kael, "looks like a masterpiece and has a super-banal metaphysical theme (death versus life) . . . It's a handbook of art-film mannerisms; it's . . . austere and studied. . . . Woody Allen's idea of artistic achievement (for himself, at least) may always be something death-ridden, spare, perfectly structured—something that talks of the higher things. People who watch this movie are almost inevitably going to ask themselves, How can Woody Allen present in a measured, lugubriously straight manner the same sorts of tinny anxiety discourse that he gener-ally parodies?"

John Simon was just as brutal. "Woody Allen has made his first seri-ous film . . . and its condition is worse than serious, it's grave to the point of disaster. Whether it makes you bite your lips in rage or roll over with helpless laughter, you will concede that there is not one real character in it; that almost every line of dialogue is, at best, hackneyed, at worst, ludi-crously stilted; and that virtually every shot is derived from some other filmmaker, usually Bergman or Antonioni. . . . Throughout the film Allen is incapable of showing anything. Everything is *told* by one character about another, or by a character about him or herself. In endless, utterly inept palaver: 'One day an enormous abyss opened up beneath our feet,' or '[I don't want to] be swallowed up in some anonymous life-style.' Or from the poetess *in extremis*: 'It was as if I had a clear vision where everything seems awful and kind of predatory. . . . I felt precarious. It was like I was a machine, but I could conk out at any minute.' On and on, they verbalize in language that one would think was persiflage if Allen himself had not announced repeatedly that he was dead serious in the film."

The box office for *Interiors* limped in at $10.43 million. Geraldine Page was nominated for Best Actress, and Mel Bourne and Daniel Albert received nominations for Best Art Direction. Allen received two Academy Award nominations for the screenplay and direction, perhaps bearing out his low opinion of the value of the Academy Awards.

Allen's next film, *Manhattan,* would be his third collaboration with Marshall Brickman, who has remained his close friend. Brickman started out as a folksinger in the early sixties with the well-known group the Tarriers. He moved on to become head writer for Johnny Carson and later, producer and creative director for Dick Cavett. Allen had worked with Brickman in 1967 on *The Filmmaker,* a project that was never made. Allen called him again in 1972 to work on *Sleeper* with him, and they continued a ritual they'd begun in 1967—one they enjoy to this day—of walking in Central Park and talking about a film before going to one of their apartments to work on the script. They reunited for *Annie Hall,* and the shape of *Manhattan* emerged from their walks in the city: "Marshall and I walk around the city," he told Natalie Gittelson in the *New York Times Magazine.* "We review the experiences of my life. We talk about the ideas and feelings that are meaningful to us, that we would like to express. It happens in an amorphous way. 'What if your ex-wife were writing a book about me?' we ask each other. Characters begin to appear: people I know, people we both know. Then others appear that are totally fabricated, sheer flights of fantasy."

Brickman and Allen develop the screenplay, and Allen, as is his creative process, proceeds to write it. "On the set, many things change. One actor may turn out to have a slightly different quality than I expected: I rewrite. I change tons of dialogue. . . . I never thought of Meryl Streep as a possibility for the role of my wife . . . but as soon as it was suggested, it was clear to me that she would just be great. More rewriting. . . . The movie was always growing, being rewritten and rewritten on the set. . . . As I edit the film, it continues to metamorphose. Sometimes concepts get lost, or I abandon them completely, and stronger concepts emerge. Finally, I finish the rough cut, the first draft, of the film. . . . There's such a disparity between what you set out to make and what, at last, you do make that you just want to . . . die. You want never to see it again."

Lorenz Hart and Richard Rodgers wrote their beautiful valentine "Manhattan" in 1925, with the haunting lyrics that have been sung by Dinah Washington and countless others, "The great big city's a wondrous toy, just made for a girl and boy. . . ." The song itself is not used in the film, but its romantic spirit permeates it: Manhattan is the golden city. By 1979 it was a struggle to still believe in that Manhattan, with rampant crime, garbage, and pornography eroding the city on every front. New Yorkers lived in the aftermath of the city's 1975 default and the blackout in the summer of 1977. Times Square was rotting, taken over by muggers, peep shows, and massage parlors. Graffiti was everywhere.

But still it was not quite over. A few Horn & Hardart Automats, where Allen and his friends hung out after shows in the early years, held on, pale ghosts of themselves; Burger Kings had gradually replaced most of them; there were a few Schrafft's left. Howard Johnson's hung on at Forty-sixth Street and Broadway. The original raffish show business weekly, *Variety*, was still churning out Runyonesque prose on West Forty-sixth Street two blocks from the RKO Palace, where forms of vaudeville were revived and held out into the late seventies. Other stage shows were gone: the Capitol, the Roxy, the Strand, the Paramount, Loew's State. It had been a banquet Woody had feasted on in his boyhood. The world he came out of and loved was suddenly gone.

Most of old Broadway and its resplendency had vanished: The sheet-music stores on Sixth Avenue; Lindy's, where Damon Runyon, Winchell, and all the comics hung out and ate cheesecake, closed in 1969; Jack Dempsey folded his Broadway restaurant in 1974. The Copacabana, home of Martin and Lewis, Sinatra, Tony Bennett, Louis Prima, Lena Horne, and Jimmy Roselli, closed in 1973; the equally glamorous Latin Quarter (West Forty-seventh Street), which featured Ella Fitzgerald, Sinatra, Sophie Tucker, Belle Baker and Ted Lewis, folded in 1969. By the late seventies what was left of the old show-business scene was mainly situated at the Carnegie Deli, the Rainbow Room, the Stage Deli, the Brill Building, and the Colony Record Shop, which gave up the ghost only in 2013. They were among the final links to a golden past. But there was still WNEW-AM, the great radio station of the American Songbook, of Gershwin, Berlin, and Porter, the home of Sinatra—all the luminaries of classic

American pop music—which would hang on until 1992, slowly losing its grip. In 1979 William B. Williams still greeted his audience with "Hello, World" at noon for hours of Sinatra, and the station boasted other disc jockeys with real personalities, like Jonathan Schwartz, Jim Lowe, and Al "Jazzbo" Collins.

The Catskills of Grossinger's, the Concord, and Brown's (where Jerry Lewis started), the original home of the Milton Berles, Alan Kings, and Sophie Tuckers, of the waiters who would become stars, were also fading fast by 1979. (Grossinger's, the "Palace" of the Catskills, closed its doors forever in 1986.) Miles of nostalgic newsprint would be expended on all these institutions for many years to come, right up to the present.

Woody Allen would somehow bridge these years in *Broadway Danny Rose* (1984), which is an homage to the old comics and vaudevillians, the show business of his youth. He even filmed a scene at the Red Apple Diner, the old gathering place of comics when they played the Catskills, in *Deconstructing Harry*. The diner seems deserted and possibly shuttered except for the actors who play the scene (there is no sense of life behind them), which would seem likely by the time the film was made.

The vision of the magical city was bound up with these places, whose novelists, journalists, biographers, memoirists, poets, playwrights, screenwriters, songwriters, vaudevillians, comics, and singers embodied that vision of Manhattan, experienced it, created it on the page, sang of it, remembered it in lustrous works like Moss Hart's *Act One* and Alfred Kazin's *A Walker in the City*. Those who read those memoirs would always associate Manhattan with Kazin's euphoric walk across the bridge from Brownsville to Manhattan, and Moss Hart at twenty-one looking out the window of his Broadway hotel to see his name in lights for the first time on a Broadway marquee for his play *Once in a Lifetime*. It was a vision that encompassed Dylan Thomas and Brendan Behan at the White Horse Tavern, Arthur Miller and Thomas Wolfe at the Chelsea Hotel, John Lennon at the Dakota, and earlier, Maxwell Bodenheim and Kay Boyle at the San Remo Café in Greenwich Village (where Boyle, who'd been an expatriate in Paris with Hemingway, Dos Passos, and Gertrude Stein took me, a young writer and her student at the New School, for my first espresso).

Allen embodies that vision, and he has added to these classics. His *Manhattan* will help immortalize the city for generations to come. It seems a vision of an almost vanished city.

Allen himself celebrates and embodies that creative quest, that churning of mind and spirit, attempting to continue to grow artistically, to do what is fresh and has never been done before. That is why he insists over and over on the need to risk, or even attain, failure: "It's very important," he told Natalie Gittelson, "that there's a certain amount of stuff one fails with. That's very important." Failure is an indication that "you're not playing it safe, that you're still experimenting, still taking creative risks. It's fruitful to get into the habit of not trying to make hits. Compromises and concessions begin to turn up in the world. . . . If you're succeeding too much, you're doing something wrong."

Speaking of Chaplin, Allen said, "He was preoccupied with developing. He was willing to take many chances and he often failed. Some of his movies were quite terrible. But he was always trying to grow."

There is something profoundly true but also something odd about this line of reasoning: It is true that in flailing around, in wrestling with material, with testing oneself, and taking chances, the artist may reach new heights. What is unusual about Allen's reasoning is that rather than keep his struggles to himself, struggling with them in the privacy of his studio and resolving them before he rushes into filming, Allen is willing to inflict his failures on his audience. And as harsh as Allen is on himself, he does not always seem to know how bad some of his films are, or, conversely, how good some of them are. He has never seemed to admit that *Interiors* is a failure, yet he is completely candid about *Another Woman*. He told Eric Lax, "It's cold, boring, ball-less. A cure for insomnia. I was falling asleep after the first fifteen minutes. I kept feeling, 'Get past this and there's a terrific scene.' But no. . . . It's too cold. A better person could make it work. *Wild Strawberries* is about a cold man and it's hot. Well, no need to sit and beat a dead horse. It's old celluloid." When I suggested that *Zelig* and *Crimes and Misdemeanors* were among his masterpieces, Allen said firmly that he did not agree at all.

*Manhattan* was not a failure. The city had never been celebrated so incandescently before, shot in black and white by cinematographer Gordon Willis, and Allen had never exposed himself with such depth and openness.

But here's that famous, glib, but typically irresistible Pauline Kael quote on the film: "What man in his forties but Woody Allen could pass off a predilection for teenagers as a quest for true values?"

Natalie Gittelson, unlike Kael and other critics who have searched every crevice of Allen's work to find evidence of something unhealthy in his relationship with younger women (and, for some, evidence of a squalid episode with Dylan Farrow years later), perceived Isaac's relationship with seventeen-year-old Tracy differently:

> Manhattan *testifies with eloquence and candor that Allen also may have a soft spot in his heart for young, young women. But there is little of Humbert ("Lolita") Humbert here. Although sex is by no means devalued, the real attraction lies between kindred spirits. The older Allen grows, the more he seems to value innocence in women—not sexual innocence, but that shiningness of soul that age so often tarnishes.*

Another writer wrote of such a relationship between a soldier traumatized by the war and a precocious young girl—J. D. Salinger's *For Esmé— With Love and Squalor.*

The city landscape in *Manhattan* is as redolent as the characters who inhabit it. The landscape evokes indelible memories for me and for so many of its fans. I know that spot on Fifty-ninth Street by the bridge; I went there with a girl I loved a long time ago. It's on Sutton Place; there's a town house beside it I wanted to live in (rent-free, I suppose; I was twenty-one). There was no bench, but we stood by the gate looking out onto the gleaming water and the miraculous city.

In the opening sequence of *Manhattan,* in a breathtaking, overpowering cascade of images (some filmed from Allen's balcony), we recognize almost every iconic location: sections of Central Park, the Manhattan skyline at dawn, parking lots, the Brooklyn Bridge, a neon Coca-Cola sign, lamplit streets of Park Avenue and Central Park, Washington Square, the Empire Diner, Grand Central Station, laundry on clotheslines hanging from a tenement building, construction men drilling on the streets, smoke billowing from open grates, Times Square, a flashing Broadway sign, the garment center, the Staten Island Ferry, kids in schoolyards, laundries, the waterfront, Manhattan Center, snow in Manhattan, women walking on Fifth Avenue, workers ogling them, children in private-school uniforms running down the school steps, two elderly women huddled in winter coats, a fruit stand, the Guggenheim Museum, three men loitering on a corner, horsedrawn carriages in front of the Plaza Hotel, a gay pride march in Greenwich Village, Gramercy Park, the Twin Towers, a man and woman kissing on a balcony, the blazing lights of empty office buildings at night, Yankee Stadium, Madison Square Garden, the Fifty-ninth Street Bridge, joggers in Central Park, the Fulton Fish Market, a fruit stand, high school boys playing basketball, buses on Fifth Avenue, Central Park in snowy winter, and, finally, fireworks exploding across the Manhattan skyline at night to the crescendo notes of "Rhapsody in Blue."

"*Manhattan* captures a sense of New York City as filtered through the unique consciousness of old movies," Douglas Brode told Stephen Spignesi in *The Woody Allen Companion*. "It is 1979 New York viewed, thanks to the glorious black-and-white cinematography and accompanying Gershwin music, by the last man who refuses to admit that the 1940s era is gone."

Isaac, struggling to begin his novel, has made various attempts, including "He was too romantic about Manhattan as he was about everything else. He thrived on the hustle . . . of the crowds and the traffic." He finally settles on "He was as . . . tough and romantic as the city he loved. Behind his black-rimmed glasses was the coiled sexual power of a jungle cat. . . . [Isaac comments: 'I love this.'] New York was his town. And it always would be."

"After *Interiors*," Allen told Gittelson, "I wanted to try and go farther on the serious side than I had done before, that continues along a path I would like to follow." The film, he said, was "my own feelings—my subjective, romantic view of contemporary life in Manhattan. I like to think that, a hundred years from now, if people see the picture, they will learn something about what life in the city was like in the [1970s]. They'll get some sense of what it looked like and an accurate feeling about how some people lived, what they cared about."

He spoke of the musical score by George Gershwin that accompanies the magnificent montage of Manhattan sights with songs that shine through the entire film, from "Someone to Watch Over Me" to "He Loves and She Loves" to "But Not for Me." "The Gershwin music fits in with Isaac's comprehension of the city," Allen told Gittelson. "He sees Manhattan in black and white and moving to the tones of George Gershwin. The score helps to vibrate several themes in the picture: the passing of time, the poignancy of where the city's gone; the fact that, in a certain sense, Isaac's living in the past, when things seemed better to him."

Allen has sometimes made fun of his psychoanalysis over the years ("If

I don't make a breakthrough soon, I'm going to try Lourdes"), but in his conversation about it with Gittelson, when he'd already had twenty-two years of treatment, a picture of a reflective, judicious Allen emerges, one who has greatly benefited from the process. The changes in him were almost ineffable, but they were nonetheless real, and they had helped him in his work: "You don't learn anything in a dramatic rush. It's very slow and unnoticeable. But an hour a day, talking about your emotions, hopes, angers, disappointments, with someone who's trained to evaluate this material—over a period of years, you're bound to get more in touch with feelings than someone who makes no effort. I think that [process] has a tendency to liberate your natural gifts. Possibly you work more produc-tively, too, because you don't obsess over self-destructive things."

Those changes may well have led to the deeper portrait of himself that Allen offers in *Manhattan,* a portrait in which comedy is harnessed to the needs of the dramatic script and does not overwhelm it; comedy and drama are fused and the tone is consistent and controlled.

Isaac Davis is a highly successful TV comedy writer who hates what he does for a living. His best friend, Yale, an avowed intellectual, is really a fool who, instead of concentrating on writing his biography of Eugene O'Neill or starting a literary magazine, is obsessing about a Porsche he wants to buy. He will betray Isaac in the end. Isaac's TV show, which sounds like early reality television, is called *Human Beings—Wow.* Isaac, confronting his stoned writing partners, quits the program and decides to spend a year writing a serious novel. Isaac's proposed novel has a familiar ring. Isaac's critiques of society sound like Allen's: He tells his friends it's about "decaying values." With no TV money coming in, he has to move from his lush duplex apartment with its spiral staircase into a normal noisy life-size apartment. (People live in very spacious, luxurious apart-ments in almost all of Allen's films, no matter what they do in life.)

We learn that Isaac has two alimonies to pay to two former wives, and child support. In addition he helps out his parents, and he will have to give up his share on a Hamptons summer house. Most significant, "My ex-wife left me for another woman." This rings a bell because in *Annie Hall,* Annie informs Alvy that she's told her analyst that she has to "give up my wife." She thinks she said "my life," but we hear her and she definitely said "wife." That's apparently Alvy. Allen never pursues this thread; he leaves it hanging. Nor does he explore, in *Manhattan*, the implications of Isaac trying to run down his ex-wife's girlfriend with his car—this is played for laughs, yet it suggests a level of hostility that at least needs to be treated with some concern. For that matter Allen doesn't spend a minute on the implications of Isaac having chosen a bisexual woman to marry in the first place.

We meet Tracy, Isaac's seventeen-year-old girlfriend, seated with him, Yale, and his wife, Emily, at Elaine's. Isaac quips that he's dating a girl who's doing homework. The radiant Mariel Hemingway is the kind of discovery that Allen has excelled at uncovering from the start. Hemingway has said that Allen worked closely with her and helped her find her way in the part. She is the resonant, authentic heart of the film, and the scenes between Allen and Hemingway are always genuine and truthful. She is unerringly real.

We understand Isaac's hesitation in getting more involved with her because of the disparity in their ages and his fear of increasing her dependency on him. The motif of fear of commitment and marriage (and parenthood), which runs through all of Allen's films, is well drawn here. Isaac does not criticize Tracy the way that Alvy puts down Annie Hall; he treats her purity of heart with a delicate kindness. When he asks Tracy what she would most like to do, we find out in the next moment when they ride in a horse-drawn carriage in Central Park at night, with the music of "He Loves and She Loves" in the background. There is nothing prurient in Allen's treatment of the relationship. There are even traces of Cliff's mentorship of his niece in *Crimes and Misdemeanors*. Embracing Tracy in the carriage, he tells her that "You're God's answer to Job. . . . You would've ended all-all arguments between them. I mean, H-H-He would've pointed to you and said, you know, 'I do a lot of terrible things, but I can also make one of these, you know.'" He buries Tracy's head in his shoulder and kisses her hand. "And then-then, Job would've said, 'Eh, okay—well, you win.'" This is passion and it is true love—which Isaac will realize too late.

When Yale (Michael Murphy) introduces Isaac to his pseudointellectual girlfriend, Mary (Keaton), Isaac is at first repelled by her affectations as well as her shallow putdowns of the writers and artists he most admires. Every word out of her mouth is phony, and he cringes with distaste and even rage. She is lonely, hollow, and a narcissist at the core, with no real belief in herself; She is everything Tracy is not. "I'm a beautiful woman," Mary announces, "I'm-I'm young, I'm highly intelligent, I got everything going for me . . . the point . . . the point is—that, uh, I don't know. I'm all fucked-up. I'm just . . . shit. I could go to bed with the entire faculty of M.I.T. if I wanted to. . . ." She is the perfect match for Yale. Yet Isaac is soon enmeshed with her (for the usual Allen reasons: being drawn to the most disturbed, unreliable, and stormy woman available), and he breaks up with Tracy.

In a scene with Tracy at a soda fountain, Tracy has brought a birthday present for Isaac: a harmonica, which she hopes will help him to shed some of his gloom. He is touched and moved and yet he informs Tracy just after getting the present that he loves someone else. This is surely the most poignant and emotionally powerful scene that Allen had written to this point in his career. It is unforgettable. One does not doubt for a moment that Hemingway is shedding real tears; she is living the scene.

Both *Annie Hall* and *Manhattan* were breakthrough films for Allen, but *Manhattan* was his arrival film, as he understood. Alvy is still partly the nebbish and is left alone at the end, not really understanding why Annie has left him, still filled with rage at authority (crashing his car and fighting with a policeman), still feeling morally superior to Los Angeles and the rest of the world, still an army unto himself, as Annie has called him. But there are portents of change in Alvy: He is proud of having instilled something in Annie when he sees with delight that she is returning to *The Sorrow and the Pity* with her new boyfriend. But in *Manhattan* many more changes are taking place. Isaac reaches beyond himself to the other person, racing to catch Tracy before she leaves for London. He recognizes what he has lost, what is truly important, a soulmate whose values are not "expedient," who is not bound by the empty lifestyle around him. He has created his own list of what is valuable and timeless in life, from Bechet and Sinatra to Cézanne and Satchmo. This is his own list, coming out of his soul. There's only one writer—Stendhal—on that list: This is what the real Allen loves. And the list ends with Tracy's face. As he races toward Tracy, he will not keep her from getting away. But he has raced away from his old self toward something far better.

"*Manhattan*," Allen said, "is about the problem of trying to live a decent life amidst the junk of contemporary culture—the temptations, the seductions."

"Not everyone gets corrupted," says Tracy.

Allen has resisted that corruption.

And yet—Pauline Kael had a good point: "Allen based his case for general moral decay on the weaknesses (not even cruelties) of two or three selfish, confused people. You could indict Paradise on charges like that."

In *Manhattan,* following what he started with *Annie Hall,* Allen continued to emerge as a real artist. The film not only had artistry, it had audacity. What was it about? A man in love with a girl twenty-five years his junior—and underage as well. A man dating a girl "who did homework." He would win an Academy Award for it—and world renown. He went on to other works in which the theme of a man's love for a much younger woman was prominent, and he's still doing them. And he acted out that theme in real life. And got away with it.

Andrew Sarris wrote that *Manhattan* had "materialized out of the void as the one truly great American film of the '70s." J. Hoberman, who had been critical of the film as "bourgeois bushwah" when it came out, reassessed *Manhattan* in 2007 in the *Village Voice.* Like John Simon, he was much more admiring, although he continued to maintain that Allen would never create a film as good as *Manhattan* again:

> *Allen was never more vividly himself than as the self-absorbed, Nazi-obsessed horny TV writer and babe magnet Isaac. . . . Whether or not* Manhattan *is Allen's most personal movie, it enshrines everything from his morality to his milieu. . . .* Manhattan *is the Woody Allen movie where it all came together. The city is gorgeously rendered by cinematographer Gordon Willis. . . . Every line is a one-liner, but the dialogue flows—it's not only funny but also seamless. For the first (and also the last) time, he graced the screen with a fully realized vision. . . . Allen's subsequent attempts to recapture* Manhattan *have often been embarrassing, but he (and we) will always have this.*

Hoberman's reassessments of Allen did not end there; in 2014 he would publish a review of *Crimes and Misdemeanors* in the *New York Times* in which he would again revise his original opinion of a film.

Allen has spent a lifetime writing for himself and about himself.

Steven Bach, an executive at United Artists, recalled in his memoir, *Final Cut,* that when he read Allen's script, he was worried that the large number of "esoteric" references in *Manhattan*—to Strindberg, Mahler, Jung,

Dinesen, Kafka, Cézanne, Flaubert, Scott and Zelda Fitzgerald, Noël Coward, Heinrich Böll, Brecht, Mozart, Nabokov, and O'Neill—would not be recognized by the film's audience. He compiled a list and carried it with him. When he spotted a young couple he knew—a pharmacist and a health-food entrepreneur "who were as representative of the general public as anyone I was likely to meet"—he read off the list of names to them. They knew all of the names except Heinrich Böll. Bach put the list back in his pocket.

Some initial reviewers were ecstatic: Vincent Canby wrote in the *New York Times* that *Manhattan* was "extraordinarily fine and funny." He continued, "As Isaac Davis is Mr. Allen's most fully realized, most achingly besieged male character, so is *Manhattan* his most moving and expansive work to date." He praised the "marvelous scene set at a soda fountain" when Isaac breaks up with Tracy and wrote, "The movie is full of moments that are uproariously funny and others that are sometimes shattering for the degree in which they evoke civilized desolation. . . ." He concluded, "Mr. Allen's progress as one of our major filmmakers is proceeding so rapidly that we who watch him have to pause occasionally to catch our breath."

Robert Hatch in *The Nation* had both praise and reservations; Allen was still, he wrote, "the quintessential New Yorker, exhausting his days and nights in a treasure hunt for the meaning of life, which he believes must surely be hidden somewhere east of Fifth Avenue. . . . There is a good deal of honest concern in Allen's wrestling with the Angel, not to mention that he is a man of uncommon charm and wit . . . [but] all in all, I doubt that Allen can get much further by plucking obsessively at his own bosom." As for Woody, he was characteristically self-critical with a dash of melancholia. He told William Geist of *Rolling Stone* in 1987 that he didn't have "any extra regard" for either *Annie Hall* or *Manhattan*.

*Manhattan* was the deeper portrait that Allen began in *Annie Hall* and a long way from the cartoonish characters he once drew. It's a leap from *Interiors* so astonishing that it seems to have been written by a different person. Allen can both see himself more clearly and has the confidence and objectivity to look beyond himself at the people around him, most notably Tracy, as well as Mary and Yale. And he grows: He is a different person at the end of the film than he was at the beginning.

In Phillip Lopate's view, "As in *Annie Hall,* once again I felt that the pain of the human situation was being muffled and aestheticized more than I felt comfortable with. And the whole unpleasantness of this older man hitting on this high school girl is finessed. I think that on the one hand he's brave to deal with these taboo things, and on the other hand, he almost always seems to sweep them under the rug.

"What was really at stake?" Lopate continued. "What did the Woody Allen character really want? Allen is often protective of the Woody character and makes him the only one who can deliver aphorisms, who has a shred of self-insight, while the other characters tend to dither on. In other words, he certainly protects his own character. Diane Keaton's character is full of clichés and platitudes. So that didn't seem fair. It was not an even playing field. Both *Annie* and *Manhattan* had the trappings of the art film, but they were pandering to the audience, playing to the audience's prejudices."

What is unquestionable is that, unlike the WASP world of *Interiors*, Allen knows the smug, insular upper-middle-class intellectual subculture that nestled around Elaine's very well. He catches the inane patter around him perfectly. *Manhattan* reaches the level of Renoir's *Rules of the Game* as a high-comedy work.

There still remains the problem (pinpointed by Pauline Kael) of Isaac's judgmental insistence in voiceovers that "he saw New York as a metaphor for the decay of contemporary culture." What exactly does that mean? How does this intellectual babble differ from the pretentious proclamations he satirizes in Mary and so many others? Allen expressed more of it in interviews, saying that the context for the film was a society "desensitized by television, drugs, fast-food chains, loud music and feelingless, mechanical sex." Isaac also speaks into his tape recorder a common plaint of Allen's (and a more grounded one) that "people are constantly creating these unnecessary neurotic problems for themselves because it keeps them from dealing with the terrible, unsolvable problems of the universe."

Allen took on the role of intellectual scold when he told an impressed Natalie Gittelson that "until we find a resolution for our terrors, we're going to have an expedient culture." She was so taken with this exhortation that she (or her editors at the *Times Magazine*) used it as an outtake caption at the top of the article. In addition, the magazine asked, could this be possible: "Is this Woody Allen speaking? Yes, the new Woody Allen . . . an uncommonly serious artist at work." Actually Allen shows what he is talking about much more clearly in his art, when in the film both Mary and Yale are all too eager to shed whatever integrity they think they possess for expediency: Mary, working on a novelization for a movie; Yale, prizing that Porsche above his book and his magazine.

"A Comic Genius: Woody Allen Comes of Age." Allen's picture was on the cover of *Time* with that headline on April 30, 1979. It was written by one of Allen's most astute critics, Richard Schickel. He said that *Manhattan* was "tightly constructed, clearly focused intellectually . . . a prismatic portrait of a time and place that may be studied decades hence to see what kind of people we were."

"We have to go at it the hard way," Allen told Schickel, "and come to terms with the fact that the universe seems to contain only the grimmest possibilities. We have to develop structures of our own that encourage us to believe that it genuinely pays to make the moral choice just from the pragmatic point of view."

The late Charles Joffe told Schickel that Allen could be "extremely arrogant and extremely hostile. He has to be goddamn comfortable with you before he'll show it, and it's not really related to his ego. It's related to the demands he makes on himself."

In one of the best character portraits of Allen ever drawn, Schickel wrote: "Everything is submerged into his work, at which he labors compulsively, since it is the vehicle through which he exercises his self-determined imperative to keep growing intellectually and spiritually."

Allen was forty-three years old.

# 7. The Woman Who Saves Leonard Zelig

BEGINNING IN 1980 and continuing to 1994, Allen made a series of mostly great and remarkable films—one a year, year in and year out. After the problematic *Stardust Memories,* in which he seemed to flay both his fans and his enemies alike, and the radiant *A Midsummer Night's Sex Comedy,* the masterpieces and near-masterpieces practically cascaded over themselves: *Zelig, Broadway Danny Rose, The Purple Rose of Cairo, Hannah and Her Sisters, Radio Days, Oedipus Wrecks, Crimes and Misdemeanors, Alice, Husbands and Wives,* and *Bullets over Broadway.* Soon he would have yet a third wave: *Mighty Aphrodite, Everyone Says I Love You, Deconstructing Harry, Anything Else, Match Point, Cassandra's Dream, Vicky Cristina Barcelona, You Will Meet a Tall Dark Stranger, Midnight in Paris,* and *Blue Jasmine.*

These films, Richard Schickel wrote, "constitute one of the great runs of movies ever made by any director in a relatively short span of time." There were also three disasters: *September, Another Woman,* and *Shadows and Fog,* although Schickel didn't think so, and *Manhattan Murder Mystery,* the kind of film Woody might describe as one of his "baubles." Woody wouldn't be Woody without some fumbling attempts at higher meaning. As long as he stayed centered, as long as he stuck to what he knew or could conjure up out of his own experience and imagination, he was terrific. And many great films would come still later—and there isn't the slightest indication that they will end soon.

First in line was *Stardust Memories,* a flawed film, but one that proved to be a watershed for Allen: It was the first time that he openly expressed ambivalence about fame and celebrity, and especially about his fans, for whom he seemed to have contempt. The film's protagonist and point of view feel so close to the real Allen that his denials were not very convincing. (There had been actual retrospective cinema weekends like the one depicted in the film, conducted by film critic Judith Crist, honoring Allen.)

*Stardust Memories* begins on a crowded train car and seems to depict a dream. Allen is seated with a group of very sad, ugly, desolate-looking people. He peers out the window and sees a train on a parallel track. It is filled with glamorous, beautiful women and couples, drinking and carousing. One of them, the young Sharon Stone, blows him a teasing kiss. Bates springs up and desperately tries to open the door so he can cross over to the other side, but the door is firmly locked. He is stuck with the uglies. When the train finally reaches its destination, the protagonist, Sandy Bates, finds himself in a garbage dump, the final destination for the people in both cars. There are Holocaust echoes here, but the scene more specifically evokes thoughts of Allen's comments about life itself being a Holocaust—a point of view that I have never understood.

Bates, a famous comic filmmaker, is trying to leave his comic films behind and strive for something more serious, but his fans constantly tell him they loved his films the way they were, "especially the early funny ones."

He is attracted to three women, two of whom are borderline mental cases: the skeletal Dorrie and the bisexual, manic-depressive Daisy— the kind of women Allen has always asserted he is drawn to—and the more grounded Isabel, who has two children and about whom Bates cannot make up his mind. Allen has insisted that the film is about Bates going through a breakdown. And that it is really partly a series of Bates's dreams, anxieties, and fantasies, partly scenes from the new movie he is unveiling at the hotel, and partly realistic moments that occur during that weekend at the Stardust. It is difficult to know which of these elements various scenes represent. Allen has said that the film might have been more successful if he had not appeared in it, since his fans confused the character of Bates with the real Allen.

Its atmosphere of brittle bitterness and sour dislike of Bates's fans hurts the film. It feels misanthropic. Bates does not encounter a single person among the throngs of fans for whom he feels any liking or respect. They are always loathsome, stupid, envious, self-seeking grotesques. They want to use him for charitable or social causes; they want to feed off him and somehow profit from his success. The fans are damned if they praise him or if they criticize him. They are stupid either way. Bates does not see himself in the glorified way his fans see him at all. He doesn't share their worship. Sometimes the atmosphere is leavened by a light, perceptive touch: the young woman who turns up in his bed with a Woody/Bates T-shirt. Bates asks her if her husband knows what she's doing, and she replies that he's sleeping in the van downstairs, and he would be honored if Bates would fuck her. Bates lectures her about the emptiness of anonymous sex. She replies, "Listen, empty sex is better than no sex, right?" and flicks off the bedside light. The scene rings true about the nature of fandom. On the other hand, did this actually happen to Allen? Probably more than once.

Another nice note is the arrival of aliens from outer space who also badger him about no longer making funny movies. The film does have these highlights, including the childhood friend who turns up, filled with self-defeat and jealousy of Bates. Bates tries to console him by telling him that life is all a matter of luck and chance; that if Bates had been born in Poland during the war, he would have ended up as a lampshade. But this is precisely the Allen philosophy of life. It reinforces our awareness that Bates represents Allen, despite his denials.

Another clever scene illustrates one of Allen's often-expressed dilemmas with women. Two women lie unconscious on operating-room tables. Sandy, dressed as a doctor, says he's never been able to find the perfect woman. He touches the head of one of the women, Doris, who has a great personality and is a wonderful woman, but doesn't turn him on. He touches Rita, the other woman and tells us she's nasty, an animal, "trouble. And I love going to bed with her." After sex, he says, he always wishes he were with Doris. He decides the answer is to put Doris's brain in Rita's body. He performs the operation and switches their personalities. "I took all the badness and put it over there," he says. "And I made Rita into a warm, wonderful, charming, sexy, sweet, giving, mature woman." And then, he says, "I fell in love with Doris." Again, this is the same Allen we know from scores of his accounts of his experiences with women. A scene that seems prescient is of Bates's fantasy of being murdered by an adoring fan who first tells him that he loves him. Ten weeks after the film's release, John Lennon would be murdered by a fan in front of the Dakota.

Allen would later tackle the subject of celebrity more successfully in *Zelig* and *Celebrity*, a film that successfully combines elements of comedy and humor with pathos, and in which his character is portrayed by Kenneth Branagh. But Allen's presence is not the stumbling block in *Stardust Memories*, nor is it burdened by its obvious debt to Fellini's *8½*. Allen has often managed to pay homage to films he has admired without imitating them. The real problem in the film is the deep ambivalence of the filmmaker, an almost unguarded expression of sour contempt that lingers long after the film is over. "One critic said my audience's left me," Allen told Sean Mitchell of the *Los Angeles Times* in 1992, "but the truth is I left my audience. The backlash really started when I did *Stardust Memories*. I still think that's one of the best films I ever made. I was just trying to make what I wanted, not what people wanted me to make."

Pauline Kael would have none of it. "Woody Allen calls himself Sandy Bates this time," she wrote. "But there's only the merest wisp of a pretext that he is playing a character; this is the most undisguised of his dodgy mock-autobiographical fantasies. . . . Allen degrades the people who respond to his work and presents himself as their victim. He seems to feel that they want him to heal them; the film suggests a *Miss Lonelyhearts* written without irony. . . .

> *He's trying to stake out his claim to be an artist like Fellini or Bergman—to be accepted in the serious, gentile artists' club. And he sees his public as Jews trying to shove him back down in the Jewish clowns' club. Great artists' admirers are supposed to keep their distance. His admirers feel they know him and can approach him; they feel he belongs to them—and he sees them as his murderers. . . . If Woody Allen finds success very upsetting and wishes the public would go away, this picture should help him stop worrying.*

John Simon was equally tough: "Almost everything we are told or shown about Sandy Bates is true of Woody Allen, yet with enough deviations from strict autobiography to allow Allen to declare it presumptuous to equate him with his protagonist. . . . [The fans] are all such super-Fellinian grotesques and behave like stampeding pigs . . . the kinds of loathsome pests that do not leave you a private minute . . . when Bates-Allen mentions 'Art and masturbation—two areas in which I am an expert,' I say there is no doubt about it—he just has difficulty figuring out which is which."

Kael and Simon could not have foreseen that Allen's finest achievements—another lifetime's worth—lay ahead of him.

Allen's relationship with United Artists dissolved after the financial failure of *Stardust Memories*, and he began to look elsewhere for financing. Steven Bach was eager to keep him, but with Arthur Krim's departure for Orion Pictures, there was little doubt that Allen would join Orion. Allen would have left UA in 1978 when Krim formed Orion, but he was always true to his word and honored the original contract.

Steven Bach met with him at the Russian Tea Room and tried to persuade him to stay with UA. Allen told him, "You've been wonderful . . . everyone's been wonderful." He continued, "But it's not about business, exactly."

"It's about loyalty," Bach said: It was about Krim.

Allen nodded. "It's not possible sometimes *not* to disappoint *some*body. I don't want to disappoint *anybody*."

Several weeks followed. During that time Michael Cimino's *Heaven's Gate*, which would prove to be one of the greatest financial film disasters of all time, opened to reviews so terrible that UA's very survival came into question. (The film did, in fact, soon sink the studio.) Allen could not have been unaware of what had occurred, but there was no question that he would not have gone with UA in any case. He would not betray Krim. He called Bach with his regrets.

In December 1980 a contract was drawn up with Orion. Allen signed to make three films over the next five years, and to star in at least two of them. The new contract gave Allen 15 percent of a film's gross receipts, which he would share with his producer, Robert Greenhut, and Rollins and Joffe, instead of first waiting until the studio had recouped its costs.

It was during this period that Allen first met Mia Farrow in 1979 at

Elaine's. Michael Caine and his wife had taken Mia to dinner there—she was appearing on Broadway in a play by Bernard Slade called *Romantic Comedy*—and spotted Allen at another table. When Mia expressed interest in him, the Caines urged her to send him a note. He quickly came over to meet her, and invited her to his New Year's Eve party. Allen and Farrow didn't actually get together until April 1980, when he invited her to dinner at Lutèce. By this time, the still-angelic-looking Farrow had two marriages with famous older men—Frank Sinatra and André Previn—behind her. She also had left in the wake of her second marriage a devastated ex-wife who was hospitalized for a breakdown.

Maria de Lourdes Villiers Farrow, born in Beverly Hills on February 9, 1945, was the fourth child and first daughter of the actress Maureen O'Sullivan and the director-writer John Farrow. She was show-business royalty; the gossip columnist Louella Parsons was her godmother and the director George Cukor her godfather. She contracted polio at nine and spent three weeks in an isolation unit in Los Angeles. Her brother Michael died in a plane crash at thirteen. When she was seventeen, her father died of a heart attack.

She had been involved with older male celebrities her entire life, beginning with Kirk Douglas and Yul Brynner. She had a platonic relationship with Salvador Dalí; they ate butterflies in the Terrace Room of the St. Regis Hotel in Manhattan. The writer Michael Thornton told Sarah Rainey of the London *Daily Telegraph* that Mia was "very intelligent, tremendously attractive and underrated. She was neither one sex nor the other. She was androgynous. She looked like a denizen of another planet. And she was very young—not mentally, but to look at."

Despite Farrow's penchant for pop spirituality and mysticism, she was tough and wildly ambitious. According to Kitty Kelley, Farrow said, "I want a big career, a big man, and a big life. You have to think big. That's the only way to get it." Her father was as complex and difficult as the men she would be drawn to, a volatile, brooding alcoholic, a Roman Catholic scholar (he wrote reputable histories of the papacy and the life of Thomas More), a womanizer, and a director, producer, and screenwriter. He won the Academy Award for Best Adapted Screenplay in 1957 for *Around the*

*World in Eighty Days*, and he had been nominated as Best Director in 1942 for *Wake Island*.

Mia met Frank Sinatra in 1964 when she was nineteen, the same year she starred in the TV series *Peyton Place*. She spoke to Sinatra on the set of a film he was shooting, *Von Ryan's Express*. The two—the greatest singer of any generation, a man who lived hard and nastily, and the mystical, ethereal waif with long flowing blond hair who always kept a box of charms, relics, and amulets with her—were instantly drawn to each other and married on July 19, 1966. They were soon battling, however. The director Roman Polanski had offered Farrow the starring role in *Rosemary's Baby* and arranged with the top international hairdresser Vidal Sassoon to give her a boyish haircut for the film. Sinatra was upset by the trendy haircut and by Farrow's anti–Vietnam War stance.

Polanski was taking too long to finish shooting the film, and the controlling Sinatra insisted Farrow leave it to costar with him in *The Detective*. Mia refused. Sinatra replaced her with Jacqueline Bisset. The marriage didn't last much longer, and they divorced in 1968.

Farrow and Sinatra seemed to fare better as friends later than they did as husband and wife. She does not exactly skirt his maniacal, violent side in her memoir, *What Falls Away*, but insists that few people knew the hidden, sensitive Sinatra: "They can't see the wounding tenderness that even he can't bear to acknowledge—except when he sings. Maybe if they looked at the earliest photos of Frank, when he was a skinny kid singing in his big bow ties, if they really looked at that face, almost feminine in its beauty, they'd see exactly who it was that Frank Sinatra the tough guy has spent his life trying to protect."

She went on to write with a cloying sentimentality and stunning lack of clarity: "He was absolutely without falseness, without artifice, in a world of pretenders. He had a child's sense of outrage at any perceived unfairness and an inability to compromise. He was tough in his judgments of others, and of himself."

This rationalized interpretation of Sinatra's actions led Farrow to write that he phoned her on the Paramount set and told her that he'd been in a fight, the caps were punched off his teeth, "some other guy had been hurt," and that "his dentist was on the way with new teeth." To Farrow it "didn't matter much what started the fight"; it was because of Sinatra's "powerful

Sicilian sense of propriety . . . which could get a little cloudy. . . ." Sinatra sounded "bewildered and upset . . . because he loved and needed me." She went on to find his behavior—he didn't tell her what had actually happened—a matter of honor: "Although the armies of his heart and mind did frequent battle and left him isolated and restless, in matters of conscience and of human hope, they were one."

Mia had been part of a wild ride on a golf cart with Sinatra on a rampage heading toward the plate-glass window entrance of the Sands Hotel in Las Vegas. Sinatra, wearing a shoebox over his head to keep the sun out of his eyes (Mia perched on the cart behind him), suddenly swerved and smashed sidelong into the window. Unhurt, Sinatra hurried into the hotel, threw some chairs into a heap, and tried to set them on fire with a lighter. "When he couldn't get a fire started," Mia wrote, "he took my hand and we walked out of the building."

What followed the next night was the incident that Mia called Frank's "matter of conscience and human hope." She was no longer at the hotel.

The Sands Hotel was the center of entertainment on the Sunset Strip and the birthplace of the Rat Pack. Sinatra had owned 9 percent of it and considered it his personal playground and domain. He had also bought into the Cal-Neva Lodge in Lake Tahoe, with the help of the mobster Sam Giancana, who helped Sinatra get a $1.75 million loan to refurbish it. Sinatra always hosted Giancana at his homes and hotels. In July 1963 Giancana was secretly staying at the Cal-Neva. When the Nevada Gaming Control Board discovered that Sinatra allowed an outlawed person into the lodge, he lost his gambling license and was forced to sell his interests in both the lodge and the Sands. Howard Hughes bought the Sands in 1967 and cut off Sinatra's line of credit.

Furious at Hughes, Sinatra had exacted his revenge, including the scene with the golf cart and refusing to perform his show, claiming he was ill. As a result he took out his rage on Carl Cohen, the executive vice president of the Sands. Sinatra was anything but an anti-Semite, but in his alcohol-fueled rages, he was capable of great cruelty. According to Kitty Kelley:

> [Sinatra] returned to the Sands and went on a drunken rampage at five a.m. . . . [He] called Carl Cohen, demanding to see him at once. Cohen agreed, and at five forty-five a.m. he . . . sat down at a table with Frank and [Stanley] Parker. . . .

*"I'll get a guy to bury you, you son of a bitch motherfucker. You kike!"*
*Sinatra screamed.*

*He [Cohen] smashed his right fist into Frank's face, splitting his upper lip*
*and knocking the caps off two front teeth.*

The marriage between Farrow and Sinatra was soon over. Mia took no alimony, only a nine-carat diamond ring, a bracelet encrusted with diamonds, and other pieces of jewelry. Mia and her sister Prudence retreated to seek enlightenment with the Maharishi in New Delhi at his ashram in 1968. (Allen would later draw upon this aspect of Mia's life at the conclusion of *Alice* by depicting Alice—played by Farrow—as journeying to work with Mother Teresa in India.) Participants were supposed to meditate for twelve hours of the day. Mia couldn't manage that many hours, but read the Bhagavad Gita. The Beatles also arrived, with "their cheerful chatter and guitars and singing," and brightened up the place. Before they left, they wrote the song "Dear Prudence" for Mia's sister. Farrow describes her weeks in India as a "long hallucination." She rode in buses, cars, rickshaws, a bullock cart; slept in huts, hotels, and dives; rode an elephant; and explored temples, monasteries, and palaces. "I did not feel at home" in India, she writes, and departed to take a role in a film, *Secret Ceremony,* in London. There she went through a time of "disorder" and "mounting depression" and an overdose of pills. Farrow recovered and went to work on the film, lunching every day with Elizabeth Taylor and Richard Burton.

Back in Malibu, the "new me [Farrow] celebrated spring," marched against the Vietnam War, met people "who awakened a vision of countless thousands of golden threads streaming, spinning, weaving through time and space, connecting all of humanity, creating a shimmering cloth, a fragment of Being, through which we could transcend our separate selves to touch an infinite whole." This beatific and psychedelic vision seemed to sustain her as she traveled with Roman Polanski and Sharon Tate to Joshua Tree, a spectacular stretch of desert in Southern California, Big Sur, Paris, London, New York, Texas, and Acapulco.

The ambitious flower child then went to work on a film called *John and Mary,* with Dustin Hoffman, and began to form a telephone relationship with the gifted pianist and composer André Previn, who at the time was the conductor of the London Symphony Orchestra. Farrow had known

Previn and his wife, Dory, a prolific lyricist, for years and was considered a friend by Dory. She would visit the Previns, chat with Dory, admire her wedding ring, and knit in the corner by the fireplace. Dory Previn was the lyricist of three Oscar-nominated songs, two of which she wrote with her husband. She also received a third Oscar nomination for her song "Come Saturday Morning" (written with Fred Karlin), the theme for the film *The Sterile Cuckoo.*

Mia joined the Previns at musicales, still knitting in the corner, in her white tights and frilly outfits. Dory Previn, who had suffered from a lifetime of schizophrenia and depression (she'd been hospitalized for a nervous breakdown in 1965), was devastated by the relationship that developed between Previn and Farrow. She wrote a song about it, "Beware of Young Girls," which gained considerable attention. She warned wives of girls: "Wistful and pale of twenty and four / delivering daisies with delicate hands. . . . I thought her motives were sincere . . . this lass . . . had a dark and different plan / She brought me pain." In 1969 Dory discovered that Mia was pregnant, and she left her husband. She had another serious breakdown soon afterward and was treated with electroconvulsive therapy. (Many years later, in 1997, Dory would collaborate again with André Previn—who continued to be a supportive friend throughout her life—on a piece for soprano and ensemble, *The Magic Number,* which was performed by the New York Philharmonic. She died in 2013.)

And so Mia did to Dory what Soon-Yi would do to her twenty years later.

Farrow wrote in her memoir, *What Falls Away,* published after her breakup with Allen, that André "had conducted a discreet, separate life [from Dory] for some years, but did not seek a divorce until he met me. Dory Previn experienced things quite differently, and made that clear publicly through her songs. . . . I am sorry to have contributed to her pain," Mia concluded rather tersely.

Farrow had begun the affair with Previn in 1968, when she was twenty-three, and gave birth to twin sons by Previn, Matthew and Sascha, in February 1970. She took her babies along in strollers for antiwar demonstrations, marching beside Vanessa Redgrave. The couple married in September 1970. Farrow and Previn adopted two orphans from Vietnam. Farrow appeared in five plays from 1974 to 1977: *The Three Sisters, A Midsummer Night's Dream, The Marrying of Ann Leete, The Zykovs* (Maxim Gorky), and *Ivanov*, the last three with the Royal Shakespeare Company. By 1977 she grew tired of Previn, who was traveling around the world for his work and was rarely at home with her, and had an affair with Roman Polanski. Near the end of the marriage, she and Previn, with the help of her friend the writer William Styron, who utilized his contacts in Congress, won permission to adopt the child of a Korean prostitute: seven-year-old Soon-Yi, who had been abandoned in the slums of Seoul by her mother and was eating food and soap out of dustbins. The pictures Mia and André had of Soon-Yi were of a sad child with shaved head and sores on her lips. Farrow traveled to Korea to meet Soon-Yi. "When I arrived at the orphanage, a dozen or so little girls combed and clean were lined up on the pavement in front of the entrance. Standing behind the children was a nun who must have pushed Soon-Yi toward me. Out of respect, and not to frighten her, I knelt down, took her hand and smiled."

Soon-Yi had never seen a mirror before, and was frightened by the image of herself in it, jackknifed with fear, and kicked the mirror hard, knocking both herself and Mia backward. "Soon-Yi didn't know about mirrors," Mia wrote, "or revolving doors, or carpets, or elevators, or ice, or eggs (I picked the shells out of her mouth), or grass, or flowers, or in fact most of the things that most of us took for granted. Whatever caught her fancy—paper clips, peanuts, money, flowers, rubber bands, chewing-gum wrappers, Cheerios—she stashed in her underpants."

The tone of Farrow's book informs us that it is the work of a very virtuous woman. The sheer fact of Farrow's fourteen children dares us to make any other less favorable assumptions about her. As Kathryn Harrison wrote in her review of *What Falls Away* in the *New York Times*, "The desire to transform a life, to offer love and security to a destitute and ailing orphan, is not one that requires explanation. But adopting ten children, added to four of one's own, ten children whose frailty and need are increasingly equated with their desirability, prompts curiosity. What drives it? . . . The reader begins to suspect that what Ms. Farrow is really collecting is order, solace, meaning, redemption."

Mia then proceeded to leave Previn, as Dory had predicted in her song: "She will leave him, one thoughtless day." Polanski, indicted for having had sex with a thirteen-year-old model and giving her drugs, fled to Paris. Mia would be outspoken in her defense of him. Mia took the children and moved into her old family home in Woods Hole in Martha's Vineyard.

She and André Previn were divorced at the end of 1979. Out of money, she took the role in *Romantic Comedy* in December 1979.

Another of Dory's songs, "With My Daddy in the Attic," has come to shadow, if not haunt, Mia. Its lyrics about a child being the victim of incest with her father in an attic are uncannily prescient of the charges Mia brought against Allen in 1992 and repeated (along with daughter Dylan) in 2014. The coincidence—not to mention that the song was on the same album with Dory's other song about Mia, "Beware of Young Girls"—is striking. It is impossible that Mia had not heard the song. Is it possible that she drummed it into her brain and found inspiration in it for her charges against Allen? Surely the detail of the father playing the clarinet—Allen's instrument—could also have resonated with her.

The lyrics in part go like this:

*In the terrifying nearness*
*Of his eyes*
*With no*
*Window spying neighbors . . .*
*To intrude*
*Upon our attic*
*he'll play*
*His clarinet . . .*

I am not the first to wonder whether there's a connection here. The writers Robert Weide and Andrew Sullivan, among others, have raised this question. And so, of course, has Woody Allen himself, in his op-ed piece of Feburary 9, 2014, in the *New York Times:*

"Undoubtedly the attic idea came to [Mia] from the Dory Previn song, 'With My Daddy in the Attic.' It was on the same record as the song Dory Previn had written about Mia's betraying their friendship by insidiously stealing her husband André, 'Beware of Young Girls.' "

Mia's romance with Allen sparked quickly. Allen was forty-five; Farrow was thirty-four. After they met in April 1980, they exchanged gifts on a daily basis and began to spend all their free time together, roaming through Manhattan and, carrying a bottle of Château Margaux and two wineglasses in a paper bag through Central Park. They went to record stores like the Colony and Tower (where Mickey runs into Holly in *Hannah*), to bookstores like the Pageant on East Ninth, where Allen gave Farrow the poems of e.e. cummings (as Elliot gives them to Lee in *Hannah*), and to Allen's favorite art house movie theaters. Allen's chauffeured Rolls-Royce took them to their favorite restaurants and picked them up at the end of their strolls. Their apartments were across the park from each other; they claimed they blinked their lights, waved towels, and scanned each other with binoculars. It became part of the romantic mythology that surrounded them.

It does appear from Farrow's memoir that the two had genuinely fallen in love. They were not terribly young, and they had already lived several disparate lives. They shared a love of Mozart, Mahler, Yeats, Dostoyevsky. They would meet for lunch and talk for hours until they looked up and discovered that the sky was dark. Allen would leave notes and gifts for her with her doorman, and she would do the same for him. They watched classic films like *The Bicycle Thief* in Allen's screening room, sipping wine and cuddling. She was impressed with his intelligence, his talent, his celebrity, and his wealth; to him, she represented the Hollywood upper crust that he was in awe of, and she was both magnetic and beautiful. There was a romantic gloss to the relationship for both of them; life must have seemed easier and more challenging, more promising to her, a single mother of seven children, with Allen's chauffeur waiting at attention outside beside the white Rolls-Royce; his penthouse apartment, his constant trips to Paris. It was a world, Farrow wrote, "of expensive restaurants, fine wines, chartered airplanes, enough caviar for even the littlest kid, and chauffeur-driven stretch limos. . . . I struggled to keep things in perspective for my kids." And there was no question that as America's premier film director, Allen could be of great help to her acting career.

This is not to say that either Mia or Woody was exploitative; they were genuinely impassioned with each other in the beginning. She wrote him that she couldn't wait to see him; he wrote that he couldn't take not seeing her for a whole week. He sent her a 1935 postcard that featured a man in a bowler hat with five children. Woody had printed across the top, "YOUR FUTURE HUSBAND—YOUR FUTURE CHILDREN." They were seen everywhere, walking in Central Park with the children in hand, and they seemed to be the most romantic and chic couple in town, quintessentially New York, rich and successful. Mia seemed like an earth mother, warm and maternal but glamorous and sensual at the same time. Allen, remote and neurotic, was just Woody; his tics and mannerisms were by now part of his charm.

There were warning signs, but Farrow chose to ignore them: Allen never phoned her (his secretary did); she claimed that he did not like to call her "Mia" and instead would refer to her as "her" and "she"; his hypochondria was somewhat alarming; and he was not fond of children. (That last must have particularly worried a mother of seven.) As a director, his "icy sternness pushed my apprehension toward raw fear" when she acted in her first movie with him, *A Midsummer Night's Sex Comedy.* "There are certain directors," he told her, "who have affectionate relationships with actors, but I've never been able to work that way. I give as much contact as is required professionally." There was the beach house he bought for millions in East Hampton and had decorated lavishly before moving in. He and Mia spent one night at the house, and Allen, unable to tolerate the country, never returned to it and sold it immediately. There was also the famous issue of the shower at Frogs Hollow, Mia's country estate in Bridgewater, Connecticut. Allen would not use a bathtub, so she had a tile shower built for him. He entered the bathroom and exited instantly, complaining that the drain was in the middle and that he could not use it or stay in the house more than one night. Farrow then had built an entirely new bathroom with a shower that had a drain in the corner.

There was the scene in front of William F. Buckley, Jr.'s, town house on East Seventy-third Street. According to Farrow, Buckley had a symbolic importance to Allen, and his presence in that neighborhood was significant to him. (Allen and Buckley had appeared on television together, and it was obvious that they had respect for and cordiality toward each other.) Farrow wrote that when she misidentified the location of Buckley's house, Allen launched an attack on her greater than any she had experienced in her life, which left her sobbing and "vaporized" on the sidewalk. While the latter part of her book is written in great anger toward Allen, the first part, which includes this account, seems relatively free of distortion. Furthermore, the account of Allen's tantrum may ring true, since Allen's obsession with WASPs is certainly a part of his psychic makeup, and Buckley, more than anyone else, symbolized the elegant, handsome, bril-

liant, rich, and wise WASP with a mellifluous voice—*the* preeminent representative of the breed—although he happened to be Catholic.

And, most significant, Allen had no intention, really, of marriage or
even of living with Farrow and the children. He would not alter that stance
for the duration of their relationship. He was not the more malleable, if
neurotic, Woody of the struggling years with Harlene and Louise. His work
schedule had always been paramount. But by now, when he had achieved
enormous success for many years, Allen was set in his ways and totally
committed to cementing his reputation with more expansive and serious
work. He lived to write. Absolutely nothing was going to get in his way.
"The subject of marriage came up a few times over the years," Farrow
wrote. "'It's just a piece of paper,' he would say. . . . He was never kinder or
more reassuring. . . . 'Do I not behave as if we are married?' . . . I would
answer that he did." Allen maintains that his attitude changed when Farrow adopted Dylan as a newborn in 1985. He was transformed. "At that
point," he said, "I just became what I consider a wonderful, wonderful father to Dylan. It became the single most important thing in my life."

The *New York Times* reported that Allen described Farrow, who had
eleven children at the time, "as a woman obsessed with motherhood, who
would become fixated for a time on one child to the exclusion of others."

Allen never slept over at Farrow's apartment on Central Park West
and Seventy-third Street, but Farrow occasionally stayed at his penthouse
on Friday and Saturday nights with the seven children. She had deposited
toothbrushes, coats, and dressing gowns for them at his apartment. He
provided shelves for sleeping bags, dolls, stamp animals, and pajamas. He
even bought bunk beds. In 1980 she adopted a new child, a sensitive
Korean boy christened Misha Amadeus Farrow, who would be called
Moses. A warm and loving child, he suffered from cerebral palsy. She
now had the ten-year-old twins, Matthew and Sascha; Lark and Soon-Yi,
who were seven; Daisy and Fletcher, who were both six; and Misha. Farrow wrote in her memoir that Woody was not comfortable with the children but made an effort with them, trading in his white Rolls-Royce for a
stretch limo to accommodate them all, and would screen movies for
them on weekends at his Park Avenue offices. Once she left the children
with him at his apartment, and when she returned, "he was throwing his
hats and gloves into the fire. The kids were ecstatic. 'I ran out of things to
do,' he shrugged."

A key to Farrow's psychological mind-set and her supposed subjugation to Allen was her retrospective reflection about why she put up with so much, including what she considered to be Allen's indifference to most of her children: "But then he was king in our midst: the one who knew everything, whose concerns were greater than most, a *superior* person. His opinions were the final word. And he could cut you quicker than you could open your mouth. We admired him and we were afraid of him, each in our own way."

Allen's first Broadway play, *The Floating Light Bulb*, with its poignant clues into his early childhood, had opened in September 1980 at Lincoln Center's Vivian Beaumont Theater. The director, Ulu Grosbard, told director and screenwriter John Andrew Gallagher, "Woody was absolutely ruthless with his own stuff. If a line wasn't working I'd have to stop him from cutting it out. If he wasn't satisfied with something he'd walk into another room at the rehearsal hall and come back with four alternatives. He would say to me, 'Okay, pick the one you like best and I'll work off that.' I mean, it was instant. I was really amazed."

Allen's friend, Jean Doumanian, one of the women he would stay very close to for a long time, had recently been fired from a directing role on *Saturday Night Live*. The day before *The Floating Light Bulb* opened, depressed, she decided to fly to Paris, and in a gesture of friendship, Allen and Farrow joined her. The play would run only sixty-five performances, but it remains one of Allen's two best dramas.

Farrow's second film with Allen was *Zelig*, in 1983. Allen is sometimes taken for granted, and *Zelig* is a case in point. This film alone would have established any other director-writer as a filmmaker of the first rank. But in Allen's case, it is quickly submerged in the flood of his output, future and past films, that come at us with such speed that it is difficult to digest them and place them in proper perspective. There is inadequate time to assess each one.

*Zelig* was the first film in which Mia and Woody appeared as a couple. Their relationship was two years old. Allen's films with Farrow offer some clues about the nature of their relationship at different points. In *Zelig*, Mia plays the psychiatrist who saves Allen's character and marries him. (Allen in his ambivalence named her Dr. Eudora Fletcher, the real name of the school principal he detested in his boyhood.)

Allen was very much in love with Farrow when the film was made. It is one of the few Allen films in which the woman saves the man. It is unique in the Woody canon. The woman takes on the man, suffers through him, and saves him. In many of his films, Allen's protagonists try to save the women. He often grapples with women bitches who reject him, who can't be pleased (Annie Hall) or are crazy, lost, and abrasive (Mary in *Manhattan*), clinically psychotic (Dorrie in *Stardust Memories*), or heartbreakers (Halley in *Crimes and Misdemeanors*). Only once, in *Zelig*, does the perfect woman take on the difficult man and save him. Usually the *women* are the Zeligs.

Can this have been Woody in 1983? Zelig is the self-loathing Jew. The shiksa rescues him. She's perfect. She's not only a psychiatrist; she's ahead of her time.

Zelig wants to fit in, but he always gives himself away. The public always turns on him. Allen, who was in analysis, is saved by a female psychiatrist (an even more groundbreaking concept in the film's 1930s setting). She saves the self-hating Jew who tries to be like the pope, who tries to be like Hitler. And Leonard Zelig and Dr. Eudora Fletcher live happily ever after. *Zelig* is a fascinating glimpse into how Allen might have seen Farrow—and their relationship—in 1981.

If Allen cast Mia as the psychiatrist who takes on the difficult man and saves him because he actually perceived her that way in life, there is at least the possibility that Soon-Yi, who works with special-needs children, is, as Jerry Epstein speculated, playing that role now with Allen.

If that is the case, Allen has once again proved a genius at getting what he wants.

Allen bristled in disagreement when I wrote him that I considered *Zelig* a masterpiece. Yet I believe that to be true—the first of a new series of truly great films from Allen. The film is a pseudodocumentary about Zelig, the "Human Chameleon," for which Allen, his cinematographer, Gordon Willis, and editor, Susan Morse, utilized thirty hours of stock footage from old newsreels, photographs, and radio broadcasts. Newly shot black-and-white footage that simulated historical scenes was superimposed on the old footage. It is a remarkable technical feat. Zelig is seen standing behind Hitler at a real Nazi rally, and he is seen with Eugene O'Neill and many other historical figures. The new footage and trick effects were aged to match the graininess of the old. Allen went to a tremendous effort. He supervised the compilation of still photographs and archival film materials onto which his fictional character was superimposed. The result is startlingly real, but Allen felt that the technical innovations of the film overshadowed what he was trying to say. He is wrong.

The portrait of the insecure man who tries to meld into his environment by agreeing with whomever he meets, assuming their personality and even their appearance, resonates so deeply with our own experiences that *Zelig* is unforgettable. It is the parable of fascism and communism that Allen intended, unique and absolutely original. The style and content of the old newsreels, even the ancient sound of the microphones (actual 1928 microphones were used), feel authentic. In *Zelig* Allen achieved some of the blazing strengths and originality of Orson Welles's *Citizen Kane*, which was also framed as a mock-documentary. *Zelig* was Allen's greatest triumph as a filmmaker up to this point in his career. The comedy does not overwhelm the drama, nor does the drama swamp the comedy.

The film is relatively short; it goes on only as long as it needs to in order to make its statement. Allen's use of real major writers and personalities throughout the film as commentators (Allen wrote their dialogue) lends further credibility to the film even though we know they are participating in a fiction. Saul Bellow, Irving Howe, Bruno Bettelheim, and Susan Sontag are among the participants. At least one—Saul Bellow—in retrospect, felt he had been tricked, although what Bellow expected from America's foremost comic director is unclear. Warren Beatty's *Reds*, which also utilized famous historical and literary figures, came to life only when they were present. In *Zelig* the real characters further the impact of the film, but they are only one of its many highlights. *Zelig* as a whole is mesmerizing.

The film is also another meditation by Allen on the nature of celebrity, but unlike *Stardust Memories*, everything in *Zelig* feels objective, compressed, compassionate, and in the service of a theme beyond Allen's own personal problems and history. The film is deliciously funny: It's the Woody wit, but Zelig is not just another version of Woody the nebbish; the humor is geared to Zelig's specific character. It's a sweet humor, an aspect of Allen that surfaces in many of his films, like *Broadway Danny Rose* and *Midnight in Paris*. When Zelig is sued for bigamy, adultery, plagiarism, negligence, performing unnecessary dental extractions and medical operations, among

other things, he humbly apologizes: "I should like to apologize to everyone
I . . . I'm awfully sorry for . . . for marrying all those women, it . . . it just,
I don't know, it just seemed like the thing to do. And to the, to the gentleman whose appendix I took out. . . . I . . . I'm . . . I don't know what to
say . . . if it's any consolation I . . . I may still have it somewhere around
the house. . . . I-I my deepest apology goes to the Trokman family in
Detroit. . . . I, I never delivered a baby before in my life and I, I just
thought that . . . ice tongs was the way to do it."

Because Zelig becomes whomever he is with, he is a psychiatrist when
he is with Dr. Fletcher. To help cure him, she tries reverse psychology. She
tells him that she is very insecure, and she outlines the fears and uncer-
tainties that she knows are Zelig's. She tells him she is not really a psychiatrist: "You see, I want so badly to be, to be liked, to be like other
people so that I don't stand out."

Zelig comments, "That's natural."

She says that she goes to such extreme lengths in order to blend in.
Zelig comments, "Well, you're a doctor, you know, you know how to handle that." Fletcher responds, "The truth of the matter is, I . . . I'm not an
actual doctor."

ZELIG: You're not?

DR. FLETCHER: No doctor. No. (*shaking her head*) I've been pretending
to be a doctor to, to fit in with my friends. You see, they're
doctors.

ZELIG: (*scratching his head*) Sss . . . that's something. (*fidgeting*)
That's . . . tsss.

Fletcher goes on to say that her whole life has been a lie, that she has
been posing as one thing after after another.

Zelig responds, squirming: "Well—you need help, lady. . . ."

She tells him of her dreams and asks him what she's suffering from.
Zelig responds, "How should I know? I'm not a doctor!"

There is the love scene laced with delicate humor in which, under hypnosis, Zelig murmurs to her, "I love you," and then, "You're the worst
cook . . . those pancakes. I love you. . . . I want to take care of you. No
more pancakes."

Allen's sly parodistic humor permeates the film: He creates within the

documentary yet another pseudofilm that is supposed to be a dramatiza-
tion of Zelig's life, and which also satirizes the biographical films of the
past; he creates songs and dances that capture the spirit of the period but
are supposed to be about Zelig. Zelig's name is interposed not only in
films but in the lyrics of contemporary songs like "I'm Sitting on Top of
the World": "Glory hallelujah, I told Leonard Zelig / Hey Len get ready to
call . . ." and he himself is the subject of songs like "Leonard the Lizard,"
and dances like the "Chameleon." Allen also uses the real historic figures
like Howe and Sontag who are supposed to be experts, but whose commentary on Leonard Zelig and other matters are sometimes so abstract,
obvious, and boring that they lose our attention even though they speak
briefly. Allen makes one of his favorite points about pretentious historians
and writers overtaken by abstraction. Famous as they are, the experts
don't have much insight, we don't always know what they are talking about,
and we can't wait to get back to Zelig. The film clips of Hearst, Marion
Davies, Marie Dressler, James Cagney, Irving Berlin, Dolores del Río are
utterly fascinating, not the ghostlike film relics they might seem out of this
context. The use of real film clips combined with simulated footage keeps
us glued to the screen; we see James Cagney chatting with Dr. Eudora
Fletcher, and he affectionately pokes her chin, that famous Cagney gesture we know so well from scores of his films. Zelig and Dr. Fletcher are
given the key to the city, and Dr. Fletcher is honored at City Hall for her
work in curing Zelig; we switch to Dr. Fletcher standing on a flag-draped
platform swinging a champagne bottle against the hull of a ship. The an-
nouncer in voiceover comments in a style we've heard a thousand times
on those ancient newsreels: "Quite a success story for a little girl from the
backwoods." Another voiceover asks the tongue-in-cheek question: "Who
says women are just good for sewing?" Allen gets every detail right.

John Simon wrote that *Zelig* was "the most daring idea for a film Woody
Allen has had so far," and Jack Kroll in *Newsweek* wrote that the film was
"a brilliant cinematic collage that is pure magic, and allows Woody to sati-
rize all sorts of things, from nostalgia, psychoanalysis and The American
Dream to critics, himself and much more. . . . His Zelig is a romantic
who desperately wants the supreme cocktail of realism mixed with glory—
the Great Gatsby as schlemiel."

Pauline Kael, amazingly patronizing, damned the film with faint and
sometimes convoluted praise. She wrote that *Zelig* "is a lovely small com-

edy, but it can't bear the weight of the praise being shoveled on it. If it is a masterpiece, it's a masterpiece only of its own kind. . . . Allen had a vertiginous, original idea for a casual piece, like his Madame Bovary story ['The Kugelmass Episode'], and he worked it out to perfection. The film has a real shine, but it's like a teeny carnival that you may have missed— it was in the yard behind the Methodist church last week. Insignificance is even its subject."

But one of Allen's toughest critics, Stanley Kauffmann, wrote: "The skill is so clever as to approach brilliance. I ignore dozens of gifted artists and technicians when I single out Santo Loquasto for costume designs that combine accuracy with slyness. Allen, as a director, shows a keen eye for the way people looked, and thought they looked in the period: the way they glanced at cameras, posed themselves for photographs, or invented 'business' for newsreels. Behind all this is not only a careful study of period materials, which many directors have done, but a sensitivity to cultural change. Allen, looking back from the present, perceives that this moment is a point of transition from the film camera as an ornament of civilization to a central component of consciousness."

I spoke to Irving Howe's widow, Ilana Howe, a therapist, about Howe's participation in *Zelig*. Woody had referred to Howe's socialist magazine, *Dissent*, in *Annie Hall*, saying he'd thought *Commentary* and *Dissent* had merged to form "*Dissentary*." "Irving was amused," Ilana Howe said, and wrote Woody a note. "You used *Dissent* in your movie. Contribute some money."

"Woody responded," Howe continued. "They met at the Russian Tea Room. There was something ironic in meeting there, where people knew him. He was terribly shy. People approached the table. He shrank; he felt so embarrassed. So why make an appointment there? Choose a dive. He is a walking paradox.

"Anyway, Woody promised to send money. Letters arrived from Woody. He asked Irving how much money he should contribute. Irving said 'As much as you can.' It continued back and forth, but no check. Finally it came. I think it was five hundred dollars. Woody agonized over it for a long time.

"Sometime later the phone call came. Woody would like you to participate in his movie. Irving hung up. He thought it was a practical joke. The phone rang again. The caller asked how much Irving would charge Woody. Irving said he had never appeared in a movie; he didn't know. The caller was quick: 'How much do you charge for a lecture?' He told her. She said, 'Okay, that's what you will get.'

"Irving did not know in advance what the movie was about. One day he received a page or two of a monologue. This was his role. He read it, but he didn't know the context. He received a note that Woody would film him that day. A car would come to pick him up. He left. I hadn't finished my coffee when Irving was back. 'He fired you?' He said, 'No, Woody said I'm a natural.' Irving told him, 'In your next movie I want to get Diane Keaton.' Woody replied, 'You're not ready yet.' When the movie came out, Irving was happy; he loved it.

"Woody invited Irving to come to Michael's Pub to hear him play. When Woody played, he was so alive. He came alive! He came to our table and was so talkative. And he was really a charmer. It was the clarinet, playing the music. It was not the man Irving met at the Russian Tea Room. It was the prince kissing the sleeping beauty and she came to life." Ilana Howe paused, and then offered her psychological take on Allen. "You know, Woody is jealous of women. He gives birth to a movie every nine months, not even a year. The antidote to fear of death is giving birth—to give life. This possibility of hope."

Marilyn Michaels, whose cameo as Mae West in *Zelig* was cut by Allen when he decided to use clips of West instead, expresses the resentment that some actors feel about Allen's remoteness on the set. "Look, my assessment of him is huge. He is gifted as a comedian, writer, director," Michaels told me. "Of course he is a genius—no, not just talented: a genius. And he observes his women the way an artist observes fruit. Then he uses all that stuff to write his female characters. He writes great women characters. Actresses, including Mia, will do most anything to get those kind of parts. Sad.

"I met him at his place on the Upper East Side," Michaels continued. "He was cordial. That was very exciting for me at that time. I was in awe of him. But I have no such good memories of him as a person. He has no class as a human being—or inhuman being, I should add.

"He is disrespectful, at least he was to me when I worked with him. He spoke to me as if through an interpreter. I stood right next to him, and he said to an assistant, 'Tell her to do such and such.' He makes his own morality. He doesn't follow the rules of society, or anyone else's rules for that matter. He is deeply self-involved and indulgent. As a director he was terse, concise, distant, ogling (I was doing a very sexy Mae West impression).

"I do think that the way he treats his Jewishness is important. Even if you send it up, whatever you do, you make the joke first so that they can't. Humor undercuts the whole thing, the hatred. So the fact that Woody does that, it's like saying, I know what I am. You can't make fun of me. I'm doing it first. That's very important. You put yourself in *peyes* [sidelocks running down the sides of your ears, as Woody did, turning into a Hasid in *Take the Money and Run* and *Annie Hall*] so they won't, because you've done it already. I don't think it had ever been done before, where he sends up the Orthodox aspect of Judaism by envisioning having Annie Hall's grandmother see him like that in the complete getup. The images are extremely funny and true to life. But anyone who mentions the Holocaust as Woody does, and does not let anyone forget it, that is important. That is the best of him."

"Actors are upset if he doesn't talk to them," Ric Menello observed. "Nobody wants to admit this with all this rigamarole about directors: John Ford said that 80 percent of being a great director is casting. If you cast it right, the actors should be able to do it from what you already saw of them. Sometimes Ford said 'Making them sweat is part of it. Let them figure it out themselves.' Ford did a movie about Mary of Scotland with Katharine Hepburn. She said 'What's my part? What am I supposed to do?' Ford said, 'You're a comedienne.' 'What?' she said. 'I'm a comedienne? Explain that.' 'I don't have to. Go away,' he said. And you know what? You find yourself that way. And the actors hate it."

An actor who auditioned for Allen recently and wants to remain anonymous told me, "I was very nervous to begin with. I really wanted the part. Then I started to say the lines. Woody came up close to me, stared up at me about six inches from my face, screwing up his eyes, examining me from all angles. It was impossible to do it under those circumstances. Of course I didn't get the part."

But Allen can also be warm, humorous, and encouraging. Elliott Gould was Allen's choice to play Harry Block in *Deconstructing Harry,* but he was locked into another commitment. Allen considers him to be a wonderful actor. Gould later auditioned for a role in the one-act play Allen contributed to an off-Broadway show, a trilogy called *Death Defying Acts*. "I went in and read for him," Gould told me. "I had had dinner with the producer and was told I was going to have a cue. But I was given the wrong cue. So I didn't say a word, and it went on for a very long time, minutes of dead silence. And Woody finally said, 'Let's go, Elliott. I have to be in temple tomorrow morning.'"

By 1986, when Allen directed *Hannah and Her Sisters,* he cast Mia in a more ambiguous role as Hannah. By that point in their relationship, Allen saw Mia in a different light. Hannah is an enigmatic character. She is shaped by people's perception of her. She is "good" and "extraordinary," but there is an air of exasperation in the filmmaker's feelings about her. There is the suggestion that she is emasculating. Her husband, Elliot, can't get her pregnant. Hannah's former husband Mickey (Woody Allen) will sleep with her sister Holly (Dianne Wiest) and later marry her. Hannah is wronged by two husbands and by her sisters. Allen presents these events as if they were perfectly normal. Everyone in the film is always attacking and wronging Hannah and getting away with it. Her sister Holly writes a book lambasting her after taking money from her to write it. And proceeds to marry her ex-husband and gets pregnant by him. And finally, we are told that Mickey Sachs couldn't impregnate Hannah when they were married. It was supposed to be his sperm count, which is why they had to go to his best friend (Tony Roberts) for sperm. But Mickey has no problem with Holly. We learn in the last scene of the film that he's gotten Holly pregnant. It's an interesting boomerang back at Hannah, as if there's something wrong with her. And so both of Hannah's sisters one-up her: One gets her husband, one gets her ex-husband—and a baby on top of it.

*Hannah* was originally a single plot about a man who falls in love with his wife's sister. "Then," Allen told the *New York Times* in 1986, "I reread *Anna Karenina,* and I thought, it's interesting how this guy gets the various stories going, cutting from one story to another. I loved the idea of experimenting with that." He was particularly intrigued by Nicholas Levin, who "can't seem to find any meaning to life, he's terribly afraid of dying. It struck home very deeply. I thought it would be interesting to do one story about the relationship between three sisters, then one story about somebody else and his obsession with mortality." The most difficult part to write, he said, was his own as Hannah's former husband: "I didn't have anything at first, just that he had been married to Hannah, and that he'd had this terrible scare. Then I thought, 'What is he going to do for the rest of the picture, just walk the streets and think?' Finally, I thought 'That's O.K. in a novel, that's what you would do.' Of course, it's not a novel, so I had to make his walking the streets nice-looking. But I had a unique possibility there, since I had been a monologist, so for me it was natural. I thought, 'I'll let him walk the streets and obsess over the fact that life has no meaning. We'll hear him think.'"

There is a feeling throughout of latent hostility toward Hannah. Hannah, like the real-life Mia, who plays her, is perfection itself. But is she? No one in the film really seems to be comfortable with her. The film has an air of false resolution—of resignation—which Allen recognized and disliked. Holly doesn't seem like a likely candidate for a stable marriage. And Elliot (Michael Caine) resigns himself to Hannah because Lee rejects him in the end. (It's much the same outcome Allen implies in *Husbands and Wives* [the Mia-Woody relationship was a "dead shark," as Woody puts it in in the film], when, spurned by Judy Davis, Liam Neeson resigns himself to marrying Mia, who nags the hell out of him for preferring Judy Davis, making him feel guilty and finally wearing him down.) There are scenes in *Hannah*, which was released in 1987, that seem right out of Mia Farrow's autobiography. In her memoir she writes of Allen's growing coldness and the distance between them because of the presence of someone else, in this case, supposedly, Dylan. "He had grown remote since our first years together. . . ." She says to him, "You're so cold," and he shouts defensively, "*That's a lie, that's an out-and-out lie!*"

In *Hannah*, Elliot is having an affair with Hannah's sister Lee (Barbara Hershey). When Hannah questions him about his growing coldness and says, "Are you in love with someone else?" he shouts angrily, "My God! Wha-what is this? The Gestapo? No."

Ronan Farrow, whose original name was Satchel O'Sullivan, was born on December 19, 1987, by cesarean section. The name was Allen's choice—Satchel Paige was the black baseball pitcher whose race barred him from the major leagues for many years—although he originally wanted to call the baby Ingmar, and Mia vetoed it.

The baby's arrival only worsened their relationship. Allen has said that his relationship with Farrow soured long before, and that by 1987, when she was pregnant with Satchel, she told Allen, "Don't get too close to him, because I don't think this relationship is going anywhere." Farrow contended that Allen was turned off by her sexually after Satchel's birth because of the cesarean and because Satchel was a difficult, fractious baby. The stormy seas ahead between Woody and Mia can be previewed in *Hannah and Her Sisters*.

## 8. Dick and Woody

DICK CAVETT HAS been Allen's closest friend for fifty-five years. They are the same age, and they have been walkers in Manhattan and especially in Central Park since 1961, when they first met. In 2015 I spoke to Cavett at length about their friendship of a lifetime.

**DAVID:** You're Woody's closest friend, and your relationship goes back to the Blue Angel in 1961. What has the friendship been like?

**DICK:** It was the day before George S. Kaufman's funeral at Frank Campbell in New York. It was the first thing we talked about. I was sent to scout him for the *Tonight Show* that night. I decided to go to the funeral, and Woody didn't. That's where I met Groucho Marx. Much stemmed from that twenty-four-hour period.

**DAVID:** What was meeting him like for you?

**DICK:** It was right after his set at the Blue Angel. Woody was a reluctant performer at that point. Our mutual manager was Jack

Rollins; Rollins and his partner, Charles Joffe, had encouraged him to perform. He was very reluctant. He saw himself as a writer and an actor and vomited a number of times, he said, before going on. He came onstage. Stood sort of behind what in those days was a wider stand mike than they have now, so that much of his face was obscured. Almost like a man holding a fan in front of himself. And then he began. And out came this string of gems, of pearls of comedy, every one of which was as good or better than the best line of any other comedian. I couldn't believe that he could do that for about a half hour. It probably seemed like a hell of a lot longer to him. Partly because the audience *talked*. They just tuned him out. Have you ever been to a convention where a dull speaker starts and suddenly the entire audience is just speaking to each other? That's how it went. And I resented it like hell. I called it an arc, from him, over their heads, in the full sense of the phrase, to me in the back, eating it up. Line after line, some of the audience didn't get, they were too hip, but all funny. . . .

**DAVID:** It was a comedy that had never been done before?

**DICK:** Well, I had never heard anything like it. I'd heard comedians come out and do a string of jokes. Gags, routines.

**DAVID:** The Catskill guys.

**DICK:** Yeah. Or Catskill style. And other styles. I'd seen Bob Hope do twenty minutes of hilarious jokes, but not like these. I think Woody wrote for Bob Hope once. Anyway, I went out and I thought, I don't know what to say to this guy. It went so poorly. But I probably ought to tell him how much I liked it. But there he was sitting in the lounge, in the club. Where everybody who came out went past him.

**DAVID:** They ignored him.

**DICK:** Yes. Nobody complimented him that I saw. There was sort of a wake. He made himself sit there. He could have stayed backstage. That was a ballsy thing to do. And I wondered what he thought he would learn from it. Or maybe hoping someone would say, "Hey kid, you'll be better soon. You're pretty good." And I said to him, "What do you get, that?" And he said "No, I get, 'That was a wonderful guitar player, but Jesus, that

comedian.'" That was one he had just heard. So that shows what
he was learning from sitting there.

And he stayed there. There was a time when I heard Jack
Paar say to some guy, "This Allen performing may not be one
of our genius ideas." I don't know if I've ever told Woody that.
And yet it *was* a genius idea, and he kept going, and he got
considerably better. He was good *then*; it was just that the dumb
audience didn't tune in.

**DAVID:** He went on Paar after that?

**DICK:** Yes.

**DAVID:** You must have told Paar how great he was.

**DICK:** Yes, and he almost endangered my job. Why was I a booker
at that point? It was because they were waiting for an opening
on the writing staff for me. Why there could be only four I don't
know, because today there are twenty. I said, "This guy is very
funny." Jack did that usual neurotic nasty little thing that was
part of his fabulously electric personality, saying [on TV], "A
guy on my staff tells me this guy is funny." For the intro. Jack
was even capable of saying, "Better be funny, pal," backstage to
a trembling newcomer. But he did this for Woody's intro. So
Jack couldn't be blamed. "Tom O'Malley on my staff tells me
this guy is wonderful." It was one of Jack's least attractive
traits. But I worshipped Paar and continue to. Anyway, Woody
came out, and then he offended Jack. I was a little surprised by
a couple of lines that he did, because he was a new comic, he
didn't have prestige behind him. He did his bit about Sweden,
where they get erotically excited about food rather than sex. So
he did that bit, the bit about the cream cheese. But the audience
loved it. It was a great feather in my cap. And Jack to the
camera, to the nation, said, "That was something interesting;
some of it may get on the air." And I get cold now thinking of
that moment.

**DAVID:** And he never warmed up to Woody?

**DICK:** I don't think he did. He later was willing to say that he
started him. Like Streisand and other people that Jack didn't
quite start.

**DAVID:** What was it that he disliked so much about Woody?

**DICK:** I don't know. He didn't have any Nixonian anti-Semitism that I knew of. He might have been shocked; there was a puritan side to Jack even though he could be as racy as anybody. As there was with Groucho. I don't know. Woody warned me once that I was about to meet the worst person in the world when I joined the Paar staff. Of course I said, Who could that be? I talked about this once on a show finally where I said—I don't want to give the guy's name but his initials are Paul Keys. He was Jack's head writer, and a backslapping treacherous son of a bitch. But you still can't slander the dead, can you?

**DAVID:** I think you can. I think you just did.

**DICK:** I'm told you can't. No, truly. Say something nice about Hitler, I guess, to protect yourself. Anyway this was a treacherous gentleman, let's put it that way. I heard him in there the next day fanning Jack's anger because people expressed astonishment that Jack had said what he said about Woody. Because everyone liked him on the show. Even the rest of the staff except PK. Who was down in Jack's office going, "Well, you licked some cream cheese off my bagel," totally misquoting him. Well, that was Woody's first appearance on the show. I'm sure Jack died remembering it as a triumph that he supported Woody.

**DAVID:** He kept booking him?

**DICK:** He was back. I don't know the number of Woody's appearances on Paar. I'm virtually certain that Jack realized he'd made that kind of mistake.

**DAVID:** You were also a magician, stand-up comic, and a writer who wanted to perform. So there was a lot you had in common with Woody.

**DICK:** Yes, it was odd that we had a number of things, except of course, growing up in Nebraska. But so many other things. The fact that we immediately saw that we both sat in the dark worshipping Bob Hope on the screen and Groucho in every way. And disliking many of the same people. We really were well matched, and at that time we were together a lot. Sometimes two or three days in a row we'd throw a baseball in the park or go see a movie or play or see Mort Sahl multiple times at the Blue Angel with Ella Fitzgerald and so forth. I remember the second night we went to see Mort, afterwards Woody used the phrase, "that great canine intelligence," which is somehow perfect without being able to explain it totally to a skeptic.

**DAVID:** They were so different.

**DICK:** Mort had that great keen-featured face. And really an apt use of the language. Woody also took Mort a box of cookies. I thought that was touching and amusing. They had never met. We all met together. Woody and I went back and met Mort after his set at Basin Street East that night.

**DAVID:** What was that like?

**DICK:** He was very cordial. Very likable. We were both in awe. There was a funny moment. As we were on our way backstage, Woody clutching his box of expensive cookies, saying, "I hope this gesture doesn't seem to border on homosexuality." And I laughed aloud.

**DAVID:** I was thinking about your sense of wonder about New York, coming from Nebraska. In some ways it seems related to Woody's feelings about coming from Brooklyn to New York. You both loved it so much.

**DICK:** That's an interesting—as people are taught to say when they're going on shows—that's a very good question. I said to him once, "I feel sorry for people who don't have the experience I had coming to New York for the first time. The city of your dreams. From the Midwest. Of course that never happened to you." And he said, "Well, in effect it did." His father brought him, I think. They came up in Times Square on the subway train. There it all was, emerging from Grand Central into the city of my dreams.

**DAVID:** I remember your talking about the radio show *Grand Central Station.*

**DICK:** It went right through my head as the train arrived. There's a line about "Past a red row of tenement houses south of 125th street—dive with a roar into the two-and-a-half-mile tunnel. . . ."

**DAVID:** Radio made that so real.

**DICK:** Have you seen the thing that Woody and I did at the 92nd Street Y?

**DAVID:** No.

**DICK:** You can. You can Google it. They showed *Radio Days* and hired Woody and me to talk about old radio. Do you know of this thing Woody did putting together highlights of Bob Hope's screen career?

**DAVID:** No, I don't.

**DICK:** Typically, he didn't come to the evening. But what happened briefly on a PBS show of mine with Woody, I wanted people to know how Woody felt about Hope. Woody said, "A master screen comedian. I would love someday to be able to put together some of the great moments." Seeing the show, one of us said, Let's do it. Woody and I looked at some movies, reliving our childhood, in screening rooms. And Bob Hope at Lincoln Center . . . me working onstage with him. The night that resulted from that . . . the showing of that movie . . . educating the viewers on Hope's screen skills. I have never seen it since. I keep hoping the evening itself exists.

**DAVID:** Hope was seen as only an establishment figure by the time Woody was famous. He was considered a mogul, a Nixon type.

**DICK:** Well, you know about the new book on him [*Hope: Entertainer of the Century*, 2015]. How he stayed on too long. Stunned when he was booed—this was announced by John Kerry in his soldiering days on a show of mine. Reported that Bob Hope had just been booed in Danang by the troops who wanted no more of the war. It stunned him, almost killed him. Woody has always been willing to admit that much of Hope's television career was crap. He was the highest rated until he began to slide, and unfortunately he stayed on too long.

**DAVID:** He always seemed to be reading the teleprompter.

**DICK:** I was taping with Jackie Gleason—Woody laughed at this— and he had just done one of the Bob Hope NBC specials. I said, "When Hope's working with you like that, are you in contact with each other?" And Gleason said, "Hope hasn't seen a guest in years." And the cue cards, stupidly, were downstage.

**DAVID:** I was wondering if your history of clinical depression and what Woody calls his history of low-level depression were factors in bonding you?

**DICK:** It could very well have been. We certainly spoke about it enough. He came and visited me when I was incarcerated with it. I just realized he didn't bring any cookies. Somebody interviewed Woody way back and said, "Your friend Cavett, are you very close?" And Woody said, "I'm not sure he would bring me chicken soup." And the interviewer laughed, and then I assured Woody that I would if I could get ahold of it.

I wish I'd gone home and written down or had worn a wire over the years, to record all the gems while hanging out with Woody. And also with Groucho. I thought I'd remember.

**DAVID:** I'm surprised you didn't take notes.

**DICK:** I did take some, in both instances. God knows where they are. On one walk twenty-five or thirty years ago, Woody said something unforgettable. We were walking in Central Park on a nice spring day. After a silence on both our parts, Allen suddenly said, "Cavett, can you think of anything that's getting *better*?" All I could come up with was "Maybe some French wines, aging in their caves somewhere. But that's about it." Some silent walking followed.

**DAVID:** You're completely yourselves.

**DICK:** Whereas many people have succeeded by being just like most other comedians or most other actors. I guess we are ourselves.

**DAVID:** Are you close now?

**DICK:** Yes. We haven't been able to get together as much. As years went by—I started to say neither of us was married, but Woody was. The first night I met Woody I also met Harlene. After the club we went to his—the smallest of his apartments I've known—I met Harlene. There was something wonderful that struck me. Where some actors have pinup pictures of themselves in show business—even then Woody had been around famous people and had probably got snapped in Rollins's office with Nichols and May or Bob Fosse or somebody. There was nothing, anything like that. . . . But he did have a tackboard of notes and things. And in the upper-right corner, cut out from the back dust jacket of a book, Woody had S. J. Perelman, carefully cut out. He didn't post the whole thing, just Perelman's face in profile. Painfully, carefully cut out. So there it was. I probably said something original, like "I guess you like S. J. Perelman." We talked about his writing. His admiration for Perelman was palpable, clear, and moved me a great deal.

**DAVID:** And what was Harlene like?

**DICK:** I don't remember Harlene at all except she left us alone. She talked, she was nice, a sweet young woman. We probably only spent a couple of minutes with her.

**DAVID:** Did you get to know Louise?

**DICK:** Oh God, yes. Louise is wonderful. We've pretty much lost touch with each other. When you have somebody in your life where you just look at each other and you both start laughing and other people can't explain it. Louise and I had that funny, odd reaction in our relationship, laughed a lot. Somehow it just clicked with us. We worked together only once and that was improvising Excedrin commercials.

**DAVID:** She was a great improviser, wasn't she?

**DICK:** Yes. And they got a bunch of improvisers up at an ad agency. And they gave a premise, and we all ad-libbed until we struck joke, as a friend of mine used to say. And Louise, as I recall, won a prize for one of those. And it was called "Liver." And at some point we were ad-libbing a husband and wife, and suddenly I said, "I can't stand liver. I've got to stop serving it." And then I said, "Somebody's got to take a stand on liver. And I'd rather stand on liver than eat it." This was considered hilariously funny. That little commercial won a prize. So that's Cavett and Lasser together.

**DAVID:** I've always thought that of all those early women, Louise was the one who had the most affinity with Woody.

**DICK:** Easily. Well I didn't know early women with Woody other than his first wife. And a couple of times we went out on things together. And then Keaton, of course, entered the picture. I don't know how anyone could have a closer affinity with Woody than Louise. And he always gave her credit for jokes she finished for him.

**DAVID:** He said once that he became a human being when he met Louise.

**DICK:** That's quite believable. They were getting on so well. I remember one night a joke she sort of finished for him. You may have to check it with him for accuracy. At a restaurant in the Village, I think he raised the subject of constructing a joke about a Reform rabbi. I think he said he was such a Reform rabbi, he was a Nazi.

**DAVID:** He used that! I've heard it in his stand-up routine.

**DICK:** Ask him if I'm slandering him by saying Louise came up with the line "He was a Nazi." Oh, and Woody took a match cover from the table next to him, and he wrote it down. And that's a habit I wish I had gotten into. He *instantly* scrambled for paper or pencil whenever a good joke came to his mind. In his disciplined way he failed to make the mistake of thinking he'll remember it.

**DAVID:** I would imagine he writes down scraps of dialogue as well.

**DICK:** Oh, he would empty his pockets.

**DAVID:** I believe you said that Woody once said to you a long time ago that he couldn't live long enough to write all the ideas he had.

**DICK:** Yeah, that put me on the floor. Maybe more than once. Once was in Trader Vic's in Beverly Hills. We each had a lobster. And he astonished me by saying, "Write movies, make movies." He said he hoped to do that. This was while he was appearing at the—whatever was upstairs at the Crescendo on the Hollywood Strip. And I was writing for Jerry Lewis. I think we hung out together every night. I would go and watch him at the club and hang out between shows. We even played a word game between shows. Filling in squares with letters. And it was one of those nights . . . this guy sitting here with me is going to make movies—moving pictures on the screen and *write* them? I remember thinking I wouldn't know how to think of a movie to write. That's when he said, "I have so many ideas, I probably won't live long enough to write them." I nearly fell into a faint.

**DAVID:** And we're talking forty-four movies later. And a lot of them are masterpieces, although he doesn't seem to think so.

**DICK:** I'd love to know all his true thoughts on those things. . . . But I can believe that. Knowing him. Something in him, you can believe what he said: "I don't care if I ever see any of them again." He doesn't have his house festooned with posters of his movies.

**DAVID:** He doesn't keep anything, does he?

**DICK:** I don't know. I think he once said, "I keep all personal letters." When I first met him.

**DAVID:** As a friend, how would you characterize him? He seems to have an incredible sense of loyalty.

**DICK:** He does have that, yes. Oh, a random thought: vocabulary lists. First time I was in his Park Avenue apartment, he took some stuff out of a closet, and he had this big bundle of papers. Sort of double-spaced lists of something on them. I said, "What's this?" They were arcane words, many undoubtedly from S. J. Perelman, who was the king of using words that sent you to the dictionary.

**DAVID:** I think that all started when he was trying to educate himself when Harlene was taking philosophy courses.

**DICK:** Yes, he once told me he was tutored on the great books.

**DAVID:** He was.

**DICK:** I made a few notes before you called. Your genius has led you to most of them. Let me see here. I remember when he uttered the words "I've got to meet Groucho." And that was to me. I had met Groucho at [George S.] Kaufman's funeral on the street afterward, and that's how the relationship [with Woody] over the years began. I couldn't wait to tell Woody that I had lunch with Groucho. As in the voice from his quiz show, we talked for a while on the street; he said, "You certainly seem like a nice young man, I'd like you to have lunch with me." We'd meet at the Plaza. I called Woody and said, "They can shoot me now. I just had lunch with Groucho." Shortly after that he said, "I've got to meet Groucho." I was the tool that engineered their meeting. We had lunch in Lindy's. We were in the cab together and we were both kind of nervous. Woody afterwards said it was this rare combination of meeting this gigantic figure and at the same time, he said, very like talking to a Jewish uncle.

**DAVID:** It's interesting: When I saw your interview with Groucho, that's a thought that crossed my mind; he looked like an old Jewish uncle.

**DICK:** Yeah, who used occasional Yiddishisms, but very rarely.

**DAVID:** But the voice.

**DICK:** Yes. And if he didn't say brilliant things he could have been a guy playing an old Jewish uncle.

**DAVID:** Or a Jewish butcher. Or waiter.

**DICK:** No Jewish accent. Strong New York. People always mis-imitate him by saying "soytainly." It's not what Groucho ever said. There's no phonetic symbol for that. If you were transcribing it, you would be better to write "Sight" than "Soit," for the first part of "certain." It's close, oddly, to Oliver Hardy's "Let me do it foist." One night as we were worshipping Mort Sahl from the back of Basin Street East, Woody said, "Cavett, when I see him I think everyone else should quit the business." So there you are. That's all the preparation I did. And you can continue to elicit if you like.

**DAVID:** As to the whole business with Mia—is she crazy?

**DICK:** I don't know what to say. I think what you have there is an example of pathological vengefulness. She has always been, as people say, very sweet to me. I think it was best summed up by Woody first at the time when on some late-night news show they shoved a mike into his face—when it was all coming out—and he said "Is it really credible that as a middle-aged man—I think fifty-seven—that I should decide to be a child molester?" As we know from the science about that, it's not a one-time thing. There are always many signs. . . . But the idea that Allen would do that is preposterous. An event that supposedly is taking place in a house *full of people*—and in an *attic*—where people would have seen him coming and going. It just doesn't hold a drop of water. Dylan's a kid I feel awful about, who's had a terrible life. And Mia, in league with her powerful journalism friend [Nicholas Kristof], has taken this child who has nightmares. . . . She finally got through that—now that she's finally found a life that's out of the spotlight, the stranger again that she wanted to be. And Mama outs her. [In 2014] for whatever demented reasons, there she is now going through it all again. Have we forgotten induced sexual memory of those years—the 1980s and 1990s—inducing sexual memory in children? Moses Farrow says Mia, not Woody, was the abuser. Certainly the child was abused. But by whom? What I think is revealing is a case of mental disorder taking the form of psychopathic vengeance. That's my take on that.

**DAVID:** You saw them together?

**DICK:** I remember when Woody started his relationship with Mia. I think he once said he had seen her getting out of a car and what a striking woman she was.

**DAVID:** In *Zelig*, he had only known her for two years when that film was made. And that's the only film where she is his savior; she's the psychiatrist who cures him. I'm just wondering if in the early years of their relationship he felt that way about her.

**DICK:** God, I'd forgotten about that. I have no idea.

**DAVID:** What do you talk about when you and Woody walk around the city?

**DICK:** It doesn't help you much to say, Anything and everything. Some political stuff sometimes. Magic. Show-biz gossip. Recollections of things. Checking with each other to see if we remember things correctly. And hearing. As in—I remember the first time Woody and I went for a walk years ago and he said, "Cavett, would you walk on my right side?" I said sure, and I remember thinking, Is this a religious thing? He went on to explain about his left ear starting to go. And one of mine started to go, quite a bit later. There was a moment in history when I was able to say, "Allen, we're running out of sides of each other to walk on."

**DAVID:** Why do you think he feels comedy is so much less important than drama? He said that the comedy writer doesn't sit at the grownups' table.

**DICK:** I don't know. I don't necessarily agree with that. What's so hot about drama that's better than masterful practitioners of comedy writing? I would love to have him elaborate on that.

**DAVID:** Can you tell me about why you think the ebb and flow of the media elite's feeling about him seems to go up and down? What do you think the feeling is now toward him?

**DICK:** I would think if they're mentally sound they would see him as a genius practitioner of his art. And if people have their half-assed moral objections, they've chosen the wrong side of that perversion. . . . What I wanted to mention was an article about child molesters through history, and that people think of them as evil monsters. More than likely, I read, they're made up of authority figures like babysitters, teachers, coaches, ministers, Scout leaders, and choir directors.

We were walking on Park Avenue early on in our relationship. And I said, "Do you have any reason to not want to run into Doc (Neil) Simon?" He said, "Why?" I said, "Because he's coming toward us on the block beyond the next one." In those days I had twenty-over-five vision. Eight times better than twenty-twenty. I could read departing license plates from two blocks away. On the eye chart the bottom line was as easy for me to read as the top. The doctor couldn't believe it. And just to piss off the doctor, who accused me of memorizing it, I'd say, "Way down at the bottom it says Brunswick Printing Press." I had made that up. Allen liked that. I guess he had thought Neil Simon and I had rigged it somehow.

**DAVID:** Do you think Woody has a sense of the magnitude of his accomplishments?

**DICK:** I would think he would have to because it's impressed on him all the time by tributes and so on. Perhaps to some people, one of his most attractive traits was "Sorry, I can't come to pick up an Oscar; my band is playing tonight." There are people who claim they don't care what people think. He has survived because he *doesn't*. He's managed, he's brought it off. It's genuine. He might care what you and I think, but not the Academy.

**DAVID:** And in that dog-eat-dog show-business world, my conclusion is that he seems to have always been loyal and honest.

**DICK:** That's the point; I learned not to be surprised by such things as the fact that he was not coming to Kaufman's funeral, though he admired Kaufman as Groucho did. Then the Bob Hope thing, putting the Bob Hope tribute together. I got to be onstage with Hope. And I impressed Woody by sitting in the wings while Hope was emceeing the thing, and I wrote some new lyrics to "Thanks for the Memory," that involved him and me: "And Woody slick and dear old Dick and neither ten foot tall, so thank you so much." I wrote it very heavily and large so Hope could sight-read it. And he did.

**DAVID:** Lovely. What do you think Woody's legacy is? The scope of his achievement?

**DICK:** The work. Eminently collective comedy recordings of such a high level they're extreme gems. Oh, one other thing I'd be ashamed if I left out. You know Philip Larkin's poem "Aubade"? It's a kind of form of a hymn to morning at the beginning of the day. You'll see why I forwarded it to Woody. Woody didn't know it, but he knew Larkin: "In time the curtain-edges will grow light. . . . Then I see what's really always there: Unresting death, a whole day nearer now . . ." It's a long poem; that's just part of the opening. And it goes on considerably. So I sent it to Woody. And it wasn't too long after he had told me that somebody had to point out to him that in his first book of collected pieces, something like ten out of fourteen stories had to do with death.

**DAVID:** His number one concern.

**DICK:** In fact his most recent e-mail to me was just about that. Because I told him that I was reading *The Denial of Death,* Ernest Becker's masterpiece.

**DAVID:** That's his favorite.

**DICK:** I forgot that's the book he hands to Keaton.

**DAVID:** That's right.

**DICK:** In the movie that we're all in together, *Annie Hall.* Anyway, there are lines in that poem "Aubade" that chill you and him and anybody who reads it.

**DAVID:** Did he respond to you about it?

**DICK:** Oh God, yes. That's the nice part. He didn't right away. And then we were out walking, maybe two weeks later. And I said, "Did you ever get Larkin's poem 'Aubade,' I sent you? I hope it didn't ruin your day." And he said, "Not my day." One of Allen's best lines. And of course we talked about it. It's a stunning poem.

It has the hyphenated phrase "furnace-fear" at some point. . . . Here it is: "Most things will never happen: This one will, and realisation of it rages out in furnace-fear, when we are caught without / People or drink."

I think it's clearly Larkin's masterpiece. I read it aloud at Lincoln Center at a poetry event they have every year. And it just chilled the audience.

**DAVID:** When did you send it to Woody?

**DICK:** About four years ago.

**DAVID:** It must have made an enormous impression on him.

**DICK:** Well, he said, "Not my day." I'll remember those three words the rest of my life. What do you make of the fact that when the Mia stuff resurfaced again in 2014, two newspapers that I saw with my own eyes gave the date of their wedding? Of course they were never married. Another gave the beginning and end date of their wedding.

**DAVID:** And that all leads to the whole notion that Soon-Yi was his daughter.

**DICK:** Not living there helped. I mention him in my new book, *Brief Encounters*, and someone wrote me, "How could you sully your book with a convicted criminal?"

**DAVID:** But the amazing thing is how he's gone back to the writing table again and again and just persisted. And with his music as well.

**DICK:** That's got to be a great tonic for him. I wish I still played the clarinet. That's another thing we have in common. And being short.

**DAVID:** Did you ever meet his parents?

**DICK:** His dad. I loved his dad. Short, maybe shorter than Woody. Very stocky. The body was almost rectangularly solid. There was a very funny incident. We were at the Stage Delicatessen. His dad ordering something, a burger. Anyway it involved his dad saying, "This is not the first meal I'm gonna eat today." And I remember Woody laughing. When I first asked Woody about his father, he said he was a short and stocky man, he was a bouncer, carried a .38, and heaved people out.

**DAVID:** He was a Damon Runyon character?

**DICK:** Straight out. Someone a creative-writing teacher would throw out as too improbable.

**DAVID:** That's what I loved about *Broadway Danny Rose*. That whole world that Woody evokes. That really was a tribute to Jack Rollins, wasn't it?

**DICK:** And he's in it.

**DAVID:** Yes, at the table at the Carnegie Deli. And it's a tribute: to the manager who is a selfless character who gives his all to his clients.

**DICK:** That element is in there strongly.

**DAVID:** What are your favorites of his movies?

**DICK:** That one is way up there. *Crimes and Misdemeanors* very much. And there are some I didn't know I hadn't seen. *Anything Else*. And here's my role in that. An old eccentric, alcoholic four-foot-nine solidly built lady housekeeper that my late wife [Carrie Nye] and I had out in Montauk was hilariously funny, kind of the "Tugboat Annie" type. And she had a repeated phrase. And you talked to her. She had had an elegant secretarial job in later years, with I think Helena Rubinstein. But alcohol and age had turned her into a really funny character. And you'd say something to her, and if she had no answer she'd say, "Well, it's like anything else, you know what I mean?"

**DAVID:** Did you mention that to Woody?

**DICK:** Yes.

**DAVID:** That's where he got it.

**DICK:** He was so taken with "It's like anything else." I said to Woody, "I wanted to say to Mrs. Bolder once, 'It's like *anything* else? Is it like anthracite coal? Like the Hanseatic League? Is it like toenail hygiene?'" And Woody used "Anything Else." And I was flabbergasted. I made that great contribution. . . . He certainly made his contribution.

**DAVID:** And he continues on and on. That's another thing about his working through these scandals. Nothing stops him. There's a lot of crap that was thrown at him.

**DICK:** We agree on that. But you know, "It's like anything else."

# 9. "Startling Intimations of Greatness"

In 1984 Allen released one of his most heartfelt films, *Broadway Danny Rose,* his tribute to Jack Rollins and his valentine to the old show business of the Catskills, vaudeville (eight big acts at the RKO Palace, five small acts at the RKO Jefferson on Fourteenth Street), and an old, raffish Broadway full of vibrant Damon Runyon characters, struggling thespians with worn suitcases trudging up and down the stairs of all the fleabag hotels on Broadway's side streets: acrobats, tap dancers, hypnotists, ventriloquists whose lips could not cease moving while their dummies cracked jokes, singing-bird acts—all waiting for the big break that never came. (I saw one comic, Frank Marlowe, throw himself from the stage into the orchestra pit of the RKO Palace as the climax of his act every time he played there.) It was the Broadway of *Guys and Dolls*; Abel Green, Sime Silverman, and Joe Laurie, Jr.'s, *Variety*; the Broadway of big cigars, big stomachs, checkerboard sports jackets, racing sheets sticking out of side pockets.

*Broadway Danny Rose* is steeped in that atmosphere of a show-business subculture he knew well and could not help but love. There were Irish, Italian, and black troupers, and as always in show business, a big percentage of Jews. The Borscht Belt comics gathered at Lindy's, the Stage, or the Carnegie Deli (the quintessential hangout for the fading show-business world), and they serve as the narrative focus for the film. The well-known comics Jack Carter, Sandy Baron, Jackie Gayle, Morty Gunty, Will Jordan, and Jack Rollins himself sit around a table at the Carnegie recalling and laughing at the pathos of Danny Rose ("He was such a failure," they remember). It's possible to view the film as a "what-might-have-been" fate for Allen, the Woody Allen who is the young protagonist of *The Floating Light Bulb*, the stuttering, isolated boy who takes refuge in the world of magic.

The film is funny, moving, and richly textured. Chaplin said that he loved Allen and particularly admired *Broadway Danny Rose*. Allen plays Danny Rose, a loser stranded on the far shores of show business, where the wannabes, hangers-on, and old vaudevillians gather to commiserate with one another over their hard luck. The film is suffused with Allen's heady mixture of drama, absurdity, and comedy, as well as a strong current of deep feeling. Danny is a loser who exhorts his bottom-of-the-barrel acts to "say the three s's: strong, smile, star."

The sappy, likable, fat Italian lounge crooner has-been-who-never-was, Lou Canova, is a close approximation of the real personality of the actor who plays him, Nick Apollo Forte. I asked Juliet Taylor, Allen's casting director, how she found Forte. "Woody's response to actors is very visceral and intuitive," she told me. "I mean, he is also very discerning about good actors. But someone strikes him like, This is who I wrote. And there have been a lot of times over the years that we have cast real people at times when we feel their kind of essential quality will get them through it. And Woody likes actors who make things sound real and aren't acting up a storm.

"Obviously some of the fun things are when we find real people," Taylor continued. "Like the whole *Broadway Danny Rose* cast was such an adventure. We had to search for the acts. The lady who played the water glasses and then the comics, and that whole family on the lawn at the party—they were a real Italian family. They were actually in the undertaking business in New Jersey. So that was really such an adventure. To find the lounge singer for Lou Canova, we decided we were going to do this big search. So I asked Ellen Lewis, my assistant at the time, who's gone on to be a very successful casting director in her own right, to go over to the Colony Record Shop and just look through the records of male vocalists. So she came back with a number of these albums of obscure singers. In the meantime we were also looking into people you've heard of, the Vic Damones and Jimmy Rosellis. And then we found the album with Nick Apollo Forte's picture on the cover, and that was it. He was singing at the Holiday Inn in Waterbury, Connecticut."

Even Joe Franklin, the lovable king of nostalgia, who never met a dead performer he didn't love, the avatar of bottom-of-the-barrel old-time show business and the host to thousands of has-beens and never-weres for half a century on radio and television, pops up to interview Danny's latest loser act, Canova, on his TV show. Franklin's words introducing Canova were scripted by Allen, but Franklin might easily have come up with them himself: "I—I hope my enthusiasm is generating, because I love this man, I really . . . I mean it, if you can love a man, I love Lou Canova."

The love story at the heart of *Broadway Danny Rose* is told with hilarity, specificity, and tenderness. The love object is Mia Farrow in her best role as Tina Vitale, the ex-Mafia wife, tough as nails, with a heart and conscience suddenly awakened by the vulnerability and wacky integrity of Danny Rose. Danny, a "theatrical manager" with a Chai necklace on his chest, is an unformed version of a Woody Allen, in his frowsy, chintzy checkered jackets; his folded-up copy of *Variety* under his arm; his hackneyed Broadway language of "God bless you, darlings" and "It's the *emes* [truth]"; his "May I interject a concept at this juncture?"; his fierce loyalty to his balloon folders, blind jugglers, one-legged tap dancers (one of them was actually a headliner at the Palace and the Apollo in the old days, Peg Leg Bates); his yearnings for the girls he cannot get; his frozen TV dinners and dilapidated apartment—who may get the girl in the end.

Mia Farrow is almost unrecognizable as an ex–Mafia moll in dark glasses that conceal her soft eyes. It was Farrow who remarked to Allen after a dinner at Rao's restaurant in East Harlem that she would like to play a character like Mrs. Rao. That was all Allen needed to create a character, a film, a masterpiece—and he did. And he gave Farrow the greatest part of her life.

The movie is a marvelous tapestry with an intricate plot that constantly surprises, an atmosphere that is lovingly observed—right down to the hapless ventriloquist perfectly named "Barney Dunn"—and never dissolves into sentimentality. While no more religiously Jewish than any of Allen's previous characters, Danny Rose, with his Chai necklace, is more explicitly Jewish, and his Jewishness is linked to his decency and compassion for the underdog. Allen twice uses the haunting words of simple wisdom that Danny ascribes to his uncle Sidney about how to conduct a moral life: "Acceptance, forgiveness, love." (The words are first spoken by Danny and later quoted back to him by Tina when she pleads with him to forgive her for her betrayal.)

Allen's concern about achieving a balance between drama and comedy is fully realized here. *Broadway Danny Rose* is dramatically resonant and poignant; its funny Runyonesque characters are not cutouts; they are fully drawn and accorded dignity and respect. The film is a parable about integrity and morality. Danny, like Jack Rollins, never sacrifices his commitment to his clients. Allen here pays back the man who believed in him from the start and made him believe in himself as a performer. While Rollins is the inspiration, it's probable that Allen's acquaintance with another talent agent, Dave Jonas, who really did deal with hopeless acts and was constantly getting screwed by them if they attained any success, was another source. Jonas had an office directly across West Fifty-seventh Street from Rollins and Joffe.

This story is also about loyalty: Rollins's to Allen, Allen's to Rollins. Tina, who has betrayed Danny by finding a powerful new manager for Lou, is haunted by her bad conscience, and she seeks his forgiveness on that Thanksgiving Eve while Danny is serving TV dinners ("Dig in! Don't be shy!" he shouts) to his collection of consummate Broadway losers.

Allen has paid Rollins back over a lifetime, both financially and by crediting Rollins on every single one of his pictures. But this story is just as much about Woody Allen, his morality, his sentiment, his gift for loyalty, and what makes him tick.

Writing in *The Guardian,* film critic Andrew Pulver noted: "Even in Allen's exceptional gallery of schlemiels, nebbishes and putzes, Rose stands out as something special: no book smarts, zero sexual presence, appalling dress sense. But Allen's affection for his character is palpable." Pulver praises the film for its moral compass, "its commitment to humanity, and to love, and to righteousness.

"This story," Pulver continued, "is not about consummation, but about reconciliation. It's a recognition that we want wrongs to be righted, that good will prevail, and that the faithless will be punished or reformed." He concludes by writing of the "innate Jewishness" he perceives in the film:

> *What other culture would see the heroism in such an apparently inconsequential failure of a human being? Danny Rose is useless in a fight, can barely run up a hill without being sick, is a loser in business, is deserted by all except those even more troubled than him. But he is unquestionably a beacon of hope in a moral wasteland—because of, not despite, his refusal to take people on. Rose's Jewishness is a defiantly non-religious identity; something that modern commentators on religion and identity just can't seem to get their heads around; but in Allen's generation . . . was entirely the norm. We need to bring it back. I think every ethnic group could learn something.*

Two poor films appeared in 1987 and 1988: *September* and *Another Woman*, two more Bergman-inspired efforts that seemed to come from a foreign part of Allen. The films seem dissociated from Allen's identity as a writer, filmmaker, and director, all humor, warmth, brilliance, authenticity, originality, spontaneity, and irony drained out of them. Even remaking *September* a second time did nothing to improve it. Trying to reach higher as an artist, Allen overreached and missed his target completely. It is telling that Allen could say that he was inspired not by characters but by a house to create both *Interiors* and *September*. "Just like in *Interiors*, the house is a character," he told Stig Björkman. "The house was the initial inspiration for the script, so it was important; I wanted you to see it, just like I wanted you to see the house in *Interiors*. In *Interiors*, the main figure, the mother, was also an interior decorator, so there the house had a further significance. But in *September* there is also some question about selling the house. So the house was an important character for me." Björkman asked Allen how he proceeded when he constructed the house together with Santo Loquasto, the production designer. "It was very important," Allen replied, "since the whole movie took place in the house, to provide the house with a lot of perspectives that were interesting. I wanted to be able to see deep all the time, that the rooms were not too flat off and separated from each other. And I wanted a warm color for the house. That was important for me. It should be warm and homey . . . so that you wouldn't get bored with the house, or claustrophobic." But it *is* claustrophobic, and no matter how good the house looks, *September* is comprised of stick figures and devoid of any resonant characters. It seems like yet another pale replica of a Bergman film. About *September*, Allen would say later, "I knew full well it wouldn't make a dime. Not a dime," he told Sean Mitchell of the *Los Angeles Times* in March 1992. It didn't bother him in the slightest. Artistic truth was the goal, but there was little artistic truth in these two films. The ultimate satirist of abstraction, the painter of warm, vivid, and specific palettes, the supreme parodist of cerebral, boring, pretentious characters, succumbed to cerebration and abstraction here once again, as in *Interiors*.

True to form, in 1989 Allen followed up the two disasters with a genuine masterpiece, *Crimes and Misdemeanors*. Allen tackled Dostoyevsky's theme of crime and punishment in this film but removed the punishment part. Allen's characters commit murder merely to protect their lives of wealth and privilege (a theme that would be repeated in *Match Point* and *Cassandra's Dream*). Despite their anxiety about being caught, they ultimately return to their normal lives without much ado. When *Crimes and Misdemeanors* was released, Allen told Stig Björkman, "In real life high ambitions don't mean anything, only success does. People commit murders, and they get away with them. They're not punished. Good people go blind. But there's also a fantasy life that people live by and escape into all the time, and it juxtaposes fantasy against the reality of real life." In this film Allen confronts some of the stark realities of our times (and perhaps all times) and concludes that evil has triumphed over good without the slightest qualm in the people perpetrating it. Allen's view of the world is encapsulated in this film, where darkness and comedy merge inextricably, but where darkness wins out. He manages to deal with these momentous issues with a mixture of realism and comedy.

Inherent in the script is the death of all meaningful religious belief and the urgent need to replace that belief with a relative morality without any religious moorings, without any conviction that there is a moral center to life. Here, at last, Allen revisits his Orthodox Jewish past with respect and without satire, irony, or comedy. Judah Rosenthal (Martin Landau), a highly successful ophthalmologist, recalls that his Orthodox father told him, "The eyes of God are on us always."

Rosenthal is struggling with what to do about a mistress (Anjelica Huston) who is threatening to destroy his marriage and his career (he is also guilty of malfeasance and she knows about it). He consults his patient, Ben, a rabbi who is going blind, who tells him, "I couldn't go on living if I didn't feel with all my heart that there was a moral structure with a real love and forgiveness. Some kind of higher power. Otherwise there's no basis to know how to live. I know the spark of that . . . is somewhere in you."

Rosenthal ultimately arranges the murder of his mistress—a remarkably easy task with the help of his connected, lowlife brother—and gets away with it. At first he is stricken by remorse. He returns in memory to the bimah in the synagogue and to scenes of family seders at the table, where questions of moral behavior are at the center of family life. A key role is played in the film by the brilliant writer, psychoanalyst, and teacher Professor Martin Bergmann, portraying Dr. Louis Levi, who is a composite, Allen wrote me, of Primo Levi and Bergmann himself. It is Bergmann who concludes the film by holding out the hope that, despite Allen's despair about the absence of a moral structure, "Most human beings seem to have the ability to keep trying to find joy from simple things like their family, their work, and from the hope that future generations might understand more." (Many of Professor Levi's lines came from Dr. Bergmann when Allen initially interviewed him and asked him a series of questions.) Allen undercuts a sense of hope, however, by having Levi, a Holocaust survivor, suddenly commit suicide. His final words of hope and optimism about the human condition run after we know he's dead.

In his first appearance in the film, Professor Levi speaks of an inherent dilemma in Judeo-Christian thought: "Now the unique thing that happened to the early Israelites was that they conceived of a God who cared. He cared, but at the same time demands that you behave morally. But here comes the paradox: What is one of the first things that God asks? God asks Abraham to sacrifice his only son, his beloved son, to him. In other words, in spite of a millennium of efforts, we have not succeeded to create a really and entirely loving image of God. This was beyond our capacity."

The wise and haunting words of Levi/Bergmann/Allen are spoken periodically through the film on a flickering screen in Cliff's (the Woody protagonist) office:

> *When we fall in love, we are seeking to re-find all or some of the people to whom we were attracted as children. On the other hand, we ask our beloved to correct all the wrongs that these early parents or siblings inflicted on us. So,*

*love contains in it the contradiction, the attempt to return to the past and the attempt to undo the past.*

*Events unfold so unpredictably, so unfairly. Human happiness does not seem to be included in the design of creation. It is only we, with our capacity to love, that give meaning to the indifferent universe.*

*We're all faced throughout lives with agonizing decisions, moral choices. Some are on a grand scale, most of these choices are on lesser points. But we define ourselves by the choices we have made. We are in fact the sum total of our choices.*

Cliff, Allen's prototypical idealistic schlemiel with high ideals, no money, and no practical means of surviving in the real world (another Danny Rose, but with a much higher intellect, awareness, and wit) screens Levi's lectures to the woman he is falling in love with, Halley (Mia), with the ostensible purpose of persuading her to sponsor his film about Levi for her major TV network program. A deeper motivation is to communicate his love for her, his need to convey the thoughts, yearnings, and feelings he cannot express to his pedestrian, career-climbing wife and hopefully to win Halley in the process. Cliff is contrasted with his celebrity brother-in-law, Lester (Alan Alda), a very successful TV writer-producer whose fame is juxtaposed with his shallowness, vanity, and banality. Allen deepens his portrait by making Lester, against all odds, actually likable and well-intentioned toward his nebbishy brother-in-law. When Lester commissions Cliff to write a flattering PBS documentary about him, tossing him a crumb, Cliff cannot resist telling the truth about him—even exaggerating it, comparing Lester to Mussolini—thus losing his one decent-paying job and his marriage in the process. Soon he will lose Halley, the woman he adores, to Lester, his nemesis, as well. Most important, Allen, like the most gifted of novelists, is able to endow his murdering protagonist, Judah Landau, with sympathetic and likable qualities that force us to experience his descent into criminality and murder with both horror and sorrow. Unlike his brittle brother, Jack (incisively portrayed by Jerry Orbach), who hasn't a flicker of conscience but seems more honest with himself than Judah, Judah observes his own betrayal of upbringing and conscience with shock and despair at how easy it is to kill—even as he eventually comes to relax and decide it wasn't so bad after all.

The two plot lines are loosely connected by the character of Ben, Cliff's other brother-in-law, a rabbi whose sight is fading but whose faith in God is unwavering. He is the moral center of the film, played with restraint by Sam Waterston. Here, as with the religious scenes of his childhood, Allen for the first time does not mock a rabbi. If anything, he yearns for the faith that Ben so unwaveringly believes in. Only the blind man believes in God; only Ben has a moral vision. "By visiting this affliction on the only character in his movie who has remained close to God," Richard Schickel noted in *Time*, "Allen is suggesting that if the Deity himself is not dead, then he must be suffering from severely impaired vision."

In an interview with Schickel, Allen said—with characteristic low-key modesty and hiding his volcanic intensity—that he "just wanted to illustrate in an entertaining way that there's no God, that we're alone in the universe, and that there is nobody out there to punish you, that there's not going to be any kind of Hollywood ending to your life in any way, that your morality is strictly up to you. . . . If you are willing to murder and you can get away with it, and you can live with it, that's fine. People commit crimes all the time, violent crimes and terrible crimes against other people in one form or another. . . ." Allen does a great deal more than "just illustrate" this concept. He is showing us how we live now and how the moral code has been eroded. *Crimes and Misdemeanors* is a meditation on greed and how it has encroached onto every sector of society, from high to low.

Schickel noted that there was a yearning for God in the film. "Yes, there is," Allen replied. "We wish that we lived in a world where there was a God and where these acts would be adjudicated in some way. But we don't. And [Judah], if he had his choice, yes, would rather live in a world—before he committed his crime . . . where there was a God, or where there was some kind of justice, and then maybe he wouldn't have committed his crime. . . . But he lives in a world where it's simply up to you . . . to make your moral choices. And if you can get away with it, you get away with it. Just like at the seder scene in the movie, where they're saying that history is written by the winners, and if the Nazis had won World War II, our history books would look very different today. You would not get the same history books that you have now. They didn't win, fortunately."

Professor Martin Bergmann, who saw the film in its entirety only when it appeared in theaters, was surprised by Professor Levi's suicide; even more startled, however, were Bergmann's real-life patients. "It was a little bit of a shock," Dr. Bergmann told Michael Bamberger of the *Philadelphia Inquirer*. "It was essential for Woody Allen, to develop the plot. It wasn't so nice for me. Some of my patients were quite upset." He went on to say that Levi's suicide was plausible even though his philosophy was "large and life-affirming." There were two kinds of suicides, he said, the planned and the impulsive. In the latter "the darkest forces of the unconscious suddenly emerge, creating total despair. Primo Levi's suicide was probably impulsive. [Levi hurled himself down a flight of stairs to his death and left no suicide note.] The suicide was most likely Levi's final reaction to his experience of the Holocaust." Dr. Bergmann also wrote to Allen, "An article of Cynthia Ozick in *The New Republic* of March 11, 1981 was sent to me. She points out convincingly that Primo Levi's last book was his suicide note. Eventually the oppression released by the Holocaust overwhelmed his capacities to transform the experience."

Bergmann had a notable career as an outstanding psychoanalyst whose primary preoccupation was with Holocaust survivors and their children. His history is a significant part of the genesis of the film and an illumination of Allen's methods, philosophy, and objectives as a filmmaker. Here Allen chose a real exemplar, a significant and venerable figure in the history of our times. Bergmann had taught for many years in the postdoctoral program in psychoanalysis and psychotherapy at New York University. His classes and seminars, which he held in the dining room of his home, were legendary, and he conducted them until his death at the age of one hundred in 2014. His father, Hugo Bergmann, was a noted philosopher in Prague, a close friend of Kafka and Martin Buber, after whom Martin Bergmann was named. Hugo Bergmann could not obtain an academic post at the University of Prague because of anti-Semitism, and in 1920 he and his family emigrated to Palestine, where he became a professor at the Hebrew University of Jerusalem. After Israel was declared a state, he was elected the first rector of the university.

As a young man Martin Bergmann gravitated toward kibbutz life, becoming involved in progressive education and later psychology. He began his teaching career in 1952, leading a seminar on dream analysis. He was the author of the seminal studies *The Anatomy of Loving*, *Generations of the Holocaust* (with Milton E. Jucovy), and *Understanding Dissidence and Controversy in the History of Psychoanalysis*.

I asked Juliet Taylor how she and Allen had located Professor Berg-mann for the film, had plucked him from real life as Allen and Taylor have done so often with their actors. "We wanted authenticity, as we do in all our films," she told me. "I have several friends who are analysts," she continued. "I went to a Christmas party of the New York Psychoanalytic Society and Institute. It was actually like a scene out of a Woody Allen movie. I mean, this is like over twenty years ago. Back then they were all wearing Earth Shoes and had goatees. It was hilarious. A friend of mine who is a psychoanalyst recommended Dr. Bergmann when I told her what we were looking for. I went to his office, and I sat and chatted with him."

Professor Bergmann told the *New York Times* of meeting Allen: "He took me into a room and asked me questions. He wanted me to talk. He wanted me to talk about love, death and religion. I spoke about all of these topics for an hour and a half. I was also supposed to teach a class on the Holo-caust [for the film]." Bergmann went on to tell the *Inquirer* that after he finished answering Allen's questions, Allen said, "You'll do." "He is not the example of a polite person," Dr. Bergmann commented, "but he is direct, which I appreciate more."

"But there I was [in a scene for the film], trying to ask the students ques-tions but all the students were dummy actors who were not supposed to answer any questions. I am accustomed to an exchange but none of my questions were picked up." That scene did not work out. Allen had also scheduled a walk in Central Park for Cliff (Allen) and Professor Berg-mann to reflect on the Holocaust, but inclement winter weather made the walk unfeasible. (There is one silent shot in the film of Professor Bergmann walking alone on a gray winter day in the park.) Commenting on the psy-chological truthfulness of the film to the Associated Press, Bergmann said, "You have the character of Clifford that Woody Allen represents, who is kind of idealistic but very unsuccessful. He falls in love with this woman [Halley] and eventually she, too, disappoints him. You have to ask yourself not whether it makes sense as an isolated event, but whether it makes sense in the framework. I must say it does make sense. There is a kind of Chaplinesque idea there—that life is very mysterious and you are a very small man."

I met with Dr. Maria Bergmann, who is ninety-five, a psychoanalyst, and was Dr. Bergmann's devoted wife for sixty-seven years, and their son, Michael Bergmann, a screenwriter, director, and producer, shortly after

Dr. Bergmann's death. Dr. Maria Bergmann was born in Vienna and married Dr. Bergmann in 1946. "My husband was at first dismayed by [Professor Levi's] suicide," she told me. "Woody came and talked to my husband here. Woody let him speak his own words at the film's conclusion because my husband said that the final words of the film had not really represented his views. And so there are a few words at the very end which are completely my husband's. Those words replaced what Woody had written before. Woody allowed them to stand.

"My husband was forever glad to do something new," Maria Bergmann told me. "That was him. One scene was supposed to take place [with] my husband and Woody walking in the park. But it never took place. Because Martin, who was much older, felt fine. But Woody Allen was cold. So that scene never took place."

Maria Bergmann shared with me the letter Dr. Bergmann wrote Allen after the film came out:

*December 29, 1989*

*Dear Mr. Allen,*

*The year has come to an end and the fever called "Crimes and Misdemeanors" has subsided at last and I am returning to my traditional identity as a psychoanalyst after a brief leave of absence as a movie star. I want to thank you for this holiday. You did more with me than I ever imagined, to the point where Vincent Canby even thought I was an actor . . . as if being natural was some kind of a gift. What was to me more interesting was that you found an artistic replica of the role of psychoanalyst in the analysand's life. I am nowhere to be seen, not even in the wedding where everybody else meets. And yet the impact of my work is felt throughout the film. . . . Acting was never part of my fantasy life, but I can say that working with you was as close as a man my age can come to playing. So for that too I want to thank you. . . .*

*Martin Bergmann*

Allen replied on January 2, 1990, with both a warm appreciation of Dr. Bergmann and a joking reference to himself:

*Dear Professor Bergmann,*

*Thanks for your note. I'm glad everything went well for you in your cinema debut. I wish I had known you earlier in my life, before I began the last 25 years of psychoanalysis and psychotherapy. You might have been able to cure me.*

*Best,*
*Woody Allen*

Mrs. Bergmann told me, "My husband didn't take out everything that Woody had written at the end of the film, but he objected to some of it, and he deepened it. Woody very much respected my husband. He was very much taken with him, as he expresses it in his letter."

While both Mrs. Bergmann and her son Michael had objections to the suicide, they emphasize that there was no anger or bitterness in their disagreement with Woody.

Michael Bergmann told me, "I think Woody Allen was happy to let my father improvise. When my father was originally given the script, he read it and said to Woody, 'Do you really want me to say this or would you rather hear my own thoughts on these subjects?' And Woody Allen said he would first try with my father's own thoughts. It seems to me that Allen gave him talking points that he wanted my father to hit. And he hit them from the beginning in his own way. And then the whole rest of it is my father riffing on them.

"My father thought he was deprived of the opportunity to play Professor Levi the way he would have if he were headed for suicide. He thought it would be a very different kind of characterization. He disliked the kind of joking suicide note, something like 'I went out the window.' But that was fair game. My father just thought that committing suicide was a *crucial* character trait. But it was up to Woody Allen to create the characters he wanted to create, the way he wanted to create them. This was just my father's feeling that he would have done it differently. He wasn't upset. My father didn't get upset about things like that. There was no bitterness, nothing like that."

In *New York* magazine David Denby called *Crimes and Misdemeanors* "Allen's most ambitious and completely organized film yet; swift, resourceful, exciting, with surprising twists and turns." Unlike Alvy Singer in *Annie Hall* or Sandy Bates in *Stardust Memories,* Allen is hardly self-congratulatory in his depiction of Cliff. As Denby wrote, "Allen's Cliff is a witty man, yet also one of the bitterest studies in failure ever put on the screen. Cliff puts himself and everyone else down. Rolling his eyes in disgust, Allen gives Cliff sarcasm without courage, intelligence without self-knowledge. Funny? Yes, but in an intentionally curdling way—the jokes are there to expose the weakness of the joker." Richard A. Blake, a Catholic writer for *America* and the author of a thoughtful study of Allen, wrote: "In his best films, Woody Allen prowls through the darkest alleyways of the twentieth century psyche, uncovering and describing the roots of our tragic sense: fear of death, failure in love, and loss of God. The tragedy, however, is filtered through the Woody Allen screen persona: the small, nervous survivor in the affluent urban wasteland. The character is comic, and so he transforms these most profound of human concerns into comedy. . . . [Woody] is, once again, the comic Everyman, a surrogate for the audience, who observes an enormously complex and at times hostile world and tries to make sense of it."

Pauline Kael wasted no time in irrationally trashing the film, and Leon Wieseltier, a literary critic, frothed at the mouth about Allen and about the film ("a stain on the culture that produced it"), but three of the finest film critics who had had some earlier reservations about Allen would be forced to reconsider and take Allen's full measure as a result of *Crimes and Misdemeanors*: John Simon and Stanley Kauffmann in 1989 and J. Hoberman—belatedly—in 2014.

"The chief strength of the movie," Simon wrote, "is its courage in confronting grave and painful questions of the kind the American cinema has been doing its damnedest to avoid. . . . [The film is] Allen's first successful blending of drama and comedy, plot and subplot. It is the Shakespearean technique of making the subplot comically echo and comment on the main plot. Judah, the big man, can get everything: the mistress he wants, when he wants her; her removal by assassination (at the cost of a little distress) when she becomes a burden. Cliff, the little man—less charming than Judah, but better and wittier—gets nothing. Crime pays; misdemeanor, like innocence . . . is severely punished. . . . What distinguishes the film most, though, is its technical savvy. Allen cuts between present and past, plot and subplot, the film and other films or videotapes within the film, grimness and levity with a sure eye and hand. . . . Moreover, he frames his shots unusually. . . . Notice Allen's handling of the music, more assured and less obtrusive than ever. . . . Both the use of Schubert in an otherwise pop score, and his use at this point [the murder of the mistress], are daring strokes. Allen now uses art for purposes beyond mere namedropping. . . . The casting . . . is generally excellent. Alan Alda's Lester, Jerry Orbach's Jack [Judah's brother] and Martin Landau's Judah could not be improved on. Even from amateurs, such as the psychotherapist Martin Bergmann . . . Allen gets exactly what is needed." Stanley Kauffmann wrote in the *New Republic* that "*Crimes and Misdemeanors* is outstanding among his films, because this time Allen the writer has addressed large themes in his own familiar, manageable mode, not imitatively."

On March 14, 2014, J. Hoberman reviewed the newly issued Blu-ray of *Crimes and Misdemeanors* for the *New York Times*. He wrote that of the three dozen or so films of Allen's he had seen, "One stands alone: *Crimes and Misdemeanors*. . . . Featuring one of the finest casts Mr. Allen has ever assembled, *Crimes and Misdemeanors* has novelistic richness in delineating character. . . . The cinematic texture is unusually complex as well. . . . [The film] is also hyperverbal, with an abundance of zingers delivered mainly by Cliff. (Mr. Allen is as funny as he has ever been, and Mr. Alda makes an excellent straight man.) At the same time, this may be the only Woody Allen movie in which Jewishness functions less as a shtick than as a moral code."

Hoberman moved on to the film's clear link to Dostoyevsky: "Mr. Allen's title consciously echoes that of *Crime and Punishment,* and the comparison is not altogether specious. Like Dostoyevsky's, his characters are notably prone to agonized self-analysis, and seldom in an Allen picture have the stakes been so high. The various crimes and misdemeanors committed include murder, suicide and adultery (among other forms of deceit and betrayal), as well as the most unspeakable sexual act in Mr. Allen's entire oeuvre; the movie ends with a wedding that brings everyone together to consecrate the notion of an unjust world.

"An agnostic with regard to Mr. Allen, I first reviewed *Crimes and Misdemeanors* for *The Village Voice*," Hoberman continued. "I thought I saw 'startling intimations of greatness.' Revisiting the movie nearly a quarter-century later, I was struck by the skill with which he pulls off this unlikely amalgam."

I am haunted by two images of Allen. One from *Broadway Danny Rose* and one from *Crimes and Misdemeanors*. These two painful, exposed moments linger perhaps longer than any other images of Allen in any of his films. They are both moments of betrayal. In *Broadway Danny Rose*, it slowly dawns on Danny that Lou Canova is about to dump him at the very moment that, through the most arduous efforts of many months and perhaps years, during which Danny has devoted himself wholeheartedly to saving Canova from his own self-destructiveness and has finally put him on the path to success in his career. He realizes not only that Canova is betraying him but also that the woman he has fallen in love with, Tina Vitale, has been colluding in the betrayal, pressuring Canova to leave Danny. In *Crimes and Misdemeanors*, it is the moment when Cliff, deeply in love with Halley, sees her and the despised Lester at the wedding ceremony of Ben's daughter and realizes that they are engaged. Cliff is crushed. Halley's motivation, very much like Tina's, is a materialistic one: Lester is a celebrity and can help Halley in her career and carry her up the ladder of fame and fortune. Tina sees Danny as a drag on her aspirations for Lou Canova. In addition, Lester is convivial and perfectly pleasant to be with, not the ogre or total vulgarian Cliff sees him as. Danny and Cliff are the unattractive ones. They do not exert any hold based on looks or sex appeal for either woman.

In both of these films Allen reaches well beyond comedy to profound depths of feeling.

In 1988, the year he was working on *Crimes and Misdemeanors*, Allen reviewed Ingmar Bergman's autobiography, *The Magic Lantern*, for the *New York Times*. His identification with his hero, Bergman, whom he called "the voice of genius," was transparently clear. He cited many examples of Bergman's painful life: "Day after day I was dragged or carried, screaming with anguish, into the classroom. I vomited over everything I saw, fainted and lost my balance"; a mother who pushed and slapped him when he tried to embrace her; a father who administered "brutal floggings"; a sister he regarded as a "repulsive wretch" and wanted to kill; thoughts of committing suicide; a household that "accepted" Nazism; and, summing up life: "You were born without purpose, you live without meaning. . . .

When you die, you are extinguished." "With this kind of background," Allen wrote, "one is forced to be a genius." Allen wrote that when he saw *Wild Strawberries*, "I still recall my mouth dry and my heart pounding away from the first uncanny dream sequence to the last serene close-up."

Bergman's life, unlike Allen's, had real brutality in it, but many passages of the review suggest a self-portrait of Allen as well. Allen writes, "He also works cheaply. He's fast; the films cost very little, and his tiny band of regulars can slap together a major work of art in half the time and for a tenth the price of what most take to mount some glitzy waste of celluloid. Plus he writes the scripts himself. What else could you ask for? Meaning, profundity, style, images, visual beauty, tension, storytelling flair, speed, economy, fecundity, innovation, an actor's director nonpareil."

And this: "Finally, the picture one gets is of a highly emotional soul, not easily adaptable to life in this cold, cruel world, yet very professional and productive and, of course, a genius in the dramatic arts."

This "highly emotional soul," this "genius," whose invented persona is cool, calm, and remote, would never make a great Bergman film, and he would fail totally when he tried to *be* Bergman. But he would make—and will continue to make—many, many of his own films with "startling intimations of greatness."

# 10. Sex, Lies, and Videotapes

IN THE LATE 1980s, the rupture between Allen and Farrow was on its way to the breaking point. Farrow maintains some balance in the earlier sections of *What Falls Away*, her 1997 memoir about the breakup, in which she puts forth her charges about Allen molesting Dylan. But she seems to diverge from reality in the later part—not so much in depicting Allen's ambivalence toward her, but in trying to build her case against Allen as a sex abuser.

She presents many instances of normal stresses between herself and Allen, and even some moments when she admits that Allen make an effort with her or with the children, but then seems to suddenly remember that she has to keep to her narrative focused on the sexual abuse of Dylan. She does this by writing of Allen's facial expressions with Dylan, of his letting her suck his thumb, and of warning comments from her friends. But in 1985 she had told *McCall's* magazine that the children "are very close to Woody and I'm glad about that. They have a good [father] substitute— he's there for them in important ways. He shares leisure time with them— he takes them to the park and plays ball with them and takes them around the city. Whenever they want to see him, he's available."

Farrow depicts Allen as a disinterested father toward Satchel, but it appears he was actually caring and, if anything, overprotective. Allen found it hard to stay away from the preschool Satchel attended, Episcopal Nursery School, annoying the other parents, who'd been told to drop off their children for classes and leave. Allen would pace up and down the sidewalk outside the school waiting for Satchel. *Newsday* reported that Satchel's teacher told Allen that he was upsetting the other parents and would have to allow Satchel to break away. "Satch has no problem breaking away," he told the teacher. "I do." Allen transferred Satchel to Park Avenue Christian School, where he repeated the same behavior. Asked by Jack Kroll of *Newsweek* in August 1992 about his affair with Soon-Yi, Allen denied he was a father figure to her, but insisted he was a devoted father with his own children: "She's not part of my family. Soon-Yi has a very high-profile father," he said. "I was not a father figure to those children. I was a father figure to my own children, period. Those are the three in my will."

There are other contradictions in Farrow's account. After telling us over and over again of Allen's obsession with Dylan, in the spring of 1991 she consults Allen about adopting an orphaned six-year-old boy in Vietnam. Allen seems amenable, and then he notices and expresses interest in Tam, the pretty girl of ten or twelve standing beside the boy in a photograph. Allen suggests looking into adopting her as well. Farrow writes that she is delighted with this suggestion: "You could have knocked me down with a feather. I hugged him tight." But if Farrow was so concerned about Woody's sexual predilections, why would she be so happy about bringing another little girl into Allen's lair?

Mia and Woody both had concerns about their relations to one of their children. Allen felt that Farrow was too close to Satchel, that her behavior with him was abnormal. Farrow had the same opinion of Allen's relationship to Dylan. They decided to bring the children to Dr. Susan Coates, a clinical psychologist, for evaluation. Coates referred Dylan to Dr. Nancy Schultz, a clinical colleague dealing with emotionally disturbed children.

At the same time Dr. Coates worked with Woody, helping him to modify some of his behavior, especially putting his face in Dylan's lap and letting her suck his thumb. Allen made progress as a result of these sessions, according to the psychologist.

There are revealing parallels between Farrow's self-portrait in her book and Allen's portrayal of Farrow in his films. Just as Alice—in the eponymous film—goes to work with Mother Teresa, Farrow writes that Mother Teresa is her idol. She tells of bringing her children to the United Nations in the early eighties to see a documentary on Mother Teresa and to meet her. When she goes to Hanoi in 1991 to fetch the two children she plans to adopt (the little girl was not available until later), she again meets Mother Teresa, this time by chance, and she writes that she "almost genuflects" when she greets her.

It appears, at least on the basis of her memoir, that Farrow failed to notice Allen and Soon-Yi's mutual attraction. By 1990 there were clear warning signs, observed by many others who saw Allen holding hands with Soon-Yi at basketball games, that something was going on between them. A New York Knicks fan observed Allen stroking her hair and kissing her cheek. The columnist Cindy Adams ran an item, not identifying Soon-Yi and Allen by name, about them in the *New York Post*. Farrow questioned Allen about it, and he denied it. Farrow told Allen that Soon-Yi had a crush on him and that she might misinterpret his behavior. Allen said, "Don't be silly," and Farrow let it go. But the sexual relationship between Allen and Farrow had been dormant for some time, and she could not have been unaware of the implications of the gossip even if she chose to ignore it. The deadness of the relationship seemed apparent to those who observed them. Kristine Groteke, the children's nanny, wrote in her book, *Woody and Mia*, "That summer of 1991 they didn't seem to have much contact with each other. They didn't talk much. They floated about and around each other, as if suspended in a huge cloud of indifference. Sometimes they reminded me of an old married couple who have been together for forty years and no longer have much interest in each other." She also wrote: "I never saw them kiss. Never. Not once. Nor did I ever see them hold hands affectionately or spontaneously touch."

Allen presented a similar picture of the relationship. Following the adoption of Dylan in 1985 and the birth of Satchel in 1987, he said, "The only thing holding us together was the children. There was really nothing else. . . . There was a burned-out undercurrent, but there was no rage or hostility and there was great mutual professional respect. It was that way for a long time, at least five years and maybe more." Groteke also drew a picture of Allen as an involved father that was sharply at odds with Mia's:

> *During the summer of 1991, whenever Woody would come up he would spend hours with the children. He had taught Moses how to play chess, and sometimes I would walk into a room, and they would be sitting at the chessboard in a quiet corner, deep in strategic thought. . . . Early in the evening . . . Woody, and sometimes Mia with him, would take Dylan and Satchel up to their room where he would either read to them or tell them a story. . . . The children would listen, enrapt.*

Allen legally coadopted Dylan and Moses with Mia on December 17, 1991. Mia had filed an affidavit with the court affirming that Allen was an excellent father. Dylan was squirming with impatience, but Moses was grinning and overjoyed; it had been his greatest desire that Woody be his father.

Allen has conceded that he originally had no interest in children and that Farrow thought of little else. Paraphrasing, he said she had told him, "You have your work, and my big aim in life is having copious amounts of children." He told author Walter Isaacson that "a month after [Dylan's adoption], I found myself bonding with her. She was just the greatest little girl. Suddenly I got tuned into the joys of parenthood." Allen said that Dylan's arrival "sort of resuscitated" the relationship with Mia for a while. "We had something in common, co-parenting the kids. But when Satchel came along, it drifted down to a polite and cordial end. . . . I was not involved with the other kids. They had their own father."

Apparently Soon-Yi later told Farrow that she and Allen became intimate in 1990, although Allen would testify under oath that it wasn't until Soon-Yi's Christmas break from college in 1991 that "we started talking about following her [graduation] from college, what would happen, and that was when I put my hands on her."

That year Soon-Yi had begun her senior year at Marymount, an all-girl parochial prep school opposite the Metropolitan Museum of Art. She secretly visited Woody, who lived five minutes away, on her lunch breaks. She also began seeing him on weekends, dressing up and going out, telling

Mia she had a new, older female friend she went shopping with. In the fall of 1991 she left New York to attend Drew University in Madison, New Jersey.

Allen was filming *Husbands and Wives* with Mia during this period. Just as *Hannah* reflected some of the tensions between Allen and Farrow and focused on the nature of her passive-aggressive, sacrificial personality and the ways in which she drove her husbands away from her, and just as *Alice* told us of some of Mia's spiritual quests for perfection and virtue, *Husbands and Wives* presents Judy, a Mia-like character who is a meek yet shrewish version of Hannah. In the film two husbands whose marriages are moribund choose younger women over their wives. These are trapped characters who can't break free. They are never going to change. They revert to form; they are drawn unceasingly back to what they were.

As in *Hannah*, the characters in *Husbands and Wives* resign themselves in the end to relationships that are "dead sharks." Jack (Sydney Pollack) returns to his frigid wife, Sally (Judy Davis); Michael (Liam Neeson), rejected by Sally, gives in to the emotional blackmail of Judy and ultimately marries her against his own will. Gabe (Woody Allen) resists the blandishments of the young girl, Rain (Juliette Lewis), and is rootless and alone at the end. Of course we know that Allen in reality did exactly the opposite: He did not resist the blandishments of a young girl (nor did he give in to the constricting relationship he'd had with Farrow for years). Instead Allen went with the young girl, broke free of his chains, and seems to be thriving. (Or, alternatively, Allen's going to Soon-Yi was almost an act of convenience: She was right there.)

If you keep in mind that Allen made this film while his life was falling apart personally and professionally, the technique he chose to use is telling. He abruptly changed his perspective. He had formerly used a more composed, rigorous style of filming and had never used a handheld camera extensively before *Husbands and Wives*. Allen chose to use jump-cutting in this film for the first time. Jump-cutting is not a fluid cut; it jumps in time and space. He chose this herky-jerky, less formal and composed way of shooting just as his life was in crisis and seemed near collapse.

Compared with all his prior films, *Husbands and Wives* seems borderline free-form and chaotic. Allen changed his visual aesthetic to make a film about people who are trapped, who are creatures of habit. At one point the interviewer in the film asks Gabe why he was drawn to such an unlikely candidate as Rain for a stable relationship. He shrugs and says, "My heart does not know from logic"—a line that encapsulates the theme of the film and a line spoken often, in one form or another, by Allen about his life and particularly about his romance with Soon-Yi. "The heart wants what it wants," he told writer Walter Isaacson in *Time* magazine of this real-life relationship.

The final scenes of the film, in which Judy (Mia) and Gabe (Woody) acknowledge that their marriage is over, that they have a "dead shark" on their hands, was actually filmed after their breakup. Needless to say, it feels real. Intentionally or not, Allen once again got exactly what he wanted.

Farrow wrote in her memoir that on January 13, 1992, "I accompanied one of the children to a therapy session at Woody's apartment. I let us in with the key Woody kept under the umbrella stand and sat down . . . in the corner room where I usually waited. Knowing I'd be there, Woody phoned from work. We chatted lightly as we always did several times during the day, then I hung up the phone, and as I turned toward the center of the room, on the mantel, there was a stack of pornographic Polaroid pictures, a naked woman with her legs spread wide apart. It took me a moment to realize it was Soon-Yi."

On January 18, reeling with rage and humiliation, Mia addressed a missive to her children, which she included in her book:

*My children,*

*An atrocity has been committed against our family and it is impossible to make sense of it. You know that I share your pain and bewilderment and anger. But I feel the need to talk and think further with you. It is essential that none of us permit ourselves to be in any way diminished by these events—we must struggle to find a way to learn and perhaps even grow stronger through them.*

That "calm," enlightened perspective and embroidered language didn't last for long. Farrow, who had beaten Soon-Yi on the day she discovered the pictures, now cut Soon-Yi's face out of a photo that hung framed on the wall and replaced it with a picture of her newly adopted child, Tam.

On Valentine's Day, Allen sent Mia a heart-shaped box filled with chocolates and a pincushion. Mia handed Allen a red satin box of chocolates with an embroidered heart cushion in a wrapped box. When he opened it later, he told *60 Minutes* in November 1992, it was "a very, very chilling valentine, meticulously worked on, one hesitates to say psychotically worked on." A white heart decorated with entwined pink buds and green vines framed a portrait of Mia surrounded by her children. She had jabbed steel turkey-roasting skewers through the hearts of the children. She gashed her own heart with the tip of a large steak knife. The handle of the knife was wrapped in a Xerox of a Polaroid of Soon-Yi in the nude. Mia wrote in rhyme, "Once my heart was one and it was yours to keep. My child you used and pierced my heart, a hundred times and deep." The effect, Allen said, was "quite frightening." He took it as a serious threat.

Farrow's treatment of Soon-Yi was disclosed by Allen in his 1992 interview with Walter Isaacson. The interview is very probing and quite candid on Allen's part. Allen told Isaacson that Soon-Yi "told me things that were surprising to me about the family, and that it was not exactly as happy as I thought it was. She and the other kids had problems with their mother. Soon-Yi did not have a good relationship with her, and we spoke about that. She said her mother had been very cruel to her. Physically and mentally. Mia was very impatient with her. She had hit her with a brush. She had written English words on her hand because she couldn't learn them, and made her go to school with them on her hand, and that humiliated her. I believe also she threatened to put Soon-Yi into an institution because she was impatient with her for having trouble learning the language. There were many other things. . . . She was worse to Soon-Yi because she stood up to her. And there was a definite difference in the way she treated the adopted children and her own children." When Farrow learned of the naked pictures on January 13, Allen said, Farrow "locked Soon-Yi in the bedroom in her apartment—there's a lot of corroboration of this—beat her on numerous occasions, smashed her with a chair, kicked her, raised black-and-blue marks so the kids at school said, Where did you get those? Finally, through the intervention of, I believe, a doctor, she got out of the house and went to live up in the [Drew University] dormitory." Moses Farrow would echo some of these accusations when he publicly disassociated himself from his mother in 2014, and even Mia conceded that she had hit Soon-Yi.

Isaacson asked Allen about the "moral dilemma" of his relationship with Soon-Yi. "I didn't find any moral dilemmas whatsoever," Allen replied. "I didn't feel that just because she was Mia's daughter, there was any great moral dilemma. It was a fact, but not one with any great import. It wasn't like she was my daughter. . . ." Allen spoke of his distance from some of the children in much the same way that Mia had described it in her memoir. Isaacson asked: "But didn't you become a father surrogate to the children she had adopted with André Previn?" Allen replied, "I was not involved with the other kids. They had their own father. I didn't spend much time with them, particularly the girls. I spent absolutely zero time with any of them. This was not some type of family unit in any remote way."

Isaacson asked, "Soon-Yi never treated you as a father figure?"

Allen replied, "Not remotely. She never said two words to me. For years I thought Soon-Yi was studying to be a nun. She was going to Sacred Heart, so I thought, well, I had no idea what she was doing. I was only interested in my own kids."

Following the discovery of the pictures, Farrow had bombarded Allen with dozens of threatening phone calls every night and into the early hours of the morning. Allen said that Farrow threatened to kill him, screaming in the middle of the night that he was "the devil" and should die and "burn in hell."

Farrow wrote in *What Falls Away* that she then began to shift her attention to Allen's behavior with Dylan, which she now regarded in a "completely different light"—wondering whether his "inappropriate" and "intense" behavior with Dylan was not sexual—but she also wrote in the same memoir that the shift supposedly took place long before the events of January 13. This contradiction is never resolved. "At exactly what point," she asked, "does it become child abuse?" The most telling sign for her, one she cites several times, was that Allen would continue to put his thumb in Dylan's mouth.

Speculating on Allen's motives in leaving the Polaroids out in his office, she wrote that she could not believe that Allen left them there accidentally. Allen was meticulous; he knew she would be in the room; he phoned her knowing his call would bring the pictures to her attention.

She was right about that. Allen, who had no taste for confrontation, must have wanted to tell her the truth and could not bear to do it in person. It was his confession. She wrote, "What rage did he feel against me, against women, against mothers, against sisters, against daughters, against an entire family?" She called the pictures a grenade he had tossed into the home.

Even if some of this were true, it would not be so easy to translate that behavior into acts of sexual abuse of Dylan, although to Farrow they were practically the same thing—and of course would be even more damaging to Allen's reputation.

Shortly afterward she wrote another note to her friend Maria Roach. She had, she wrote, come perilously close "to a meltdown of my very core." Allen would lead her daughter into a betrayal of her mother, her family, and her principles, "leaving me morally bankrupt." Allen had no respect for everything she held sacred—"not for my family, not for my soul, not for my God or my purest goals." Allen deserved pity, she wrote; he had spoiled and mutilated "that part of himself which is improved by right conduct and destroyed by wrong; is there any part of us that is more precious? Together I stand, with washed eyes, gazing clearly into an unknown future." She "would travel lightly there, carrying only the essentials, trusting that a new life will create itself." Finding a new comfort in her long-dormant Catholic faith, Mia proceeded to baptize all of her children in a traditional ceremony, and told Allen that she had found God and had found peace. Allen would comment that "not for a second" had she mentioned God or religion in their entire relationship.

Mia vacillated between this sense of virtue and the desire to violently punish the man who had symbolically jabbed skewers into the hearts of her children and gashed her own heart with a knife—who was, to her, a murderer. Allen told *60 Minutes* that she would sometimes act forgiving and full of religious fervor. "And twenty-four hours later, she was threatening my life, threatening to stick my eyes out."

Allen was concerned that Mia might take her own life when she wrote a suicide note to him in April. She told Groteke, "I called Woody to tell him what I was going to do. I went outside and stood by the edge of his terrace, and I looked down. But I couldn't jump. . . ." Instead she went back inside the apartment and lay on the couch, weeping. Allen had rushed home and found her there. That was Mia's version of events. According to Allen, they had been quarreling in his apartment, and Allen had gone upstairs. When he returned he saw the drapes blowing. Mia had disappeared. He raced to the terrace. He found a note from her on the floor that said: "I have decided to end my life because you have fallen in love with my daughter."

A panicked Allen leaned over the railing to see if she had jumped. There was no sign of commotion in the street. He then came upon Mia hiding in the kitchen. She grabbed the note and tore it apart, screaming at him. She ran out of the apartment. Allen phoned her psychiatrist and alerted her as to what had occurred.

On August 6, 1992, four months later, Farrow struck. She alleged that Allen had molested Dylan on August 4 in an unsupervised moment when he was visiting Frog Hollow. Her account of Woody's abuse of Dylan has a certain ambiguity in terms of when these events occurred. On the same day two events supposedly transpired: (*1*) Her friend Casey Pascal told her she saw Woody kneeling on the floor, putting his head in Dylan's lap on the couch. (Farrow said that Dylan was not wearing panties.) Farrow wrote that when she quizzed Dylan about this, Dylan replied that he "touched my privates."

(*2*) According to Farrow, Allen then took Dylan up to the crawl space in the attic, where he kissed her and "touched her private parts with his finger." The two accounts seem so similar that it's difficult to understand why Allen would have taken Dylan up into the attic at all, since he would be repeating what supposedly occurred on the couch. Allen was notoriously claustrophobic as well. These events were supposed to have taken place at a time when Allen was anathema to the family, an object of hatred, totally unwelcome in the household, and when his every movement was supposed to be watched by Farrow's nanny, Kristine Groteke, and the rest of the household. Farrow had written Groteke a note in June: "From now on, Kristi, I want you to keep a very close eye on him [Allen] when he's with Dylan. I want you to follow him around and be very careful, because I'm suspicious of his behavior when he's with her." Yet Groteke was out shopping that day, apparently not very alarmed about Allen.

Farrow had immediately taken a video camera and taped an interview with a naked Dylan about what had transpired. Many of those who watched the film concluded that it had been doctored by Farrow.

Earlier, on July 11, 1992, Groteke wrote, the family celebrated Dylan's birthday with a party. Woody came up from New York for it. Mia had implored him not to spend all his time with the child. Nevertheless he gave all his attention to Dylan and did not socialize much with the others. Far-row was enraged, and in the evening she composed a note and tacked it to the bathroom door: "CHILD MOLESTER MOLDED THEN ABUSED ONE SISTER. NOW FOCUSED ON YOUNGEST SIS-TER." Groteke does not indicate what the children made of this note.

But Farrow seemed to be getting ahead of herself. She wouldn't make the charge official until August 4. Allen's alleged behavior that day in July was the last straw. The note was a highly curious harbinger of what was to come. Farrow later petitioned Surrogate Court in Manhattan to have Allen's adoption of Dylan annulled.

Groteke's own account in her book, *Woody and Mia*—a book that Farrow encouraged her to write but was unhappy about and tried to stop publica-tion of when she read it, according to Groteke—has an ambiguous, un-certain ring to it, and was not the clear-cut accusation Farrow wanted her to level against Allen. She states that she does not know if Allen actually molested Dylan. Among the reluctant and highly pertinent questions she raised was this: "With all her . . . doubts about his behavior toward her daughter, why did Mia allow Woody to adopt Dylan (in 1991) in the first place?"

Groteke had told Farrow that when she returned from her shopping on August 4, Allen and Dylan were missing for about twenty minutes. Another question that bothered Groteke was the authenticity of the videotape. "The tape had undeniably . . . stopped and restarted several times," she wrote. "I suppose it's possible that in the interim Mia *could have* told her daughter what to say. Some viewers have watched it and said that it looks rehearsed, as if Dylan is acting. . . ." Groteke didn't think so, but as with other matters, she raised enough questions to create doubts. Com-ing from a "true believer" in Mia's veracity, they were startling. She went on to write about the events of August 4: "Still, I had been puzzled by the vigilance with which Mia herself had been watching for signs of molesta-tion; it had sometimes seemed as if she were *willing* the incident to happen. For instance, take the child-molester note that she tacked onto the bathroom door after Dylan's birthday party. Of course, Mia said that she was refer-ring to Soon-Yi. In light of events to come, her accusations seem eerily prophetic. But of what? Of Woody's actions? Of her own vindictive need to make the punishment fit the crime?" Even Groteke had to wonder about the possibility of Farrow's pathological vengeance.

Apparently Farrow first called the Connecticut State Police sometime on August 4, although she doesn't specify the date of her call. The police told Farrow to bring Dylan in to be interviewed by child welfare authorities. Farrow writes that the interviewing caseworker felt there was cause to believe that sexual abuse might have occurred. The police opened an investigation.

Allen believed that Mia had been brainwashing Dylan for weeks before the accusations of August 4. "She had told me on the phone several weeks earlier," he said in court testimony, "that she had something nasty planned for me. . . . That I had taken her daughter, she was going to take mine. And she put a 'child molester' note on my door. I believe she was brainwashing Dylan at that time planning to do that nasty thing she had planned for me."

Elkan Abramowitz, Allen's attorney, asked Allen how Mia could have brainwashed her daughter *before* August 4 to accuse Allen *after* August 4 of abusing her *on* August 4. Allen replied, "I don't think she brainwashed her to say I did something on August 4 . . . the opportunity presented itself on August 4. That became the date that the fruits of her brainwashing came to fruition. I think she was telling her [before August 4] that 'your father did a dirty thing to Soon-Yi.' That 'he did a terrible thing to her.' That 'please be careful. Does he ever touch you? Does he ever put his hand on you?' I think she was speaking to her in that way constantly. And to the other kids around there who're also reinforcing this."

On August 13 Allen went forward with his legal battle for custody of Dylan, Satchel, and Moses. He filed papers in State Supreme Court in Manhattan.

Groteke wrote that "Mia's molestation charges and Woody's lawsuit together unleashed a media circus that did not let up for an entire year." A mob of reporters and photographers flocked to Bridgewater, Groteke said, "stationing themselves at the top of the hill, right outside [Mia's] driveway."

On August 17 Allen released a statement that he was in love with Soon-Yi.

Abramowitz and his legal team had Allen take a lie detector test given by the former FBI agent who led the FBI's Polygraph Quality Control Program. Allen passed it. Kathryn Prescott, Allen's psychiatrist, filed a two-page affidavit stating, "There has never been any suggestion that

Mr. Allen was suffering from a sexual perversion / deviant behavior." Another psychiatrist, Fred Brown, professor emeritus of psychiatry at the Mount Sinai School of Medicine and an expert in pedophilia, wrote that his tests of Allen indicated a "child-like" personality characterized by "obsessiveness, vulnerability to anxiety, discomfort with adults, and feelings of safety and security in the presence of children and young women. Sexual abuse of a child and especially his daughter would be both alien and repulsive to Mr. Allen." Brown concluded that "the allegation made against him is false."

While all this furor was going on, Allen, almost incredibly, was at work on a new film, *Manhattan Murder Mystery*, and, of course, continuing to perform every Monday night with his jazz band at Michael's Pub. A lesser, middling effort, the film was in an old Hollywood tradition: the married couple who encounter a murder mystery and become obsessed with solving it. The film was an Allen indulgence: re-creating the kind of old-style film he had watched as a boy—here he treats it somewhat seriously, while the film-within-a-film of *The Purple Rose of Cairo* was given a whimsical, satirical touch. Mia was originally cast to play opposite Allen, but as the relationship burst into flames, Diane Keaton was recast in the role. (Farrow sued for her $350,000 fee.) But before it, in addition to *Zelig*, *Broadway Danny Rose*, *Crimes and Misdemeanors*, *Husbands and Wives*, and *Hannah and Her Sisters*, Allen had also done splendid work with *The Purple Rose of Cairo* (1985), *Radio Days* (1987), *Oedipus Wrecks* (1988), and *Alice* (1990). He would stumble once more with his German expressionist / Brecht / Kurt Weill–inflected film, *Shadows and Fog*, based on his one-act play, *Death*.

In *Manhattan Murder Mystery*, Larry and Carol Lipton (Allen and Keaton) are a middle-aged married couple who become friendly with their neighbors, Paul House (Jerry Adler) and his wife, Lillian (Lynn Cohen). When Lillian suddenly dies mysteriously and Paul seems supremely indifferent about it, always with a smile on his face, Carol becomes suspicious and sneaks into his apartment. She discovers human ashes stuffed under the sink and two tickets to Paris, and overhears his conversation with another woman. She becomes convinced that he murdered his wife.

Carol persuades their friend Ted (Alan Alda) to help her search for clues, and Larry encourages an author, Marcia Fox (Anjelica Huston), to meet Ted, who is recently divorced. The four of them get involved in tracking down the mystery. The film is fairly charmless and perfunctory;

it's not rock-bottom Allen *(Hollywood Ending; The Curse of the Jade Scorpion)*, but it's an indifferent piece of frivolity. But—still—Allen had kept working.

"I was in the middle of the chaos," Lynn Cohen, an actor in *Manhattan Murder Mystery*, told me. "I was hired. The next day they announced that Mia had left the film. I thought, Oh no, there's not going to be a film. Diane Keaton came to his rescue. So I only had the part of the script with my lines. I had no idea I was the one that was murdered.

"The scandal was in the paper every day. He was a gentleman during the trouble he was going through all that time. It was horrific. People on the street, wherever we were, they would scream, 'We love you, Woody. We're with you.' I never saw any negativity, never. And he never showed any stress. I never saw him lose his temper. And he was in an extraordinarily desperate situation, being accused of terrible things, most of them not true. But he was a gentleman at all times, and a *gentle man*. And there are people who have spent a lifetime tearing him down. I know people who can't stand him. His films. People who don't understand his films. He's a loyal, trusting human being. And he's had relationships that have lasted for fifty years, Jack Rollins, Diane Keaton. I think he has a deep love for people. I loved *Everyone Says I Love You*, and when he sang I was very touched. Because he was very exposed, very uncovered.

"So we started working," Cohen continued. "I thought it was heaven working for him. I understood everything he said. There's nothing remote about him. I think that he shows up: intellectually, emotionally. Cares deeply. And he's not a hack. A great artist. He has much more to say. You have more to say when you're eighty than when you're seventy. Woody's going to do it until the day he dies.

"He's very instinctual. He told me at first, 'You don't have to take the words exactly as I wrote them.' There was a lot of improvising. Some actors are afraid of it; I love it. His taste in women seems to be catholic. Embraces everything. From Louise Lasser to Soon-Yi. I knew Louise. Louise Lasser was a hundred miles away from Mia Farrow, Diane Keaton, and Soon-Yi. Nobody could be more different from Louise Lasser than they, in every way. He loves women, which is a joy. And I don't think he's afraid of them. Because women don't always fare so well in many films. He writes complex roles for them. He doesn't write one-noters.

"So Diane came to his rescue. I think she loved him. And he loved her.

Love is not always predicated on who you go to bed with or whose children you have. There was a great bond between them. And I was extraordinarily lucky because improvisation with her was second nature or first nature. There was nothing that I could say improvisationally that she wasn't right there with me.

"I think he gives actors a chance they haven't had. Owen Wilson in *Midnight in Paris*. Nobody else would cast him like that. He has a wonderful eye for actors. Mia in *Broadway Danny Rose*. That may be the one piece of acting she's done outside of who she was. She's not someone who transforms easily. But Woody gave her that chance. And she acted in one thing after the other with him. That's a wonderful gift he gave her. Otherwise she could have been stuck in a little-girl role forever. So he allows that.

"Working with him, he was very present. He wasn't an actor who just did his stuff. You work with actors, some very good ones, that when the camera is not on them, they give you nothing. He's there immediately.

"You have to weep, he's so in love with this city. We live in a time of genius, with him. This is not a fluke, this man. There are certain people— thank God I lived in a time when they exist."

The Connecticut State Police opened an investigation in September 1992 in response to Farrow's accusations and commissioned the Child Sexual Abuse Clinic of Yale–New Haven Hospital, headed by Dr. John Leventhal, to conduct interviews, administer tests, and evaluate the merit of the allegations. In December, Richard Marcus, a retired New York City police lieutenant who spent six years in the Manhattan sex crimes unit, viewed Mia's videotape of Dylan. He wrote that it "violated every rule" of objective interrogation. "Many of the questions are suggestive and there are numerous gaps in the continuity of the videotape which give me cause for concern." He concluded that the tape "has not convinced me of the child's credibility."

Allen was interviewed by Jack Kroll of *Newsweek* on August 25, 1992. Kroll asked him if he had sexually molested Dylan. He replied, "Of course not. I'm on record with the most unequivocal denial that you can possibly imagine." About Dylan, he said, "[Mia's] either been up to it, or in some frightening way, in an atmosphere rife with hostility toward me and lectures about how evil I am, this has crept into her psyche in some way. . . . I've been a model, model father with these kids."

Allen contended that when Farrow accused him of child molestation, he decided to seek custody of them. "When that happened, that was so grotesque," he said, "and so fraudulent and so sick that I felt I've got to get those children out."

Kroll asked, "Many people have invoked what they think of as your preoccupation with considerably younger girls—especially because of certain plot lines in your films."

Allen replied, "Well, that's just a smear. Where, where are these young women? It's absurd, a stupid perception. It just doesn't bear out against the realities, the relationships of my life. I've been married twice, and have long-term relationships with Diane Keaton and Mia Farrow. So the four most major relationships of my life are all age-appropriate."

Allen was interviewed by Steve Kroft on *60 Minutes* on November 22, 1992. Asked about the alleged visit to the attic, Allen replied: "Well, be logical about this. I'm fifty-seven. Isn't it illogical that I'm going to, at the height of a very bitter, acrimonious custody fight, drive up to Connecticut where nobody likes me in a house—I'm in a house full of enemies. I mean, Mia was so enraged at me and she had gotten all the kids to be angry at me, that I'm going to drive up there, and suddenly, on visitation, pick this moment in my life to become a child molester. It's just—it's just incredible. I could have—if I wanted to be a child molester, I had many opportunities in the past. . . ." He told Kroft that several weeks or a month before the allegations, "Mia called me on the phone and said—in the course of an argumentative phone call, she said, 'I have something very nasty planned for you.' And I said, 'What are you going to do, shoot me?'" He added, "And on many, many occasions, many occasions, over the phone and in person, Mia had said to me, 'You took my daughter, and I'm going to take yours.' . . . She meant by it that I had formed a relationship with her twenty-one-year-old daughter and she was going to get my daughter, who's Dylan. . . . She's threatened my life many times. . . . She's threatened to have me killed and to kill me. And to—and to stick my eyes out, to stick my eyes out, to blind me because she became obsessed with Greek tragedy and—and felt that this—that that would be a fitting, you know, vengeance."

Kroft asked if Allen took Farrow's threats seriously. "I took it seriously in the middle of the night," he replied. "When you get a phone call at four in the morning saying that you're going to be killed and that your eyes are going to be put out, you get scared because it's the middle of the night and your heart's beating, that's what—you know, when it got to be daytime, you know, I felt better, and I—moving around in New York City I always feel—you know, I always feel scared anyhow, so this was no worse."

Allen went on to state that many people saw him as guilty of abusing Dylan because he had a relationship with Soon-Yi. "There has been an attempt to link my relationship with Soon-Yi with charges of child molestation. They're two completely different things. I have an adult relationship with Soon-Yi. These people that feel . . . it's questionable and not their taste or they—she's too young for me or she's Mia's daughter. . . . I'll take that heat. I-I'm responsible for that. I accept all the criticism that they want, you know, that—it's my life and it's Soon-Yi's life, and I-I accept that. That does not mean that I should be charged with child molestation."

Allen told Kroft that after Mia's accusation of August 4, most strangely, she spent the rest of the week preparing for her costume fitting for Allen's next movie, *Manhattan Murder Mystery*. Allen said, "August 5, 6, 7, 8 and 9—you know, the week after, she's fully saying, 'When do we begin our new movie? I'm going for my costume fitting next week.' And I—she made an appointment with the costume designer on the movie, and she— and I said, 'What do you mean, the new movie?' And she . . . said, 'Well, you know, I-I'm supposed to go in and see the costume designer. I've got to get my fitting, and I—we're going to begin shooting in another five weeks.' And I said, 'Are you kidding? You're accusing me of child molestation, and you think we're going to just go on with the movie? This is insane.'" Allen continued that he told his lawyer to call and terminate Farrow's contract, and went out and hired Diane Keaton to play the role.

Allen appeared in State Supreme Court in Manhattan for a hearing about the custody battle on December 16, 1992. The presiding judge, Elliott Wilk, was a social activist. He had a photograph of Che Guevara on his wall and had represented Attica prisoners when he was in private practice. He was known to have particular sympathy for women, especially mothers. He despised Allen from the start.

Wilk ruled that Farrow, who was not present, had to turn over a copy of the videotape of Dylan. Wilk rejected Allen's request that the court appoint a psychiatrist to treat Dylan and guardians to supervise the welfare of all three children until custody was resolved. Harvey I. Sladkus, one of Allen's lawyers, accused Farrow of "systematically and intentionally trying to drive a wedge between Mr. Allen and the three children." He said that Farrow had prevented Allen from seeing Satchel for more than a month, and Dylan and Moses for more than four months. Eleanor Alter, Farrow's lawyer, brought up the photographs of Soon-Yi taken by Allen and stated, "These are not model pictures. These are Polaroid pictures of a young woman with her legs spread, naked." The *New York Times* summed up the day's proceedings with the headline, "Vitriol Is Order of Day in Allen-Farrow Case."

On January 12, 1993, Wilk held a preliminary hearing to consider Allen's petition requesting visits with his three children. Eleanor Alter told Wilk that Allen had had intercourse with the sister of his children when they were in the room. She quoted Mia's affidavit that the children had seen Allen and Soon-Yi having sex while visiting Allen's apartment. She said that "visitation with Dylan is unthinkable." Wilk agreed.

It was an excruciating time for Allen. There were negative news stories about him daily. In addition to his custody suit and a petition to broaden his visitation rights, he was opposing Farrow's suit in Surrogate Court to invalidate his adoption of Moses and Dylan. He was also awaiting the outcome of the criminal investigations in Connecticut and New York. He agreed to take a lie detector test. Meanwhile, work was his salvation. In spite of the intense pressure, he wrote steadily, and began a collaboration with Douglas McGrath on a screenplay that would become *Bullets over Broadway*.

The Yale–New Haven investigation was under way in the fall of 1992. Dylan's inconsistency was noted in Kristine Groteke's memoir: "On October 20, Dylan dropped a little bomb in New Haven. She recanted her testimony. When Mia brought her for her session that day, Mia explained to the social workers that Dylan had not wanted to come. In addition, as Mia testified, Dylan had earlier confided to her that Woody 'didn't do anything; nothing happened.' Later that afternoon, however, Dylan reversed herself and *denied her denial*."

On February 2, 1993, the *Los Angeles Times*, in an article headlined, "Nanny Casts Doubt on Farrow Charges," reported that Monica

Thompson, the former nanny, swore in a deposition to Allen's attorneys that Farrow pressured her to support the charges of Allen's sex abuse of Dylan. She stated that as a result of the pressure, she quit her job as nanny. Speaking of the videotape, she said, "I know that the tape was made over the course of at least two and perhaps three days. I recall Ms. Farrow saying to Dylan at that time, 'Dylan, what did Daddy do . . . and what did he do next?' Dylan appeared not to be interested, and Ms. Farrow would stop taping for a while and then continue." Thompson also mentioned a conversation she had with Kristine Groteke: "She told me that she felt guilty allowing Ms. Farrow to say those things about Mr. Allen. [Groteke] said the day Mr. Allen spent with the kids, she did not have Dylan out of her sight for longer than five minutes. She did not remember Dylan being without her underwear."

There were other instances of Dylan's contradictory statements. The *New York Times* reported on March 26, 1993, that Farrow testified taking Dylan to a doctor on the same day as the alleged incident. Farrow said, "I think [Dylan] said [Allen] touched her, but when asked where, she just looked around and went like this." Farrow patted her shoulders to indicate Dylan's gesture. Farrow said that she then took Dylan to another doctor four days later. Allen's attorney, referring to the findings of the latter doctor, asked Farrow, "There was no evidence of injury to the anal or vaginal area, is that correct?" Farrow replied, "Yes."

After six months of investigation, which included medical examinations, Yale–New Haven Hospital issued its report on March 17, 1993, "Child Sexual Abuse Clinic Evaluation of Dylan Farrow." It was compiled by Dr. John Leventhal, a pediatrician and director of the hospital's Child Sexual Abuse Clinic, and two clinical social workers trained to detect child sexual abuse. Leventhal had interviewed Dylan nine times and had met with Allen and Farrow.

The interviews were exhaustive, and forensic tests were conducted; Allen had to contribute samples of hair from every part of his body. The report completely exonerated Allen of all charges, and recommended that Woody and Dylan be reunited quickly. Referring to Farrow's "very disturbed" relationship with Dylan and Satchel, it said it was "absolutely critical" for Mia to undertake "intensive psychotherapy to address these relationships."

The report stated:

Dylan Farrow. . . . was referred to the Child Sexual Abuse Clinic of Yale–New Haven Hospital in September 1992. The referral was made by the Connecticut State Police . . . State's Attorney Frank Maco, and members of the Child Sexual Abuse Team. At that meeting, the history that the police had at the time was briefly presented, and the videotape (taken by Ms. Farrow) of Dylan telling what had reportedly happened to her was reviewed. Two major questions that were posed in the referral were:

Is Dylan telling the truth, and did we think that she was sexually abused?

To determine the meaning of Dylan's statements and whether they were true, we interviewed her on nine occasions. In addition, because the family context and Dylan's past psychiatric history are important in understanding the meaning of her statements, we met with both of her parents, two baby sisters, and two psychotherapists who had evaluated and treated Dylan and Satchel.

After a detailed chronology of the lengthy evaluation, the report continued:

In summary, Dylan presented as an intelligent, verbal 7-year-old whose story-telling was quite elaborate and fantasy-like at times and who manifested loose associations in her thinking. She appeared confused about what to relate to the interviewers and was very controlling of what she would say. In her statements and her play she elaborated interrelated themes. She was upset by the loss of her father and Soon-Yi and worried that her father might take her from her mother's care. She felt protective of and worried for her mother. Dylan was very much attuned to her mother's pain, and her mother reinforced Dylan's losses and her negative view of her father.

Assessment of Whether Dylan was Sexually Abused:

It is our expert opinion that Dylan was not sexually abused by Mr. Allen. Further, we believe that Dylan's statement on videotape and her statements to us during our evaluation do not refer to actual events that occurred to her on August 4, 1992. Our initial impression was formulated in December 1992 before reviewing any outside materials and before meeting with anyone outside the family except the Connecticut State Police and Kristine Groteke, a babysitter. Our opinion was reinforced by the additional information that we gathered throughout the rest of the evaluation.

The major reasons for our opinion that Dylan was not sexually abused are the following:

(1) There were important inconsistencies in Dylan's statements in the videotape and in her statements to us.
(2) She appeared to struggle with how to tell about the touching.
(3) She told the story in a manner that was overly thoughtful and controlling. There was no spontaneity in her statements, and a rehearsed quality was suggested in how she spoke.
(4) Her descriptions of the details surrounding the alleged events were unusual and were inconsistent.

The *New York Times* reported on May 4, 1993, that Dr. John Leventhal, who interviewed Dylan nine times, had released a sworn statement in which he theorized "that the child either invented the story under the stress of living in a volatile and unhealthy home or that it was planted in her mind by her mother, Mia Farrow. . . . [He] said that one reason he doubted her story was that she changed important points from one interview to another, like whether Mr. Allen touched her vagina."

Leventhal noted that Dylan's statements at the hospital contradicted each other and contradicted the account she gave on the videotape. "These were not minor inconsistencies," he said. "She told us initially that she hadn't been touched in the vaginal area, and she then told us that she had, then she told us that she hadn't." He felt Dylan's words had "a rehearsed quality," and she told him, "I like to cheat on my stories."

The *Times* added, "The doctor suggested a connection between Miss Farrow's outrage over Mr. Allen's affair with her adopted daughter, Soon-Yi Farrow Previn, and the accusation made by Dylan, who he said was unusually protective of her mother. 'It's quite possible—as a matter of fact, we think it's medically probable—that she stuck to that story over time because of the intense relationship she had with her mother,' he said.

"Even before the claim of abuse was made last August, he said, 'The view of Mr. Allen as an evil and awful and terrible man permeated the household. The view that he had molested Soon-Yi and was a potential molester of Dylan permeated the household.'" Leventhal also noted that Dylan kept referring to "her poor mother, her poor mother," whose movie career was destroyed.

What disturbed Farrow's supporters was that the Yale investigative team had destroyed their notes before submitting the report, and that the three doctors who were part of the investigative team did not testify in court except for the sworn deposition of its leader, Dr. Leventhal.

Allen said the report confirmed that "I never ever used my daughter, that no sexual abuse took place." But he was not buoyed by the outcome. Although he regarded it as vindication, he was being cleared of something that had no basis in fact to begin with. He still had no access to his children. "I'm just breaking even," he told the *New York Times*. "I never did anything. I would never molest a child." He was most concerned with Mia's manipulation of Dylan. "A terrible, terrible crime has been committed against my daughter," he said. "My daughter is a virtual prisoner in her house. Her statements might have been the result of stress. Or she may have been programmed. The videotape was fraudulent from the start. The tape has been doctored. . . . There is a strong recommendation [in the Yale report] that Mia herself seek psychiatric help."

Mia was devastated by the report, most especially by the suggestion that she needed psychiatric treatment. She did not comment on the report at all to journalists. Denis Hamill, writing in the *New York Daily News*, wrote of the many tranquilizers and sedatives Mia was taking. He also wrote of Mia's breast-feeding Satchel until he was three and a half years old "and [that she] even had a special harness constructed to do so over Woody's objections." Allen noted Mia's despair over the report, even though it concluded that Dylan had not been abused. "So deep is her venom," he said, "that she actually sees this as a loss."

Speaking to Denis Hamill on March 20, 1993, Allen said that he had avoided visiting playgrounds and toy stores while the allegations against him were investigated because any connection to children was too painful: "When I saw a father on the street with his child, it sent a pang through me. Physical pain."

Farrow had gone to Frank Sinatra about Woody. According to the *Los Angeles Times* of March 27, 1993, she testified that month that she told a therapist that one of her ex-husbands offered to break Allen's legs. Allen's lawyer quickly cut off a question about which husband made the offer, and Acting State Supreme Court Justice Elliott Wilk sustained the objection. "It was a joke," Farrow added.

It was not a joke. "When Sinatra heard what Woody did to Mia, he was livid," Len Triola, a former programmer at WNEW-AM and manager of the Crystal Room, the former music venue of Tavern on the Green, told me. "Frankie Randall [the singer and close friend of Sinatra] told me that Frank wanted Woody fucking clipped. Taken out. That's what he wanted. Frank loved Mia. He spoke to three people every day: Nancy, Sr.; Chicken [Nancy, Jr.]; and Mia. Mia remained close to Nancy and Tina. She was their age when she was married to Frank.

"But Frank didn't have the juice. The boys wouldn't sanction it for him. The guys Frank dealt with, the old-timers, reputable people who aren't with us anymore or in jail, wouldn't sanction that. It would set a bad precedent."

"Mia went to Frank, she claimed, because she was afraid Woody was going to have her offed," I said to Triola.

"Well, she had nothing to worry about," Triola said. "I don't give that weight. Woody had power with unions, but he didn't have the type of power like the Old Man [Sinatra] had. What are the Teamsters going to do to her? But Frank couldn't pull the trigger on it. Not that kind of pull. Look, I heard it from many guys. Frank really wanted him offed. But they wouldn't do it. They're not ethical people to begin with, but they're not going to just go and kill a movie director because he cheated on a guy's ex-wife. Then you're open to everything, if a politician says something to you or a fan writes you a letter. But that's what went down. Listen, Frank hated him. Hated him. There was even a story going round that Lou Canova in *Broadway Danny Rose* was less like a Jimmy Roselli and more like a Sinatra, that type of singer. Woody was nervous."

The custody proceeding of *Allen vs. Farrow* began on Friday, March 19, 1993, the day after the team of investigators at Yale–New Haven Hospital had cleared Allen of Farrow's charges. Judge Wilk asked Allen that afternoon if he had thought of the effect on the children of his affair with Soon-Yi. "I felt nobody in the world would have any idea," he replied.

"Wasn't that enough, that you would know you were sleeping with your children's sister?"

"I didn't see it that way," Allen said. "I'm sorry."

On March 25 the State Supreme Court heard Allen's application for custody of Satchel, Dylan, and Moses. Mia Farrow read a letter from Moses to Allen in which he described Allen as "needy"—an odd word for a young boy to use; far more likely a term coming from his mother—and said, "I hope you get so humiliated that you commit suicide."

On March 29 Dr. Susan Coates testified that she warned Allen that she feared for his safety because of Mia Farrow's threats. Dr. Coates, the clinical psychologist who treated Satchel from 1990 to 1992 and often met with Mia and Woody, portrayed Mia as filled with escalating rage after discovering Allen's affair with Soon-Yi.

The *New York Times* reported that "Ms. Farrow's actions in the following months, which included angry phone calls and a gift to Mr. Allen of a valentine with skewers through the hearts of her children, had convinced her [Dr. Coates] that Ms. Farrow might harm herself or Mr. Allen. . . . 'I felt it was a really dangerous situation,' she said, explaining she told Mr. Allen that he should not visit Ms. Farrow and her children at their country home because Ms. Farrow remained so distraught. In my clinical evaluation, this was a place where protection was needed.'"

The article stated that "Dr. Coates characterized Ms. Farrow's behavior as increasingly erratic as the months progressed. Dr. Coates testified that on Aug. 1 of last year [1992] Ms. Farrow called her after having learned that the affair with Ms. Previn was continuing. Ms. Farrow described Mr. Allen as 'satanic and evil,' Dr. Coates said, adding that Ms. Farrow pleaded with her to 'find a way to stop him.'

"Dr. Coates testified she was taken aback after Ms. Farrow mentioned at another point in the conversation that she and Mr. Allen had the week before been discussing the possibility of getting married. 'Do you think I should marry him?' said Dr. Coates, reading from the notes she took at the time and quoting Ms. Farrow.

"I said, 'Are you serious?' Dr. Coates said. 'She heard my reaction to it, and realized there was something absurd about it.'"

The reporter, Peter Marks, wrote that four days after that conversation, Farrow called Dr. Coates again and said that Dylan had told her that Allen had abused her. Coates was puzzled that Farrow sounded "extremely calm" during this phone call in contrast to her previous agitated ones. Dr. Coates testified that she broke the news to Allen of Dylan's allegations: "He sat on the edge of his chair and his eyes were very wide," Dr. Coates recalled. "He said, 'I'm completely flabbergasted. I'm completely flabbergasted.' He said it over and over again."

Dr. Coates also testified that while she thought that Allen's relationship to Dylan was "inappropriately intense," she never observed him acting in a sexual way toward her. She noted that an evaluation of Dylan made in 1990 found that she easily "would be taken over by fantasy."

On March 31 Gerald Walpin, a lawyer for Farrow, attempted to discredit Dr. Coates. He described her as "a sloppy record keeper" who was "mesmerized" by Allen and gullible in accepting his version of Farrow's behavior.

"In dramatic back-to-back appearances on the witness stand," Elizabeth Gleick of *People* magazine wrote in an overview of the trial on April 12, "Woody Allen, 57, and Mia Farrow, 48, showed just how miserable their lives had become since their 12-year-old relationship ended last summer in a firestorm of charges and countercharges. . . . The raw, underlying issue of the trial was not whether Allen was a child molester. It was his continuing affair with Soon-Yi Previn, Farrow's 21-year-old adopted daughter. On the opening day of testimony, as Farrow quietly wept in her seat just a few yards from the witness stand, Allen described how he and Soon-Yi began seeing each other in the fall of 1991 and started sleeping together that December. . . . Farrow's testimony painted a lurid picture of Allen as a man lost in his obsession with Dylan. . . . Despite Allen's denials and the Yale–New Haven findings, the actress reiterated her charges that Dylan had told her Allen had touched her in a sexual manner. She also said Allen acted inappropriately toward Dylan. She told the court, 'He was constantly wrapping himself around her, constantly hovering over her.'"

The hearing went on for six and a half weeks and concluded on May 4. "In closing arguments," John J. Goldman of the *Los Angeles Times* wrote, "each parent, through lawyers, accused the other of being unfit, of lying and disregarding the welfare of the children. Allen's lawyer called for reconciliation, a time to heal. Farrow's attorney dismissed the plea outright, arguing that her client's family needs protection. Eleanor Alter said that Allen 'has violated the fundamental trust of a family, created an irreparable break. His actions have beeen morally unacceptable, socially confusing and sexually baffling as a role model for a child. . . . A family is supposed to be a safe place . . . if this family is to have any peace, they need protection from this court.'"

Elkan Abramowitz, speaking for Allen, said, "Miss Farrow persists in placing her needs and feelings ahead of Dylan's . . . Her children are soldiers and pawns in a publicity barrage to denigrate Mr. Allen." He charged that after Farrow learned of Allen's relationship with Soon-Yi, "She understood best how to get her revenge. It is all summed up in what she said: You took my daughter and I am going to take yours. She understood how vulnerable Mr. Allen was to this threat. She pursued it with a singleness of purpose that Mr. Allen underestimated." He also charged Farrow's lawyer, the Harvard law professor and celebrity attorney Alan Dershowitz (who had represented Claus von Bülow, Mike Tyson, and Leona Helmsley, among others), had sought a $4 million settlement from Allen on Farrow's behalf after the charges of child abuse were made. Abramowitz commented that, "If someone asks you to pay for something you didn't do, that's extortion." Abramowitz said that if Allen were granted custody, he would share time spent with the children fifty-fifty with Farrow.

On June 7, Judge Wilk rendered his decision. He rejected Allen's request for custody of Dylan, Moses, and Satchel because of a lack of evidence of his parenting skills. He described Allen as a "self-absorbed, untrustworthy and insensitive" father. The *New York Times* wrote that Wilk "denounced Mr. Allen for carrying on an affair with one of Ms. Farrow's daughters, trying to pit family members against one another and lacking knowledge of the most basic aspects of his children's lives." Wilk left the children in Mia's care because he thought she was the better parent. Allen would be able to visit with Satchel three times a week, two hours at a time, which was an increase from the two visits per week already allowed, under the supervision of a third party. Wilk would not grant immediate visiting privileges for Dylan, but left the door open based on psychological counseling for her. A therapist would decide in six months if a relationship with Allen would be harmful to Dylan. Wilk would evaluate her therapy at that time and review the case. Wilk said that the psychotherapists who had interviewed Dylan had their judgment "colored by their loyalty to Mr. Allen," according to the *Times*.

In his decision Wilk wrote that "Mr. Allen has demonstrated no parenting skills that would qualify him as an adequate custodian for Moses, Dylan and Satchel. . . . He did not bathe his children. He did not dress them, except from time to time, and then only to help them put on their socks and jackets. He knows little of Moses' history, except that he has cerebral palsy; he does not know if he has a doctor. He does not know the name of Dylan and Satchel's pediatrician. He does not know the names of Moses' teachers or about his academic performance. He does not know the name of the children's dentist. He does not know the names of his children's friends. He does not know the names of any of their many pets. He does not know which children shared bedrooms. He attended parent-teacher conferences only when asked to do so by Ms. Farrow."

Wilk in effect rejected the Yale–New Haven report, and said the evidence was inconclusive that Dylan had not been sexually abused by Allen. He doubted that Allen could ever be prosecuted but decided to leave the question of Allen's guilt open nevertheless so that doubts could always persist: "We will probably never know what occurred on August 4, 1992." Farrow had but one shortcoming: "her continued relationship with Mr. Allen."

Wilk further ruled that he would accede to Moses Farrow's request that he not be forced to see Allen. "In almost every way," the *Times* reported, "the opinion was a repudiation of the parental role of Mr. Allen. . . . Judge Wilk, however, had few unkind words for Ms. Farrow, whom he commended as a caring and loving mother who had tried to protect her children from what he characterized as Mr. Allen's manipulativeness and insensitivity." Wilk ordered Allen to pay Farrow's legal fees because he had brought a "frivolous petition." Costs were estimated at $1 million on each side of the case.

Farrow and her lawyers celebrated their victory. "You got everything!"

Farrow's lawyer, Eleanor Alter, exulted when she read to her from the ruling over the telephone.

Allen could not have gotten a more prejudiced and hostile judge. What infuriated him most was Wilk's assertion that the circumstances of what had happened with Dylan were unknowable—permanently so. Wilk let a shadow of doubt pursue Allen forever. He clearly seemed to imply that although Allen was guilty, there was insufficient proof—"We'll never really know what the truth is." But Elkan Abramowitz pointed out that the molestation charge was totally disproved: "I don't think any one person could do more to prove that this did not happen."

Farrow held a news conference in Eleanor Alter's office. She was glowing. According to the *New York Times*, she said through tears: "For so many, many months my family has been living through a nightmare. . . . My children have been ripped apart emotionally. I'm so proud of how they've held themselves together, stood by one another and stood by me."

In September 1993 Allen received another blow. Connecticut state attorney Frank S. Maco announced that while he found "probable cause" to prosecute Allen, he was dropping the case because Dylan was too fragile to cope with a trial. He said that Farrow agreed with the decision. He made it clear that he was certain that Dylan had been molested. This unusual statement—that Allen was guilty but wouldn't be prosecuted—was condemned by Allen as coming from a "cowardly, dishonest, irresponsible state's attorney." He filed an ethics complaint with the State Criminal Justice Commission of Connecticut, demanding that Maco be disbarred for professional misconduct. Many in the legal profession agreed with Allen's evaluation of Maco's decision.

The *New York Times* wrote that "Mr. Maco's remarks about the case were criticized by some legal scholars, who said it was an unfair attempt to have it both ways by claiming victory without taking the case to trial." Stephen Gillers, a professor at New York University Law School and an expert on legal ethics, criticized Mr. Maco, saying, "You don't declare the man guilty and then say you're not going to prosecute, leaving him to defend himself in the press. It's a violation of Mr. Allen's constitutional rights, in my view. I can't overemphasize how remarkable this is."

Gerald E. Lynch, a federal judge, law professor at Columbia University, and a former prosecutor, said of Allen's action, "This is not a frivolous threat. It's always inappropriate for a prosecutor to say anything about a case in which no charges are brought. And to say 'We think the guy is guilty' is outrageous."

Kate Smith, a law professor at Yale University and a former federal prosecutor, told the *New York Times*, "I've never heard of another case where a prosecutor spoke so directly and so inappropriately about a case he wasn't going to prosecute."

On October 13, 1993, Allen asked for disciplinary action against Maco. He filed complaints with two state agencies, and said that Maco was guilty of misconduct for his handling of the child molestation complaint. Allen lodged one complaint with the statewide bar counsel, Daniel B. Horwitch, who had the power to disbar lawyers, and the other with the Criminal Justice Commission. Allen wrote Horwitch: "The clear objective of Mr. Maco's press conference was to achieve a conviction of me in the media in circumstances where he could not possibly obtain a conviction in court." Due to Allen's complaint, Maco was suspended from trying cases. The suit would take four years to settle.

A Connecticut criminal-justice panel voted unanimously on November 3, 1993, to dismiss Allen's complaint against Maco, but several members of the panel qualified their decisions. William Mottolese, a Superior Court judge, stated that Maco's remarks were "insensitive and inappropriate." On February 24, 1994, Maco's handling of the complaint against Allen was cause for "grave concern" and "may have prejudiced the legal battle between Allen and Farrow," a disciplinary panel found. According to the *New York Times*, "Its decision . . . amounted to a stern rebuke of the prosecutor, Frank S. Maco," but concluded that Maco had not violated any provision of the state's code of conduct for lawyers.

"The grievance panel," reported the *Times*, "revealed that on the same day Mr. Maco sent a copy of his statement to the Surrogate Court judge in Manhattan who will decide whether to void Mr. Allen's adoption of Dylan and another of his and Ms. Farrow's children, Moses, now 16. That act, the panel wrote, 'was inappropriate, unsolicited and potentially prejudicial.'"

Kate Smith commented: "This amounts to a public reprimand, though they're not calling it that." She said that the decision was "quite damning," but said she was not surprised that the panel did not punish Maco, "because lawyers are rarely disciplined for their public statements."

Dorothy Rabinowitz, a Pulitzer Prize–winning columnist for the *Wall Street Journal* and the author of the notable book about child sex abuse witch hunts of the 1980s and 1990s, *No Crueler Tyrannies: Accusation, False Witness, and Other Terrors of Our Times*, and of *New Lives: Survivors of the Holocaust Living in America*, told me in 2014, "It should be very clear that to say, as Judge Wilk did, 'We can never know,' is a monstrosity. We can certainly know that this did not happen within the realm of human probability. And in keeping this case open, this is absolutely in keeping with the predilections of fanaticism—of everybody who's invested in the idea that if a child says this happened (which of course the child didn't say), then it happened. It's an absurdity and yet the number of people who over the years have told me, 'Of course it happened'—confident people, people I know, normal, brilliant, healthy people. 'How do you know?' 'I know.'"

Satchel visited Allen at his apartment, where Woody would hug him and say, "I love you as much as the stars." Satchel replied, "I love you as much as the universe." According to Marion Meade, Satchel confessed to Allen that "I'm supposed to say I hate you," and on another occasion he said, "I wish you were dead." Allen was waiting anxiously for December, as Judge Wilk had spoken of the possibility of a reunion with Dylan at that point.

However, in September, Dylan's psychiatrist [Dr. Susan Coates] advised against a resumption of Allen's visits. She claimed that Dylan had made several remarks about Allen's "touching her." The psychiatrist asked for an extension until March 1994, and Wilk granted her request. The pattern was repeated in March: The therapist again convinced Wilk it was against Dylan's interests for Allen to see her. In the following months Judge Wilk vented his hostility against Allen in the press. "I don't trust him," he told Cindy Adams of the *New York Post* in 1995. "I didn't trust him two years ago, and I don't trust him now. I don't trust his instincts. I don't trust his insights. I don't trust that he does not represent a danger to this child, because the fact that he won't beat him up and throw him out the window does not mean Satchel is safe." The months passed torturously for Allen. It was clear that Wilk was permanently biased against him.

A year later the Appellate Division of the Supreme Court confirmed Wilk's ruling. It also upheld Wilk's restrictions on Satchel's time with

Allen (he could not sleep at Woody's apartment, take toys home, or see Soon-Yi). Allen took his appeal of the Appellate Division's ruling to the State Court of Appeals, New York's highest court, where it was dismissed. The case was finally over.

Allen's financial resources were greatly reduced by the three-year ordeal. His expenses for seven lawyers at the start and many attorneys and private detectives were huge. He had paid to fight Farrow in Surrogate Court, to appeal Wilk's ruling, and to lodge his complaints against Frank Maco. The ultimate injury was Wilk's ordering him to pay the $1.2 million for Farrow's lawyer, Eleanor Alter.

Linda Fairstein, a former prosecutor who was head of the Sex Crimes Unit of the Manhattan District Attorney's Office from 1976 to 2002, focuses on crimes of violence against women and children. "I had questions about the accusations against Woody Allen," Ms. Fairstein told me. "It was very apparent to me at that time, as it would be to any professional who worked in that business—meaning sex crimes prosecutors, prosecutors in general, and people who practice at the matrimonial bar, lawyers and judges—that when there is an acrimonious divorce proceeding, there are frequently allegations of sexual abuse that are not made until the proceedings are under way. A very disproportionate number of these allegations are false in proportion to false reporting in the general community. It's generally believed that it's the worst thing you can say about someone, that he sexually abused his own child. So it's become a part of a high-stakes litigation. At that point I'd been prosecuting for twenty years and in charge of sex crimes for sixteen; the cases that were referred to us all the time had this element in the middle of a divorce. So I was pretty keenly attuned to it.

"There were strange things, anomalies in this to begin with. For example, the allegation came four months after [Farrow's discovery of the naked pictures]. Soon-Yi was not one of Allen's children but one of Mia Farrow's adopted kids. Dylan was also not Woody's child; she was André Previn's adopted child. So now Allen's in the middle of this firestorm that's a publicity event, to put it mildly. And he's in Connecticut for visitation of, I believe, one of his kids. It's four months in, and there's nannies and a lot of other kids around. The idea that he would be left alone with another child seems unlikely, as angry as Mia Farrow was. So that's one way; I mean, I'm looking at this as a prosecutor.

"And Mia Farrow did not call the police or doctors right away. She began to videotape the child. This, I remember well, was disturbing to many prosecutors. She took the child naked into the bathtub, stood her up, and had her start telling stories about what Woody Allen supposedly did. And the big problem with the videotape? It starts and stops; it's done at different periods. The psychiatrist who interviewed the child came to the conclusion in 1993 that the videotape was stopped for coaching purposes, that the child does not tell on the videotape a consistent story. And so the reason it stopped was so that somebody could coach her and say, No, remember what you're supposed to say? This is where you were touched, this is where you were not touched.

"That was a big problem at the time. The third problem was that Dylan's statement was inconsistent. Very common with children; it's hard to determine. But at one point the child was supposed to have replied, to where did he touch you? and she put her hand on her shoulder and she said, 'On my shoulder.' Under no circumstances would that be sexual abuse. And finally, the last part that was very meaningful and made it probable that the Connecticut prosecutor would not be able to move forward even if he had wanted to, were the findings of a great facility in New Haven, the child abuse center, Yale–New Haven, where they do physical and psychiatric evaluations. Dylan was in treatment there for six months. The determination by Dr. John Leventhal, very well respected in this field, was that there was no sign of any physical abuse. And there was a suggestion that the child either had emotionally disturbed problems from either or both parents and from her upbringing, or that she had been coached by someone, or, Dr. Leventhal found, a combination of both. So with that medical finding, that case could never have gone forward.

"Summing up: Number one was the matrimonial situation, the outspoken ugliness of it. What I call the vitriol, the ugliness of the relationship with Mia Farrow breaking up because of the affair with Soon-Yi. What you look at in matrimonial court, whether it was Soon-Yi or whether it was Mia's next-door neighbor or whether it was a complete stranger—in any ugly situation with a marital dissolution, child sexual abuse is a very common false report.

"Second was that it happened at a time when the courts had issued very strict guidelines for visitation. The risks to whoever the alleged perpetrator was, that anybody would offend under the eye of those restrictions, would suggest an extreme pathology [on Allen's part] that I didn't find to be evident. Thirdly, the fact that this was a household unlike many, where often visitation occurs where there aren't such restrictions. Or where somehow the alleged perpetrator manages to be alone with the child. This was a household with many other children, with nannies around, and many, many people in the house when this was alleged to have occurred. This would be very unusual and very-high-risk behavior for someone with no history of sex offenses. You look for that in someone who has had other very-high-risk behavior. And fourth, apparently Woody Allen was publicly known as a claustrophobic. The idea of going into an attic seems implausible.

"So custodials—when there's a marital dispute—who's going to get the kids, is the biggest time for false reporting. It's hugely common. I'm not saying this is a false report, but that's what a judge looks at; that's what a prosecutor looks at: Why is this happening now?

"How easy it is for a child," Fairstein continued, "especially in the middle of something so highly charged as the Allen case was, to be coached unintentionally and intentionally. Unintentionally in the sense that 'he's just a bad man' and you're getting the kid to believe that, the kid's hearing Mom and the older siblings think he's a horrible man. So it feeds into the kid's buying into that idea that he did something awful.

"So in this case: 'Did Woody hurt you?' This is a kid who's living in a household where for weeks Mom's been hysterical because 'Woody's been doing bad things to Mom.' Woody is the monster in that household by the time these allegations are made. So that's all internalized by the child. It's the kind of thing we saw over and over again. I believe there were a lot of histrionics involved. It was not just a cold, clean 'Let's keep the kids away from this story.' The drama was acted out in front of the kids.

"And then: 'The monster's coming; don't let him do anything bad to you. He's a horrible man; he did horrible things to Mommy.' The allegation was not of a completed, sexual penetration. I believe the allegation was a touching. So that's something that (*a*) doesn't hurt, and (*b*) doesn't leave marks. What we do often in these cases, to test the reliability of a child, when a child describes what seminal fluid feels like, and the child is five, and the rapist has ejaculated on him, the child would have no reason to know that's what happens when somebody becomes aroused. But the child describes the texture of something sticky, that's wet, and you sort of know that the kid's been there. That's the kind of thing you're looking for. Obviously it's less clear when it's only touching. So it's harder because the touching may not hurt at all, and it could have been an act of very short duration: an act that didn't hurt."

"How do you prove it?" I asked Ms. Fairstein.

"Yes," she said, "proving it is hard, but suggesting it is pretty easy: 'Daddy touched you here.' And again, I go back to the red flag. I'm recalling two other things: One was that the child's story changed from time to time. At one point it was touching in front, then at a later point it was touching in the back. The kind of inconsistencies you are interested in for either proving something truthful, or the inconsistency.

"And then a separate point, absolutely: that the videotape was stopping and starting. A separate, very critically bad point of its own. Very bad. And I can remember just the idea being shocked that a mother would film her child naked talking about this. So that was another factor in the alarm that went off that I was listening for in determining what I believed had happened."

In 2014 Robert Weide, who directed a superb documentary on Allen in 2013, *Woody Allen: A Documentary*, listed the ten most common misconceptions about Allen and Soon-Yi in the *Daily Beast*, followed by his responses:

1. Soon-Yi was Woody's daughter. *False.*
2. Soon-Yi was Woody's stepdaughter. *False.*
3. Soon-Yi was Woody and Mia's adopted daughter. *False. Soon-Yi was the adopted daughter of Mia Farrow and André Previn. Her full name was Soon-Yi Farrow Previn.*
4. Woody and Mia were married. *False.*
5. Woody and Mia lived together. *False. Woody lived in his apartment on Fifth Avenue, Mia and her kids lived on Central Park West. In fact, Woody never once stayed overnight at Mia's apartment in 12 years.*
6. Woody and Mia had a common-law marriage. *False. New York State does not recognize common-law marriage. Even in states that do, a couple has to cohabitate for a certain number of years.*

7. Soon-Yi viewed Woody as a father figure. *False. Soon-Yi saw Woody as her mother's boyfriend. Her father figure was her adoptive father, André Previn.*

8. Soon-Yi was underage when she and Woody started having relations. *False. She was either 19 or 21. (Her year of birth in Korea was undocumented, but believed to be either 1970 or 1972.)*

9. Soon-Yi was borderline retarded. *Ha! She's smart as a whip, has a degree from Columbia University, and speaks more languages than you.*

10. Woody was grooming Soon-Yi from an early age to be his child bride. *False. . . . According to court documents and Mia's own memoir, until 1990 (when Soon-Yi was 18 or 20, Woody "had little to do with any of the Previn children, (but) has the least to do with Soon-Yi," so Mia encouraged him to spend more time with her. Woody started taking her to basketball games, and the rest is tabloid history. So he hardly "had his eye on her" from the time she was a child.*

Among those who were skeptical of Mia's accusations against Allen was Steve Stoliar, whom Allen had befriended from a distance over the years. Stoliar could have been a biased party in this instance, but his reasons were based on more than loyalty to Allen. Stoliar's late wife, Angelique, had been the victim of severe sexual abuse as a child at the hands of her father and her brother. Her memories had been repressed until she had a bad fall and began therapy to deal with the pain of her physical condition. At that point her memories began to surface, and she was filled with terror and shame. She had good reason to be suspicious of Allen. "We were extremely sensitive from then on to reports of child abuse," Stoliar told me. "We hated the news stories where supposed experts would debunk repressed memories. When the Dylan scandal hit, suspiciously close to the Soon-Yi scandal, I initially felt caught between an allegiance to Allen and of course a hatred of child abusers. And here's Woody, this guy I have admired all my life and who has always been supportive of me. I wasn't about to give him the benefit of the doubt just because I didn't want to believe that.

"However, in the course of the investigation, Angelique kept up with it and concluded that Woody did not do anything wrong, that Mia was being vengeful, and that the abuse that was occurring was Mia brainwashing Dylan into saying those things. And we understood that the team that examined Dylan, the Yale–New Haven clinic, was the team that Mia had pushed for. This is who she wanted. If anyone was entitled to think the worst about someone about whom a child had said, He molested me, it would have been my wife. She concluded that Mia was a woman scorned.

"Angelique died in 2008," Stoliar continued. "And then when this thing resurfaced in 2014, people didn't understand my defense of Woody. I'd try to explain that I am a crusader against child molesting; I would still like to use Angelique's father as a piñata. The repercussions of molesting a young child on the rest of their life are incalculable. However, falsely accusing someone has repercussions as well. And I'm guessing that Dylan has probably come to believe the things she's saying. I had hoped that as time went by the children might think maybe Mom's version of the truth isn't the whole story. And that perhaps there would be some kind of rapprochement with the kids and Woody. It seems to have happened with Moses, but not with Dylan.

"I know that Angelique more than anyone would be entitled to say to me, 'I know you like his movies; I like them too. I know he answers your letters and that's great. But I'm sorry, kids don't make things up like that. You have to believe the children or else they're weirded out the rest of their lives.' It's a delicate line for me to walk. But I can see the boundaries of it distinctly. It's a narrow one when I flip between wishing great harm on child molesters and wishing harm on people who falsely cry wolf and screw up the lives of people who didn't do anything. And you get 'I guess we'll really never know' even when there's a ton of evidence.

"The Soon-Yi stuff is completely separate, but people staple it together. And there's so much misconception that he married his daughter. She was never his daughter. He was never in a parental role. But they think—if someone can do that—it's just a hop, skip and a jump."

The question that still mystifies is this: How did Allen keep going in such an atmosphere—and *thrive*? He would soon make one of his best films, *Bullets over Broadway,* and two more excellent ones would follow that: *Mighty Aphrodite* and *Everyone Says I Love You.*

"So people just stopped caring about the scandal—it's like, I got enough problems," Mark Evanier recalled about the events of 1992–93. "Woody didn't grovel in public. He didn't run around and apologize. He didn't do a mea culpa. He just kept working, and from all outward appearances didn't change his life much.

"People have a resentment of the untouchable person," Evanier continued. "People who were assaulting him: 'You have to come out and play our game. You have to attend our film festivals. You have to come to my parties, do a personal appearance. And do the interviews we want.' And he just said, 'No, I'm going to do what I want.' And Woody doesn't want to play anybody else's game.

"But there was the one time he was on the Oscars; he made that wonderful surprise cameo. Whoopi Goldberg hosted. It was the first Oscars after 9/11. About a third of the way into the show Whoopi announced a tribute to New York, 'and we've got a person to come out to talk about New York whose films epitomize New York.' She gave him a really, really big buildup. As she was describing it, you could kind of hear the audience going, Well, she can't be talking about Woody Allen. He wouldn't be here. And when she finally said, 'Woody Allen,' the place erupted. And there was kind of a moment of hesitation in the audience. You could see they weren't sure, Are we going to stand for this guy? A bunch of big stars stood up, and everybody stood up.

"So Woody comes out onstage and the audience goes nuts. And he did, for the first time in I don't know how long, a bit of stand-up, an actual kind of a stand-up act. Six or so minutes. All over America comedy buffs were thinking, Hey, he's still got it. And it was all new, fresh material. He obviously wrote it for that occasion. And he's on a stage at the Academy Awards in front of the largest audience that anybody's ever had. He's in a tuxedo in front of the elite of Hollywood. He's just gotten a standing ovation. And he's still talking about being a nebbish. 'I don't deserve this. You could have gotten somebody better to come out and do this than me.' He did a joke. 'When they called me, I said, Why don't you get Martin Scorsese? And they said, We would but he wasn't available.' It was like: Do I deserve this? And 'I thought you were going to give me the Jean Hersholt Humanitarian Award. Because I gave a beggar on the street fifty cents once.' Anybody else would have said, 'I gave the guy twenty bucks.' He understood enough that when he stepped on the stage he had to start by being Woody Allen: He owed the audience Woody Allen jokes. He owed them a monologue. And it was a little way of sort of apologizing for not being there in the past.

"But it was all about New York. He introduced a film that someone else had made, a montage about New York. And he finished it, and he got the hell out of there. I had TiVoed the thing. It was running, and I was in the other room. And I came back and heard a voice. And I thought, Gee, that sounds like Woody Allen. He wouldn't be at the Oscars. And I walked in and there he was, and I rewound it to the beginning and saw his full entrance. And he came out, and he was very humble. There was not the slightest trace of, I honor you with my presence. It was like, Thank you for the honor of letting me come out here and talk about New York. Because here's a guy who doesn't need anything from Hollywood. He doesn't need awards, he doesn't need publicity, he doesn't need to suck up to people for deals. He doesn't need anybody."

Terry Gross of National Public Radio asked Allen in May 2012: "Do you care what people think of your personal life? Or is that just irrelevant to you?" He replied, "Well, you know, if I say I don't care, it sounds so cold and callous. But let me put it this way. How could you go through life . . . taking direction from the outside world?" Perhaps thinking of Leonard Zelig, he continued, "I mean, what kind of life would you have . . . if you made your decisions based on, you know, the outside world and not what your inner dictates told you? You would have a very inauthentic life."

But how did Allen get through it? He worked. It is almost certain that his work ethic got him through. Before the scandal broke, he said in 1988:

> *I never think of being "Woody Allen Inc.," of being a "mini mogul," or whatever they are now called in Europe. I just think of the old Puritan work ethic: a day's work. My day is my own. I get up when I feel like it. I take a break when I want to play my clarinet. I write when it is all in my head, buzzing along. But it has to all be there in my head before I start. I have to see the last shot before I begin to set down the first one. It may not be the most perfect of lives—but I don't know a better one.*

And so he picked up where he had left off and kept going.

"This short Brooklynite has produced some of the most invaluable, heartening testimony to all that distinguishes our popular culture," Dorothy Rabinowitz says. "Films like *Crimes and Misdemeanors*, *Hannah and Her Sisters*, and others contain the reassurance, the reminder, of the best of our times."

In 2002 Woody Allen wrote of his reaction to Elie Wiesel's novel *Night*: "Wiesel made the point that the inmates of the camps didn't think of revenge. I find it odd that I, who was a small boy during World War Two, and who lived in America, unmindful of any of the horrors Nazi victims were undergoing, and who never missed a good meal with meat and a warm bed to sleep in at night, and whose memories of those years are only blissful and full of good times and good music—that I think of nothing but revenge."

"Those are words," Rabinowitz said, "I could have spoken. I had a childhood that was secure, happy—I was born in America, was oblivious to what was going on in Europe. I had the cookies and milk when I came home from school, a warm bed, a family—and I, too, think of nothing but revenge. Except I don't think it's odd to feel that way. Woody said what no one else in his position has dared to say."

# 11. Woody Pulls the Rabbit Out of the Hat—Again

THE QUESTION AFTER THE SCANDAL of 1992 was whether it would affect his audience. Almost no reviewers held the scandal against him, except film critic Georgia Brown in the *Village Voice,* who ripped his 1993 film, *Manhattan Murder Mystery,* to shreds because of his treatment of women. But Allen's audience was so small that he lucked out. *Manhattan Murder Mystery* came out in the depths of his career, and it was called a success, yet it made only $11 million.

"The scandal didn't destroy him," Gary Terracino said. "It was a low ebb of popularity for him anyway. That's why he survived it. And then he hooked up with Tri-Star. So that gave him the air of a bounce back. Woody is lucky. He didn't have mega-huge smashes, not *Pulp Fiction* or even *Taxi Driver.* He had hits, not smashes. But they were consistent and different. In the end he does what no one else can do: He manages to make really bright intellectual films that aren't talky. You always think his films have more dialogue than they do."

Allen had been with United Artists until *Stardust Memories*. He was then with Orion from 1982 until 1991. He had been close to Mike Medavoy, the chairman of Tri-Star, since Medavoy had been chairman of Orion, which financed the majority of Allen's films. But Orion did not want to distribute his movies anymore because they weren't making money, and because Allen demanded total control. In September 1991 he agreed to make one new film for Tri-Star. In July 1993 Allen announced that he was leaving Tri-Star to make his next three films with private funds. The new arrangement involved Sweetland Films, which was funded by his old friend Jean Doumanian. The principal investor in Sweetland was Doumanian's boyfriend, Jacqui Safra, a member of a Swiss-Lebanese banking family.

Allen's contract was not renewed by Tri-Star simply because his so-called hits were failures by commercial standards. Both *Husbands and Wives* and *Manhattan Murder Mystery* had lost money. *Manhattan* (1979), his one big hit, had grossed $40 million. He would have no mainstream hits after it for many years, until *Hannah and Her Sisters* in 1986, which also grossed $40 million. But he would always find a new audience because he made new films every year; he was not dependent on the old audience, and his audience diversified.

Doumanian's reign would usher in a new atmosphere for Allen's staff. She decided to issue steep pay cuts for the staff as a way of trimming the production budget. Almost the entire tight-knit production team, who had been working with Allen for many years, would leave in the next two years. Robert Greenhut, Allen's producer since 1976, was among the first to go, followed by coproducer Helen Robin, associate producer Thomas Reilly, costume designer Jeffrey Kurland, cinematographer Carlo Di Palma, set photographer Brian Hamill, and film editor Susan E. Morse. They were all replaced with cheaper staff members. Only Juliet Taylor and production designer Santo Loquasto were retained and not asked to take pay cuts.

"The team that helped fashion movies like *Annie Hall, Manhattan* and *Hannah and Her Sisters* has largely broken up amid an intense effort to cut costs and overhaul the management of [Allen's] operation," the *New York Times* reported on June 1, 1998. Allen told the *Times*, "If I had my way, and the money, everyone who started with me would still be with me." The article noted that "Mr. Allen's films may cost an average of $18 million to $20 million to make, but their recent box office has been poor." Most of the criticism of Allen was based on his hands-off attitude about the matter and his delegating responsibility to others to make the cuts and deal with the situation. He wanted to keep writing, and nothing would stand in his way.

The year 1998 may well have been the nadir of Allen's career. While much of his staff was being disbanded, Allen told the *New York Times* that he was leaving his agent, Sam Cohn, because he wanted to "vigorously pursue an acting career." An "associate" of Allen told the newspaper that Allen "is keen on acting; he wants more choices and opportunities." A big motivation for the move was money. At this time Allen needed—or just was worried about—money. Cohn's power had slipped and nearly all his big clients had left before Allen did. Meryl Streep and Mike Nichols had left Cohn in the early nineties. With the commercial failures and the recent custody case, Allen needed a change. He went with Diane Keaton's agent, John Burnham at William Morris, which soon became WME— William Morris Endeavor. Several years later Burnham left WME and went to ICM, and Woody followed him.

Allen was momentarily stymied again in 2001 with the intrusion of messy real life. In May of that year he sued Jean Doumanian, his closest friend for thirty years, in New York State Supreme Court in Manhattan, stating that he had been cheated out of at least $12 million in profits from eight movies—*Bullets over Broadway, Mighty Aphrodite, Everyone Says I Love You, Deconstructing Harry, Wild Man Blues, Celebrity, Sweet and Lowdown,* and *Small Time Crooks.* He claimed that he had never seen accounts for the films despite calling Doumanian repeatedly. According to the *New York Times,* Allen's business manager, Stephen Tenenbaum, had been quietly urging Allen to examine the financial accounts of the films for years, and he had been reluctant to do so. Allen was always reluctant to engage in confrontation, and this situation must have been an especially painful moment for him. Robert Greenhut, who chose to stop working with Allen three and a half years earlier because of Doumanian's influence, told the *Times,* "It's amazing that Woody has taken this long to say, 'Where are the dollars and cents?'" "Under Mr. Allen's agreement with Ms. Doumanian and Mr. Safra," the *Times* wrote, "he earned a salary for each film as well as a percentage of the profits after the film's costs were recouped. During most of Mr. Allen's career before his partnership with Ms. Doumanian, he had an arrangement similar to that enjoyed by only a handful of film-makers, like Steven Spielberg: a percentage of every dollar earned by each film, as well as a salary." Allen had been willing to enter into the new arrangement, in which he didn't earn money beyond his salary until the films' investors were paid back, because Sweetland was financing the projects itself. Robert Greenhut told the *Times* that "I would have sued five years ago. But everyone was so friendly. When you're doing business with close friends, sometimes you let normal business practices go by the wayside. It's awkward to bring things up. The problem is there were never any financial reports issued on the films."

Allen's complaint said that Doumanian and Sweetland Films "failed to pay Mr. Allen's company, Moses Productions, its share of adjusted gross profits [money received after payments are made to theater owners] from the last eight movies they made together and refused to provide accurate information about the films' earnings."

Doumanian denied the allegations on June 25, 2001, and accused Allen of being "self-indulgent" and "fiscally irresponsible." She told the *New York Times* that she and her companion, Jacqui Safra, "took significant financial risks" for Allen. She said they had supported him "at a time when Allen stood accused of betraying others who trusted him" (referring to the custody battle). Doumanian and Safra filed their response in New York Supreme Court in Manhattan in response to Allen's suit the previous month. "Ms. Doumanian and Mr. Safra," the *Times* reported, "said that a full accounting of the movies—which included 'Mighty Aphrodite,' 'Bullets Over Broadway' and 'Everyone Says I Love You'—had been made to Mr. Allen's company, Moses Productions."

Doumanian and Safra also maintained that their company, Sweetland Films, took over the financing of Allen's movies in the early 1990s "almost as a favor to the filmmaker." They added that Allen and his company "had complete access to any and all financial information that they wanted regarding the pictures."

On June 12, 2002, Allen reached a settlement in his civil suit against Doumanian. Allen and Doumanian agreed to end the case. According to the *Times*, none of the parties would reveal the terms of the settlement. Allen received some money but would not say how much. Allen's lawyer, Michael Zweig, stated, "We're very pleased with the settlement."

Allen proceeded to open up a relationship with Jeffrey Katzenberg of Dreamworks, His sister, Letty Aronson, had begun to work with Allen as a co-executive producer of *Bullets over Broadway* and took over as lead producer starting with *Curse of the Jade Scorpion* in 2001.

Allen's creative surge—with its usual sidetracks—had never abated. A dizzying, erratic roller-coaster ride of films had continued in the nineties. *Deconstructing Harry* (1997) and *Celebrity* were solid achievements, followed, as usual, by one notable effort, *Sweet and Lowdown*, and a failure, *Small Time Crooks* (the latter somewhat reminiscent of *Big Deal on Madonna Street* and *A Slight Case of Murder*). But these two were masterpieces compared to what came next: *Curse of the Jade Scorpion* (2001) and *Hollywood Ending* (2002). Then came the impressive *Anything Else* (2003) and the mediocre *Melinda and Melinda* (2004). Allen hurried on to the excellence of *Match Point* (2005)—a fresh financial success at $23.2 million—followed, naturally, by a bomb, *Scoop* (2006), the excellent *Cassandra's Dream* (2007), and the brilliant *Vicky Cristina Barcelona* (2008). *Whatever Works* (2009) was stupefyingly bad; next came the intoxicating charm of *You Will Meet a Tall Dark Stranger* (2010) and then the splendid *Midnight in Paris* (2011), a huge financial hit at $56.8 million. A quick descent followed with *To Rome with Love*, ascendency again with *Blue Jasmine* (worldwide gross: more than $100 million), and near torpor with *Magic in the Moonlight*. Allen gave one of his best performances in a film he didn't write or direct, John Turturro's *Fading Gigolo*, as an unlikely pimp, in 2011, receiving wonderful reviews and revealing a new dimension to his talent. He had been flailing about in some of his own later films in which he appeared, looking older and uncomfortable, yet here he was totally relaxed, light as a feather, serene and whimsical. He was aging with grace and humor.

*Blue Jasmine* was singled out for its depiction of a complex, fully dimensional woman—an aspect of Allen's films that has been widely noted by scores of critics. He has been praised for creating extraordinary female characters without revering women. "That's what makes him so vital and alive and human and relatable," said Gary Terracino. "He's fascinated by women but I don't think he particularly adores them. They all need a Valium and a polo mallet. He uses that line in *Annie Hall* and at the end of *Manhattan Murder Mystery*. He says that to Diane Keaton.

"The key to Allen's appeal," Terracino continued, "is that women dropped off the cinema radar in the eighties; you had a lot of the titans of the seventies, Streisand, Fonda, Clayburgh—their careers just ended or they walked away. Women were absent except for Woody's films. It was not a female decade in Hollywood. The indie film is still male-centric. So Woody became the female director by default. Only Woody cast women; they just weren't working. I think that's one reason the press and the industry wanted him to succeed. We only had Bette Midler. He just does great roles for women. Even a bad Woody Allen role for a woman is better than what Hollywood is offering to this day. It was one of the many things that kept Woody going. Plus he has heart. There's so much heart in Woody's films."

Yet Woody's fecundity in creating complex women's roles and casting those roles is not a universally held opinion. A decidedly different point of view comes from Annette Insdorf, sometimes an enthusiastic fan of Allen's films. "Woody's depiction of female characters has often been problematic," Professor Insdorf e-mailed me. "My favorite Woody Allen films are the ones with sympathetically developed heroines, namely *Annie Hall, Manhattan, Another Woman, Hannah and Her Sisters* and *The Purple Rose of Cairo.* But many of his other movies present unsympathetic women: The female is nosy or abrasive in *Scoop, Match Point,* and *Crimes and Misdemeanors*; how easily an irritating mistress becomes the target of her lover's murderous intent!

"In *Anything Else,* the heroine is profoundly unsympathetic—Christina Ricci—and her mother—Stockard Channing—is not much better. *Deconstructing Harry* has mostly problematic women, including first wife, Demi Moore, and Harry's angry Jewish sister. Moreover, in *Husbands and Wives,* the characters played by both Judy Davis and Mia Farrow are de-eroticized; they think or talk too much during lovemaking, destroying the moment." Cate Blanchett, on the other hand, told author Charles McGrath in the *Wall Street Journal* that Allen writes a lot of good, juicy parts for women: "I think he understands what fabulous, unusual, complex, volatile creatures we are."

And if Woody is guilty of creating neurotic female characters, what about his own superneurotic persona, what about his murderous or befogged male protagonists, and just about every other neurotic character he can conjure up? Perhaps he feels this is simply what the messy world is really like, and he has been a master at delineating it. This kind of feminist realism strikes me as an offshoot of the socialist realism that yearned for perfect, sensitive workers of brawn and heft with positive, healthy, and sunny outlooks who had no faults and were shining examples to all Soviet workers. The stubborn elephant in the room remains the human condition, male or female.

David Denby wrote of this universal restlessness in his review of *You Will Meet a Tall Dark Stranger* in *The New Yorker:* "In this movie, no one is satisfied with what he or she has; everyone attempts to get more and, with one ironic exception, winds up with less. . . . The world is ruled by egocentricity and meanness, and much of what we do approaches grubby comedy." Denby wrote that "the men come off far worse than the women. . . . Anthony Hopkins' obvious intelligence makes Alfie's last grasp at sexual happiness pitiable and touching—even a man this shrewd, we think, is capable of falling for a woman a third his age. . . . Allen the moral rationalist can't help pointing out that there isn't any connection between virtue and happiness, intelligence and satisfaction."

Stuart Klawans, writing in the *Nation,* saw that Allen had achieved great depth in his portrait of a woman in *Blue Jasmine.* Applauding Allen for "a new departure" in examining "chicanery as a systemic problem of the kind that was exposed in the 2008 financial crisis and the Bernie Madoff affair," he said, "I admire, and am moved by, his decision to look at his new subject obliquely, through the experience of an enabler of the crimes: a woman who is fully individuated as a character and yet exemplary of the privileged class from which she has now been drummed out." Klawans wrote of Cate Blanchett that she is "the ferocious mistress of a hundred emotional nuances."

Allen's move to making films in Europe in 2005 with *Match Point* seems to have been the catalyst for a new burst of creativity. It was commonly assumed that a change of venues gave him a new freshness of vision, but in fact he had never lost that vision. It came in fits and starts as always. The latest triumph was *Blue Jasmine.* He was at yet another peak of his career.

The year 2012 was a hugely successful year for him: "A Comeback Fit for a Prince" was the title of Carl Unegbu's article in *ComedyBeat.* "First off," Unegbu wrote, "there was the blockbuster movie *Midnight in Paris,* followed later in the year by the rare honor of a two-part presentation on PBS entitled *Woody Allen: A Documentary,* a glowing tribute to Allen, co-produced by the renowned PBS series *American Masters,* and directed by

Robert B. Weide. Allen went on to win a Golden Globe Award for Best Original Screenplay for *Midnight in Paris*."

Yet if one is to take Allen literally in his interviews, he was in a morose but candid state of mind when he spoke to Tim Teeman of *The Times* (London) in 2012. "I've squandered an opportunity that people would kill for," he said. "I have had complete artistic freedom. Other directors don't get that in their lifetime. But I have a very poor record given the opportunities I've had. Out of 40 films I should have 30 masterpieces, eight noble failures and two embarrassments, but it hasn't worked out that way. Many of the films are enjoyable by the mean standards of movies, but look at what has been accomplished by people who have done beautiful things—Kurosawa, Bergman, Fellini, Buñuel, Truffaut—and then look at my films. I have squandered my opportunities, and I have nobody to blame but myself."

He named six films he prized: *The Purple Rose of Cairo, Match Point, Bullets over Broadway, Zelig, Husbands and Wives*, and *Vicky Cristina Barcelona*. "You reach a certain age and you come to the conclusion that greatness is not in you," he said. "You aspired to greatness when you were younger, but either through lack of industry or lack of discipline or simply lack of genius you didn't achieve greatness. The years go by and you realize, 'I'm this mid-level guy.' I did the best I could."

It is difficult to understand this wall of depression. Allen has experienced one of the longest records of creativity in the history of film. Many directors (and novelists, for that matter) experience early points of greatness, and we are accustomed to the diminution of their talents with time. The early glories of Fellini's *I Vitelloni, The White Sheik, Variety Lights, La Strada*, and *8½* were hardly matched by such later works as *Satyricon, Roma, Amarcord*, and *Ginger and Fred*. Sometimes an artist even seems to become a pale echo of himself. Ralph Ellison achieved one timeless masterpiece, *Invisible Man*; this is true, as well, of Sherwood Anderson's *Winesburg, Ohio* and Henry Roth's *Call It Sleep*, and countless others. Arthur Miller, whom Allen admired as a young man, went from the heights of *All My Sons, Death of a Salesman, A Memory of Two Mondays*, and *A View from the Bridge* to the turgidity of *After the Fall* and, beyond that, to the thinnest of didactic plays, regurgitating his early themes with thoughts seemingly to be culled from newspaper editorials and the palest stick figures as characters. Allen, lurching forward and backward, has an amazing record of work, work that is never confined to one note; work that is fresh, innovative, new, startling, vivid, and alive, with resonant and startling characters. It is work that has the impact of a deep emotion or a crystalline thought or dialogue captured in a way we could not express ourselves—an impact that does not diminish over time.

We will remember (and those who will follow us in time will remember) that bench on Fifty-ninth Street under the bridge in *Manhattan* with the figures of Isaac (Allen) and Mary (Keaton) finding each other, we will remember Linda Ash (Mira Sorvino)—the character's porno name was "Judy Cum"—telling Kevin (Michael Rapaport) when they meet, "I bet you're built like a horse," and Mia (Tina Vitale) telling Danny Rose in the car that her ex-husband was "a juice man for the mob," and Danny asking innocently: "He made juice for the mob?" I know that I will never forget the moment when the secret writing genius and mafioso, Cheech (Chazz Palmintieri), shoots Olive (Jennifer Tilley) in *Bullets over Broadway* in the name of art because her horrible voice was ruining "my play." Or the look on Isaac's face when he digests the meaning of Tracy telling him, as she leaves for London, "Look, you have to have a little faith in people." Or, of course, Danny running after Tina in the rain and kissing her in front of the Carnegie Deli, or Cliff in *Hannah and Her Sisters* leaping into the air with joy in front of Mount Sinai Hospital when he learns he isn't dying, and then collapsing with depression when he realizes he will eventually anyway.

Across the world millions and millions of people have such memories of Allen's films. It is not easy to give enduring laughter to the world, laughter based not on glib one-liners but on a deep comprehension of the human condition.

If Allen did not have one transcendent work, as he contends—and I think he has many—his record of consistent, memorable films would accord him a permanent place as one of the great directors of all time.

Javier Aguirresarobe is Allen's brilliant cinematographer on *Blue Jasmine* and *Vicky Cristina Barcelona*. Aguirresarobe has also worked with Miloš Forman, Pedro Almodóvar, and Imanol Uribe. "Woody Allen is a man of few words," he told me. "He assumes those who collaborate with him know his way of working. With *Vicky Cristina Barcelona*, I had a very short phone conversation with him before his trip to Spain. He told me he wanted a 'warm' film. 'Very warm,' he repeated, I remember. 'We will speak about the rest upon arrival.' But we never spoke more. My strategy was to carefully study Woody's movies. I recall now that my technical communication with him was more fluid than I thought because through all his movies, you could discover a specific style of filmmaking and a very personal language. I had strong and memorable emotions shooting his movies. I also cannot forget the huge hug Woody gave me at the movie's premiere in San Sebastián; it was something unusual and memorable. For *Blue Jasmine* I very much enjoyed working alongside Mr. Allen. He always wants the most simple route for developing complex scenes.

"Woody Allen is a very active director on the set," Aguirresarobe continued. "He enjoys trying to figure out the perfect choreography for each scene so that the actors move at ease and act as naturally as possible, that the dialogue sounds right, and the camera captures the mise-en-scène in an attractive way. *Blue Jasmine* contains many examples of this, such as the dentist's sexual harassment of Jasmine, one of the finest scenes. In the original script this scene covered just three pages, but we saw the possibilities for lengthening his stubborn pursuit of her and establishing more credibility for it.

"Allen tends to use one or two long uninterrupted shots for his scenes, with the camera moving but almost no cutting." What Aguirresarobe meant was that for this very long scene with the actors jumping around a lot (the two actors were literally jumping around each other) in a tiny space, Allen decided to use just *one* long take with no cutting/editing to create the tension and claustrophobia of Jasmine being harassed.

Another director might create tension with a lot of cutting and extreme close-ups, such as a close-up of a flared nostril, cut to Jasmine's eyes rolling in fear, cut to a wide shot of the dentist chasing Jasmine behind the desk, cut to extreme close-up of Jasmine's hands fluttering nervously, close-up of the phone ringing ominously. Allen created the tension by putting the two actors in an actual tight space and shooting them continuously.

"While shooting *Vicky Cristina Barcelona* I realized there weren't any monitors on the set, takes, or rehearsals. Woody stood behind the camera with his headphones just watching the scene, as it used to be done in the old days. I had to adapt to the old style. And I found a director who accurately communicated what he wanted.

"For light and camera movement, there are special rules in Woody's grammatical language. This can be described with concepts such as simplicity, naturalness, and an attractive choreography. In his movies stridencies, unusual angles, strong lights, excessive contrast in lighting are avoided. He loves the camera flying over the situation until the scene is resolved/concluded. He likes a warm tone. His palette is fed from warm tones like crème, brown, gold. Only a few times or perhaps never do blue tones appear in his films. On the other hand, I think that Woody Allen still aspires, as if from an old dream, to shoot a black-and-white movie again.

"During the shooting of *Vicky Cristina* I was initially puzzled by the lack of monitors on the set, or a video assist. And then I realized that Woody didn't use video playbacks for rehearsals or takes. I found the movie very difficult because I didn't have any reference images, so I usually had to make a lot of changes during the shot itself. I also had to adapt to this old style. I measured light as accurately as possible and changed the lens. Yet what I keep in memory is that I shot this movie like being a little bit 'blind.'"

I asked Aguirresarobe to assess Allen's style in terms of cinematography and how different it was from other directors he had worked with, like Almodóvar, Forman, James Ivory, or Alejandro Amenábar. "Woody Allen is more audacious than any of them when it comes to cinematographic language," he replied. "He takes risks that nobody else takes. He tells his stories with a great technical economy. I don't recall, for example, his even once using a crane or something like that in his films. Woody Allen is different from all the others. He trusts a good cast so he won't have to spend any time giving instruction to the actors. He gives them a lot of freedom on the set. On the other hand, Woody never shoots covers [extra additional shots that may or may not be used]. It is the words, the dialogue, that give birth to the movie with such technical simplicity. I don't remember ever having seen this with other directors."

"What are your impressions of him as a human being?"

"Woody Allen is a very quiet man on the set, very polite, but keeping a distance from everyone, including his closest collaborators who have been working with him for a very long time. It's very difficult to figure out what is going on in his mind.

"I have a feeling that he is at a very good moment in his creativity. And

*Blue Jasmine* proves it. I consider myself a very authentic fan of his work, and I feel proud and honored to have participated in two of his productions."

It may have been the announcement of Cate Blanchett's nomination for both the Golden Globes Award and the Academy Award for *Blue Jasmine* in January 2014, as well as the announcement that the Globes would give Allen a lifetime achievement award, that brought Mia Farrow's simmering resentment to a boil. Her rage had been building through 2012 and 2013. Allen was not even really experiencing a "comeback"; he had never actually gone away, his films continuing to exert a powerful fascination and interest. Audiences continued to love his films, and the films kept coming, every single year. Actors competed frantically to work for him, not caring about the small salary they would receive. The prestige associated with working with him more than compensated for that, and they genuinely admired, often loved, his work with a passion. He was more popular and successful than ever. He was too committed to the work to let momentary setbacks sink him.

Allen's period of renewed success coincided with what had been a dark time for Farrow. Publicly she had concentrated on good works, serving since 2000 as a UNICEF international Goodwill Ambassador, with a focus on children in conflict zones. She traveled to Sudan's Darfur region thirteen times and spoke out against genocide at Senate and congressional hearings. In 2010 she appeared at The Hague, testifying at the war-crimes trial of Charles Taylor, the former Liberian president.

She was named by *Time* as one of the most influential people in the world. She received humanitarian awards including the Refugees International McCall-Pierpaoli Humanitarian Award for "extraordinary services to refugees and displaced people." But her acting career had been dormant for many years, a source of tremendous frustration for her, and she was enmeshed in personal and family crises as well. Two of her later adopted daughters, Tam and Lark, died. Tam died of heart failure in 2000. She was twenty-one. Lark died in 2008 at the age of thirty-five of an undisclosed illness. Farrow continued to support her close friend, the convicted sex offender Roman Polanski, who was still evading extradition to the United States. She went to London in 2005 to testify in his 2005 libel suit against *Vanity Fair*. In addition, her own troubled family history tragically resurfaced with two other events in close sequence. In June 2009, her older brother Patrick Farrow committed suicide in Vermont. He died of a single gunshot wound to the head.

Then, in 2012, her brother John Charles Villiers-Farrow was indicted on charges of sexual abuse of two ten-year-old boys over a period of several years in Maryland. Farrow pled guilty while maintaining his innocence and was sentenced to ten years in prison.

The abuse ended only in 2007 or 2008, when the boys reached their midteens. The charging documents alleged that Villiers-Farrow abused the boys together and alone, showing them pornographic movies and performing oral sex on them.

Tim Pratt, a reporter for the *Capital Gazette News* in Maryland, told me that the presiding judge at the trial, Laura Kiessling, "made mention of Villiers-Farrow being abused as a child. Then she said: 'What I think of when I hear that statement is [that] a victim of child sex abuse should know better than anyone else what it is to suffer at the hands of an abuser, and I didn't hear that from Mr. Villiers-Farrow.' She said she felt that Villiers-Farrow was only expressing regret because he got caught."

"The indictment was on November 30, 2012," Kathleen Rogers, the deputy state's attorney of Anne Arundel County, Maryland, told me. "We started a jury trial on July 25, and we picked a jury that day. We did opening statements, and then the next morning, the twenty-sixth, the defendant decided to enter pleas in both of the cases. . . . We proceeded by way of what we call an Alford plea."

"What are the implications of that?" I asked.

"What that means," Ms. Rogers said, "is that he is saying that he believes that the state has enough evidence to convict him, but he's maintaining his innocence. But he wants to enter this plea basically because he believes that he'll be convicted if he goes to trial. It allows him to maintain his innocence, I guess, for himself, but in terms of the effect on the court and the judicial system, it's equal to a guilty plea."

"Tim Pratt," I said to Ms. Rogers, "told me that he was startled by one thing, and the judge alluded to it also: that Villiers-Farrow stated that he'd been the victim of sex abuse as a boy himself. Is that right?"

"Yes, his attorneys said that at the sentencing."

"Was Mia Farrow present at the trial?"

"She was not."

"Was any member of the Farrow family there?"

"No. I think the other person there was his wife."

"How strong was the case?"

"I think it was really strong," Ms. Rogers replied. "The details that the boys gave of the abuse made it so clear that it was real. I've been prosecuting sex offenders for twenty-four, twenty-five years now, and I have to say one of the boy's versions . . . if you closed your eyes you would believe it. Because in my experience, if kids are making something up, you don't get the details. Details about things Farrow would say, terms he would use, besides the actions, the other little things that kind of make you believe that it's true. And in addition to that, the one-party-consent phone call, where the one boy spoke to Farrow. It wasn't as if Farrow confessed to everything in the phone call, but there were certainly some very incriminating statements by him."

As a young man Villiers-Farrow had traveled to India with Mia and encountered the Beatles with her. At the time of the allegations against Woody Allen in 1992, Villiers-Farrow, standing beside Mia, had told *People* that Allen "is going to be indicted and he's going to be ruined. I think when all of it comes out, he's going to go to jail."

Mia Farrow has remained silent about her brother's imprisonment.

She did, however, begin to speak out again about Woody in 2012, along with Satchel—now Ronan Farrow—and it soon became clear that she was still obsessed with her old lover and director. It was Ronan, twenty-five, who made news first. On June 18 he had tweeted a Father's Day greeting to Allen: "Happy Father's Day—or as they call it in my family, happy brother-in-law's day." Mia then retweeted the message, adding the word "Boom." The message became major tabloid news, and Ronan was soon the media's flavor of the week. Handsome and articulate, Ronan was only eleven years old when he entered Bard College. He graduated at fifteen, the school's youngest graduate. He was a Rhodes Scholar and a graduate of Yale Law School; he had worked for the State Department under Hillary Clinton in 2011. He was also a gossipy tweeter. He was the subject of extensive newspaper coverage, including a profile in the *New York Times Magazine,* and he would soon be hired by MSNBC and given his own daily program (which was canceled in February 2015). In November 2013, in a

*Vanity Fair* article by Maureen Orth titled "Mama Mia!" Mia was quoted as stating that Ronan was "possibly" the son of Frank Sinatra. She told Orth that while she was with Allen, she continued seeing Sinatra, and was uncertain about Ronan's paternity. The story made front-page headlines. As Robert Weide wrote in *The Daily Beast*, "To even say that Ronan is 'possibly' Sinatra's son implies that Mia was fooling around with her ex-husband decades after their divorce. Backdating from Ronan's birthdate, it means that Farrow and Sinatra 'hooked up' in March of 1987 when Mia was forty-two and Old Blue Eyes was seventy-one. This sort of dispels the myth that Woody and Mia had this idyllic, loving, monogamous relationship until Woody threw it all away in 1992, since Mia was apparently diddling her ex five years earlier."

Weide also noted that those who hated Woody "for what he did to Mia . . . should be reminded that if Sinatra was indeed Ronan's biological father, it's not the first time Mia had a child by a married man. In 1969, at the age of twenty-four, she became pregnant by musician/composer André Previn, forty, who was still married to singer-songwriter Dory Previn."

On January 16 it was announced that Cate Blanchett had been nominated for a Best Actress Oscar for her performance. The Golden Globes had also nominated Blanchett for best actress and announced on January 9 that they would give Allen a lifetime achievement award.

While the Globes ceremony was going on, Mia tweeted, "A woman has publicly detailed Woody Allen's molestation of her at age 7. Golden Globe tribute showed contempt for her and all abuse survivors." She later tweeted again: "Is he a pedophile?" and linked to the *Vanity Affair* article by Maureen Orth.

There had been an odd incident at the time of the preparation for the Golden Globes. Robert Weide was asked to work on the clip montage of Allen's films that would precede the award to Allen. Weide and the montage editor, Nicholas Goodman, wanted to include a clip from *The Purple Rose of Cairo* in which Mia appeared. The producers were concerned about whether Mia would sign a release. She instantly agreed to its use for the occasion honoring Allen. She would, therefore, participate in the event that "showed contempt for [Dylan] and all abuse survivors." It was an echo of her eagerness to appear in *Manhattan Murder Mystery* despite her horror over Woody's alleged sexual abuse of Dylan, and also of the memorable question she put to Dr. Susan Coates after accusing Allen of abuse: "Do you think I should marry him?"

On February 1 two documents appeared in the *New York Times*: an article by Nicholas Kristof introducing and quoting from an open letter from Dylan Farrow and Dylan's letter itself.

# 12. **Balls of Steel**

WRITING FOR THE OP-ED PAGE of the *Times* on February 1, Nicholas Kristof said that "one person who hasn't been heard out" about the accusations against Allen was Dylan Farrow. Dylan, Kristof wrote, "tells me that she has been traumatized for more than two decades by what took place; last year, she was belatedly diagnosed with post-traumatic stress disorder. She says that when she heard of the Golden Globe award being given to Allen she curled up in a ball on her bed, crying hysterically." Kristof quoted Dylan as writing:

> *That he got away with what he did to me haunted me as I grew up. I was stricken with guilt that I had allowed him to be near other little girls. I was terrified of being touched by men. I developed an eating disorder. I began cutting myself.*
>
> *That torment was made worse by Hollywood. All but a precious few (my heroes) turned a blind eye. Most found it easier to accept the ambiguity, to say, "who can say what happened," to pretend that nothing was wrong. Actors praised him at awards shows. Networks put him on TV. Critics put him in magazines.*

*Each time I saw my abuser's face—on a poster, on a T-shirt, on television—I could only hide my panic until I found a place to be alone and fall apart.*

Kristof then, remarkably, came to a conclusion based on no evidence. He said that "none of us can be certain what happened," but nevertheless accused the Golden Globes of "siding with Allen, in effect accusing Dylan either of lying or of not mattering." And so, after stating that no one could be certain of what happened, he wrote "Do we really need to leap to our feet and lionize an alleged molester?"

Dylan's "Open Letter"—the same letter, but in full—was published on Kristof's blog on the same day, on February 1 in the *Times*, thus providing maximum media impact. She began, "What's your favorite Woody Allen movie? Before you answer, you should know: when I was seven years old, Woody Allen took me by the hand and led me into a dim closet-like attic on the second floor of our house. He told me to lay on my stomach and play with my brother's electric train set. Then he sexually assaulted me. He talked to me while he did it, whispering that I was a good girl, that this was our secret, promising that we'd go to Paris and I'd be a star in his movies." Dylan went on to repeat the same charges Mia had made in 1992, most of which also appear in the Kristof article.

There are some curious comments here: "I didn't know that my father would use his sexual relationship with my sister to cover up the abuse he inflicted on me." How exactly did Allen manage to "cover up" anything by his relationship with Soon-Yi? On the contrary, it would appear that the relationship with Soon-Yi is used as ammunition by those who believe that Allen is also guilty of abusing Dylan.

In the final part of her letter, Dylan gets to what seems to be the point, that the Golden Globes and the Academy can send a message on her behalf by not giving awards to Allen or Blanchett: "What if it had been your child, Cate Blanchett? Louis CK? Alec Baldwin? What if it had been you, Emma Stone? Or you, Scarlett Johansson? You knew me when I was a little girl, Diane Keaton. Have you forgotten me?"

Linda Fairstein commented on the letter by saying, "The psychological suggestion from those who work in this field is that the letter is either very real and that Dylan lived with this for twenty-one years and is reporting it—or, as often happens, if she was coached to believe, that this happened, then that's remained with her. She may think it happened. It took fourteen months for the prosecutor to investigate and decide. During that fourteen months, if it did happen, she was being encouraged to recall that it happened. If it didn't happen, she was still being encouraged to recall that it happened. I've seen commentators on TV in the last twenty-four hours say, 'I read the letter, therefore it happened.' You just can't do that without looking back at the contemporaneous facts.

"But I'm sort of in the camp with the people who are saying there was a timing to this that had to do with the Academy Award show and her half brother's [Ronan's] new show. It just seemed very staged. And I was shocked that none of the mainstream media went back to Dr. Leventhal's [Yale–New Haven Clinic] report. In his findings there was no sign of abuse, and in fact he believed there was manipulation by an angry parent. Dylan may really believe that Woody abused her. I just don't think he did, and I don't think there's any evidence that he did.

"But nothing will happen now. This was investigated by a Connecticut prosecutor in the county where it occurred. And he came to the conclusion that he had no evidence with which to mount a prosecution. There's a statute of limitations; it's over. This is, I think, all just part of a campaign that began when Woody Allen got his award [for *Blue Jasmine*] at the Golden Globes and the Academy Award nomination."

On February 5 Moses Farrow, who was adopted by Farrow and Allen in December 1991, spoke out for the first time in defense of his father. "Of course Woody did not molest my sister," he told *People*. "[Dylan] loved [Allen] and looked forward to seeing him when he would visit. She never hid from him until our mother succeeded in creating the atmosphere of fear and hate toward him." Moses said that on the day of the alleged abuse there were several people present in the house the whole time, and "no one, not my father or sister, was off in any private spaces. I don't know if my sister really believes she was molested or is trying to please her mother. Pleasing my mother was [a] very powerful motivation because to be on her wrong side was horrible." Moses also told Robert Weide that life at Mia's home amounted to "brainwashing."

I received the following response to an interview request with Moses from attorney Eric J. Broder on January 12, 2015: "I spoke to Moses and he advised me that he does not want to be interviewed at this time and would only say that a terrible and dishonest thing was done to his father. He further explained that he knows this to be true because he was there."

Woody responded to Dylan's letter and Kristof's article on Feburary 7, 2014, in the *New York Times*. He wrote:

> *Twenty-one years ago, when I first heard Mia Farrow had accused me of child molestation, I found the idea so ludicrous I didn't give it a second thought. We were involved in a terribly acrimonious breakup, with great enmity between us and a custody battle slowly gathering energy. The self-serving transparency of her malevolence seemed so obvious I didn't even hire a lawyer to defend myself. . . .*
>
> *I naively thought the accusation would be dismissed out of hand because of course, I hadn't molested Dylan and any rational person would see the ploy for what it was. Common sense would prevail. After all, I was a 56-year-old man who had never before (or after) been accused of child molestation. I had been going out with Mia for 12 years and never in that time did she ever suggest to me anything resembling misconduct. Now, suddenly, when I had driven up to her house in Connecticut one afternoon to visit the kids for a few hours, when I would be on my raging adversary's home turf, with half a dozen people present, when I was in the blissful early stages of a happy new relationship with the woman I'd go on to marry—that I would pick this moment in time to embark on a career as a child molester should seem to the most skeptical mind highly unlikely. . . .*
>
> *I very willingly took a lie-detector test and of course passed because I had nothing to hide. I asked Mia to take one and she wouldn't. Last week a woman named Stacey Nelkin, whom I had dated many years ago, came forward to the press to tell them that when Mia and I first had our custody battle 21 years ago, Mia had wanted her to testify that she had been underage when I was dating her, despite the fact this was untrue. Stacey refused. I include this anecdote so we all know what kind of character we are dealing with. One can imagine in learning this why she wouldn't take a lie-detector test.*

Allen went on to write about the finding of the Child Sexual Abuse Clinic of the Yale–New Haven Hospital and quoted their conclusion as to his innocence in full. He wrote of Judge Wilk's bias: "He thought of me as an older man exploiting a much younger woman, which outraged Mia as improper despite the fact she had dated a much older Frank Sinatra when she was 19." He wrote that he and Soon-Yi had been happily married for sixteen years "with two great kids, both adopted," and pointed out that he and his new wife were extra-carefully scrutinized "by both the adoption agency and adoption courts, and everyone blessed our adoptions."

He said that he was heartbroken when Mia took custody of the children: "Moses was angry with me. Ronan I didn't know well because Mia would never let me get close to him from the moment he was born and Dylan, whom I adored and was very close to and about whom Mia called my sister in a rage and said, 'He took my daughter, now I'll take his.' I never saw her again nor was I able to speak with her no matter how hard I tried. I still loved her deeply, and felt guilty that by falling in love with Soon-Yi I had put her in the position of being used as a pawn for revenge. . . ."

Allen quoted Moses: " 'My mother drummed it into me to hate my father for tearing apart the family and sexually molesting my sister. . . . Of course Woody did not molest my sister. . . .' "

Allen went on to comment on the question of whether Ronan was his son or Sinatra's. "Is he my son or, as Mia suggests, Frank Sinatra's? Granted, he looks a lot like Frank with the blue eyes and facial features, but if so what does this say? That all during the custody hearing Mia lied under oath and falsely represented Ronan as our son? Even if he is not Frank's, the possibility she raises that he could be, indicates she was secretly intimate with him during our years [together]. . . ."

Allen said he didn't doubt that Dylan had come to believe she'd been molested, but if from the age of seven, "a vulnerable child is taught by a strong mother to hate her father because he is a monster who abused her, is it so inconceivable that after many years of this indoctrination the image of me Mia wanted to establish had taken root? . . ."

Allen also addressed the issue of where the molestation was supposed to have taken place: the attic of Mia's house. He pointed out that he was a "major claustrophobe." He suggested that the idea of the attic came from Dory Previn's song, "With My Daddy in the Attic," which was on the same recording as the song Dory had written about Mia's betrayal of her with Dory's husband, André Previn. He raised the question of whether the letter was even written by Dylan or "at least guided" by Mia. He acutely observed that movie stars were dragged into the letter, "which smells a lot more like Mia than Dylan."

Allen quoted Moses again: "'Knowing that my mother often used us as pawns, I cannot trust anything that is said or written from anyone in the family.'" Allen finally raised the question of whether Mia herself really believed he had molested Dylan. He noted Mia's granting permission for the Golden Globes to use a film clip of her for a ceremony in his honor. "Common sense must ask: Would a mother who thought her 7-year-old daughter was sexually abused by a molester give consent for a film clip of her to be used to honor the molester at the Golden Globes?"

In his conclusion he said, "Of course, I did not molest Dylan. I loved her and hope one day she will grasp how she has been cheated out of having a loving father and exploited by a mother more interested in her own festering anger than her daughter's well-being. . . ."

"I knew that Mia would come out swinging around now," Gary Terracino told me. "From her angle it makes sense . . . while Woody is having a career resurgence and still in the public eye, and just as Ronan is making his debut as a public person on MSNBC, Mia wants to set the record straight, make Woody squirm one last time, have one last shot at permanently tarring his rep—and launch Ronan into the public eye in the process.

"But it has spectacularly backfired, because Mia has exposed her own moral transgression and self-absorption in the process. To wit: 'I don't know which wealthy powerful man is Ronan's father . . .'; 'I'm all about protecting children—but am forcing Ronan and Dylan to trot out these allegations in detail'; 'People are protecting Woody because he's famous—but I am going to brag about all the famous men I've slept with—Woody, Frank, Philip Roth, et al.' And her gleefulness in dredging all this up again after twenty-two years—it didn't go over well. She overstepped and ripped the halo off of Saint Mia." Terracino added, "But here is Woody at his best and worst. Effectively denying the allegation that he molested Dylan, but surprised that people even care that he ran off with Mia's twenty-one-year-old [adopted] daughter."

In an article in the *Wall Street Journal*, "On Woody Allen and Echoes of the Past," Dorothy Rabinowitz wrote that it was impossible to read Allen's response without being struck by its haunting echoes of other people who had been falsely accused. "He had thought that the charges were so ludicrous he didn't think of hiring a lawyer," she wrote. "It was a kind of naiveté evident in virtually every person known to me who had been falsely charged in the high-profile sex-abuse cases that had swept the country in the 1980s and early 1990s—people convicted and sentenced to long prison terms on the basis of testimony from children coaxed into making accusations. Accusations made, at ages 5, 6, or 7, that many of them would continue to believe fervently were true, into adulthood."

What these accused did not know, she wrote, was "what Woody Allen didn't recognize in 1992 . . . the deadly power of a child-sex-abuse accusation." Despite the straightforward conclusion about Allen's innocence by the Yale–New Haven investigators, "the judge in the custody case wrote in his opinion that 'we will probably never know what occurred.'" This was, she wrote, "the sacrosanct status of the child sex-abuse charge. Resorting to the comfortable 'we will never know' remains the evasion of choice for authorities in terror of acknowledging the innocence of anyone accused of the charge."

Ms. Rabinowitz concluded, "For no one, perhaps, is the importance of keeping alive the charge of guilt greater than for the person who was, as a child, part of a famous child-sex-abuse case built on false charges. These children, reinforced again and again in the truth of the accusation, would believe as adults that their horrific victimization early in life has caused them psychic injury of untold depths.

"Such was the predicament evident in one of the Amiraults' [Violet Amirault and her daughter, Cheryl, falsely imprisoned for eight years, and Violet's son, Gerald, imprisoned for nineteen years] child accusers, grown to adulthood who arrived at a parole hearing for Gerald Amirault in a state pitiable to behold, afire with fury, tearful as she recounted the terrors, the failures in her life, that she attributed to his victimization of her. That this was suffering brought on by a lifetime educated in the belief of her victimization, it would be hard to dispute. It is similarly hard now, witnessing the public raging of Ms. Farrow's daughter, Dylan, not to recall the sight and sound of that witness in the hearing room, and to recognize, again, the costs exacted by a lifetime of such belief."

All the sound and fury did not impede Allen's continuing artistic quest, a quest that was crowned by more success than he had ever achieved before. Cate Blanchett won the Academy Award for Best Actress on March 3, 2014. She was the seventh actor who won on the basis of a role in an Allen film (seventeen have received nominations).

There were bitter recriminations from Dylan Farrow, who said that she did not expect "a betrayal of this magnitude" from so many people after she'd finally had the courage to tell her story. She issued her response on February 6. About Moses, she said: "My brother has broken my heart. . . . His betrayal is the lowest form of evil that I could ever imagine."

None of it mattered. Writing in the *New Republic*, Adam Kirsch said that Dylan's letter had not technically added anything to the public record and "asks more from us than any audience has ever been willing to grant"—that is, missing out on a Woody Allen movie. Kirsch cataloged a long list and range of evildoers, including a few murderers. Kirsch wasn't sure if Allen belonged in this list, but rather carelessly included him anyway without much effort at examining the facts of the case. But he was certain of one thing: Allen's audience would not desert him. "Time will lessen that reaction [to Dylan and Mia's charges]—if the public could forget the charges in 1992, they can forget again in 2014." The bottom line: "If people are still watching movies a century from now, there's no doubt that they will be watching *Annie Hall* and *Crimes and Misdemeanors*."

Allen continued to insist that he kept working because the work kept him from obsessing about mortality or the human condition: "You know in a mental institution they sometimes give a person some clay or some basket weaving?" he asked Charles McGrath in the *Wall Street Journal*. "It's the therapy of moviemaking that has been good in my life. If you don't work, it's unhealthy—for me, particularly unhealthy. I could sit here suffering from morbid introspection, ruing my mortality, being anxious. But it's very therapeutic to get up and think, Can I get this actor; does my third act work? All these solvable problems that are delightful puzzles, as opposed to the great puzzles of life that are unsolvable, or that have very bad solutions. So I get pleasure from doing this. It's my version of basket weaving."

But even with his therapeutic moviemaking, Allen continued to voice his darkest reflections. In August 2014 he told Kevin Maher of *The Times* (London), "I really don't care about anything that happens after my death. I don't care if they take all of my movies and burn them. There is no God.

There is no magic. There is nothing other than the cold hard facts of what you see with your eyes. It begins. It ends. There is no reason for anything."

In sunnier moments, though, Allen can tell McGrath in the *Wall Street Journal,* with serene self-acceptance: "It's an inevitable disaster of aging. If I think of parts for myself now, all I can be is Pop, the lovable doorman, or the amiable Dad at the wedding. I'd like to be the lover."

There is no trace of age in the prickly energy, creativity, and skill he brings to the film set: Cate Blanchett told McGrath that Woody was "brutal and electric. Everyone is on tippy-toes," she continued. "I think he thinks the more he says, the more he screws it up. He wants to get out of the actors' way, and they want as much as they can get of him. He's incredibly restless, and that creates a sort of nervous energy on the set. He wants to get it done now. He wants all the energy of that day and then he wants to go and have dinner." Judith Malina, the cofounder of the Living Theater, appeared in *Radio Days.* She told me how perturbed she was by Allen shouting at her, "No dramatics! No dramatics!"

Allen bounces back from depression as soon as he is working, and Diane Keaton said it best: He has "balls of steel." He has never been blocked in his work. "People always ask . . . do you think you'll wake up one morning and not be funny or have writer's block?" he told Stuart Husband of *The Telegraph.* "But that wouldn't occur to me. It's not a possibility to me." He is certain that failure is okay, that it won't last: "You throw enough stuff against the wall, something's eventually gotta stick, right?"

He spoke of his "incredible luck" for making people laugh: "I've parlayed that little gift into an entire career. If I hadn't had that, I'd be waiting tables or trying to sell you insurance."

In January 2015, Allen announced he was embarking on another new journey. Amazon had signed him to write and direct his first television series. The company ordered a full season of half-hour shows, which would be available exclusively on the company's Prime Instant Video service. Allen will earn a minimum of $5 million for the series.

Harlene Rosen Allen, Woody's first wife, who had not spoken publicly in many years, sent me an eightieth birthday message for him:

> *Wondrous Woody, you inspired me with your enormous energy, creativity and charisma. I loved going to movies with you. I loved making music with you, Jack Victor and Elliott Mills. After our teenage summer of love, marriage*

*was difficult. You established a career. I completed four years of college. We supported each other, learned about life, and became adults. There was sadness, tears, laughter, and love. Happy 80th birthday.*

*Harlene*

## Epilogue
## Touching the Entire World

In April 2015 I wrote Woody Allen requesting that we meet. He wrote back that he would meet me, but that "This must not be construed as cooperation with your book but merely a friendly response to a friendly invitation." This was a characteristic demurral; while usually answering my questions, he always wanted to make it clear that his responses should not lead to a surmise on my or the public's part that he was participating in the book. And in fact, while being friendly and collegial, he has absolutely not cooperated with or authorized this book. He has not cooperated in the traditional biographical sense of opening up his Rolodex and his time.

I visited Woody at his cozy, very lived-in, dark-hued office with its rust and brown couches. He greeted me warmly. I found innocence, curiosity, intensity, total responsiveness, and deep emotion in him. He was nearly eighty, yet he had the youthfulness of the committed artist who cannot wait to get back to his work. I have known many writers, and he is among the most youthful I have ever met.

We talked about Israel, about anti-Semitism, about the Holocaust: "It can happen in a minute," he said. He talked of Victor Klemperer's diaries of life in Nazi Germany, of Michael Thomas, a resister to Nazism he'd known, of Rossellini's *Il Generale Della Rovere.* He was enthusiastic about the CDs I had sent him of the New Black Eagles Jazz Band. I mentioned what I thought were the improvisational scenes of disputes and arguments in *Husbands and Wives* and *Vicky Cristina Barcelona.* He confirmed they were improvised and that he didn't even know what Javier Bardem and Penélope Cruz were saying when they were speaking Spanish. "If you have a skilled artist, they will know what to do if I get out of their way." And he lamented the sudden death of Sydney Pollack, who seemed so vigorous and was so brilliant in *Husbands and Wives.*

I noted that in recent years Woody appears to have reached a certain self-acceptance and happiness, a quality that seemed evident in his recent screen performances, especially in John Turturro's *Fading Gigolo.* He said he was still unhappy about not having achieved a masterpiece. I mentioned John Simon, who had sometimes been brutal toward his early films. I shared with him Simon's comments to me (see chapter 1) that Woody always seemed on the verge of something wonderful, and that one might reasonably conclude that his having made so many excellent films could be equated with having achieved a masterpiece. He considered this with surprise and interest. He also said that he thought that Simon's film criticism would endure more than that of any other critic.

I asked him about the novel he'd written. It hadn't worked out, he said. "You know, I was not a reader in my youth."

I asked him what was his greatest joy in life. His face became radiant. "My marriage to Soon-Yi. And my children. If you told me I'd find someone thirty-five years younger, Korean, who'd been through such horrors in her childhood. . . . That kind of experience can mold a person into something terrible or something wonderful.

"I learned a lot from all my wives," he said. "I put Harlene through college. She studied philosophy, she spoke German, she read Jaspers. I learned from her. And Louise was wonderful."

We talked a lot more, about the thrilling double bills of classics at the original Thalia, of Brooklyn, typewriters, and the Internet—"How can kids watch *Citizen Kane* on that tiny screen?"—and about the Automat. I mentioned the mashed potatoes and the creamed spinach. "What about the baked macaroni?" Woody said. We talked about the decline of night-clubs, how they had had their curious moments—such as John Carradine reading Shakespeare at the Blue Angel nightclub—and he spoke with admiration of Mort Sahl, Nichols and May, and Max Gordon.

I returned to the subject of a masterpiece and asked him if he'd thought of tackling the Holocaust. He had considered it seriously and I think he keeps considering it.

And so our conversation encompassed the moral realities of the world we live in: discussion of the Holocaust, discussion of art and the idea of a masterpiece versus frivolity.

If you look at his work ethic, the richness of having had this kind of loving marriage for nineteen years, and building a real family, reaching eighty with all this, and, with luck, with many years to go (his father, after all, reached a hundred; his mother ninety-seven)—it rather seems as if he figured it all out. Woody may be ambivalent still; it's possible to remember he's gone for thirty years and more playing in his band without talking to anybody and rarely making eye contact; it's easy to remember him throwing his tennis racket in the air when he saw a bug, hiding his head and ducking. There are countless stories like that. And he may still be exploring depression. But at the same time, he's pretty put together. He managed to get the business deals he wanted. He managed to get an enviable marriage. He got everything he wanted except the masterpiece, and from my glimpse of him, that may well be in the offing. If not, there are at least twenty-five terrific films so far.

All the time we thought he was a neurotic mess he was playing the ultimate magic trick on us. Broken, needy, an impractical dreamer, a shlepper on-screen, in life he was the artist who kept going, was never destroyed, who got it all.

This "short Brooklynite" has imposed his talent, his dramatic vision, his romance with Manhattan and his love of women, his capacity to create characters we feel we've known all our lives, his irresistible wit, his acceptance of failure as one route to the sublime, his discovery of the hidden talents of actors, his dreads, his neuroses, his brilliance, his magic, his movies that continue to move and inspire us no matter how often we see them, his capacity for endless invention—this writer for all seasons, this filmmaker has touched the entire world.

# Filmography

## Woody's Best

*Take the Money and Run* 1969
*Bananas* 1971
*Sleeper* 1973
*Annie Hall* 1977
*Manhattan* 1979
*Zelig* 1983
*Broadway Danny Rose* 1984
*The Purple Rose of Cairo* 1985
*Hannah and Her Sisters* 1986
*Radio Days* 1987
*Oedipus Wrecks* 1987
*Crimes and Misdemeanors* 1989
*Alice* 1990
*Husbands and Wives* 1992
*Bullets over Broadway* 1994
*Mighty Aphrodite* 1995
*Everyone Says I Love You* 1996
*Deconstructing Harry* 1997
*Celebrity* 1998
*Anything Else* 2003
*Match Point* 2005
*Vicky Cristina Barcelona* 2008

*You Will Meet a Tall Dark Stranger* 2010
*Midnight in Paris* 2011
*Blue Jasmine* 2013

*What's New Pussycat?* (Famous Artists/UA, 1965)
Director: Clive Donner
Screenplay: Woody Allen
Woody Allen, Peter O'Toole, Peter Sellers

*What's Up, Tiger Lily?* (American International Pictures, 1966)
Director: Senkichi Taniguchi
Screenplay and dubbing: Woody Allen, Len Maxwell, Louise Lasser, Mickey Rose

*Casino Royale* (Famous Artists/Columbia, 1967)
Directors: John Huston, Robert Parrish, Val Guest, Ken Hughes, Joseph McGrath
Screenplay: Wolf Mankowitz, John Law, Michael Sayers, from the novel by Ian Fleming
Woody Allen, David Niven, Peter Sellers, Ursula Andress, Orson Welles, Jacqueline Bisset, Jean-Paul Belmondo, William Holden

*Don't Drink the Water* (Avco Embassy, 1969)
Director: Howard Morris
Screenplay: R. S. Allen and Harvey Bullock, from Woody Allen's play
Jackie Gleason, Estelle Parsons, Ted Bessell, Joan Delaney

*Take the Money and Run* (Palomar Pictures, 1969)
Director: Woody Allen
Screenplay: Woody Allen and Mickey Rose
Woody Allen, Janet Margolin, Louise Lasser, Jackson Beck, Howard Storm

*Bananas* (United Artists, 1971)
Director: Woody Allen
Screenplay: Woody Allen and Mickey Rose
Woody Allen, Louise Lasser, Howard Cosell

*Play It Again, Sam* (Paramount Pictures, 1972)
Director: Herbert Ross
Screenplay: Woody Allen, from his play
Woody Allen, Diane Keaton, Tony Roberts, Jerry Lacy

*Everything You Always Wanted to Know About Sex (But Were Afraid to Ask)*
(United Artists, 1972)
Director: Woody Allen
Screenplay: Woody Allen, from the book by Dr. David Reuben
Woody Allen, Gene Wilder, Lynn Redgrave, Lou Jacobi,
Tony Randall, John Carradine, Burt Reynolds, Louise Lasser

*Sleeper* (United Artists, 1973)
Director: Woody Allen
Screenplay: Woody Allen and Marshall Brickman
Woody Allen, Diane Keaton

*Love and Death* (United Artists, 1975)
Writer-director: Woody Allen
Woody Allen, Diane Keaton, Jessica Harper, James Tolkan

*The Front* (Columbia, 1976)
Director: Martin Ritt
Screenplay: Walter Bernstein
Woody Allen, Zero Mostel, Herschel Bernardi, Michael Murphy, Andrea
Marcovicci, Lloyd Gough

*Annie Hall* (United Artists, 1977)
Director: Woody Allen
Screenplay: Woody Allen and Marshall Brickman
Woody Allen, Diane Keaton, Tony Roberts, Carol Kane, Paul Simon, Janet Margolin, Colleen Dewhurst, Shelley Duval, Christopher Walken,
Sigourney Weaver

*Interiors* (United Artists, 1978)
Writer-director: Woody Allen

Mary Beth Hurt, Diane Keaton, Geraldine Page, Maureen Stapleton, Sam Waterston, Kristen Griffith, E. G. Marshall

*Manhattan* (United Artists, 1979)
Director: Woody Allen
Screenplay: Woody Allen and Marshall Brickman
Woody Allen, Diane Keaton, Michael Murphy, Mariel Hemingway, Wallace Shawn, Meryl Streep, Karen Ludwig, Tisa Farrow

*Stardust Memories* (United Artists, 1980)
Writer-director: Woody Allen
Woody Allen, Charlotte Rampling, Jessica Harper, Daniel Stern, Marie-Christine Barrault, Tony Roberts, Louise Lasser, Sharon Stone

*A Midsummer Night's Sex Comedy* (Orion Pictures, 1982)
Writer-director: Woody Allen
Woody Allen, Mia Farrow, Mary Steenburgen, José Ferrer, Julie Hagerty, Tony Roberts

*Zelig* (Orion Pictures, 1983)
Writer-director: Woody Allen
Woody Allen, Mia Farrow, with Dr. Bruno Bettelheim, Saul Bellow, Susan Sontag, Irving Howe, Bricktop, and Professor John Morton Blum as themselves

*Broadway Danny Rose* (Orion Pictures, 1984)
Writer-director: Woody Allen
Woody Allen, Mia Farrow, Nick Apollo Forte, with Milton Berle, Howard Cosell, and Joe Franklin as themselves

*The Purple Rose of Cairo* (Orion Pictures, 1985)
Writer-director: Woody Allen
Mia Farrow, Jeff Daniels, Danny Aiello, Stephanie Farrow, Van Johnson, Ed Herrmann, Zoe Caldwell, Dianne Wiest

*Hannah and Her Sisters* (Orion Pictures, 1986)
Writer-director: Woody Allen

Woody Allen, Mia Farrow, Michael Caine, Maureen O'Sullivan, Lloyd Nolan, Dianne Wiest, Sam Waterston, Barbara Hershey, Max von Sydow, Julie Kavner, Carrie Fisher

*Radio Days* (Orion Pictures, 1987)
Writer-director: Woody Allen
Woody Allen (narrator), Julie Kavner, Mia Farrow, Dianne Wiest, Seth Green, Wallace Shawn, Diane Keaton, Danny Aiello, Jeff Daniels, Kitty Carlisle Hart, Josh Mostel, Judith Malina

*King Lear* (Cannon Films, 1987)
Writer-director: Jean-Luc Godard
Woody Allen, Burgess Meredith, Peter Sellers, Molly Ringwald, Norman Mailer

*September* (Orion Pictures, 1987)
Writer-director: Woody Allen
Mia Farrow, Elaine Stritch, Dianne Wiest, Jack Warden, Denholm Elliott, Sam Waterston

*Another Woman* (Orion Pictures, 1988)
Writer-director: Woody Allen
Gena Rowlands, Ian Holm, Mia Farrow, Blythe Danner, Gene Hackman, Martha Plimpton, Sandy Dennis, Betty Buckley, John Houseman

*Oedipus Wrecks* (from *New York Stories*) (Touchstone Pictures, 1989)
Writer-director: Woody Allen
Woody Allen, Mia Farrow, Julie Kavner, Mae Questel, George Schindler

*Crimes and Misdemeanors* (Orion Pictures, 1989)
Writer-director: Woody Allen
Woody Allen, Martin Landau, Alan Alda, Mia Farrow, Anjelica Huston, Claire Bloom, Jerry Orbach, Sam Waterston, Joanna Gleason

*Alice* (Orion Pictures, 1990)
Writer-director: Woody Allen
Mia Farrow, William Hurt, Joe Mantegna, Judy Davis, Blythe Danner,

Alec Baldwin, Bernadette Peters, Cybill Shepherd, Keye Luke, Blythe Danner, Gwen Verdon, Julie Kavner

*Scenes from a Mall* (Touchstone Pictures, 1991)
Director: Paul Mazursky
Screenplay: Paul Mazursky and Roger L. Simon
Woody Allen, Bette Midler, Bill Irwin

*Shadows and Fog* (Orion Pictures, 1992)
Writer-director: Woody Allen
Woody Allen, Mia Farrow, John Cusack, John Malkovich, Madonna, Julie Kavner, Donald Pleasence, Kathy Bates, Jodie Foster, Lily Tomlin, Kate Nelligan, Wallace Shawn

*Husbands and Wives* (Columbia-TriStar, 1992)
Writer-director: Woody Allen
Woody Allen, Mia Farrow, Juliette Lewis, Sydney Pollack, Judy Davis, Liam Neeson, Lysette Anthony, Benno Schmidt, Blythe Danner, Jeffrey Kurland

*Manhattan Murder Mystery* (Columbia-TriStar, 1993)
Director: Woody Allen
Screenplay: Woody Allen and Marshall Brickman
Woody Allen, Diane Keaton, Alan Alda, Anjelica Huston, Jerry Adler

*Bullets over Broadway* (Sweetland/Miramax, 1994)
Director: Woody Allen
Screenplay: Woody Allen and Douglas McGrath
John Cusack, Dianne Wiest, Jack Warden, Chazz Palmintieri, Jennifer Tilly, Rob Reiner, Tracy Ullman, Mary-Louise Parker, Jim Broadbent

*Mighty Aphrodite* (Sweetland/Miramax, 1995)
Writer-director: Woody Allen
Woody Allen, Mira Sorvino, Helena Bonham Carter, Michael Rapaport, Claire Bloom, Jack Warden, F. Murray Abraham, Olympia Dukakis, Jeffrey Kurland

*The Sunshine Boys* (Hallmark, 1995)
Director: John Erman

Writer: Neil Simon
Woody Allen, Peter Falk, Liev Schreiber

*Everyone Says I Love You* (Sweetland/Miramax, 1996)
Writer-director: Woody Allen
Woody Allen, Goldie Hawn, Alan Alda, Julia Roberts, Tim Roth, Drew Barrymore, Natasha Lyonne, Edward Norton

*Deconstructing Harry* (Sweetland/Fine Line Features, 1997)
Writer-director: Woody Allen
Woody Allen, Judy Davis, Bob Balaban, Julie Kavner, Amy Irving, Stanley Tucci, Kirstie Alley, Billy Crystal, Hazelle Goodman, Demi Moore, Elizabeth Shue, Robin Williams, Mariel Hemingway, Richard Benjamin, Julia Louis-Dreyfus, Eric Bogosian

*Wild Man Blues* (documentary) (Sweetland/Fine Line Features, 1998)
Director: Barbara Kopple
Woody Allen, Soon-Yi Previn, Letty Aronson, Eddy Davis, and others as themselves

*Antz* (Dreamworks Pictures, 1998)
Directors: Eric Darnell and Tim Johnson
Screenplay: Todd Alcott, Chris Weitz, and Paul Weitz
Woody Allen, Sharon Stone, Dan Aykroyd, Danny Glover, Jane Curtin, Anne Bancroft, Gene Hackman, Jennifer Lopez, Sylvester Stallone, John Mahoney, Christopher Walken

*Celebrity* (Sweetland/Miramax, 1998)
Writer-dirctor: Woody Allen
Kenneth Branagh, Judy Davis, Leonardo DiCaprio, Melanie Griffith, Joe Mantegna, Winona Ryder, Gretchen Mol, Charlize Theron, Bebe Neuwirth

*Sweet and Lowdown* (Sweetland/Sony Pictures Classics, 1999)
Writer-director: Woody Allen
Sean Penn, Uma Thurman

*Picking Up the Pieces* (1999) (Comala Films Productions)
Director: Alfonso Arau
Woody Allen, Sharon Stone, Cheech Marin, Fran Drescher, David Schwimmer

*Small Time Crooks* (Sweetland/Dreamworks, 2000)
Writer-director: Woody Allen
Woody Allen, Hugh Grant, Jon Lovitz, Tracey Ullman

*The Curse of the Jade Scorpion* (Dreamworks, 2001)
Writer-director: Woody Allen
Woody Allen, Greg Stebner, John Tormey, Elizabeth Berkley, Wallace Shawn, Dan Aykroyd

*Hollywood Ending* (Dreamworks, 2002)
Writer-director: Woody Allen
Woody Allen, Téa Leoni, Bob Dorian, George Hamilton, Treat Williams

*Anything Else* (Dreamworks, 2003)
Writer-director: Woody Allen
Jason Biggs, Christina Ricci, Danny DeVito, Jimmy Fallon, Stockard Channing

*Melinda and Melinda* (Fox Searchlight, 2004)
Writer-director: Woody Allen
Will Ferrell, Radha Mitchell, Vinessa Shaw, Chiwetel Ejiofor, Wallace Shawn, Chloë Sevigny

*Match Point* (Dreamworks, 2005)
Writer-director: Woody Allen
Jonathan Rhys Meyers, Scarlett Johansson, Emily Mortimer, Matthew Goode

*Scoop* (BBC Films, Ingenious Film Partners, UK Film Council, 2006)
Writer-director: Woody Allen
Scarlett Johansson, Hugh Jackman, Woody Allen, Ian McShane

*Cassandra's Dream* (The Weinstein Company, 2007)
Writer-director: Woody Allen
Colin Farrell, Ewan McGregor, Tom Wilkinson

*Vicky Cristina Barcelona* (Mediapro, Metro Goldwyn Mayer, 2008)
Writer-director: Woody Allen
Rebecca Hall, Scarlett Johansson, Javier Bardem, Penélope Cruz, Patricia Clarkson

*Whatever Works* (Sony Pictures Classics, 2009)
Writer-director: Woody Allen
Larry David, Ed Begley, Jr., Evan Rachel Wood, Patricia Clarkson

*You Will Meet a Tall Dark Stranger* (Sony Pictures Classics, 2010)
Writer-director: Woody Allen
Antonio Banderas, Lucy Punch, Josh Brolin, Anthony Hopkins, Gemma Jones, Naomi Watts, Freida Pinto

*Midnight in Paris* (Sony Pictures Classics, 2011)
Writer-director: Woody Allen
Owen Wilson, Marion Cotillard, Rachel McAdams, Kathy Bates, Adrien Brody

*To Rome with Love* (Sony Pictures Classics, 2012)
Writer-director: Woody Allen
Woody Allen, Alec Baldwin, Penélope Cruz, Judy Davis, Jesse Eisenberg, Greta Gerwig

*Blue Jasmine* (Sony Pictures Classics, 2013)
Writer-director: Woody Allen
Cate Blanchett, Sally Hawkins, Alec Baldwin, Louis CK, Andrew Dice Clay, Bobby Cannavale, Peter Sarsgaard

*Fading Gigolo* (Antidote Films, 2013)
Writer-director: John Turturro
John Turturro, Woody Allen, Vanessa Paradis, Liev Schreiber, Sofía Vergara, Sharon Stone

*Magic in the Moonlight* (Sony Pictures Classics, 2014)
Writer-director: Woody Allen
Colin Firth, Emma Stone, Hamish Linklater, Marcia Gay Harden

*Irrational Man* (Sony Pictures Classics, 2015)
Writer-director: Woody Allen
Joaquin Phoenix, Jamie Blackley, Parker Posey, Emma Stone

# Bibliography

Allen, Woody. *Death*. New York: Samuel French, 1975.

———. *Don't Drink the Water*. New York: Random House, 1967.

———. *The Floating Light Bulb*. New York: Random House, 1982.

———. *Four Films of Woody Allen*. New York: Random House, 1982.

———. *Getting Even*. New York: Random House, 1971.

———. *God*. New York: Samuel French, 1975.

———. *Hannah and Her Sisters*. New York: Vintage, 1976.

———. *Mere Anarchy*. New York: Random House, 2007.

———. *Play It Again, Sam*. New York: Samuel French, 1968.

———. *Side Effects*. New York: Random House, 1980.

———. *Three Films of Woody Allen*. New York: Vintage, 1987.

———. *Three One-Act Plays*. New York: Random House, 2003.

———. *Without Feathers*. New York: Random House, 1975.

Bach, Steven. *Final Cut: Art, Money, and Ego in the Making of* Heaven's Gate, *the Film That Sank United Artists*. William Morrow: New York: 1985.

Bailey, Peter J. *The Reluctant Art of Woody Allen*. Lexington: University Press of Kentucky, 2001.

Baxter, John. *Woody Allen: A Biography*. New York: Carroll & Graf, 1999.

Becker, Ernest. *The Denial of Death*. New York: Free Press, 1973.

Berger, Phil. *The Last Laugh: The World of Stand-Up Comics*. New York: Ballantine Books, 1975.

Bergman, Ingmar. *The Magic Lantern: An Autobiography*. New York: Viking, 1988.

Bergmann, Martin S. *The Anatomy of Loving: The Story of Man's Quest to Know What Love Is*. New York: Columbia University Press, 1987.

————, and Milton E. Jucovy, eds. *Generations of the Holocaust*. New York: Columbia University Press, 1982.

Blake, Richard A. *Woody Allen: Profane and Sacred*. Lanham, Md.: Scarecrow Press, 1995.

Brode, Douglas. *The Films of Woody Allen*. Secaucus, N.J.: Citadel Press, 1992.

Burrows, Abe. *Honest, Abe*. New York: Little, Brown, 1980.

Burton, Dee. *I Dream of Woody*. New York: William Morrow, 1984.

Björkman, Stig. *Woody Allen on Woody Allen*. New York: Grove Press, 1993.

Carroll, Tim. *Woody and His Women*. New York: Little, Brown, 1993.

Dawidowicz, Lucy. *The War Against the Jews: 1933–1945*. New York: Holt, Rinehart and Winston, 1975.

de Navacelle, Thierry. *Woody Allen on Location*. New York: William Morrow, 1987.

Desser, David, and Lester D. Friedman. *American Jewish Filmmakers*. Urbana: University of Illinois Press, 1993.

Farrow, Mia. *What Falls Away: A Memoir*. New York: Bantam, 1997.

Fox, Julian. *Woody: Movies from Manhattan*. Woodstock, N.Y.: Overlook Press, 1996.

Gabler, Neal. *An Empire of Their Own: How Jews Invented Hollywood*. New York: Crown, 1988.

Gelbart, Larry. *Laughing Matters: On Writing* MASH, Tootsie, Oh, God!, *and a Few Other Funny Things*. New York: Random House, 1998.

Girgus, Sam B. *The Films of Woody Allen*. Cambridge, UK: Cambridge University Press, 2002.

Gordon, Max. *Live at the Village Vanguard*. New York: St. Martin's Press, 1980.

Groteke, Kristine, with Marjorie Rosen. *Woody and Mia: The Nanny's Tale*. London: Hodder and Stoughton, 1994.

Hirsch, Foster. *Love, Sex, Death and the Meaning of Life: The Films of Woody Allen*. New York: McGraw-Hill, 1981

Insdorf, Annette. *Indelible Shadows: Film and the Holocaust*. Cambridge, UK: Cambridge University Press, 2002.

Isaacson, Walter. *American Sketches: Great Leaders, Creative Thinkers, and Heroes of a Hurricane*. New York: Simon & Schuster, 2009.

Jacobs, Diane. . . . *But We Need the Eggs: The Magic of Woody Allen*. New York: St. Martin's Press, 1982.

Kael, Pauline. *5001 Nights at the Movies*. New York: Henry Holt, 1982.

————. *For Keeps: 30 Years at the Movies*. New York: Plume Books, 1994.

Kapsis, Robert E., and Kathie Coblentz, eds. *Woody Allen Interviews*. Jackson, Miss.: University Press of Mississippi, 2006.

Keaton, Diane. *Then Again*. New York: Random House, 2011.

Kellow, Brian. *Pauline Kael: A Life in the Dark*. New York: Penguin Books, 2011.

Klemperer, Victor. *I Will Bear Witness: A Diary of the Nazi Years, 1933–1941*. New York: Random House, 1988.

Lahr, John. *Show and Tell*. Woodstock, N.Y.: Overlook Press, 2000.

Lax, Eric. *On Being Funny: Woody Allen and Comedy*. New York: Charterhouse, 1975.

————. *Woody Allen: A Biography*. New York: Knopf, 1991.

McCann, Graham. *Woody Allen*. Cambridge, Mass.: Polity Press, 1991.

McKnight, Gerald. *Woody Allen: Joking Aside*. London: W. H. Allen, 1983.

Meade, Marion. *The Unruly Life of Woody Allen: An Unauthorized Biography*. New York: Cooper Square Press, 2000.

Moor, Jonathan. *Diane Keaton: The Story of the Real Annie Hall*. London: Robson, 1990.

Nathan, Debbie, and Michael Snedeker. *Satan's Silence: Ritual Abuse and the Making of a Modern American Witch Hunt*. New York: Basic Books, 1995.

Nichols, Mary P. *Reconstructing Woody: Art, Love, and Life in the Films of Woody Allen*. Lanham, Md.: Rowman and Littlefield, 1998.

Oates, Joyce Carol, ed. *Best American Essays 1991*. New York: Ticknor & Fields, 1991.

Rabinowitz, Dorothy. *No Crueler Tyrannies: Accusation, False Witness, and Other Terrors of Our Times*. New York: Wall Street Journal Books, 2003.

Richler, Mordecai. *Belling the Cat: Essays, Reports, and Opinions*. New York: Knopf, 1998.

Rosenblum, Ralph, and Robert Karen. *When the Shooting Stops . . . The Cutting Begins: A Film Editor's Story*. New York: Viking Press, 1979.

Sahl, Mort. *Heartland*. New York: Harcourt Brace Jovanovich, 1976.

Schickel, Richard. *Schickel on Film*. New York: William Morrow, 1989.

————. *Woody Allen: A Life in Film*. Chicago: Ivan R. Dee, 2003.

Simon, John. *John Simon on Film: Criticism, 1982–2001*. New York: Applause Books, 2005.

————. *Movies into Film: Film Criticism, 1967–1970*. New York: Delta, 1971.

————. *Something to Declare: Twelve Years of Films from Abroad.* New York: Clarkson N. Potter, 1983.

Spignesi, Stephen J. *The Woody Allen Companion.* Kansas City, Mo.: Andrews and McMeel, 1992.

Wernblad, Annette. *Brooklyn Is Not Expanding: Woody Allen's Comic Universe.* Rutherford, N.J.: Fairleigh Dickinson, 1992.

Wiesel, Elie. *Night.* New York: Hill & Wang, 2006.

Wilde, Larry. *The Great Comedians Talk About Comedy.* Secaucus, N.J.: Citadel Press, 1968.

Wisse, Ruth. *No Joke: Making Jewish Humor.* Princeton, N.J.: Princeton University Press, 2013.

Yacowar, Maurice. *Loser Take All: The Comic Art of Woody Allen.* New York: Frederick Ungar, 1979.

# List of Illustrations

Grateful acknowledgment is made for permission to reproduce the following photographs:

Woody breaks on the set of *Annie Hall*. *(Courtesy of Photofest)*   1

Woody drinks in his beloved Manhattan. *(Courtesy of Photofest)*   33

Woody and Diane on a bench in Sutton Place in *Annie Hall*. *(Courtesy of Photofest)*   51

Jack Rollins in *Broadway Danny Rose*. *(Courtesy of Photofest)*   86

Standup comic. *(Courtesy of Photofest)*   113

Woody and his New Orleans Jazz Band. *(Courtesy of Photofest)*   144

Woody in the 1960s. *(Courtesy of Photofest)*   178

Mia and Woody in a scene from *Zelig*. *(Courtesy of Photofest)*   225

Dick Cavett and Woody on Dick's TV show in 1971. *(Courtesy of Daphne Productions, Inc.)*   251

Woody and Sven Nykvist discussing a shot from *Crimes and Misdemeanors*. *(Courtesy of Photofest)*   267

Woody and Soon-Yi in 2002. *(Courtesy of Photofest)*   284

Woody directing Cate Blanchett and Alec Baldwin in *Blue Jasmine*. *(Courtesy of Photofest)*   323

Woody today. *(Courtesy of Photofest)*   339

Diane and Woody in love in the early 1970s. *(Courtesy of Photofest)*   349

# Index

Abbott, George, 40

Abramowitz, Elkan, 295, 309, 311

Academy Awards, 41–42, 44, 99, 103, 123, 165, 171, 203–4, 206–7, 230–31, 320–21, 334, 337, 341, 346

*Act One* (Hart), 214

Adams, Cindy, 286, 313

Aguirresarobe, Javier, 331–34

Aiello, Danny, 80

Alber, David, 87, 91

Albert, Daniel, 212

Alda, Alan, 274, 281

Aleichem, Sholem, 181

*Alexander Nevsky* (Eisenstein), 187

Allen, Harlene Rosen, 29, 35, 91–97, 114–18, 134–35, 199, 239, 257–58, 260, 347–48, 350

Allen, Steve, 117

*Allen vs. Farrow*, 307–11

Allen, Woody, *1, 33, 51, 113, 178, 225, 251, 267, 284, 323, 339, 349.* *See also* works, Allen
adoptions by, 287, 294, 301, 343
Allen, Harlene, marriage to, 29, 35, 91–97, 114–18, 134–35, 199, 239, 257–58, 260, 347–48, 350
anti-Semitism/Holocaust observations of, 10, 18–20, 50, 52–55, 60, 63–66, 122–24, 174–75, 180–81, 184, 190, 195, 199–202, 226, 232–33, 247, 254, 273, 276, 322, 350–51
"April-October" relationships as theme of, 39, 42–43, 45–46, 207, 218–21, 299
awards/nominations for works of, 41–42, 44–45, 103, 123, 165, 171, 203–4, 206–7, 212, 330, 334, 337, 339–41, 344, 346
birth of, 66–67
casting process by, 21–23, 247–48, 268–69, 277
childhood of, 26–31, 49, 63, 67–85, 86–88
cinematography of, 241–42, 244–45, 288, 331–34
comedic development of, 86–112
custody battle of, 42, 295, 299, 301, 307–11, 313–14

Allen, Woody (*continued*)

depression of, 23, 28, 71–72, 80, 85,
143, 204, 256–57, 330, 346–47,
351

education, college, of, 88–89, 90,
121, 123

Farrow, Mia, relationship with, 18,
42–46, 117–18, 153, 229–30,
236–41, 248–50, 261–62, 265,
284–96, 298–319, 336, 337–38,
340–46

father's relationship with, 26–28,
69, 74–76, 83, 100, 103,
177

influence/legacy of, 3–14, 34–35,
38–47, 57–58, 61–62, 174, 264,
330–31

influences on, 10–12, 14–18, 37–38,
59–60, 62–66, 70–71, 75–76,
79–80, 90, 132, 137, 141,
187–88, 189, 196, 228–29,
238, 254, 256, 257–58

Jewish themes/representations in
work of, 5–9, 39, 50, 55–66,
119–20, 122–24, 139, 146,
151–52, 158, 174, 179–84, 188,
190, 195, 199–202, 226, 241,
247, 270–76, 281

Keaton's relationship with, 44,
128–29, 156–62, 165, 196–97,
198–99, 258, 297–98, 299,
340

Lasser's relationship with, 114–17,
135–36, 156–57, 161–62,
178–80, 198–99, 239, 258–59,
297, 350

magic as interest of, 28, 30–31,
67–69, 74, 81–85, 86, 143,
254, 262

molestation allegations against,
42–46, 118, 236, 284–85,
293–96, 298–306, 308,
310–17, 319–21, 336–38,
339–46

mother's relationship with, 28–29,
69, 71, 74, 83, 177

music as hobby of, 18, 68–69, 72,
77, 79, 85, 133, *144*, 159,
165–69, 246, 263, 265, 321,
350–51

political leanings of, 18–20, 25, 169,
190

Previn's relationship with, 42–43,
45, 117–18, 153–54, 234, 241,
265, 285–88, 289–94, 297,
299–301, 304–5, 307–8, 315,
317–21, 340, 342–43, 350

religious beliefs, personal, of, 9,
183–84, 190, 272–75, 346

self-criticism by, 10–12, 34–35, 180,
183, 222, 330, 350

sexuality of, 32, 52, 66, 71, 72–73,
159, 162, 198

shyness of, 21, 34, 84, 102–9, 124,
164

soundtrack/music scores of, 132,
150–51, 166, 168–69, 217,
281

stand-up comedy of, 30–31, 35, 40,
57–59, 61–62, 70, 74–75, 90,
99–112, 113–30, 154–55, 165,
175, 195, 201, 251–54, 259,
264

Almodóvar, Pedro, 331, 333

Alter, Eleanor, 301, 309, 311, 314

Altman, Robert, 25

Amazon television, 347

*American Jewish Filmmakers*, 53

*American Masters*, PBS, 12, 329

Amirault family, 345

Anastasia, Albert, 26, 74

Anderson, Sherwood, 330

Angell, Roger, 137

*Anna Karenina* (Tolstoy), 248

anti-Semitism. *See* Judaism/Jews

Aronson, Letty Konigsberg, 27–28,
45, 71, 327

Arthur, Beatrice, 80

"Aubade" (Larkin), 264–65
Aurthur, Kate, 46

Bacharach, Burt, 132
Bach, Steven, 39, 170, 174, 194,
 207–8, 221–22, 229
Baldwin, Alec, *323*, 340
Bamberger, Michael, 276
Banducci, Enrico, 127
Banker, Stephen, 183
Bardem, Javier, 350
Barer, Marshall, 94–95
Bart, Peter, 162
*Battleship Potemkin* (Eisenstein), 187
Baxter, John, 163–65
Beatty, Warren, 38, 130–32, 134,
 242
Bechet, Sidney, 68, 92, 165, 220
Becker, Ernest, 264
Beck, Jackson, 145, 150
Begelman, David, 192
Beiderbecke, Bix, 166
Belafonte, Harry, 99, 101–2, 104–5,
 111, 126
Belle, Jennifer, 43, 152
Bellow, Saul, 242
Benjamin, Richard, 56
Benjamin, Robert, 170–71
Bennett, Tony, 2, 88, 99, 213
Benny, Jack, 2, 31, 52, 61, 114, 154
Berger, Phil, 96
Bergman, Ingmar, 10, 12, 37–38, 63,
 196, 208, 210–11, 228, 271–72,
 282–83, 330
Bergmann, Hugo, 276
Bergmann, Maria, 277–79
Bergmann, Martin, 273, 275–79, 281
Bergmann, Michael, 277, 279
Berle, Milton, 31, 52, 57, 58, 75, 154
Berlin, Irving, 10, 88, 213
Bernstein, Walter, 191–93
Bernstein, William, 171
*Best Plays* (Guernsey), 80

Bettelheim, Bruno, 242
Bishop, Joey, 55
Biskind, Peter, 43–44
Björkman, Stig, 9, 17, 23–25, 37, 72,
 79, 131, 142, 145, 202–3, 206,
 271–72
Blake, Eubie, 151
Blake, Richard A., 280
Blanchett, Cate, 44–45, *323*, 328,
 329, 334, 337, 346, 347
Boone, Pat, 97
Bourne, Mel, 212
Boxer, Sarah, 10
Branagh, Kenneth, 62, 228
Brickman, Marshall, 14, 19, 41, 94,
 181, 183, 205–6, 212
*Brief Encounters* (Cavett), 265
British Academy of Film Awards, 206
Brode, Douglas, 188, 217
Broder, Eric J., 341
Brodie, Donna, 60
Brodsky, Jack, 178
Brooks, Mel, 31, 55–57, 94, 97, 98,
 150
Brown, David, 162
Brown, Fred, 296
Brown, Georgia, 323
Bruce, Lenny, 16, 25, 57, 75, 98
Buber, Martin, 276
Buckley, William F., Jr., 61, 238–39
Burnham, John, 325
Burns, George, 52, 61, 154
Burrows, Abe, 89–90, 191
Burton, Richard, 133–34, 233
. . . *But We Need the Eggs* (Jacobs), 83
Buxton, Frank, 102, 136, 142–43, 144,
 175–76
*BuzzFeed*, 46

Caesar, Sid, 57, 90–91, 94, 97, 186
Caine, Michael, 41, 62, 230
Canby, Vincent, 151, 182, 222,
 278

*Candid Camera,* 90, 117, 125–26
Cannes Film Festival, 42
*Capital Gazette News,* 335
Career Golden Lion award, 41
Carlyle Hotel, New York City, 79, 165–66
Carroll, Tim, 64, 115
Carson, Johnny, 30, 35, 114, 117, 159, 195, 212
Cavett, Dick, 19, 30, 44, 99–100, 109–10, 114, 126, 185–87, 195, 201, 212, *251,* 251–66
Cecil B. DeMille Award, 42
César Award, 41
Chabrol, Claude, 25, 40, 47
Channing, Stockard, 328
Chaplin, Charles, 3, 12, 31–32, 62, 70, 170, 202, 203, 215, 268
Cherry, Leon, 69
Cherry, Sarah, 69
Child Sexual Abuse Clinic of Yale-New Haven Hospital, 298, 301, 302–5, 307, 308, 310, 315, 319, 341, 342, 345
Cimino, Michael, 229
*Cinema* magazine, 173
*Citizen Kane,* 242, 351
City College, New York City, 89
Clay, Andrew Dice, 4
Coates, Susan, 285–86, 307–8, 313, 338
Coca, Imogene, 57, 94, 186
Cohen, Carl, 232–33
Cohen, Jonathan D., 111–12
Cohen, Lynn, 296–98
Cohen, Sarah Blacher, 181
Cohn, Harry, 52–54
Cohn, Sam, 325
*Colgate Comedy Hour,* 87, 91–92, 98
Collins, Al "Jazzbo," 214
*ComedyBeat,* 329
*Commentary,* 20, 245
*Contra Costa Times,* 126

*Conversations with Woody Allen* (Lax), 11
Corry, John, 124
Cosby, Bill, 117, 126
Cosell, Howard, 14
Coughlin, Charles, 52
*Criers & Kibitzers, Kibitzers & Criers* (Elkin), 181
*Crime and Punishment* (Dostoyevsky), 272, 281
Crosby, Bing, 52, 70
Cruz, Penélope, 350
Cukor, George, 230
Cusack, John, 62

*Daily Beast,* 45, 46, 317–18, 337
*Daily Telegraph,* 230
Dalí, Salvador, 230
David, Hal, 132
David, Larry, 4, 62
Davis, Eddy, 165
Davis, Judy, 249, 328
Davy, Dick, 96
*Death of a Salesman,* 10, 53, 330
Denby, David, 279–80, 329
*The Denial of Death* (Becker), 264
Dershowitz, Alan, 309
Desser, David, 53
*The Detective,* 231
*Diane Keaton* (Moor), 157
Diller, Phyllis, 58
Di Palma, Carlo, 324
Directors Guild of America, 41, 206
*Dissent* magazine, 245
Dixon, Stephen, 181
Donner, Clive, 131
Dostoyevsky, Fyodor, 10, 17, 28, 126, 187, 237, 272, 281
Dougherty, Marion, 21–22
Doumanian, Jean, 126, 135, 240, 324–26
Dreamworks, 327
Dürrenmatt, Friedrich, 189

Eastwood, Clint, 12, 21
*The Ed Sullivan Show*, 117
Eisenstein, Sergei, 187
Elkin, Stanley, 181
Ellison, Ralph, 330
*An Empire of Their Own* (Gabler),
     53–54
Epstein, Jerry, 26–27, 29–30, 66–79,
     89, 91–92, 126, 130, 152–54,
     165, 241
Epstein, Sandy, 73, 126, 154
*The Errand Boy*, 132
*Esquire*, 164
Evanier, Mark, 30–31, 35, 36, 52,
     57–59, 75, 319
Evans, Bob, 162


Fairstein, Linda, 44, 314–17, 340–41
Farrow, Dylan, 249
   adoption of, 286–87, 294, 301
   custody battle over, 295, 299, 301,
       307–11, 313–14
   sexual abuse accusations by, 42–46,
       118, 236, 261, 284–85, 293–96,
       298–306, 308, 310–17, 319–21,
       336–38, 339–46
Farrow, John, 230–31
Farrow, Mia, 60
   adoptions by, 235, 239, 286
   Allen molestation accusations and,
       42–46, 236, 261–62, 284–85,
       293–96, 298–306, 308, 310–13,
       336, 337–38, 340–46
   Allen–Soon-Yi relationship and,
       42–43, 45, 117–18, 153, 289–94,
       299–301, 304–5, 307–8, 315,
       317–18
   Allen's relationship with, 18, 42–46,
       117–18, 153, 229–30, 236–41,
       248–50, 261–62, 265, 284–96,
       298–319, 336, 337–38, 340–46
   birth of, 229
   in *Broadway Danny Rose*, 269–70, 298

   brother's sex abuse charges and, 45,
       335–36
   in *Hannah and Her Sisters*, 185–86,
       248–49, 288
   in *Husbands and Wives*, 288–89,
       328
   memoir by, 18, 61, 164, 231,
       234–35, 249, 284, 291
   paternity uncertainty by, 337, 343
   Previn, André, marriage to, 230,
       233–36, 265, 343
   Sinatra's relationship with, 230,
       231–33, 306, 343–44
   as UNICEF ambassador, 334
   in *Zelig*, 225, 240–45
Farrow, Michael, 230
Farrow, Misha Amadeus "Moses,"
     42, 239
   adoption of, 287, 301, 341
   custody battle over, 295, 299, 301,
       307–11, 313–14
   sister's molestation accusation
       and, 44, 262, 341–42, 343–44,
       346
Farrow, Patrick, 335
Farrow, Prudence, 233
Farrow, Satchel O'Sullivan "Ronan,"
     42, 285, 305, 336
   birth of, 249–50, 286
   custody battle over, 295, 299, 301,
       307–11, 313–14
   molestation charges and, 341, 343,
       344
   paternity of, 337, 343
Farrow, Tam, 285, 289, 334
Feiffer, Jules, 25, 39, 55
Feinstein, Morley T., 180
Feldman, Charles K., 130–32, 141–43
Fellini, Federico, 10, 16, 38, 63,
     228–29, 330
Fields, Totie, 58
*Film Comment*, 3
*Final Cut* (Bach), 39, 174, 221–22
Fitzgerald, F. Scott, 16, 52

Flatley, Guy, 210
Ford, John, 3, 25, 40, 247
*For Esmé—With Love and Squalor*
    (Salinger), 216
Forman, Miloš, 331, 333
Forte, Nick Apollo, 268–69
Franklin, Joe, 269
Frazier, Cie, 168
Freedman, Samuel G., 53
Freud, Sigmund, 181
Friedkin, William, 150
Friedman, Bruce Jay, 55–56, 181
Friedman, Lester, 53
Fuchs, Daniel, 181
Funt, Allen, 125

Gabler, Neal, 53–54
Gallagher, John Andrew, 240
Gallo, Freddy, 21
Garfield, John, 54–55, 99, 191, 192–93
Geist, William, 222
Gelbart, Larry, 5, 96–98, 110–11
Geller, Uri, 138
*Genii* magazine, 30, 67–68
Gershwin, George, 10, 88, 213,
    217
Giancana, Sam, 232
Gilette, Anita, 136
Gillers, Stephen, 311
Gilliatt, Penelope, 182
Giordano, Vincent, 175
Gittelson, Natalie, 156, 164, 208, 212,
    215–16, 217–18, 223
*The Glass Menagerie* (Williams), 82, 84
Gleason, Jackie, 137, 256
Gleick, Elizabeth, 308
Godard, Jean-Luc, 9
Goldberg, Whoopi, 320
Golden Globe Awards, 41–42, 44–45,
    330, 334, 337, 339–41, 344
Goldman, Albert, 56
Goldman, John J., 309
Goldwyn, Samuel, 52–54

Goodman, Nicholas, 337
Gordon, Max, 101–2, 351
Gornick, Vivian, 110
Gould, Elliott, 55–56, 118, 178–79,
    247–48
*The Graduate*, 6, 8, 47, 55
Grant, Hugh, 62
*The Great Comedians Talk About Comedy*
    (Wilde), 154–56
Greenfield, Robert B., 6
Greenglass, David, 14, 99
Greenhut, Robert, 229, 324–26
Grodin, Charles, 56
Grosbard, Ulu, 80, 240
Gross, Terry, 321
Groteke, Kristine, 286–87, 293–95,
    301–2, 304
*The Guardian*, 270–71
Guernsey, Otis, 80
Gurney, A. R., 347

Hack, Moe, 94, 96
Halkin, Hillel, 180
Hall, Willis, 96
Hamill, Brian, 324
Hamill, Denis, 305
Hamlisch, Marvin, 151
Hardin, Tim, 126–27
Hardy, Oliver, 31–32, 87,
    261
Harrison, Kathryn, 235
Hart, Lorenz, 213
Hart, Moss, 214
Hatch, Robert, 222
Hawkins, Sally, 45
Hawks, Howard, 40
Hayden, Julie, 175
Hayes, Peter Lind, 90
*Heartland* (Sahl), 99
*Heaven's Gate*, 229
Hecht, Ben, 40–41
Hemingway, Mariel, 15, 41, 43, 207,
    219

Hepburn, Katharine, 247
Higgins, Robert, 152
Hirsch, Foster, 157
*Hitchcock* (Truffaut), 34
Hitchcock, Alfred, 34, 36
Hitchcock, Ethan, 169
Hitler, Adolf, 20, 57, 65, 174, 194,
    204, 241, 254
Hoberman, J., 5–6, 12, 14, 24, 56,
    221, 280, 281–82
Hoffman, Dustin, 8, 55–56,
    233
the Holocaust, 10, 19–20, 50, 52, 55,
    60, 63–66, 174, 180–81, 184,
    195, 199, 226, 247, 273, 276,
    322, 350–51
*Honest, Abe* (Burrows), 89
Hope, Bob, 2, 8, 31, 52, 59–60, 70,
    90, 92, 131, 141, 196, 252, 254,
    256, 263–64
Hopkins, Anthony, 329
Horwitch, Daniel B., 312
Howe, Ilana, 245–46
Howe, Irving, 242, 244, 245–46
Hughes, Howard, 232
Humphrey, Hubert, 169
Humphrey, Percy, 169
Husband, Stuart, 347
Huston, John, 25
Hyman, Dick, 166

*I'll Be in My Trailer* (Modderno), 126
*I Lost It at the Movies* (Kael), 7
*Indelible Shadows* (Insdorf), 12
Insdorf, Annette, 1, 12, 19, 48,
    328
*Interview* magazine, 19–20, 157
Ionesco, Eugène, 189
Isaacson, Walter, 289–91
Israel, 56, 77, 174. *See also* Judaism/
    Jews
    Allen's views on, 18–19, 350
*I've Got a Secret*, 35

Jacobi, Lou, 136
Jacobs, Diane, 83
Jaffe, Sam, 55
Joffe, Carol, 99–100, 113–14, 132,
    136
Joffe, Charles, 41, 99–103, 105, 107,
    109, 112, 113–14, 128–30, 132,
    141, 144–45, 150, 170, 172,
    178, 224, 229, 252, 270
Johnson, Bunk, 165, 167–68
Johnson, James P., 166
Johnson, Lyndon B., 126, 171–72,
    179
Jolson, Al, 76, 86, 88
Jonas, Dave, 270
Jones, Kent, 3
Jones, Tom, 132
Judaism/Jews
    Allen themes/representations of,
        5–9, 39, 50, 55–66, 119–20,
        122–24, 139, 146, 151–52, 158,
        174, 179–84, 188, 190, 195,
        199–202, 226, 241, 247, 270–76,
        281
    anti-Semitism/Holocaust and, 10,
        18–20, 50, 52–55, 60, 63–66,
        122–24, 174–75, 180–81, 184,
        190, 195, 199–202, 226,
        232–33, 247, 254, 273, 276, 322,
        350–51
    Orthodox, 9, 49, 60, 69, 76, 122,
        179–80, 247, 272
"The Judgment" (Kafka), 28, 139
Junker, Howard, 143

Kael, Pauline, 4, 7–9, 37, 53, 182,
    199–200, 201, 211, 215–16,
    221, 228–29, 244–45, 280
Kafka, Franz, 25–26, 28, 32, 139,
    191, 276
Kakutani, Michiko, 11, 141
Kallen, Lucille, 97
Kaplan, James, 15

Katzenberg, Jeffrey, 327
Katz, Lehman, 174
Kauffmann, Stanley, 39, 188, 245, 280, 281
Kaufman, George S., 251, 260, 263
Kaye, Danny, 54, 88, 94
Kazin, Alfred, 214
Keaton, Buster, 31
Keaton, Diane, 60, 246, 325, *349*
    Allen's relationship with, 44, 128–29, 156–62, 165, 196–97, 198–99, 258, 297–98, 299, 340, 347
    in *Annie Hall*, *1*, 16, 41, *51*, 61, 135, 160–62, 196–202, 204, 205–6, 264, 327
    in *Manhattan*, 43, 135, 160, 219–20, 222–23, 331
    in *Manhattan Murder Mystery*, 296–98, 300, 327
    in *Play It Again, Sam*, 158–59, 161, 162
    in *Sleeper*, 181–82
Kelley, Ken, 192
Kelley, Kitty, 230, 232–33
Kellow, Brian, 8, 199
Kennedy, John F., 171–72
*Kenyon Review*, 160
Kerr, Walter, 84–85, 137
Kerry, John, 256
Keys, Paul, 254
Kiessling, Laura, 335
*The Killer* (Ionesco), 189
King, Alan, 58, 75
Kirsch, Adam, 346
Kissinger, Henry, 169
Klawans, Stuart, 329
Konigsberg, Isaac, 69–70
Konigsberg, Marty (Allen's father), 67, 71, 121, 265
    Allen's relationship with, 26–28, 69, 74–76, 83, 100, 103, 177
    background of, 69–70

Konigsberg, Nettie (Allen's mother), 26–27, 67, 69–70
    Allen's relationship with, 28–29, 69, 71, 74, 83, 177
Konigsberg, Sarah, 69–70
Kopple, Barbara, 165
Krim, Arthur, 99, 170–74, 194, 204, 207–8, 229
Kristof, Nicholas, 44, 261, 338, 339–42
Kroft, Steve, 299–300
Kroll, Jack, 244, 285, 298–99
Kurland, Jeffrey, 324


Lahr, John, 3, 20, 69, 166, 168
Landau, Martin, 272–75, 281
Lapidus, Allan, 64
Larkin, Philip, 264–65
Lasser, Louise, 151–52, 171–72, 210
    Allen's relationship with, 114–17, 135–36, 156–57, 161–62, 178–80, 198–99, 239, 258–59, 297, 350
Lasser, S. Jay, 114
*Laughing Matters* (Gelbart), 97–98
Laurel, Stan, 31–32, 87
Lax, Eric, 11, 23, 37, 71, 87, 90, 109, 132–33, 156, 215
Leonard, Jack E., 75
Letterman, David, 36, 99
Levene, Sam, 55
Leventhal, John, 298, 302–5, 315, 341
Levine, Joseph E., 137
Levi, Primo, 273, 276
Lewis, Ellen, 268–69
Lewis, George, 68, 92, 165, 167, 169
Lewis, Jerry, 31, 38, 132, 145, 213, 259
Liebman, Max, 57, 94, 96
*Life* magazine, 133
*Little Stalker* (Belle), 43
Loeb, Philip, 191, 193
*Look* magazine, 127

Lopate, Phillip, 37, 66, 141, 200–201, 210–11, 222–23

Loquasto, Santo, 245, 271, 324

*Los Angeles Times*, 152, 228, 272, 301, 306, 309

*Love Letters* (play), 347

*Love Trumps Death* (Epstein), 130

Lovick, John, 30

Lowe, Jim, 214

Lumet, Sidney, 47, 55, 200

Lynch, Gerald E., 312

Lynd, Lou, 153

Lyons, Leonard, 86


Maco, Frank S., 303, 311–13, 314

*The Magic Lantern* (Bergman), 282–83

Maher, Kevin, 346

Malina, Judith, 347

*Maltese Falcon*, 158

Mandel, Johnny, 165

Marcus, Richard, 298

Margolin, Janet, 146–48

Markfield, Wallace, 181

Marks, Peter, 308

Marx, Groucho/Marx Brothers, 2, 35, 38, 61, 63, 70, 79, 87, 111, 131–32, 147, 168, 176, 185–86, 196, 251, 254, 257, 260–61, 263

Marx, Patricia, 143

*Mary Hartman, Mary Hartman*, 135, 198

Maslin, Janet, 43, 44–45

Maxwell, Len, 93, 136

May, Elaine, 25, 56, 57, 98, 99, 101, 110, 115, 257, 351

Mayer, Louis B., 52–54

Mazursky, Paul, 55

McCarthy, Eugene, 148

McGrath, Charles, 328, 346–47

McGrath, Douglas, 19, 301

McKnight, Gerald, 96

McLuhan, Marshall, 16, 196

McPhee, John, 124–25

Meade, Marion, 46–47, 174, 313

Medavoy, Mike, 171, 324

Medford, Kay, 136

Meisner, Sanford, 115

Menello, Ric, 40–41, 247

Mezzrow, Mezz, 165

Michaels, Marilyn, 246–47

Michael's Pub, New York City, 79, 165, 206–7, 246, 296

Miller, Arthur, 10–11, 53, 214, 330

Miller, Sing, 168

Mills, Elliott, 27, 29, 63–64, 67–68, 71–72, 74–75, 77–79, 91–92, 106–7, 119, 147, 165, 347

Mitchell, Sean, 228, 272

Modderno, Craig, 126–30, 147–49, 184–85

Moore, Demi, 328

Moore, Garry, 90–91, 98

Moor, Jonathan, 157

Morse, Susan E., 205–6, 241, 324

Morton, Jelly Roll, 166

Mostel, Zero, 55, 191–93

Mottolese, William, 312

Muni, Paul, 54

*My Song* (Belafonte), 105


National Film Critics Awards, 206

*The Nation*, 222, 329

NBC Writers' Development Program, 87, 91

Neeson, Liam, 249

Nelkin, Stacey, 207, 342

Newman, Manny, 53

New Orleans Funeral and Ragtime Orchestra, 165

New Orleans Jazz and Heritage Festival, 165

*New Republic,* 44, 183–84, 188, 276, 281, 346
*Newsweek,* 115, 143, 176, 181, 188, 244, 285, 298–99
*New York Daily News,* 45, 110, 305
*The New Yorker,* 5, 7, 18, 63, 137–41, 168, 175, 182–83, 208, 329
*New York* magazine, 15, 279–80
*New York Post,* 210, 286, 313
*New York Times,* 10–11, 19, 28, 43–44, 46, 53, 63, 66, 84, 127, 137, 151, 156, 182, 204, 208, 210, 222, 235, 248, 277, 281–82, 287, 301, 302, 304–5, 307–12, 324–26
    Farrow's/Allen's open letters in, 338, 339–40, 342–44
    *Magazine,* 212, 223, 336
New York University, 88–89, 90, 121, 123
Nichols, Mike, 57, 98–99, 101, 257, 325, 351
*Night* (Wiesel), 322
*The Night They Raided Minsky's,* 150
92nd Street Y, New York City, 10, 255–56
Nixon, Richard, 8, 169, 254
*No Crueler Tyrannies* (Rabinowitz), 313
Nykvist, Sven, *267*

Odets, Clifford, 53
O'Hehir, Andrew, 46
O. Henry Award, 41
*On Being Funny* (Lax), 156, 203
O'Neill, Eugene, 10–11, 17, 241
Ophuls, Marcel, 10, 65, 195
Orbach, Jerry, 274, 281
Orion Pictures, 99, 229, 324
Orth, Maureen, 44, 337
O'Sullivan, Maureen, 230
O'Toole, Peter, 131, 142
Ozick, Cynthia, 276

Paar, Jack, 59, 105, 109, 117, 253–54
Page, Geraldine, 212
Paige, Satchel, 249
Palme des Palmes Award, 42
*Paris Review,* 11–12, 53, 87, 141
Parker, Dorothy, 53
Parsons, Louella, 230
Pascal, Casey, 293
Penn, Arthur, 145
*People,* 308, 336, 341
Perelman, S. J., 137, 141, 168, 206, 257–58, 260
*Peyton Place,* 231
*Philadelphia Inquirer,* 276, 277
Picker, David, 170, 172
*Playboy,* 35, 45
Pleskow, Eric, 171–74, 194, 204, 207–8
Podhoretz, Norman, 20, 54, 74–75
*The Point,* 115–16
Polanski, Roman, 231, 233, 235, 334
Pollack, Sydney, 20, 21, 350
Porter, Cole, 10, 88, 213
*Portnoy's Complaint* (Roth), 6, 56, 124
Pratt, Tim, 335
Preminger, Otto, 174
Prescott, Kathryn, 295–96
Preservation Hall Jazz Band, 166, 168–69
Previn, André, 230, 233–36, 285, 291, 314, 337, 343
Previn, Daisy, 239
Previn, Dory, 234–36, 337, 343
Previn, Fletcher, 239
Previn, Lark, 239, 334
Previn, Matthew, 234, 239
Previn, Sascha, 234, 239
Previn, Soon-Yi, 28, 239, *284*
    adoption by, 343
    adoption of, 235, 314
    Allen's relationship with, 42–43, 45, 117–18, 153–54, 234, 241, 265, 285–88, 289–94, 297,

299–301, 304–5, 307–8, 315,
317–21, 340, 342–43, 350
Farrow's relationship with, 289–90,
303
nude photo scandal and, 42–43, 45,
117–18, 289–93, 301
Prince of Asturias Award, 42
*The Producers*, 6, 55, 150
Pulver, Andrew, 270–71

Quine, Richard, 54

Rabinowitz, Dorothy, 313, 321–22,
344–45
Rainey, Sarah, 230
*Raised Eyebrows* (Stoliar), 185
Randall, Frankie, 306
Rapf, Maurice, 54
*Really the Blues* (Mezzrow), 165
*Reds*, 242
Refugees International McCall-
Pierpaoli Humanitarian
Award, 334
Reilly, Thomas, 324
Reiner, Carl, 5, 31, 57, 94, 98
Reiner, Rob, 5, 47, 178
Reinhardt, Django, 166
Renoir, Jean, 9, 63, 202,
223
Reuben, David, 178–79
Ricci, Christina, 328
Ritt, Martin, 191–92
Rivers, Joan, 25, 58
Roach, Maria, 292
Roberts, Tony, 136
Robin, Helen, 324
Robinson, Edward G., 54
Robinson, Jim, 168–69
Rodgers, Richard, 213
Rogers, Kathleen, 335–36
*Rolling Stone*, 126, 192, 222
Rollins, Francesca, 104–6

Rollins, Hillary, 104
Rollins, Jack, 1, 14, 27, 48, *86*,
99–112, 114, 128–29, 144–45,
150, 152, 170, 172–73, 178,
229, 251–52, 257, 266,
267–68, 270, 297
Rollins, Susan, 27, 48, 102–4, 106
*Romantic Comedy* (play), 230, 236
Rose, Judy, 135, 147
*Rosemary's Baby*, 231
Rose, Mickey, 56, 71, 79, 91, 126,
135–36, 145, 147
Rosenberg, Ethel, 14
Rosenblum, Ralph, 13, 17–18, 23, 29,
34, 61, 150–51, 201, 204–6
Rosen, Julius, 91, 92
Rosen, Milt, 91
Rossellini, Roberto, 10, 62–63, 350
Rossen, Robert, 54
Ross, Herbert, 162
Roth, Henry, 330
Roth, Philip, 25, 56, 124, 180–81,
344
*Rules of the Game*, 223
Runyon, Damon, 26, 87, 265, 267,
270

Safra, Jacqui, 324–26
Sahl, Mort, 25, 55, 57, 59, 98–99,
103, 114, 117, 254–55, 261,
351
Salinger, J. D., 216
*Salon*, 46
Sarris, Andrew, 206, 221
Sassoon, Vidal, 231
Sayer, Cynthia, 48, 166–68
Sayles, Emanuel, 168
Schickel, Richard, 1, 33–34, 37,
46–47, 48, 52, 120, 194, 224,
275
Schultz, Nancy, 285
Schuster, Arnold, 73–74
Schwartz, Jonathan, 214

Scorsese, Martin, 36, 47, 320
Scott, A. O., 46
Sedric, Gene, 68
Segal, George, 55–56
Sellers, Peter, 55, 131, 142
Shandler, Jeffrey, 56
Shandling, Garry, 3–4
Shawn, Wallace, 44
Shaw, Sam, 130
Sherman, Allan, 57, 98
Shriner, Herb, 87
Sid Caesar's Chevy Show, 97
Simon, Danny, 90, 92, 93–94, 96–97,
    99, 182–83
Simon, John, 1, 12–13, 37–39, 48, 52,
    143, 188–89, 193, 211, 221,
    228–29, 244, 280–81, 350
Simon, Neil, 55, 65, 90, 94, 98, 136,
    263
Sinatra, Frank, 10, 88, 111, 213, 220
    Farrow's relationship with, 230,
        231–33, 306, 337, 343–44
Singer, Isaac Bashevis, 181
60 Minutes, 290, 292, 299–300
Skulnik, Menasha, 110
Slade, Bernard, 230
Sladkus, Harvey I., 301
Smith, Gerald L. K., 52
Smith, Kate, 312–13
Smothers, Tommy, 126, 144
Snow White and the Seven Dwarfs, 70
Sontag, Susan, 242, 244
The Sorrow and the Pity, 65, 195, 199,
    220
Spignesi, Stephen, 217
Stanley (sitcom), 96–97
Stein, Sammy, 68
The Sterile Cuckoo, 234
Stern (Friedman), 181
Stoliar, Angelique, 318–19
Stoliar, Steve, 185–87, 318–19
Stone, Sharon, 226
Storm, Howard, 100, 114, 145,
    175

Streep, Meryl, 212, 325
Streisand, Barbra, 5–6, 8, 53, 55–56,
    115, 253
Sturges, Preston, 11, 12, 38, 79
Styron, William, 235
Sullivan, Andrew, 236
Sullivan, Ed, 90, 117
Sullivan's Travels (Sturges), 11
Sutton, Willie, 73–74
Sweetland Films, 324–26

Tamiment (resort), 1, 93–96, 108
Tanenhaus, Sam, 46, 164
Taylor, Charles, 334
Taylor, Juliet, 21–22, 268–69, 277,
    324
Teeman, Tim, 330
The Telegraph, 347
Telushkin, Joseph, 180
Tenenbaum, Stephen, 325
Teresa, Mother, 233, 286
Terracino, Gary, 2–3, 7, 35–36, 323,
    327–28, 344
That Was the Week That Was, 117
Then Again (Keaton), 159–60,
    202
Thomas, Bob, 147
Thomas, Kevin, 152
Thompson, Monica, 301–2
Thomson, David, 44
Thornton, Michael, 230
Tiel, Vicky, 106, 133–34, 157
Tikkun magazine, 19
Time, 114, 124–25, 143, 224, 275,
    289–91, 334
The Times (London), 330, 346
To an Early Grave (Markfield), 181
Tobias, George, 55
Tolstoy, Leo, 17, 159, 187, 248
The Tonight Show, 90, 114, 117, 126,
    251
Triola, Lennie, 2, 306
Tri-Star Pictures, 324

Truffaut, François, 12, 34, 330
Turturro, John, 327, 350

UA. *See* United Artists
Unegbu, Carl, 329
United Artists (UA), 170–77, 207,
    229, 324
*The Unruly Life of Woody Allen* (Meade),
    46
Uribe, Imanol, 331

*Vanity Fair*, 43–44, 335, 337
*Variety*, 206, 213, 267, 269
Venice Film Festival, 41
*Vertigo*, 34
Victor, Jack, 27, 29, 64, 67–72,
    76–79, 86, 91–92, 116, 126,
    165, 347
*Village Voice*, 55, 166, 221, 281,
    323
Villiers-Farrow, John Charles, 45,
    335–36
*The Visit* (Dürrenmatt), 189

*A Walker in the City* (Kazin), 214
*Wall Street Journal*, 328, 344–45,
    346–47
Walpin, Gerald, 308
Waterhouse, Keith, 96
Waterston, Sam, 275
Weedman, Sid, 1, 48, 95
Weegee (photographer), 26
Weide, Robert, 23, 45, 111, 154, 236,
    317–18, 330, 337, 341
Weill, Kurt, 189
Welles, Orson, 12, 36, 142,
    242
Wexler, Jerry, 165
*What Falls Away* (Farrow), 18, 61, 164,
    231, 234–35, 249, 284, 291
*What's My Line?*, 35, 180

*When the Shooting Stops* (Rosenblum),
    13, 61, 205
Whitehead, Clay, 169
Wiesel, Elie, 322
Wieseltier, Leon, 280
Wiest, Dianne, 41
Wilde, Larry, 98, 106, 107,
    154–56
Wilder, Billy, 12, 174
Wilder, Gene, 179
*Wild Strawberries*, 215, 283
Wilk, Elliott, 300–301, 306, 307–11,
    313–14, 342–43, 345
*Williamsburg Trilogy* (Fuchs), 181
Williams, Robin, 99
Williams, Tennessee, 10–11, 65, 82,
    84
Williams, William B., 214
Willis, Gordon, 215, 221, 241
Wilson, Earl, 86
Wilson, Owen, 42, 298
Winchell, Walter, 86, 88, 213
Winters, Jonathan, 144
*Wit and Its Relation to the Unconscious*
    (Freud), 181
"With My Daddy in the Attic" (song),
    236, 343
WNET, New York City, 169
WNEW-AM, New York City, 213–14,
    306
*Woody Allen: A Documentary*, 23, 154,
    317, 329
*The Woody Allen Companion* (Spignesi),
    217
*Woody and His Women* (Carroll), 64
*Woody and Mia* (Groteke), 286, 294,
    301
works, Allen
  albums
    *Woody Allen*, 117
    *Woody Allen: The Stand-Up Years*,
      175
  articles/stories
    "The Diet," 139

works, Allen (*continued*)

"Examining Psychic Phenomena," 138–39

"Fine Times: An Oral Memoir," 140

"The Gossage-Vardebedian Papers," 137

"Hasidic Tales," 184

"If the Impressionists Had Been Dentists," 140

"The Kugelmass Episode," 5, 41, 141, 245

"A Little Louder, Please," 137

"A Look at Organized Crime," 138

"Retribution," 160–61

"The Scrolls," 184

"The Whore of Mensa," 140

"Yes, But Can the Steam Engine Do This?," 137

books

*Without Feathers*, 138–39

*Getting Even*, 139

*Side Effects*, 139

films

*Alice*, 37, 80, 166, 225, 233, 286, 288, 296, 353, 357–58

*Annie Hall*, 8, 9, 13, 16–17, 19, 34–35, 37, 39, 61–63, 65, 71–72, 80, 85, 93–94, 98, 103, 119, 124, 135, 138, 139–40, 159–61, 170, 171, 194–207, 208, 212, 218, 220–23, 245, 247, 264, 280, 324, 327, 328, 346, 353, 355

*Another Woman*, 84, 208, 210, 215, 225, 271, 328, 357

*Antz*, 46, 359

*Anything Else*, 19, 37, 136, 225, 266, 327, 328, 353, 360

*Bananas*, 9, 62, 91, 135, 156, 166, 171–72, 175–77, 182, 194, 353, 354

*Blue Jasmine*, 4, 44–45, 63, 225, 327, 329, 331–32, 334, 337, 341, 346, 354, 361

*Broadway Danny Rose*, 9, 13–14, 34, 37, 46, 62, 87, 88, 99, 101, 108, 152, 225, 242, 266, 267–71, 282, 296, 298, 306, 353, 356

*Bullets over Broadway*, 19, 37, 44, 46, 62, 152, 166, 189, 225, 301, 319, 325, 327, 330, 331, 353, 358

*Casino Royale*, 34, 55, 78, 131, 141–43, 354

*Cassandra's Dream*, 152, 225, 272, 327, 361

*Celebrity*, 44, 62, 228, 325, 327, 353, 359

*Crimes and Misdemeanors*, 2, 8–9, 13–14, 17–18, 24–25, 37, 42, 46, 48, 60, 62, 152, 195, 215, 219, 221, 225, 241, 266, 272–82, 296, 321, 328, 346, 353, 357

*The Curse of the Jade Scorpion*, 43, 327, 360

*Deconstructing Harry*, 37, 44, 85, 118–19, 139, 225, 247, 325, 327, 328, 353, 359

*Everyone Says I Love You*, 9, 13, 37, 44, 62, 152, 225, 297, 319, 325, 353, 359

*Everything You Always Wanted to Know About Sex (But Were Afraid to Ask)*, 8, 178–81, 182, 189, 194, 355

*Fading Gigolo*, 327, 350, 361

*The Filmmaker*, 212

*The Front*, 191–94, 355

*Hannah and Her Sisters*, 9, 15, 37, 41, 46–47, 62–63, 136, 138, 185–86, 195, 225, 237, 248–50, 288, 296, 321, 324, 328, 331, 353, 356–57

*Hollywood Ending*, 43, 327, 360
*Husbands and Wives*, 37, 44, 46,
　135–36, 161, 225, 249, 288–89,
　296, 324, 328, 330, 350, 353,
　358
*Interiors*, 34, 37, 38, 72, 84, 203,
　207–12, 217, 222–23, 272,
　355–56
*Irrational Man*, 362
*King Lear*, 357
*Love and Death*, 9, 34, 160,
　187–89, 194, 355
*Magic in the Moonlight*, 44–46, 81,
　327, 362
*Manhattan*, 9, 13, 15, 17, 34, 37,
　39, 41, 43, 46, 62–63, 94, 98,
　111, 119, 134, 135, 160, 170,
　195, 200, 207, 212–24, 241,
　324, 328, 331, 353, 355–56
*Manhattan Murder Mystery*, 152,
　225, 296–98, 300, 323–24,
　327, 337, 358
*Match Point*, 37, 152, 189, 225,
　272, 327–29, 330, 353, 360
*Melinda and Melinda*, 327, 360
*Midnight in Paris*, 37, 42, 44, 63,
　123, 225, 242, 298, 327,
　329–30, 354, 361
*A Midsummer Night's Sex Comedy*,
　225, 238, 356
*Mighty Aphrodite*, 44, 152, 225,
　319, 325, 353, 358
*Oedipus Wrecks*, 5, 9, 28, 62, 225,
　296, 353, 357
*Picking Up the Pieces*, 43, 360
*Play It Again, Sam*, 6, 80, 162–63,
　165, 194, 355
*The Purple Rose of Cairo*, 37, 41, 46,
　49, 70, 80, 84, 166, 225, 296,
　328, 330, 337, 353, 356
*Radio Days*, 26, 37, 46, 61, 64–66,
　76, 80, 88, 152, 225, 256, 296,
　347, 353, 356–57
*To Rome with Love*, 44, 327, 361

*Scenes from a Mall*, 186, 358
*Scoop*, 327–28, 360
*September*, 21–22, 84, 172, 203,
　208, 210, 225, 271–72, 357
*Shadows and Fog*, 37, 84, 189, 208,
　225, 296, 358
*Sleeper*, 8, 36, 62, 94, 166, 168,
　181–82, 188, 189, 194, 212,
　353, 355
*Small Time Crooks*, 43, 325, 327,
　360
*Stardust Memories*, 4, 9, 135, 152,
　161, 225, 226–29, 241, 242,
　280, 324, 356
*The Sunshine Boys*, 358–59
*Sweet and Lowdown*, 166, 325, 327,
　359
*Take the Money and Run*, 6, 7, 9,
　35–36, 56, 91, 99, 144–52,
　154, 170, 176, 204, 205, 247,
　353, 354
*Vicky Cristina Barcelona*, 42, 189,
　225, 327, 330, 331–33, 350,
　353, 361
*Whatever Works*, 62, 327, 361
*What's New Pussycat*, 34, 55,
　130–33, 143, 354
*What's Up, Tiger Lily?*, 34, 55,
　136, 353, 354
*Wild Man Blues*, 28, 69, 165–67,
　325, 359
*You Will Meet a Tall Dark
　Stranger*, 37, 225, 327, 329,
　354, 361
*Zelig*, 2, 4, 6, 37, 46, 48, 166, 176,
　185, 215, 228, 240–47, 262,
　296, 330, 353, 356
plays
　*Bullets over Broadway*, 45
　*Death*, 137, 189–91, 296
　*Death Defying Acts*, 248
　*Death Knocks*, 137, 139–40
　*Don't Drink the Water*, 80, 136–37,
　　158, 354

works, Allen (*continued*)
    *The Floating Light Bulb*, 80–85,
        136–37, 191, 240, 268
    *Play It Again, Sam*, 80, 128, 137,
        156–61, 191
   television
    Amazon series, 347
    *Hot Dog*, 144
    *Men in Crisis*, 169
Writers Guild of America, 42
*Writers' Theater*, 94, 96

*Yedioth Ahronoth*, 18
*Your Show of Shows*, 57–58,
   97

Zardis, Chester, 168
Zimmerman, Paul D., 176, 181,
   188
Zinsser, William K., 114
Zweibel, Alan, 3–5
Zweig, Michael, 326